The Lives of Can

The Lives of Camphill

An Anthology of the Pioneers

Compiled and edited by Johannes M Surkamp

Floris Books

First published in 2007 by Floris Books
© 2007 Johannes M Surkamp

British Library CIP Data available

ISBN 978-086315-607-6

Printed in Great Britain
by Bell & Bain Ltd, Glasgow

Contents

Those Who Arrived in the Fifties

Those Who Arrived in the Sixties

Those who Arrived Later

Foreword

The community movement now known as Camphill, with its vision of serving children and adults with special needs, was started in Camphill, Scotland, in 1940 by Karl König and a group of young refugees from Europe. This founder group had much to deal with, in the first instance having to come to terms with their own precarious existence. They were united by their shared ideals, their commitment to each other and their intended task of educating, helping and healing others. These original eleven co-workers are presented in the book *The Builders of Camphill* (edited by Friedwart Bock, 2004). The present book came about through trying to respond to the question, "How was the Camphill-impulse carried out into the world?"

The "Camphill vision" was based on the anthroposophy of Rudolf Steiner and on the example and help of Steiner's medical collaborator, Ita Wegman. Steiner himself had given a course of lectures on curative education at Dornach, Switzerland, in 1924. Now, during the period of the Second World War, Camphill had to develop independently of the curative-educational work being done in Europe, although one centre, Sunfield, in Clent, had been established in Britain earlier.

Following the initial year spent at Kirkton House northwest of Aberdeen in 1939–40, the founder group established themselves on the Camphill estate, in the lower valley of the river Dee while the Second World War raged. The group was in due course joined, miraculously, by British people who came to live and work with them under the most basic and self-sacrificing conditions.

By 1949 the way became open for an influx of young people, mainly from defeated Germany, who had suffered many hardships and were eager to devote themselves to living with children in need of special care who at that time were deprived and often neglected. This groundswell led to the first training-course ('Seminar') under the guidance of Karl König.

This trend continued during the 1950s, by which time Camphill itself had expanded along the Dee valley to include four other estates: Murtle, Newton Dee, Heathcot (rented for 15 years) and Cairnlee. With this increased capacity, the number of children and co-workers went up dramatically. In 1956 the number of children had reached 272 and the expansion went far beyond the Aberdeen area. In England, the Sheiling Schools at Ringwood and Thornbury were started in 1951, Glencraig near Belfast started in 1954, Botton Village for adults with special needs started in Yorkshire in 1955, the school near Hermanus, South Africa started in 1957 and the work near Lake Constance, Germany began in 1958.

This phenomenal expansion followed in the wake of lecture tours by Dr König when parents got together and asked him for help to start a Camphill school or village in their area. It was at the same time a historical opportunity in the years after the war to challenge the personal initiative of many talented and dedicated young people to rise to unexpected demands. The words of Karl König in 1939 found their idealistic, as well as realistic, response: "Now when the floods of terror and warfare are once more covering the face of the earth, we too must built an ark to help as many souls as we can."

For some the intensity and commitment to work was too much, and for some others, Karl König's personality was experienced as too severe a taskmaster. These people left after a while, several starting work of their own, based on what they had learned. For others, Camphill continued to be an inspiration and they united their own work to the growing community network. Importantly, as well, other physicians gave professional recognition to Karl König and Thomas Weihs and sought roles as collaborators in what had become the Camphill movement.

The next decade was characterized by these developments, not to mention the intensive spiritual work that took place through clinics, college-meetings, house-evenings, training courses, lectures, conferences and the varied therapeutic and educational work with the children. Furthermore, none of this work proceeded in isolation: many professional contacts were made, Management Councils were formed for the charitable, non-profit companies that had been founded; while many parents formed Parents' and Friends' Groups for fund-raising and support.

The 1960s saw further important developments. In 1962, the longed-for Camphill Hall was completed and opened at a ceremony for Karl König's sixtieth birthday. The Camphill Movement Council of earlier years was dissolved by Karl König in 1964 and seven Regions with their own managers were established instead, thus decentralising the growing movement. König himself moved to Brachenreuthe in Germany. He wanted to return to Central Europe and join actively in the work there. He died on March 27, 1966. The movement had now to prove its ability to maintain itself without the vital presence and inspirational example of one of its principal founders.

During these and the following years, the movement spread further to Scandinavia, Germany, Switzerland and the United States. Even in Scotland new foundations emerged at a distance from Aberdeen; while at the same time work was started in the Republic of Ireland, Canada, Russia and Poland.

Even as more of the ideals and practices of Camphill were being adopted by mainstream movements, challenges from outside were also being faced, notably the demand from external authorities for a qualified workforce. This was bound to have an impact on Camphill training approaches. A partnership developed between Camphill Aberdeen and Aberdeen University, offering Bachelor of Art and Master of Art courses and Diplomas in Curative Education. A growing number of students availed themselves of this opportunity; others took up social work training, others opted for Scottish Vocational Qualifications. Camphill began to integrate further into local and national settings. This gain, however, also meant a certain loss of the original spirituality, communality and enthusiasm that had characterized the movement. The danger became reality in some places that only the *name* of Camphill survived with some unusual inherited habits, without the founding spirit. Other places endeavoured, with more or less success, to integrate paid work without abandoning the community ideals, referred to as *Camphill ethos.*

Yet the spirit cannot die. Life experiences and service offered with love always endure, waiting for another historic opportunity and the guidance of our friends in the spirit-world. Humanity generally is at a stage where it is endangering the very presence of life on earth, and an assertion of Christian healing, above and beyond party politics and national interests, will be ever more needed. We are all called to hear and heed Gandhi's challenging words, "We have to be the change we wish to see in the world."

JOHANNES M SURKAMP

Acknowledgements

With gratitude I wish to acknowledge Laurence Alfred for having given the challenge for the task (which turned out much more than expected) of bringing about this book. I wish to express the same gratitude to all those who were willing to share their life-story.

My thanks go to those who have given encouragement and practical help: Maria Mountain and Christoph Hanni for supplying missing issues of *Camphill Correspondence;* Sandra Stoddard for continued interest, suggestions and proof-reading; Friedwart and Nora Bock for corrections and information; John Baum for giving the impulse for a complete change of direction and for final proof-reading; Ueli Ruprecht for scanning the pictures and giving computer help when needed; Margrit Metraux for supplying dates. And thanks to all those who have given their support by giving information. Special thanks go to Tomas Zelenka for all the complicated computer work which went beyond my modest computer-literacy.

JMS

Those who Arrived
in the Forties

Christof König

February 8, 1933

I was born in Pilgramshain, in the first children's home where my parents, Tilla and Karl König, worked. From there we moved to Vienna when the Nazis came to power. In Vienna my father had a big medical practice, and that is where the founder members met and studied together for their future task of Camphill. When the Nazis moved into Austria, the founder-group had to disperse, and met up again in Kirkton House near Aberdeen.

After the first years of schooling in Camphill, my brother, Andrew and I went to the Edinburgh Rudolf Steiner School before going to Michael Hall School in Sussex.

I was called up into the army for two years and was stationed in a military hospital in Northern Ireland. After this I worked on a farm near Thornbury, Gloucestershire, for six months, and then found a job on a farm in Sweden where I stayed for two years. During this time my mother asked me to join her in starting a hostel for Camphill co-workers' children at the Grange, Gloucestershire, where they could attend Wynstones Waldorf School.

After some years the hostel changed its function and became part of the Camphill Village Trust as a new venture. During my time at the Grange I met and married my wife, Annemarie.

I then found a job as a manager on a tobacco plantation in Zimbabwe; Annemarie and I had, however, to return to Europe when Annemarie's father died. We then decided not to return to Africa as the Congo crisis was in full swing and our employer was a very racist person.

During the time back in Europe we met up with Carlo Pietzner who asked us to join Glencraig, which we then did in 1959. I took on the farm and Annemarie the nursery class, and then the laundry. We helped to start the village-community in Glencraig at that time.

After twelve years in Glencraig it was decided to found two new village communities, one in Northern Ireland and one the Republic. We offered to become part of the founding group of Mourne Grange Village in Northern Ireland in 1971. The pioneering years were the most fulfilling of our whole lives. Our two older sons were born in Glencraig and our third son in Mourne Grange.

During the first year in Mourne Grange I became a service holder and was appointed to become a member of the Camphill Movement Group as

well as being entrusted with other responsibilities. This full commitment to the spiritual aims of Camphill felt to be a fulfilment of my life.

After a few years in Mourne Grange I became very ill with arthritis, and had to give up farming for good, as my strength had decreased so much. I then took on the craft shop for some years, and also some estate work.

The Hall at Mourne Grange came about as a kind of crowning of the community in its twenty-first year. Annemarie and I then took a half-year sabbatical. After this we moved to the Mount Community in East Sussex for two years to have an experience with trainees, and thereafter moved back to Grange Village where we had met all those years ago. There we stayed for just a year before being asked to return to Northern Ireland by the friends in Mourne Grange Village, who were going through some difficult times.

We have been in Mourne Grange ever since, and retired in the summer of 2006. It has been very hard for us both not living with villagers any more but hope we will get used to it; it is the first time in our married life that we live on our own after many decades of living in extended family settings. Now at 74, I can look back on my life in Camphill with tremendous gratitude.

AUTOBIOGRAPHICAL

Bernhard Lipsker

March 6, 1913 – January 31, 1979

During the New Year's Assembly of Camphill in Britain held at Glencraig, many of us had the occasion of meeting Bernhard again. There was nothing in his cheerful and kindly way-of-being to suggest that this was the last time we would be seeing him. Barely a fortnight later Bernhard slipped away on January 31, 1979. Many of us, especially his friends in Glencraig, felt that his going was part of the New Year's Assembly event which, in a new experience of togetherness, had brought so many of us closer together.

I do not have many personal memories of Bernhard from the very early days of Camphill, but two moments I remember distinctly.

The first was the occasion of a Bible Evening in Camphill House, perhaps one of the first in which Bernhard participated. His sharp, even cutting, intellect was marked and I remember thinking: How can this man ever be one of us? Then later, in the summer of 1942, after Bernhard and Barbara had become engaged, I was sitting with Dr König in what was then the library in Camphill House and Bernhard passed by the window outside. Dr König said: "there goes the next in our brotherhood." And I experienced the peculiar pang of joy and welcome one feels when a new brother unites with the commitment which has claimed one's own life.

Barbara and Bernhard celebrated their wedding on the very last day of 1942 in Heathcot. It was a festival of double significance: their marriage to one another, and Bernhard's true entry into Camphill. A few months later when this first child was on her way, Bernhard, after attending a lecture given by Dr König in Camphill House, was going to return to Heathcot. Turning into the main road on his bicycle, he was hit by a car — a blow which changed the course of his life. He was thirty years of age.

Bernhard was born on March 6, 1913 in Hamburg of Jewish parentage. His father died before he was born and his mother moved to Berlin where she then remarried. Bernhard's stepfather was a complicated and eccentric man who could not cope with this lively and wilful stepson and later, when a little half-sister was born, the situation at home became untenable and Bernhard was placed in an orphanage run by very fine people whom he much admired, but there was a strong bond of love, too, between him and his mother and sister, which sustained him throughout his childhood and youth.

Bernhard studied physics and mathematics at the university where he led an active social and political life, but this was terminated when Hitler came to power. He then took a teaching post in a Jewish school and loved

his work, but the school was subsequently closed down. He began to think of emigrating and decided to take up agriculture as a preparation for a future elsewhere than in Germany. He had his first contact with the biody-namic method in Mark Brandenburg and with anthroposophy through a close friend.

In December 1938 Bernhard came to Britain and went to work at Broom Farm in Clent where he first met Dr König who was on a visit. He was very impressed by Dr König's descriptions of the community he was building up in Scotland. He then moved to a tree planting college in Essex and while there was interned after the fall of Dunkirk in 1940. In the big internment camp on the Isle of Man he again met Dr König and our other men from Kirkton House, but then, like all unmarried internees, he was sent overseas to an internment camp in Canada and met Carlo Pietzner on the journey. He was eventually released to Scotland, and early one morn-ing in the summer of 1941 he stood before the door of Heathcot House. This was his first entry into Camphill.

Bernhard made a very slow recovery from the severe damage he sus-tained through the accident, and re-adjustment to life was laborious, for he was bereft of some of his former faculties. He often seemed morose and irritable but through the incredible bravery and uprightness of Barbara, he had unfailing support in the difficult struggle of his existence.

Many new challenges and tasks awaiting Barbara (who by now had three small daughters) and the resulting moves meant that Bernhard had to adjust anew to other places, other people, other circumstances — other gardens, too, for he then resumed his gardening and tree-pruning.

Heathcot, Camphill, Murtle, and Heathcot again, Botton, Thornbury and finally Glencraig were the many "homes" he and his family had. Through all this, very many of us encountered Bernhard through the 36 years following his accident, but fewer were perhaps aware of his background.

Gradually as time went on, Bernhard, always kindly by nature, achieved the mellowness, steadfast good humour and acceptance of his destiny that were so warming to experience in his later years. A gracious "house-father" in the little Pestalozzi House at Glencraig, interested in people and in world events, Bernhard had become an intrinsic part of the Glencraig community and carried responsibility for the training school.

ANKE WEIHS
From Camphill Correspondence, *1979/3.*

Irmgard Lazarus

September 3, 1900 – July 30, 1994

Irmgard was one of the very first to join the group of pioneers in Scotland. She was a teacher of eurythmy wherever she went. Her later years were spent in Norway.

Believe it or not, we in Norway are lucky to have had a young pioneering spirit of ninety!

When, at the age of 69, Irmgard returned to Europe from South Africa, it was to settle for good. She was then approaching old age and seventy would be the signal to retire.

However, things turned out differently. She was returning by boat and on her way she received a letter: "Would you like to come to Norway, at least for a visit?" She agreed. She came, saw and stayed.

For the first years of pioneering Camphill in Norway we were, to put it mildly, not welcome. Endless discussions with representatives of the Anthroposophical Society, internal questionings and so on were almost daily, or at least weekly events. Now the second experienced "Camphiller" arrived, speaking Norwegian in the heavenly language of eurythmy. And she not only stayed, she conquered Norway for Camphill.

She even learned this heathen language and has now lectured in Norwegian many times. What would Vidaråsen have been without Irmgard? Through her it rose up to a single purposeful task.

Irmgard came from Berlin; she was considered to be a Jewish person although her parents as well as she had been christened. So she came as a refugee to London and was interned on the Isle of Man where she shared a room with Maria Röschl-Lehrs and deepened her link with anthroposophy.

She joined Camphill in 1941, and as a dear friend of Dr König's endured his teasing for a number of years, went wherever he asked her to go: to Thornbury, to Ireland, as well as to South Africa.

There is something about her which biographical dates do not reveal, speaking a powerful language: her name, Lazarus. This disciple of Christ, Lazarus-John, whose ear listened to the heart of Christ and who finally wrote the Gospel of St John, shines out through her name. Love worked out through her and rayed out to many.

A person very close to your heart, a friend, is hard to describe in outer details. If your soul, your spirit, has really touched and recognized this person, an invisible bond is created, a friendship that might last beyond the threshold of death.

One day, when I myself needed rest and was put up in what was the tiny old St John's cottage of Thomas and Anke Weihs, Irmgard Lazarus happened to be my companion. During those days I learned to admire her outstanding faithfulness towards the impulse of Camphill, her love for its carrying people, her steadfast inner work and her lovely sense of humour. Some time after this fortnight she left for South Africa, where she spent quite some years.

A favourite impulse of Irmgard's was Idriat.* Carlo Pietzner had asked her to join the first one to be celebrated in Chartres, and as she was wise enough to follow the advice of the still wiser brother, she joined this venture as one of its pioneers. A year later she formally dragged me against my wish and will to a similar event. I went for her sake. This proved to be the beginning of wonderful high points of our lives. Instead of holidays we joined the Idriat in Bled (Slovenia), in Budapest, Tbilisi (Georgia), Kaluga (Russia), St Petersburg and Tallinn. Eastern Europe was calling and Irmgard loved this call. Later, when she could not travel anymore, she supported those events inwardly, remembering Dr König's message about Camphill's task in Eastern Europe.

The last one and a half years of her life became a challenge for the

* An initiative to create cross-border understanding between people through music and conversation.

teacher in the art of movement. Her right side was paralysed to a great degree. Sometimes she revolted with immense strength against her hard destiny. To her and my deep gratefulness, Eleonore Kralapp, with great understanding, took on total care. She cooked and served, recognizing the great individuality behind Irmgard's outward appearance.

During the last weeks Irmgard Lazarus seemed to have accepted her destiny. Now her longing for death could slowly find its fulfilment. She was lying peacefully in bed when I had to leave for Estonia on July 17. In spite of serious setbacks during my absence, Irmgard generously waited for my return, greeting me with small gestures of joyful recognition. Then on July 30, at 11.30 pm she was freed from her earthly prison and passed away peacefully. No doubt, many friends welcomed her on the other side of the threshold. May she also now help to show the Norwegian villages their way into a creative future.

MARGIT ENGEL
From Camphill Correspondence, *1994/5*

Thesi Baum

June 22, 1913 – May 18, 1990

Thesi was born in Karlsruhe into a family who carried a lot of the intellectual stream of the beginning of the twentieth century. After the Abitur she decided to train as a nursery nurse at the Jugendheim in Berlin which her aunt, Anna von Gierke, had founded and led. She was convinced she should take on a social task, rather than an academic one favoured by her parents. Her path led her to England as the pressure of Hitler's Germany became unbearable. This was her personal decision: she was the only one in her family to take this step. Destiny led her to the children of Muckie [William] Mann for whom she cared for some years, and where she met anthroposophy for the first time. From there it was a natural step to join Camphill in Autumn 1941, during its early years. Her meeting with Alex Baum was soon followed by their marriage, February 22, 1943.

Camphill in the dawning years was full of glory, idealism and the burning wish to establish a curative place as well as the community living. These were great expectations, efforts and totally new tasks interwoven by struggles of greater self-knowledge and failures. Added to this was the task to integrate their own growing family into the framework of community-living, long meetings and high demands of the everyday activities.

Their further way pointed to Bristol, where Alex joined St Christopher's School as a teacher. There Thesi gave some handwork lessons whenever she managed to hand over her three young children to a nursery class. Having witnessed their life from close quarters, I had the feeling that the new lifestyle as a more or less private family did not fulfil their longing, not even when Wraxall House began to function as a first Camphill offspring. For Thesi especially it was not easy to make new friends, and she felt lonely and unfulfilled.

Moving back to Camphill was a relief, especially as their fourth child was soon to make his appearance. Alex during these years was the spiritual leader while Thesi with her down-to-earth attitude to life provided the practical background, bringing up their children.

Their last and final move was back to the South of England. The Sheiling at Ringwood was in need of being built up, especially as regard to the schooling and strengthening of the spiritual life. Thesi taught herself to weave and took on with great determination the task of a weaving teacher until her retirement only a few years before her death. For thirty years she faithfully and patiently initiated hundreds of children into this craft. Her standards were high as to care, exactitude and perseverance. Though the work was started as a craft, the therapeutic value was strong and helped

most of the children — however restless, fidgety or distracted — to find their own centre and dignity. The woven cloth was then made into attractive clothing by Thesi, and sold to parents and friends. This gave to even the most retarded child or youngster the impetus to achieve still more.

Thesi's activity in the realm of sewing, mending and knitting was carried on after her retirement from class work. She made herself available to the whole community, helping and healing whenever she was asked.

While Alex was alive, he was the leading spirit. After his death in 1975 a great change came about. She had to carry on, and did so without hesitation. She started to read and study as well as to give various talks and she contributed a lot to the spiritual life of the Sheiling throughout these fourteen years. With this her personality grew visibly, she became tolerant and positive towards others.

Her extended family of ten grandchildren kept her lively and busy in caring for their christenings and confirmations, birthdays and Christmas.

Looking back on her life, one can see a thread running throughout the years to take up the challenge of anthroposophy on the one hand and to put her gifts at the disposal of the community on the other. One can notice a definite trend and direction from early on. Her striving towards a social task and also towards an inner path has always been her longing. In spite of frequent rough passages, she managed to steer her boat into calmer waters as she got older. Her life was full of many real treasures.

LOTTE SAHLMANN
From Camphill Correspondence, *1990/6.*

Christopher Karl Baum

March 25, 1944 – June 27, 1992

Chris's story is placed here as a representative of all co-worker/staff-children for whom the fact of their birth into a Camphill life-situation was a determining factor for their later life which in many instances led them back to uphold Camphill in later life through their own particular capacity.

Chris was born in Aberdeen on Saturday, March 25, 1944. His parents, Thesi and Alex Baum were one of the first couples to marry in Camphill. Chris was the first of four siblings. It was wartime and he was also one of the first children born in Camphill. To the Viennese founders of Camphill those who came to them during the war belong to Camphill in a special way. I include in this the first handicapped children, the first non-Viennese co-workers and the first staff children. As a child Chris experienced this and he said to his siblings "The future of Camphill depends on us."

He was christened Christopher Karl in the Christian Community. The priest was Alfred Heidenreich. His godparents were Tilla König who had a special concern for the many staff children, and Irmgard Lazarus, who has followed Chris, faithfully, from birth to death, through all his forty-eight years.

Chris grew up with many children. He lived in Camphill, Newton Dee, Bristol, Murtle and the Sheiling. That many of these children were special dawned on him when he met a young lad called George, in a passage one day. George said to Chris, "I am in your way." That George saw himself in this way made a deep impression on Chris and called up much that was to become his imaginative approach to life.

As a child Chris was a dreamer. After the first five years at St John's School (Shirley Ravenscroft, and later Wolfgang Beverley were his teachers), it was thought necessary for the staff-children to go to a Waldorf school elsewhere. This sudden decision and change was a shock to Chris and he wondered shortly before his death what effect such a shock in his childhood had later in his life. Significantly, Waldorf schools play an important role in his life. He knew St John's School and then later Wynstones as a child and as a youth, as well as the Aberdeen Waldorf School where he was a council member and treasurer for ten years. With the last strength he possessed he continued to teach chemistry to the eleventh class in the Waldorf School in Vestfold, Norway. It was a special experience for Chris that, though afflicted by the pain of his illness, he was able to teach about the substances of the earth.

In his teens, three events marked a change in his life. His eyesight changed, his nose was broken (playing hockey), and the illness (ulcerative colitis) emerged that he endured for the rest of his life.

As a boy Chris was closely connected to animals, especially to squirrels, foxes, horses and cows. He studied zoology and chemistry and received a BSc and later an MSc. He did research for five years, working in teaching hospitals in London. Chris finally stopped this work because he did not agree with the negative proof science required. He explained how he felt by saying: "We experience the sunrise a thousand times but only if it would not rise one day, would there be real proof."

Chris and Ellen married at the turn of the year 1969/70. With his family he then moved to the Sheiling, later to Newton Dee and then Vidaråsen. Their marriage was blessed with five sons. Chris's eldest son, born before he married, grew up with his mother without contact with Chris. During Chris's last illness, to his joy, this son came into his life to join the other five.

In his many years in Camphill Villages, and despite his chronic illness which flared up intermittently, Chris was active with many ideas and initiatives. It was only when he developed cancer that he allowed illness to change his life and tempo. He was in pain and often alone but he was able to come to an inner peacefulness. Much then began to happen around him, and, in a special way he was able to sense just what each person needed. Chris died in Tonsberg, Norway in the early morning, Saturday, June 27, 1992.

JOHN BAUM
From Camphill Correspondence, *1993/1.*

Ada Mary Shaw

June 28, 1890 – April 7, 1965

Ada Mary Shaw was the second or third child of a large family. She was born in Yorkshire and brought up in the country, though I do not think her people were farmers.

The first memory of which she told me many times was the death of a little sister when she was about three years old. She trained at an early age in millinery and dressmaking and in her late teens went to the local cottage hospital to train as a nurse. She did exceedingly well and won a gold medal. She had wide experience as a ward sister in several hospitals, and eventually went to London and became a Sister Tutor. She was in many different hospitals, the last one was Brompton Chest Hospital.

I do not remember if her first contact with anthroposophy was with Mary Adams but she was deeply connected and corresponded with her.

The one who made an early deep impression — it must have been in the thirties — was Dr Eugen Kolisko with whom Mary spent many hours, working through *Occult Physiology* and the *Study of Man.*

Through him she met Dr König and straightaway she recognized her destiny with him. Around 1941 she gave up everything, her career and security, in order to join Camphill. Although she was not able to type (she wouldn't admit that) she went out and bought a typewriter and became Dr König's secretary!

She put all her savings at the disposal of Camphill which at that time was a great help as money was short. She was the first one from Britain to join the totally German-speaking community, and that was not easy. Neither was having to get used to homeopathy nor adjusting to a totally new way of life at the age of fifty.

My first meeting with her was in 1945. She showed me round Camphill House, and I was specially impressed with her nursing of a very ill Down's syndrome child with pneumonia. We walked in Camphill garden and she showed me her many beehives and the herbs she cultivated, especially arnica. She told me of her love for Camphill and Dr König, though life cannot have been easy for her, as Dr König spared her no pain for mistakes and shortcomings which she accepted as essential part of her inner training. As time went on — we knew each other better though as both of us were grounded in our own place we were never really close.

Mary's sixtieth birthday was in 1950. After this changes came about in the Community and life was very difficult for her. She had a series of small accidents; rheumatism and age began to show, and she decided to leave, I think in 1952, to join good friends in Exeter, Devon.

She was there until I met her again in 1956 at the funeral of Irene Groves, who had been a great help to Mary when she first heard of anthroposophy. I could see that she needed some help and could really not manage to work any more and invited her to Thornbury Park. We took a room for her in Thornbury and suggested she could do sewing for us. All her possessions were stored with us. She was tremendously grateful. Dr König on a visit to us greeted her most warmly and was relieved that this could be done for her.

The following year it became evident that she needed more care than we could give as she did not really know where she was. Her memory was poor and she spoke only of her childhood. We arranged for her to have an apartment close to her brother in North Wales, the expense of which Thornbury carried as long as she needed. I once visited her there, but she was really living in another world with her memory, sometimes lighting up at the name of Dr König or Camphill. She was surrounded by many nurses she had taught and by her family. Mary died in Rhyl, North Wales, April 7, 1965.

Mary was small in stature — the same height as Dr König. She was thin and frail looking, with lively grey eyes and a sense of humour. She was very English and self-effacing. She was a tremendously active person — always doing things and speaking a lot. She was always up at 4 am when, quiet as a mouse, she worked either in the garden or typing or copying out lectures of Rudolf Steiner. Her rhythm of life was unlike other people's: she ate sparsely at odd hours and also slept very little, especially in Murtle.

Yet in the early days of Camphill she had a lot to give and did so generously. For instance, both in all matters concerning correct English wording or spelling of Dr König's correspondence, as well as tireless nursing of ill children day and night.

Though it was difficult for her to follow the rapidly evolving steps of the Community, she had heard the "call" of the Community and responded immediately, leaving all she had achieved to make a humble beginning to live anthroposophy. Mary was a human being who freely sacrificed her own will for the Spirit Will.

JANET McGAVIN
From Camphill Correspondence, *1990/5.*

Marianne Gorge

June 16, 1921

Both of my parents were from Jewish families in Moravia, a German-speaking region on the Austrian-Hungarian border. They met in Vienna and married in 1918 at the end of the war. Their first child was stillborn. My older brother Peter was born in 1920, and my younger brother, William, joined the family in 1927.

I was born in the morning of June 16, 1921 with a condition that did not allow me to digest food properly, and it was six months before my mother could bring me home from the clinic. We all grew up in a flat of a large five-story house that my father had designed. It stood in a narrow cobbled street near the Naschmarkt, a large permanent food market that is still there today. We had a nanny to take care of us as children.

My older brother, Peter, could not pronounce my name when we were very young, and so he called me Ipsi. This has remained my name within my family throughout my life. My parents had artistic gifts. For Father it was the visual arts; for Mother it was dancing and music. My mother had attended Dalcroze dancing classes, and she hoped to foster these talents in her little daughter. So when not yet eight years old I was sent for several months to the famous Isadora Duncan dancing school in Schloss Klesheim on the outskirts of Salzburg. It was a boarding school, and although we received lessons alongside the dancing classes, to this day I have no recollection what we were taught! I do, however, remember the smell of burnt porridge every morning (it was an American school) and the stowaway snails which accompanied the lettuce leaves served at lunch. I did not stay at the school very long, but back in Vienna I continued dancing and ballet lessons for several years.

Between the ages of nine and ten I have retained some vivid memories that I always felt were formative in their effect on me. It was winter, there was snow on the ground and my father had collected me from school. Near our house we passed a poorly clad man with bare feet. He held a hat in his outstretched hand and he was trying to catch coins that people threw from open windows on either side of our narrow street — it was his reward for singing. Tears welled up in my eyes as we entered our house and then I just could not stop crying. I was not able to tell my father what had upset me so deeply.

After that experience, every night when I lay in bed before going to sleep, I would turn my thoughts to those who were suffering. It was my longing at this time of my life to embrace the world of suffering with my compassion. An outing to the zoo also made me cry because I was sorry

to see the caged animals. But perhaps the most significant event occurred when I was in Class 4 and one day we were informed that one of the teachers, still a young woman, had died. We had all been very fond of her, and at break-time the children stood together expressing their sadness, some crying, and all saying how terrible and awful this event was. I told them that we are only sorry for ourselves; for the teacher things are quite all right! The other children thought I was cruel and heartless. They turned away from me and were not prepared to talk to me for the rest of that day. However, I was not prepared to deny what I felt to be true, and so I suffered in silence being misunderstood.

My father's dream was for us all to live in a family house with a garden. He realized this dream in Autumn 1934 when we moved to Hietzing, a district on the outskirts of town. Four months later, on Christmas day, he died of a heart attack. He was 51 years old. A few days later, before the funeral had taken place, I experienced my father while I was sleeping; I hesitate to call it a dream because for me it was very real. I asked him how he was and he told me that he was well. Things were much easier for him now, he said, without the burden of his body. He told me that he would always stay at my side, help me and support me. He also said that I, too, could help him. When I woke up I knew I had received a message that I was not to forget, but it troubled me for many years, this question of how I was to help him.

At the funeral it was hard for me to accept the condolences of friends and family. They were all so sad, and yet I knew my father was well — they didn't seem to understand that death was only a transition.

I was thirteen years old when I changed school and met my first real childhood friend. She was Hilde Gottfried, a girl in my class, with whom I shared thoughts about literature, philosophy, questions about life and death. We enjoyed many excursions into the Vienna Wood (often when we should have been in school). I failed in French and mathematics and had to repeat the year.

Maria Selinger, our literature teacher (who happened to be an anthroposophist) suggested to my mother that I should go to a Rudolf Steiner School. There was such a small school in Vienna, with only seven classes, and I was to join the Class 8. Finally I learned to enjoy school! I loved the artistic lessons, the possibility to be creative, and the hands-on approach to doing things like woodwork, copper-work, modelling and painting which enhanced my self-awareness. Among our teachers were Dr Hiebel and Dr Unger. They had been teachers of the first Waldorf School in Stuttgart. When the Nazis closed down this school, they had moved to the fledgling Vienna Waldorf School. Georg Unger was our teacher for mathematics and, finally, thanks to him, I took an interest in this subject and achieved good results.

During break-times at school I invariably ended up in the kindergarten which was housed in the floor below us. Still to this day being with young children, playing with them and watching them play gives me great joy. Even then it gave me glimpses of a paradise not yet lost. I have maintained this experience all my life when around young children, and I could never understand that it was not the same for other people.

Hearing the story of Parsifal for the first time in class eight was an unforgettable experience for me. The art teacher used to conclude his afternoon painting lesson with lively descriptions of the story. His enthusiastic renderings allowed us to participate with all of our hearts and souls in this unparalleled adventure. When the story had finally been finished, the teacher told us that the Grail had been removed from the sight of men. Angels had carried it away — one day to be found again. He told this to us in such a matter-of-fact way that for me it was as if it was part of the imagination of the story. I still remember the words with which he concluded that lesson because they struck me like a bolt of lightning: "This is the quest that one day we are all destined to join."

A year after my father's death my mother was introduced to anthroposophy by a friend. Although Alice, my mother, attended on occasions the synagogue with her parents, she grew up to be modern, searching woman who was interested in other religions, astrology and philosophy. For her anthroposophy was a fulfilment of this search. She joined the Society, took part in lectures and study groups, and there met Karl König, the future founder of the Camphill Communities in which Alice spent the last years of her life. It just so happened that Dr König had also become her physician in Vienna! Through these connections my mother developed an enthusiasm for Rudolf Steiner's art of movement called eurythmy, which she studied for two years. It was a predilection that I was later to emulate.

In March 1938 Hitler annexed Austria and German soldiers occupied the country. It seemed to me that life in Vienna changed overnight. "Heil Hitler" from one day to the next was the morning salutation of teacher and pupils. Imagine our Jewish teachers, with their Jewish pupils, standing with arms raised in class and mouthing these words with something less than conviction, and a certain sense of fearful bewilderment! In retrospect it strikes me as perverse that the traditional greeting in the street in this part of Austria was, and still is, "Grüss Gott," and yet then, everywhere, it had become "Heil Hitler!"

The Führer-cult brought with it even more frightening dimensions: throughout the town large speech choirs gathered, chanting and stamping, proclaiming the benefits of the new regime. Men marched around in brown uniforms holding banners with swastikas emblazoned on them and shouting in loud voices: "One people; one country; one leader." This mass hysteria spread, it seemed, before anybody knew what was really happening. Hitler's photograph appeared on countless windowsills. There was always a lit candle next to it and it was surrounded by flowers. Shops put up notices on their doors that Jews were not allowed to enter. Jews were no longer allowed to sit on benches in the park. Such things, however, did not bother me greatly — I was a young blond teenager interested in life and philosophy, and mused on such while sitting on the park benches!

It became clear to us that inevitably all non-Aryans like ourselves would have to emigrate, the sooner the better. For most people this was a lengthy, expensive, and difficult undertaking. When my younger brother was eleven years old and I was seventeen, my mother told us that we could both join a "children's transport" that was arranged by the Quakers. And so we arrived in London in February 1939. My mother and older brother arrived one month later. All of our possessions from our house in Vienna had been packed up by a moving firm and were to be shipped to England. They never reached us.

I was fortunate to find a place as an au pair with a young couple who had two little daughters. I remember going to Streatham Common with them in the afternoons. The girls of course wanted to play, but the rule was that their little dresses had to remain spotless, like in the Beatrix Potter story! Life with the middle class London bourgeoisie was like going to the moon for me!

My mornings were spent in the kindergarten of the "New School" in London, which was later named Michael Hall. My job was to assist a Miss Sargent with her large group of children. My future plans at this time of my life were to attend a Waldorf Teacher training and become a Waldorf teacher. Before the children got up in the morning I studied, with great enthusiasm, the lecture course given by Rudolf Steiner at Ilkley (1923), albeit with the help of a dictionary. I also was reading Grimm's Fairy Tales in English because I knew the content and this helped me learn the language.

One of the children in the kindergarten was Lawrence, a beautiful six year old boy. I would often accompany him home at the end of the morning for the shear pleasure of his company. It was a short walk which he otherwise managed on his own. One day, however, when I brought him home, I was met on his doorstep by his mother, a Mrs Harwood, who asked me to come in and in the course of my visit invited me to spend the summer holiday with her family in Cornwall. I was to help with cooking, household chores and the care of the five children aged from two to eleven. I gladly accepted the offer.

The small stone holiday cottage just outside the village of St Goran was built on a hill a short walk from the sea. There was a pump in the lawn which provided water, and candles and tilley lamps (oil lanterns) for light on evenings. I remember that 1939 was a long and hot summer. We spent much of our time on the beach, building sandcastles, or roaming the countryside collecting blackberries. Mrs Harwood was highly educated, like her husband, and very creative but completely impractical. I expected to learn my domestic responsibilities from her. In fact it was Mr Harwood who gave me instruction on cooking. "What do I do with the cabbage?" I asked. "Put it in the water and take it out again" he replied.

In September 1939 the war broke out. We stayed in Cornwall until October, and then moved to Minehead in Somerset. This is where a large building had been acquired for the New School, which had to be evacuated from London. The children were housed in hostels or boarded in private family accommodation. My younger brother, William, was housed in one of the hostels. The Harwood family and myself (by then I was part of the family) were to occupy a wing of the school building. As it was deemed necessary to introduce this new "New School" to the local community, a number of teachers from the school gave a series of lectures in town introducing the aims and principles of Waldorf education. They were Francis Edmunds, William Mann, Jesse Darrell, and Cecil Harwood. I had the great privilege to attend some of these lectures, which I found lively and stimulating.

In January 1940 I visited my mother where she was working at Sunfield Children's home in Clent Grove (near Birmingham). This was the first anthroposophical Curative School in England which was founded by Fried Geuter and Michael Wilson with the support of Dr Ita Wegman. I was hugely impressed by the work that they were doing there, so I decided there and then to join them, to work with the children and gain new experiences. On my return to Minehead, I informed the Harwood's of my decision and it was agreed that I would stay with them until the end of Spring term. I arrived in Clent shortly after Easter and just in time to attend a performance of a "Parsifal" play and hear sung for the first time "In the quest of the holy grail."

Then, in June 1940 as I was feeding a spastic child his breakfast, two policemen entered the dining room. They informed me that I was to come with them because I was classified as an "enemy alien"! My mother told me later, a point which she always found amusing, that I asked them to wait until I had finished feeding the child his breakfast. Then gathered what belongings I could, including a copy of Rudolf Steiner's *The Younger Generation,* which I had not yet finished reading and found very inspiring, and went out to the Black Maria. In the back, which was windowless, were a few other "enemy alien" women like myself. So off we went—destination unknown.

In fact the destination was Holloway Prison. It took some time to go through reception procedures, so it was the wee hours of the morning before a warden took me to a room, pointed her torch into the corner where there was a straw matt, ushered me, closed the door and turned the key. Everything was dark, and I couldn't tell what size the cell was or if there were others already there. The only thing to do was lie down and sleep, which I did in a state of complete exhaustion.

Prison, however, was an experience which aroused great interest in me — I did not regret the experience. Renate Scholem, a girl with long brown plaits and blue eyes became my new friend. She had come to England some time before as a refugee from Berlin. She was a little younger than myself and had been attending school before she was rounded up along with the rest of us.

After six weeks of confinement the "enemy aliens" were transferred to the Isle of Man. Despite being chosen by the government specifically to house potential threats to the State, this beautiful island was no Alcatraz. I still look back on my time there as the most wonderful, albeit brief, episode in my life.

Men and women were segregated on different parts of the island, and husbands and wives were not permitted to visit each other. Mothers, however, were allowed to take their children with them. The women's camp was spread over two villages, Port St Mary and Port St Erin. The accommodation varied from large hotels and boarding houses to smaller guesthouses or private rooms in residences that at other times were offered to holiday makers. Neither we, nor our erstwhile hosts had the slightest idea how long we would be there, thus lending a timeless quality to it that Renate and I revelled in — it was like holiday time! There was so much to take in and enjoy: walks along the cliffs, swimming in the sea, finding crystals in a disused mine, collecting wool from barbed wire fences left by the sheep. Someone taught us to make wooden hand spindles for spinning this "refugee" wool. The spun wool was then knit into useful garments. Imagine the village main street with many of the internee women strolling along and chatting, each with her wooden spindle spinning away. Wartime Isle of Man had become medieval Europe.

As Autumn approached, new initiatives sprung among the internees. Study groups formed, and there were gymnastics classes and eurythmy. A small youth group, led by Kaethe Wolf, a priest in the Christian Community, met regularly. Dr Selinger, one of my teachers at the Girls High School in Vienna, led a group studying Goethe's *Faust*.

Minna Specht, a gifted teacher who was influenced by the ideas of A.S. Neil and the Odenwald School, started giving classes for us refugee children. So for several months Renate and I went to school again. Then in February 1941, Renate was released and returned to London. I was released three months later, and Sunfield Children's Home was glad to welcome me back after a nine months absence. I, however, was looking for other life experiences beyond the confines of enclosed communities, and I left Sunfield a few weeks later and joined Renate in London. We both took jobs as waitresses at "Lyons Corner House," a large restaurant on Tottenham Court Road.

We worked shifts, in the early mornings welcoming the overnight factory workers to whom we served baked beans on toast with sausages. On Saturday afternoons we would welcome the Jewish families who came in from the East End. The whole *mischpoche* treated themselves to cakes and tea, ice cream and hot chocolate. And on Saturday night a podium was erected for an orchestra which played anything but classical music. I actually enjoyed my times in between these odd-hours shifts. If I had a late morning shift, I would hire a boat and row myself around the lake in Regents Park. And if I had a late evening shift I would attend lunchtime concerts at the National Gallery. What little money I earned I spent on concerts and eurythmy lessons that I attended at Rudolf Steiner House.

In January 1942 I started a new job. Mrs Fliess, whom I had met in the internment camp, offered me a position as kitchen helper at the "Vega." The Vega, situated near Trafalgar Square, was founded by Mr and Mrs Fliess and was the first vegetarian restaurant in London. It catered for about 150 people and had a small kitchen in the basement that was lit up all day by electric light and was very hot. One day we had a visitor: a young woman who had been a former employee. She was carrying in her arms a beautiful baby boy, and had come to show him to her friends. For a brief moment everyone stopped working to gather round the child. Christmas had already passed, but now it seemed to me to repeat itself. It was as if a ray of heavenly light shone into the darkness of human existence. This humble experience was for me a great joy and reassurance that brushed all doubts from my mind.

Our eurythmy teacher, Elly Wilke, was a remarkable person. She was very small, which is saying something coming from myself, and slightly disfigured by way of a hunched back which hardly showed when she did eurythmy. Before she came to England she had been a music and eurythmy teacher at the Waldorf School in Stuttgart, chosen for this task by Rudolf Steiner himself. During this time my eurythmy lessons were becoming more and more important to me. I experienced something rejuvenating and life enhancing through this new art of movement. I decided in myself that I must train as a eurythmist and began looking for any such possibilities, which were non-existent in wartime Europe. There was no eurythmy school in London yet, and so Ellie Wilke offered to take me on as a private student. I needed to find a part-time job, and was accepted to help in a "war nursery" assisting with the care of very young children whose parents were busy with the war effort. So it was that, once again my life focused on two themes, children and movement.

It was in these eurythmy lessons that I met Marjory Dain, who was a few years older than myself and who had worked in Switzerland at the Sonnenhof, the curative home founded by Ita Wegman. Marjory told me about the community in Scotland that was called Camphill which Dr Karl König, my mother's physician from Vienna, had founded. Camphill, she told me, was dedicated to curative education and community living, and, Marjory thought, would be an ideal place for me. She told me this in the same breath as she told me that she would never live or work there herself! Nevertheless, she felt that I might find there, in Camphill, what I was looking for.

It just so happened that at the end of June, 1942, Dr König was giving a lecture at Steiner House. I arranged an interview with him in order to get some more information about Camphill. I was expecting a formal meeting, but Dr König instead suggested that we go for a walk in Regents Park which was across from Steiner House. During our talk, he made no attempt to present Camphill to me as an easy life option. Quite the opposite! He described in a matter of fact way a working day of thirteen hours, no free time whatsoever, no holidays or private life, and no wages! Besides the willingness to accept such austere conditions, all he asked was for the readiness to live and work in a community with "handicapped" children. That was all. He left me to think it over and get back to him with my decision.

Although I had already made plans to study eurythmy in London, it was quite clear to me that I should change them and apply to work in Scotland in Camphill. I had become increasingly convinced that there was a need in this world for communities to come into existence, communities that worked differently socially. Such communities, I felt and thought, would be the seeds for a new cultural life, based on spiritual insight and true human values. For such communities to have a healing effect in this world, it required people to commit themselves, together, to such aims. I felt challenged to join them and commit myself to these ideals.

I wrote to Dr König, informing that I would like to join the community in Camphill because of my awareness of my personal responsibility towards our time. I had to wait several months before I received the reply that I was welcome to join in the work of Camphill! So, at the end of October on a bright sunny day I arrived at Aberdeen Station. My older brother Peter, who was staying in Aberdeen at Heathcot House for convalescence, met me at the station. We enjoyed a beautiful bus ride to Milltimber with the Highlands visible in the distance, the Autumn leaves at their most beautiful and the River Dee sparkling in the sunlight. What a joy for someone coming from London to breathe the crisp Scottish air and experience the clarity of light. A short walk brought us to Camphill House. Tilla König, Dr König's wife, was called to welcome me and show me around. My brother was welcomed like a postman delivering a parcel. I said goodbye to him, full of expectation of what I was to meet. First of all Mrs König told me that it was necessary for me to put on a skirt because it would not be possible to come to lunch in the cornflower blue corduroy trousers I was wearing. I could not imagine why, but, as the English are fond of saying to their children: "Do as you are told!"

I was shown to my room in the Lodge, a small room to be shared with a girl of sixteen or seventeen. And later I was introduced to my main task, which was to assist Trude Amann with the care of her group—five girls with special needs. Trude was one of the few people in Camphill who had some experience in Curative Education as she had been trained in Switzerland at the Sonnenhof. Next to this task I was to help wherever help was needed in the kitchen, the laundry, with household chores and with the care of the children.

Everyone in Camphill seemed to be so much older than myself even though the age difference was only five or six years. I looked up to everyone with great admiration, and being the youngest, Dr König often called me "Benjamin" by way of Old Testament reference.

In one way or another art has always played quite an important part in my life, and in coming to Camphill I discovered a new form of art. This new art revealed itself in the way the founders of Camphill related to work. No one approached their work as if it was a "job," in fact no one was employed as such in Camphill. All the work that had to be done every day was carried out in a joyful mood, with dedication and loving care. To me it was like a magic way of transforming matter, of spiritualizing it. The dignity and divinity of human nature found an expression in this way of life. This was all very much due to Tilla König, who had lived in a community of Moravian Brethren, the "Herrenhuter." This "art of living" would permeate all practical activities: the way meals were prepared, tools handled, children's clothes folded, tables laid, shoes cleaned and flowers arranged all spoke of a loving attention to detail. This was all rather new to me, and was and is like an ideal to be attained with devotion and practice.

In those early days of Camphill the children with special needs were not "cared for" in the traditional sense. Rather, we shared our lives with them, and they accompanied us in the various tasks that had to be done. Lessons were taught to different groups of children in the mornings, and once a week Hans Schauder gave a singing lesson which was attended by everyone. Special therapies were only developed much later. The structure and rhythm of daily life was both harmonizing and healing for everyone.

In German, the word "König" means "King." He gave guidance and direction for celebrating the festivals, for ordering the structure of the day, and for the medical care and education of the children. In his youth, Dr König, who was very musically talented, had considered his chances of becoming an orchestra conductor. He was now conducting the orchestra of Camphill, which strove to articulate and demonstrate a new social venture dedicated to the theme of healing in the widest sense. Through his presence we became aware that it lies within the possibilities of human existence to be master over time and space. It was never acceptable to run after time, nor to stay behind it, but to be with it and use it. Punctuality was a must, and expected to be kept by everyone. Each object, each large or small thing in the community had to be in its right place: the books in the library, the clothes in the cupboard, the tools in the shed, the chairs in the room. It was not a pedantic or narrow fixation of order. It was an expression of the regard for each and every thing that we come into contact with. His own personal conduct was a leading example of this ideal.

In February 1943 Karl König gave a talk about Kaspar Hauser. He had started the lecture in English, but eventually reverted to German, the language he was more at home in and enabled him to express his deep connection to the "Child of Europe." As he described the events that led to Kaspar Hauser's murder, his descriptions became so vivid that I could see the falling snowflakes and the trees covered with snow in the park of Ansbach—I could experience the darkness and cold of this winters day, a day when darkness came early.

For me the past had become the present. The attack on the "Image of Man" stood out like a timeless deed that had repeated itself ever anew in the course of history and still takes place in our time. Likewise the attack on childhood, innocence, and the purity of the human heart. From then on I read all I could find about Kaspar Hauser. He had become for me a star that gave guidance and direction to my life. He was the challenge to uphold the image of man, to listen to the human heart, and a friend to stay by my side.

AUTOBIOGRAPHICAL

Morwenna Bucknall

July 27, 1919

I was born on July 27, 1919, the second of three girls in St Austell, Cornwall. My sister Joan was fourteen months older and Katharine who died age two and a half in London in a whooping cough epidemic was the youngest. My father had been in Mirfield Theological College, Leeds, which has a strong social tradition. Trevor Huddleston, of South Africa fame, was a member of the Community of the Resurrection which ran Mirfield Training College. Jack Bucknall was inducted curate in Wakefield in 1912 and later went to Cirencester in Gloucestershire as his family came from Stroud.

There he befriended a lady and her family, Clarice Thomas, who seems to have been a Rosicrucian and had heard Rudolf Steiner speak in Oxford on one of his visits to England. After ordination in Gloucester Cathedral in 1913 he became a socialist priest. When I was about two the family moved to Thaxted in Essex where Conrad Noel was a champion of the Social Gospel with all the folk dancing traditions, being the centre of the Morris Dancing ring. He used hand-woven vestments with wild flowers on the altar in earthenware pots instead of the brass vases. At the back of the church was the Red Flag (God has made of one blood all nations), flanked by the Sinn Fein Irish flag on one side and St George's flag on the other. There was the Battle of the Flags, which is well known in English ecclesiastical history!

Once lorry loads of people came from Cambridge with stones and threatened to tar and feather my father and stone the anti-Empire people at the church. One night a local gypsy woman all of whose children had been christened in the church took Joan and me to Saffron Walden's Quaker Centre for safety.

After Thaxted we moved to the East End of London to St Michael and all Angels, Poplar. I was told that as an example to the poorer folk my father wheeled my sister's coffin in a hand-cart to bury her in a common grave with fourteen other children. Later we were moved to Delabole in Cornwall, probably to be out of harm's way because of my father's socialist views. There we went to the village school, and I was told later that my sister and I were "picked on" because we were "socialist kids." The headmaster of the school was a die-hard Conservative.

Later we spent nine years in a Church of England convent boarding school for girls, St Monica's School, Warminster, close to Salisbury Plain. This is now the area where many crop circles appear. We used to go to Stonehenge for Ascension Day outings, and the surroundings of Stonehenge were quite natural then, not the cars and sightseers of today. I was at that school until I was eighteen. It was a good preparation for community life!

We were able to be at that school because we were priest's children. We got our clothes through charity and had to alter them to fit us. My memory of the school was the endless games we played in the twenty minutes or so of break times — ball and skipping games, hop-scotch and yo-yo — which were very helpful for play therapy later in Camphill when I used to give workshops on play.

Being socialists we didn't stand up to sing the national anthem and when at school the King and Queen of Afghanistan drove past, our principles wouldn't allow us to wave the Union Jack with the other girls who lined the pavement! The contrast of our school and home life was very marked.

Meantime we had moved up to the Potteries in the Black Country, my father being a Church of England socialist priest, and my mother supported him in every way. We often had missionaries to stay and were host to tramps, gypsies and all sorts of folks, so our interest in people of all kinds began very early. After leaving school I went to the Art School in Burslem in the Potteries (Midlands) for three years, and I taught part time in various local schools, travelling on my bike. I did bookbinding, woodcarving and pottery and also started to play the cello, joining in a youth orchestra which played classical music for the wireless even though I could only play open strings at the time.

Michael Hall School had been evacuated to Minehead during the war. My sister Joan had become a helper at the hostel while I was still in London and suggested that I try helping out there. I must have been about 21 when I arrived there in 1940. Outwardly my connection to anthroposophy seems to start at that point, but actually it is to be found there before I was born. Clarise Thomas had become my sister's godmother, and I still have my parents' books, *Initiation and its Results* and *Occult Science* dated 1917. The back pages packed tight with notes. In Minehead I lived with Cecil Harwood's family and became an assistant handwork teacher and through this I was able to attend the teachers' meetings. This enabled me to pick up some knowledge about what it meant to be a Waldorf teacher. We also had a study group with Olive Whicher on the *Philosophy of Spiritual Activity*.

I played hockey on the beach with the children. It was quite fun but the tide would come in, so we had to mark out the pitch again at half time. I was there for three years and when Dr König visited and talked about Camphill I was very taken by what I heard.

In summer 1943 I went up to Scotland where my father was at a Christian Community conference at Heathcot near Aberdeen. I was shown around by Carlo Pietzner. When visiting the weavery I mentioned that I had a loom unused and could send it up, to which Carlo replied, "Why don't you come with it?" And so I did.

On Christmas Eve, 1943, Joan and I arrived to attend the English-German conference on Goethe and Shakespeare! Joan had been an au pair in Stuttgart to Dr Sandkühler's family so knew a little German.

I stayed on and was the first young English person to join Camphill. I looked after a group of teenage youngsters in Camphill House and worked in the washhouse with the boilers, and in the early morning walked around the estate waking up the house communities by playing on the recorder. I also learned to milk a cow in the farm. I knew no German at all — serious meetings were held in the co-worker's own language, as was the Bible Evening until maybe Easter 1944. Irmgard dared to speak about the donkey in English! After the Bible Evening during washing up they had to tell me what they had spoken about. Birthdays were hilarious affairs with Dr König and Peter Roth playing four hands at the piano. Tilla König taught me how to make butter, and the men-folk made sauerkraut with bare feet stomping round the barrels in the kitchen yard. We all joined in the haymaking and the corn harvest propping up some of the children against the stooks to watch. The half hour's silence before the children's service was quite a challenge for me.

I can clearly remember a moment when gardening that I became conscious of the connection of St Michael in the Heaven and St George on Earth, the patron saint of England.

Dr König asked me to start a Youth Group. I was 28, so I said, "I am too old." He answered, "It can't start without you." So we did, and included one or two older pupils in the youth group! It was through this that in October 1947 a group of us went to Holland to a large youth conference. I was the contact person from Scotland involved with youth work and became associated with Tom Fiedler and his people. They were a very Michaelic group, thinking of doing something together. They were told that there was a community in Scotland and that they should visit Camphill, which they did for two weeks. Dr König gave lectures to them and Tom stayed on to carve the beautiful *Angel, Mother and Child* statue, which still stands in Camphill Hall in Murtle.

By 1947 there were co-worker children who needed education, and with a child from an anthroposophical family in Aberdeen, there was the wish to start a school. As I had been in Michael Hall people thought I could do it! I said, No! I had come to Camphill for the child with special needs, though before then I had never met one! I then said that, if by October no one has been found I would do it. No one came forward, and so on October 13, 1947, I started St John's School in Camphill with a mixture of co-workers' and special needs children and two or three children from Aberdeen. Later on there were more maladjusted and delinquent children who joined the class. Some of them have done well in life and one is also a great grandfather and still a good friend ringing me every weekend!

I took a class for six years. By then the co-worker children were able to attend Wynstones School in England. After that I was involved in play therapy and in 1953 Dr König asked me if I would go to Ringwood.

I wrote twenty-one festival plays and plays for the classes. In Thaxted the festivals were part of the socialist approach, being social together. I missed this aspect to life when I was in Michael Hall but it came back again in Camphill. I joined the Anthroposophical Society in 1949, and the School of Spiritual Science a year later, having become a service holder earlier.

I always related to the Celtic stream of history, also to those who had died, and to Robert Owen. It is strange how my Celtic origin and socialist upbringing came to fruition in the Camphill Community. I have lived my whole life with the social question and joined a group of society members for some ten years concerned with the Fundamental Social Law as formulated by Rudolf Steiner.

In Ringwood I still did some teaching but was also involved in creating the yearly festivals in the community for eight years before moving to Thornbury for another eight years. During this time I was involved in many interregional activities, also joining the Movement Core Group visiting Camphill worldwide. Finally I became the Principal in Thornbury.

It was then that one of our ex-pupils, Michael Hopkins, persuaded me that I should join him and his Austrian wife, a Waldorf teacher, in a social venture in Bristol: "The Community Toy Makers," working and living with ex-prisoners and selling pop-up dolls on the streets! It was there that the idea of a Waldorf school was brought forward under the banner of a "threefold" Rudolf Steiner School in the city, formulated by Gerry Hayn. Our anthroposophical doctor, our Christian Community priest and an artist in St Christopher's School all had children of school age; so eventually the Bristol Waldorf School was founded and I could teach games in the younger classes, in the nursery class and help in the College of Teachers.

Then came the call to found a Camphill place in the modern city of Milton Keynes. Being on their Council and only doing little teaching and toy making in Bristol I asked if I could join them in what was then the beginning of a Camphill Working Community. For four years I was able to run the Food Processing Workshop and help with the services, study groups etc.

At the age of eighteen, I can remember saying, "It is not fair, everyone else is allowed to suffer except me!" It truly was a lucky life that I was allowed to have.

AUTOBIOGRAPHICAL

Eileen Slaughter

March 26, 1893 – May 11, 1976

Eileen came from a very old family, which had its seat in Upper Slaughter in Gloucestershire. Her father was a doctor in the navy and served for a time in Egypt and later in Malta where Eileen spent the greater part of her youth. She used to tell fascinating stories about supersensible happenings in Egypt and there is no doubt that the sojourn there in her formative years stirred in her a deep sense of reincarnation and the metaphysical. Of her girlhood in Malta, little is known other than that her life there was characteristic of relatively carefree upper society.

Eileen sometimes spoke of a man with whom she had a profound bond. He fell in the First World War. She maintained this bond throughout her life and never married.

After her father's death Eileen looked after her mother at home in England, but otherwise had never to work for her living. She had some connections with a form of Rosicrucianism, and it may have been through this that she met Walter Johannes Stein during the Second World War, and through him, the teachings of Rudolf Steiner. By this time, Eileen had experienced dissatisfaction with the life she had been living and was looking for some kind of war work. Dr König, having started his work in Britain in 1939, was frequently invited to other anthroposophical centres and early in 1943 went down to Minehead to lecture in a small conference at Michael Hall and while he was there, a kind of party was given for him which was attended by Honor O'Morrhoe and Eileen. It was Eileen who immediately decided to go to Camphill.

In those early days in Camphill House, Mrs König had been wishing for an assistant matron to take from her some of the responsibilities of running the house. And now we heard of an English woman who was cooking in Michael Hall, a Miss Slaughter. *She* was going to be the ideal assistant matron.

I seem to remember that I fetched Eileen from the station in Aberdeen early one morning. It was immediately obvious that this was no English "woman"; this was an English "lady." Tall, upright, immaculately dressed, wearing a broad-brimmed brown hat and the string of pearls she wore all her life.

Mrs König gave her the task of laying the tables for breakfast, lunch and supper, not quite as mean a task as one might think, for in those days the entire estate crowded into the dining room of Camphill House. Legend has it that Eileen laid the tables with her gloves on. I do remember that she certainly laid them with her hat on. It took quite a while before the hat came off and we dropped the "Miss Slaughter" and she became Eileen to us all.

While she was still "Miss Slaughter," I remember our experiencing a kind of panic when she had finished laying the tables betimes (needless to say with great perfection) and whispering to one another in the passage: "What shall we do with her now?" Actually, I think, we expected her to go to Dr König at any moment to announce that she would be leaving this uncouth and foreign place. We didn't know Eileen.

She was the second English person to come to Camphill to stay, the first having been Sister Mary (Ada Mary Shaw), at a time when few knew how to speak English and our meetings were blandly conducted in German.

Eileen always seemed a little passive and unobtrusive. Actually, a lot of things went against her metal and she could be outraged, for instance, about German being persistently spoken in her presence. Her eyes would flash and there would be an almost imperceptible tightening of the prover-bial British "stiff upper lip," but she never lost her bearing; even in indig-nation, her manners were impeccable. Likewise, behind an almost ever-gracious mien, she was exceedingly discerning of other people's minds and hearts and motives, and it was delightful to hear her chuckle over someone's hidden foibles.

There exists a list of members of the Community in Dr König's hand, drawn up in 1953 in chronological order. Eileen's name occupies the fif-teenth place, which indicates that she was present almost from the begin-ning at the emergence and development of the Camphill Community.

When in 1945 Newton Dee Estate was acquired for delinquent (very delinquent) boys, Eileen was one of the few who volunteered to go there and help with the cooking. I know very well what it cost Eileen to live with these excruciating youngsters in Newton Dee House, for I was there, too, and knew of the power they had of instilling fear into those who worked with them. Eileen had many moments of the greatest fear. I remember going off to meetings in another estate in the evenings, leaving her to keep house with a face as white as a sheet. But never did she com-plain or give in, her innate fortitude bade her go through with anything she undertook.

Yet Eileen was restless. Much travelled in her youth, she "travelled" a good deal in Camphill, occupying many rooms in different houses and estates. Only her chosen work remained the same; it was always related to cooking.

In 1954, when Botton Hall was acquired for the founding of the first Village, Eileen decided to join the new venture which, at this time, was also a rough and uncouth undertaking.

Why did Eileen, who was such a lady, choose to go to the most difficult and untried of places and likewise choose the Cinderella's task at the hearth of the kitchen?

If I may seem to deviate — I remember that at decisive moments in the development of the Community, Eileen seemed to draw back and even go into a kind of opposition, and with a display of, to us, most aggravating emotionalism or even sentimentality, to champion all those who were likewise in opposition. Yet when the decision finally fell, Eileen was there, a veritable knight, steadfast, loyal and supportive.

At one such moment, she wrote a letter explaining that before she could truly participate in what she knew was right, she had to go through an experience of opposition"in order to test myself." This, I feel, was the essence of Eileen's way of life; she had to test her strength, her honesty, her uprightness, her "knightly armour" to see that it was worthy. And all this, if I may say, with utmost and gracious humility.

In the early days of Camphill, we experienced ourselves as being an Order, somewhat militant in character, but Dr König always insisted that Camphill must become part of the world, a socially integrated community. Yet, if there were an element of an Order within the Community, Eileen in her own, apparently unobtrusive manner, would have been one of its steadfast and most loyal carriers.

She was fifty years of age when she came to Camphill. She died after an orthopaedic operation at the age of eighty-three. Thirty-three years of her life were spent in the service of the "Order" of Camphill. In death she looked not more than fifty — serene and light and emanating a kind of active peace around her.

ANKE WEIHS
From Camphill Correspondence, *1976/7.*

Ursula Gleed

August 14, 1908 – January 17, 1996

In Ursula three qualities stand out above all others: Faithfulness, Integrity and Courage.

Ursula was an only child; her mother was a painter and her father a lawyer. An only child usually has a special destiny and like most only children, Ursula was often lonely throughout her life. Her parents were elderly and after holidays she always looked forward to return to boarding school to be with other children, although she had a warm and loving family life.

As a child she lived in Chislehurst, Kent, but her parents moved while she was still small to Ringwood where a family home was established and named the Sheiling, as it was built by a Scottish branch of the family, and it was here that Ursula had her home until she married David and lived in London. They had two sons, Richard and Charles, and it was in this early period while the boys were quite young that they took a lease on a house, 122 Harley Street.

Charles, the second son, was born with a handicap and it was through Charles that Ursula found her true direction in life. She consulted Dr König about her son and in 1944 Charles was admitted to Camphill. In no time, 122 Harley Street was offered by Ursula for Dr König to hold interviews with families of children with special needs. Other doctors also practised in the house. The house became a venue for escorts taking children on night trains from Kings Cross to Aberdeen after holidays in the south, and an early memory of mine was of Ursula, this petit elegant lady, standing on the platform at Kings Cross station with her poodle, to wave farewell to her small over-active and dependent son whom she would only see again at the end of term.

Number 122 Harley Street became not only a centre for interviews for children and from 1955 onwards for adults with special needs, but also the central office for the Sheiling Schools with their two centres at Thornbury and Ringwood. From 1951 onwards when the work of Camphill was established in the south of England, Ursula became the secretary of the Sheiling Schools and the family home, The Sheiling in Ringwood, was given over for the work with children with special needs. Ursula's parents moved at this time to The Studio, which stood in the grounds of The Sheiling estate and where her mother had been painting.

In 1955 the Camphill Village Trust was established, and again the house in Harley Street was generously made available for offices by Ursula.

Ursula herself had found her way to the teachings of Rudolf Steiner and joined the Anthroposophical Society in 1948. She became a member of the First Class in 1950 and later was appointed to be a Class reader. Her marriage came to an end in those early days with Ursula finding a new direction to her life.

From the beginning of Ursula's involvement with Camphill it was apparent that she had a heart for the mentally frail and mentally handicapped adults and there were always one or two people with special needs also at home in Harley Street and even trained by Ursula to do reception work for the doctors who practised there. Bible Evenings were held nearly every Saturday and the home became a meeting place for leading personalities of the Anthroposophical Society.

Young co-workers coming by train from the Continent in those early days would have their first contact with Camphill through Harley Street and there were often quite amusing incidents such as when one young lady phoned to say that she could be recognized when she was coming to stay, as she would have a pony. Of course, at first Ursula was daunted by where to put such an animal in the middle of London, but later understood that a "pony" in Germany meant that she was wearing her hair with a fringe.

Dr König asked me to help Ursula in Harley Street with her very heavy work load there, particularly with arrangements for interviews for children and young people who were streaming to that centre to be assessed, and recommendations made for the schools and villages throughout the country. I travelled down to London and my presence there enabled Ursula, for the first time, to live in one of the centres that she had been so involved in establishing. She moved to the Grange Village to take on a leading role there.

This made it possible for her and Charles to be together in one centre. Later Charles had to be admitted to hospital. It was as though the work he had set out to do, to lead his mother to her special path, was fulfilled. She was then able to take these life experiences to help other parents to understand that their children, now grown up, may have other directions than those they had planned for them.

After some years at the Grange, Ursula had to return to the studio in

Ringwood to be with her elderly parents. It was at this time that the Counselling Service was initiated through Ursula's efforts and has grown from strength to strength. She was also involved with the first discussions and sessions of the Mental Health Seminar. Ursula had a lively interest in the world at large, loved to travel and had many friends throughout the world. In spite of physical frailty in later years and the loss of her leg through amputation, her spirit was not deterred and even in the late autumn she was still travelling to meetings in the south of England.

She will, I feel sure, still be concerned with the work of Camphill and Rudolf Steiner from the other side of the threshold.

ANN HARRIS
From Camphill Correspondence, *1996/3.*

Reg Bould

August 28, 1920

In 1949, ten years after the beginning of work in Kirkton House and four after the end of the Second World War, the first group of student co-workers arrived from the continent to join the first Camphill Curative Education Course.

Those who have not experienced the destruction of war, or the rundown conditions after many years of "making-do" and food rationing, may find it difficult to imagine what it was like. There was relief that the fighting was over, but also a mood that among mankind something had gone seriously wrong. To us "foreigners" arriving in Camphill then, the zeal and struggle to build other than competitive, combatant relationships, the attempt to honestly embrace those who were different from ourselves, to accept the additional outer poverty due to a pioneering situation, made sense. The "unreasonable" working hours and workloads, the many meetings late into the night, the heavy and serious mood of life, which felt like that of a religious order was acceptable.

The children, of course, were British. But most of the co-workers came from the vanquished peoples of Europe. The first group had fled before the war, while we came with the experiences of war and failure that motivated us. Much of the culture, ways of expression and even the language in those days were familiar to us — German was still spoken quite often. So, although Camphill was in Britain, those few British co-workers who joined made themselves foreigners in their own country by joining this community of "enemy aliens."

Celebrating Reg Bould's eightieth birthday seems to me a fitting moment to ask a question that perhaps we should have asked long ago. What was it that they had heard? What motivated them to join this odd bunch in Scotland? In a still very class-conscious Britain, they represented a remarkable social spectrum. While most were single and could be concerned only with themselves, Reg and Molly stood out among them with their courage to maintain a family in this early community.

In retrospect one might appreciate that these friends were not deceived by victory over external enemies, not that battles could be won once and for all. They heard and were motivated by the universally human, and made common cause with others.

As a young man I had the good fortune to live close to the Bould family, to be taken along for their Sunday drives in the green Jowett. As extended family living in the huts around the Bungalow in Newton Dee — now Ronecht — we crowded twelve-plus around their family table in the small dining room. What I experienced particularly through Reg was this spirit of the generally human, not as Central European ideal, but lived and expressed, made visible with lightness of touch, brightness of laughter and often forgiving insight. So the zeal and intensity of community-building struggle and seriousness was lit up and made bearable time and again.

The family presence was a kind of substantiating hope that this community life had a sustainable future and was not just carried by the idealism of youth and the burdening experiences of our past. Reg was never a disciplinarian (that task was carried out by others), but always a mediator, even to one's own conscience. I remember a scene in front of the Bungalow. Once again, and probably once too often, I wanted to take the weekend off to hitchhike by fish-lorry to London to meet a certain lady. Reg's response was that only I could decide whether this was justified or not in the given circumstances. That put me into a freedom space, which at the same time was a tight spot, a remarkable experience! Yes, I did go. Being still married to the lady after 46 years I am sure Reg has long accepted the justification. But that is just it — the acceptance was there before I made the decision!

Beattie Warburton, Molly and Reg and Morwenna Bucknall were in Camphill, because their hearts and ears had been attuned to the universally human by the best of British Christian socialism, as expressed by Morwenna's parents, Jack and Daisy Bucknall in the Potteries. Jack Bucknall, a vicar of the Church and member of the Thaxted Movement, had recognized the depth of Christianity in Rudolf Steiner and anthroposophy — which is the only basis for a socialism capable of recognizing the individual and which does not get lost in social forms or party politics. He had grasped how threefolding was not a method or a constructed order but a tool for a living discernment; and for metamorphosis of the will, by which the individual could be responsible to others as well as to his own humanity. More than that it enabled an individual to act "vicariously" that is on behalf of, as a representative or "vicar of mankind." In this the British Spirit finds a possibility of union with the Spirit of Middle Europe.

Reg, let us use your eightieth as a celebratory moment of recognition of what you and your fellow Brits brought to the Camphill Community and movement. I salute you and with you that special group of early British Camphill Community members.

MARK GARTNER
"On the occasion of Reg's eightieth birthday," from Camphill Correspondence, *2000/6.*

Kate Roth

June 10, 1915 – October 11, 1993

Kate grew up as the only and very choleric child of middle class parents in Streatham, London. Because of her father's disappointment with the education available, he sent her to the newly founded Waldorf School, which was later to become Michael Hall School. On leaving school she

studied drama, following which she joined a travelling theatre company performing Shakespeare's plays. Later on as a young woman she went as a trainee to the Sonnenhof, the first anthroposophical home for children with special needs, in Arlesheim, Switzerland, returning to England before the outbreak of the Second World War.

After the death of her father in the middle of the war, Kate founded a nursery class in London, where her mother looked after the household side. It soon became clear that Kate's supreme gift lay in home-making, that is to say the spiritual nature of the housewife. Dr König on his frequent visits to London soon began to stay with her, and it was a natural consequence of these visits that Kate went to Camphill near Aberdeen following her friend Joan Hinchcliff with whom she had built up the nursery class.

From 1945 Kate spent the rest of her life in Camphill. After Scotland, she went to Ringwood, then to Botton where she spent thirty-seven years before moving to Delrow in May 1992.

Like most biographies in Camphill, outer events featured in only a limited way. In Kate's case she and I married in 1951 and our son Simon, who later became a doctor, was born in 1954. "Outer" life soon gave way to the "inner," when after a few years in Ringwood we went into the lush though lonely pastures of Botton in 1955. She surrounded the growing number of households, workshops, forestry and farm work with a holy halo of "home." All members of the community, whether adults with special needs, co-workers or children, all felt each other as brothers and sisters of a growing family. Through Kate, the idea of Home in the greater sense became personified; this idea, so essential for any village, had an ally, which was Truth. Kate's words, not dictated to by logic or in need of proof, were undogmatic and permeated with personal warmth; this Truth shone into the listener as if spoken with the immediacy and modesty of an angel. This was especially so in later years when she became a Class reader.

Our time is full of great personalities who, in spite of the unifying and Christianizing influence of anthroposophy, bear many frustrations. Kate was one of those personalities who carried this destiny with magnificent fortitude and courage.

PETER ROTH
From Camphill Correspondence, *1994/1.*

As I sat and listened to the tributes being paid to my mother at the memorial evening, I could not help but be amazed by the many different things attributed to her of which I was quite unaware.

The picture that emerged on that evening was of someone who could create the right condition for new innovations and then, rather then putting herself at the centre of it, enabled others to sail the ship. This was not only achieved with a choleric temperament but also with the vision that necessarily accompanies a strong will if anything meaningful is to be achieved. Not exactly appreciating these virtues in one's own mother, I realize now how I too had been the beneficiary of her far-sightedness. The following example stands out above all others. As pupils at Botton School, the natural progression was to complete secondary education at another Waldorf School. For reasons better known to herself at the time, my mother took the unprecedented decision to send me to a local school. Though this may sound like everyday stuff to today's readers, in Botton of 1968 this was a quantum leap from tradition and the first time a non-Waldorf education had been considered. Four of us subsequently went off to the Friends' School, Great Ayton. Having had twenty-six years to reflect on that move, it is now abundantly clear that I would never have been able to meet all the opportunities which have subsequently opened up for me had I not had the rude awakening which Great Ayton was able to offer. (This is of course a purely personal comment and not an indictment on Waldorf schools!) I will, however, be forever indebted to my mother for this decision.

No memory of her life could be complete without mentioning her elevation to grannyhood in the last seven years of her life. A very special and intimate relationship developed between her and Helena, which was a two-way affair. When Granny moved to Delrow last year it was a source of great joy for both of them that Helena could spend more time with her and stay overnight. They were like old friends who had known each other for a very long time.

SIMON ROTH

From Camphill Correspondence, *1994/1.*

In Kate's honour, the Kate Roth Seminar for home-makers was founded through Veronica van Duin's initiative.

Janet McGavin

November 21, 1915 – March 13, 1994

Our first child Johnnie was brain damaged at birth and when Dr König agreed to take him to Heathcot House in Aberdeen, my sister, Janet, was already in residence and took responsibility for him. He was there for seven years and I used to visit him regularly. After some years Janet decided to join the Camphill Community — a decision our family found difficulty in accepting for there was a worry about her future. However, as far as Janet was concerned it was the right decision and it gave scope for her talents undreamed of by her family.

JOHN MCGAVIN

From Camphill Correspondence, *1994/4.*

Having worked with Janet for quite some years, I know that she laid seeds into the hearts and souls of all those who have been allowed to be with her. One image I have is of Janet coming for a boy called James. He was a foundling, laid and left on the steps of a church or a hospital. He had a large head. One never did know where he came from or what his real name was. James was brought to Heathcot House where Janet worked. He became closely connected with Janet and with her help learned to stand and make his first steps. His head continued to grow. James in the end lost his sight and had to lie in a pram, not even able to sit up or lift his mighty head. But he could listen to the speech, music and songs around him. With a clear angelic voice he sang and spoke — his features were as pure as that of an angel. He became a true Camphill child. With Janet he moved to Thornbury Park (near Bristol) and there I saw Janet caring for him. To see the tenderness when she lifted him out of his pram, held him on her arms or played the lyre when he could not sleep. It was an image of Janet I never forgot.

IRMA ROEHLING
From Camphill Correspondence, *1994/4.*

It had seemed important that one or two Camphillers should become US citizens. It expressed our commitment to this country. I remember that Janet had been working in the laundry and the whorls on her fingers were not sharp enough for fingerprinting, so she had to leave the laundry to others. We had both studied the constitution, but when asked to name its three branches, Janet became slightly flustered. She was quick to name the Executive Branch — being a matron herself — and then there was a prolonged pause. "L," said the questioner. "The Legislature!" replied Janet triumphantly. There was no question that we were earnest

This was during the fifth year of Donegal Springs House. It was a glorious period for all working there. We lived in a large, historic mansion on fifteen acres of park, woods and gardens. We had thirty children in our care and they were divided into three school classes. We were a fairly closely-knit community.

Janet was born into the family of a Scottish engineer, in Shanghai, China on November 21, 1915. Her earliest memories were of China. She went to school in England, separated from her family, as was the custom. Her education culminated with a nurse's training at the Florence Nightingale School which was connected with St Thomas Hospital in London. There she remained during the Blitz. She made her rounds as midwife on a bicycle and often slept in the shelter of the Underground. It was during this period that she came into contact with anthroposophy and became a supporter of the work of Walter Johannes Stein.

Janet joined Camphill right after the war in 1945. She lived first in Heathcot and then in Thornbury Park, where I met her in 1958. During this period her work was with physically handicapped children. This ended in 1959 with the possibility to begin a new Camphill venture in Rhodesia. When this fell through she was ready to respond to the invitation of Gladys Hahn to come to America and take on her work near Downingtown, Pennsylvania.

We all moved to Beaver Run in 1967. Janet was never again to take a leading role in our work, though she always remained a helper and guide for others. She retained the ability to attract "special souls." Janet could be quite stern; and yet this does not nearly give the whole picture, for she had a warmth of heart that did not allow her to turn away any child who asked for our help.

A progression of newer ventures followed Beaver Run. First of all, Kimberton Hills, and then nine years at the Waldorf Institute in Detroit where she taught. After a time in Triform she returned to Detroit, to the Barnabas Project in the inner city. She died there, in the early hours of Sunday, March 13, 1994.

Janet had completed the grand gesture of her life's journey, from East to West.

ANDY HOY
From Camphill Correspondence, *1994/4.*

In 1945 Janet had made another oath of allegiance, namely to the muse of music, resulting in a lifelong faithfulness to learning the art of lyre playing. Less a natural inclination or disposition of talent, it was rather a new task through which she acquired the fame of introducing the new instrument to North America. She was a self-made musician.

From Thornbury House where Janet had worked with rather ill children, she once came to Glencraig, Northern Ireland, to join one of the first lyre conferences with Edmund Pracht, taking away with her an enthusiasm for the lyre that she could employ years later at the first American lyre conference in 1969. She led a crusade for the lyre, first in Pennsylvania, then in New York State and Detroit. By the time I settled in Camphill Village, Copake, and some of us decided to launch an Association for promoting the Lyre as a "new instrument" she joined the effort, bringing some know-how. So in 1982 our Lyre Association of North America was created, enjoying Janet's fullest and inspiring support as did the lyre conferences springing from it.

Her enthusiasm for the healing sound made her suggest that the Camphill Association should recognize it as a task to promote the arts and widen the participants to include needy folk to whom our classrooms and halls should be opened freely and fully. She herself forged ahead by arranging an open lyre workshop to take place in early summer and an Easter Festival at a women's club in Detroit in 1994, at which lyres were to sound, eurythmy would be practised, a choir was to sing, a Thornton Wilder play to be performed and she herself would have talked on "Meeting the Future in the New Holy Grail."

"Meet the Future? Meet the World!" she would have said. However, it became a memorial evening for her.

C A LINDENBERG
From Camphill Correspondence, *1994/4.*

Donald M Perkins

April 27, 1903 – January 29, 1992

Our friend the Reverend Donald Perkins celebrated his sixtieth birthday on April 27, 1963. This was a day of joy and happiness for all who work in Camphill, but especially to the few who belong to the founder-group of the movement.

We met Donald Perkins as one of the first who recognized our intentions and supported our efforts. Already in 1941, he invited me to lecture to his congregation at the Skene Street Congregational Church in Aberdeen. He often visited Camphill and felt quite at home. In these early times he imagined that some day he would join us and throw in his lot to help our work. After studying Rudolf Steiner's books and lectures with great zest, Donald Perkins — after much heart-searching — decided to become a priest of the Christian Community. He gave up everything — his church, his security, his conventional life, and then took a big jump into the unknown. Within a few years he was ordained and took up his new duties with great energy. When working again in Aberdeen he saw the needs of our bigger boys and girls in Newton Dee. He founded a kind of youth club for them and took a great and personal interest in many of their needs and troubles. He gradually became their spiritual father and helped them profoundly. Later on he and his family settled down in Newton Dee and are now a great support of the village community there. Donald

Perkins' human qualities and his rare understanding of the troubled heart of the adolescent personality afford help and comfort to many. He is esteemed and loved by us all.

KARL KÖNIG

From The Cresset, *Easter 1963.*

Helga Perkins

May 30, 1917 – August 24, 1980

Helga was the older of two children (her younger brother, now a medical doctor, is closely connected with the Camphill places in Germany), her father a professor of classics in Coburg, Bavaria. Her mother was a member of the Anthroposophical Society and from early childhood Helga was guided by her to anthroposophy. She received her education partly in Coburg and partly in Stuttgart, where she attended the Waldorf School. Later she took a training in commercial foreign correspondence and translating, having also trained in domestic skills, crafts and needlework.

She spent the war years in her native Coburg. Through her connection with anthroposophy she came to hear of Dr König and the work in

Scotland, and in November 1951 she joined Camphill, where she started work in the kitchen at Heathcot House. Later she moved to Cairnlee where she looked after a group of older girls, and was responsible for the kitchen and the garden. Her next move took her to Newton Dee where she spent many years caring for a village household, her own family, sometimes also a workshop and the garden, and the chapel.

In 1971, she went with her husband, Donald, to Botton where she continued to carry her personal and community responsibilities with undiminished devotion in spite of increasing ill health during the latter years. Her last year was overshadowed by the growing illness which she finally overcame, passing over the threshold peacefully on the August 24 in the brilliant sun of midday.

GOTTFRIED PRETTZNER

Dr König invited Helga to Camphill and from 1951 Camphill, Scotland, became her home. There she met the Rev Donald Perkins and in 1955 they married. She became increasingly active in the work of the Christian Community and when she came with her family to Botton she set up a workshop for making vestments, which were sent to congregations all over the world. Wherever she worked with children, trainees or adults, or within the realm of the house-community, she was permeated by love and enthusiasm for Camphill and anthroposophy. Her great modesty often hid her exceptional gifts, except from those who knew her well. One felt that in this life a great personality had worn the vestments of a server.

PETER AND KATE ROTH
From Camphill Correspondence, 1980/11.

Ann Harris

July 27, 1923 – September 8, 2006

Ann Harris, who died aged 83, was an influential figure in the development of Camphill school and adult communities where the abilities of those with special needs are nurtured and valued.

She devoted sixty years of her life to improving the support and opportunities available to people with learning disabilities and mental health problems — the last 43 years being particularly associated with the establishment and growth of the Camphill Village Trust's Delrow College at Aldenham, near Watford.

Ann Gertrude Harris was born on July 27, 1923, at Newport Pagnell,

Buckinghamshire. She was the eldest of six children, and though her father had independent means she was educated at local schools. During the Second World War she worked for Echo at Aylesbury, producing radios for the war effort. With the coming of peace she began studying at the Glasgow School of Art, which was to have an unexpected and profound influence on the course of her life.

A lecture on the therapeutic value of art led her to visit the Camphill Rudolf Steiner School in Aberdeen. It was her first contact with disabled children and the community way of life. She quickly realized that this was the path for her. Within weeks she had abandoned her studies and on St Martin's Day, November 11, 1946, moved to Camphill in Aberdeen.

The environment in which she immersed herself was considerably different from anything she had previously experienced. The Camphill Schools had been established so that vulnerable children in need of special care could live and learn with others in a healthy social relationship based on mutual care and respect. It wasn't just the children who were learning, as those who cared for and supported them were learning too, so as well as working with the children Ann attended lectures and seminars.

Soon she had to take a class, and while she taught the children, she was also being taught by Kate Roth.

Ann found the work challenging as some of the children were very difficult, but she was spurred-on by the inspiration provided by Dr König and the other Camphill founders. At the same time, König recognized that she had much to contribute.

"If he saw that you might be able to help him, he had time for you," she recalled in 2002, the centenary of his birth. "He was able to see your potential, although you might not see it yourself. People thrived on his awareness of their potential."

Ann was one of those people, and after four years in Aberdeen she volunteered to move to the South of England to help spread the Camphill approach to educating children with special needs. Initially she moved with Tilla König to assist St Christopher's School at Bristol in establishing its first facility, Wraxall, where pupils with special needs could board. Within a couple of years she was involved in starting the Sheiling School at Thornbury, near Bristol — Camphill's first school in England. From there Ann moved to Hampshire to help at the Sheiling School at Ringwood. While there, she took in three nephews when their mother died, mothering them alongside her other work until they were able to return to her brother when he remarried.

In 1955 there was a move back to Camphill in Aberdeen where at Cairnlee House she worked with a demanding group of girls. Four years later she moved to Murtle House to work with younger children, and in Camphill's true spirit of mutual support took with her an older difficult group of girls to help!

By this time Dr König and his colleague, Thomas Weihs, had consulting rooms in Harley Street, London. There they held interviews and assessed special needs children and adults who might benefit from the Camphill community life. Ann, with a group of eight people with disabilities, occupied the upper floors of the building and she was greatly involved with the medical interviews. These were much more than an assessment of the level of ability of the child or adult. They allowed the interviewees to have their say about what they wanted from life and were a holistic assessment to determine the best situation for each individual — person-centred planning long before the term was ever used.

Camphill had established its first working community for adults with special needs in Botton in 1955 and by the early 1960s Ann wanted to see one near London. She found Delrow House at Aldenham near Watford and, undaunted by the broken glass on top of the walls of this former approved school for girls, or the wet and dry rot in the three-hundred-year-old mansion, in 1963 she moved in with her group from Harley Street. Soon more were referred to Delrow, mostly with forms of mental illness.

A synergy resulted from the inclusion in the new community of people with disabilities and mental health problems with each group benefiting from the presence of the other and providing mutual support.

By then the interviews for children, young people and adults seeking places in communities were held at Delrow, so Ann was often the first contact with Camphill for those with disabilities and their families. Her caring, thoughtful way and her interest in each individual made lasting impressions which resulted in her corresponding regularly with several hundred people right up until a few days before her death.

As the community at Delrow grew, it found its role in the Camphill movement as a place where people could find their direction in life. Ann described it as "a positive space where adults can decide where their future will lie."

Sometimes that future would be in one of the Camphill Village Trust's other working communities, but Ann also recognized that the Camphill life didn't suit everyone and for some a different situation could be what was needed.

Her role at Delrow was pivotal — always encouraging and organizing, liaising with the parents and families of residents, fund-raising and publicizing the work of Delrow and Camphill in the local area. Over forty years, Delrow grew to become a community of a hundred people, with around half having special needs.

The cultural and social life of the community was important to Ann. The hall at Delrow has hosted concerts by many gifted musicians from all over the world as well as local events, such as the Radlett Music Club. She was an avid reader, and by running a bookshop at Delrow she had the pleasure of having a whole shop to choose from. Travel was one of her loves too. For 24 years she took groups from Delrow to the former Yugoslavia, and in her seventies she holidayed in places as diverse as Uzbekistan and Borneo. She gave slide-shows of her travels at Delrow and to local clubs.

While Delrow was her home from 1963 until her death, she was always involved with many Camphill communities and other organizations. As well as being a member of the management committee of her own community she was involved in the management of Camphill at Milton Keynes, East Anglia, Devon and Stroud. She was a trustee and, for many years, joint company secretary of the Camphill Village Trust. She was also a trustee of the Camphill Foundation and of Nutley Hall, a home for people with disabilities in Sussex, and was closely involved with the Association of Camphill Communities which represents the fifty communities in the UK and Ireland. For a long time she was a council member of the Anthroposophical Society of Great Britain and was also deeply involved with the Association of Therapeutic Communities, the National

Association for the Care and Resettlement of Offenders and the National Schizophrenic Fellowship.

At the age of sixty she was awarded the MBE for her work with Camphill. She didn't believe in retirement and continued to share her enormous experience, providing advice and reassurance for the many people who contacted her. She was at work in her office at Delrow until the week of her death.

Despite proposals, she never married, saying that a personal family life would not have allowed her the time to devote her energies to Camphill. The wonderful legacy resulting from her life's work is her memorial.

SANDY COX
From New View, *Autumn 2006.*

Florence Bryan

September 16, 1902 – June 2, 1995

Florence Bryan was born on September 16, 1902, in Cardiff, south Wales, as the last of eleven children. Her father was a self-taught man, who had a grocery wholesale business but, described as "something of a mystic," was also a lay preacher and wrote hymns, sold in the Welsh valleys to raise money for the soldiers' families in the First World War. By the age of twelve she was the only child left at home; the war claimed some of her six brothers and she found herself having to fight for an education, while her ailing mother increasingly claimed her attention. She must have been a bright student though, and by 1920 she was booked to go to Cambridge with the intention of working towards scientific research (which in later years she would claim could not have led her on to anthroposophy). However, her eyesight deteriorated and she opted for a relatively shorter training as a pharmacist, which was nearer home and allowed her to continue assisting her mother. On completing her studies this latter circumstance, regrettably, also prevented her taking a job in her hard-won profession.

During this time she met and became engaged to her future husband, Edgar Cooper Bryan, eventually marrying in 1926 after difficult years in the post war era. A girl and a boy were born to them and, having been introduced to the Christian Community and anthroposophy through friends in the early thirties, they decided to move to Streatham in South London in 1936 so that their two children could attend The New School (later renamed Michael Hall). The family father had a secure job travel-

ling throughout South West England for a protective clothing manufac-
turer, and Florence found time, next to being a caring mother, to attend the
first ever Michael Hall Teacher Training course. This settled existence,
however, was all too soon shattered by the outbreak of the Second World
War — her husband sent to an industrial job in the Midlands as a conscientious objector, she with the children was evacuated to the West Country.
Very difficult years followed, with the children attending Wynstones
School, where she at times helped with hostel work and handwork teaching to make ends meet. Living conditions were very "romantic" as evac-
uees housed in upstairs rooms of an old vicarage with no gas or electricity
laid on and water fetched from downstairs! Relief only came when she
was offered the post of housekeeper for the newly started Christian
Community Social Centre at 34 Glenilla Road in North London, preferring to move there despite the bombs still falling in 1944. Her warm hospitality there was quietly appreciated for some years before she and
Cooper sought a new life working together in Camphill at the end of the
war. They settled in Newton Dee, the most recently acquired estate, built
the "Bungalow" and with others set up the Central Training Workshops as
a successful extension of the work there with delinquents.

Contrary to their hopes, however, she and Cooper separated in 1950.
Not wished for on her part and selflessly accepted, this mid-life change

did at last open the way for her to realize her professional ambitions instead of accepting secondary roles for the sake of others. She took the new challenge positively and soon commenced on what was to become many years of close collaboration with Dr König and Dr Hans-Heinrich Engel, preparing and potentizing, even making new medicines and carrying out endless experiments for new diagnostic techniques with crystallization and capillary dynamolosis.

When circumstances changed in the mid sixties, some rather unsettled years of searching followed with longer or shorter periods of time spent at Brachenreuthe, Glencraig and the Sheiling at Ringwood (working with Dr Lotte Sahlmann) and ending with six months keeping the Weleda pharmacy going in Johannesburg, South Africa, before settling at Perceval, St Prex in Switzerland. There, at the age of sixty-four, she started nearly twenty years of further demanding and fruitful work in the medical department in close collaboration with Dr Leonardo Fulgosi.

For many years of her life she had been a server for the Christian Community services, later in life also holding religion lessons and the school children's and offering services — an activity continued, even in French, to the end at Perceval. Semi retirement at 81 brought some quiet years in her much beloved lakeside surroundings until need for greater care necessitated a move to Simeon Care for the Elderly at Bieldside, Aberdeen. There she remained, devotedly cared for, until her strong forces allowed her to cross the threshold in June 1995, closing her long life of service and striving.

JOHN BRYAN
From Camphill Correspondence, *1995/5.*

Lotte Sahlmann

April 22, 1913 – December 7, 2002

Dr Lotte Sahlmann died on December 7, 2002, at the age of 89 at her home in Ringwood. Two months previously she had still been working in her garden where she had spent much of the last years tending her vegetables and pondering life's ways. Having left her garden for the last time, she turned her gaze inward to reflect on her own life. It was as if she recognized that her work as a doctor was incomplete until she had lived into the experiences of dependency and vulnerability. It was with these challenges that she entered the last month of her life. Modesty and humility became hallmarks of her dying just as they had been of her living.

Lotte was born in Fürth near Nuremberg in southern Germany of German-Jewish parents. Her father traded hops and her mother ran the family home. She loved her time in school and was in a class with very able students who formed close and long-lasting friendships. Two incisions into this otherwise joyful and rich childhood made deep impressions on her. The first, at around the age of seven, was the sudden death of her elder brother in a bicycle accident. The second was the protracted illness and subsequent death of her mother when Lotte was twenty-one.

Around the age of eleven she saw a eurythmy performance, probably directed by Marie Steiner, and several years later came into possession of Steiner's *Knowledge of Higher Worlds*. However, she still searched far and wide before committing herself to anthroposophy.

Lotte left school in 1932 and followed a call to study medicine. During the first semester in Munich she witnessed Hitler delivering a speech to a huge crowd and realized then and there that she would leave Germany. Then followed the third tragedy of her life: the decision of her fiancé not to join her.

With an invitation to continue her studies in Florence, she left, Italian dictionary in hand, and spent the next three years there before transferring to, and graduating from, the University of Turin. Immediately on completion of her final exams she fled the now war-involved Italy and travelled via Paris to London, arriving on April 2, 1939. Later she related the amusing incident of mishandling an none-compliant telephone box on her arrival at Charing Cross station and receiving its entire contents in exchange! She took this as a good omen and after a two-year period as an au pair got her first medical job near Newcastle. From there to the Homeopathic Hospital in Birmingham and Grantham Hospital she joined up as a general practitioner in Buckinghamshire. This fruitful period lasted until her decision to move to Aberdeen to join Camphill.

Thus she arrived in Aberdeen, an established professional with expectations, questions and a fiery will. Between April 1946 and September 1950 she lived in several locations. Then she moved to Bristol where she served the medical needs of St Christopher's, Wraxall House, before moving to Thornbury Park. There she focused her work on children with cerebral palsy, giving daily treatments and building up a specialist knowledge. Her final move was to Thornbury's sister school, The Sheiling in Ringwood, in 1963. From there she travelled widely, still covering the needs in Thornbury as well as other places, most notably South Africa. Over the years she extended her fields of specialization to children with aphasia, Fragile-X syndrome and autism among others. But she remained *par excellence* a doctor for all children with special needs. Here she excelled in her diagnostics, her empathy, her good judgments and her teaching. She helped innumerable parents and others to understand and accompany their children. She was recognized by many as the first person to really understand their child. It was in appreciation of her tireless work in this field that she was awarded the MBE.

Lotte's modesty was apparent on this occasion in a very obvious way: her brand new outfit in which she met the Queen was purchased in its entirety from Oxfam and worn with pride! I met another aspect of this in the last month of her life when she reflected on some of her experiences. It seemed that a profound questioning had arisen in her and a humility appeared in respect to all situations she might have understood and acted upon differently. Her final wish was to recognize, accept and do better in an attempt to do the good on earth.

FRANCES TAGG
From Camphill Correspondence, *2003.*

Avril Buchanan

March 17, 1926 – February 9, 1992

It was in the summer of 1964 that we first met Avril Buchanan on one of our visits to Camphill Village, Copake, USA. At once we were attracted by her warm humour, her cheerfulness of spirit and most of all, perhaps, by her whole-hearted goodwill, which radiated to include all the Villagers and those associated with her work at the village bakery.

Our second memorable impression of Avril was our great pleasure and appreciation when we saw her unforgettable performance as the Mother in Christopher Fry's play *The Boy with the Cart,* with George Zipperlin in the leading role. This presentation took place outdoors on the site where Fountain Hall was to rise the following year. One still can recall with a chuckle of enjoyment how she clung to the sides of the cart as it lurched precariously over the rough ground, being manfully trundled by the enthusiastic son!

Among other gifts, Avril had an outstanding ability in producing Festival Plays with our villagers. Her own warmth and enthusiasm readily united them in a real community spirit. To watch her rehearse a cast in a play was an unforgettable experience, particularly her rehearsals of Karl König's St John's Play at Corbenic in the three years 1989–91.

Avril was an excellent teacher and speaker whose enthusiasm for the subject matter in hand immediately opened the ears and hearts of those with whom she worked. Indeed, her activity with trainees, villagers and co-workers over the many years of her Camphill life was a remarkable illustration of the truth of the saying that: *what goes from the heart, reaches the heart.* That was the keynote of her life and activity as we all knew her, for she was above all a person of heart — in the finest and most objective sense of the word.

Avril Buchanan was born March 17, 1926 in Assam, NE India, where her father was a manager of Rungamuttee Tea Estate. Her sister Elizabeth was born four years later while the family was on a brief visit to England. Avril's father was the youngest son of a Church of Scotland minister, her mother the eldest daughter of a Church of England clergyman.

Shortly before Avril's sixth birthday she was taken to England to live with her mother's parents in order to convalesce from the effects of recurring malaria and tropical dysentery. The parting from her mother was one of the most painful life memories, for she sensed that she would never see her again. Indeed, her mother died in childbirth in India just five months later.

Avril and Elizabeth continued living with their grandparents in Sussex where she eventually attended a convent school in Mayfield. In order to prepare for this convent education, the grandmother read the New Testament to her every evening, and the Old Testament for an hour every day in the holidays. She attended church at least once each Sunday and after confirmation at fourteen years, also taught in Sunday school.

In 1940, with the fall of France (and also the death of her grandfather), a period of unsettled wartime existence began for Avril, involving among other activities, a short period of nursing in a children's hospital in 1943. Because of dissolving family relationships, Avril experienced for the first time in her life absolute homelessness. This led to her conviction, as she later expressed it, that "reincarnation was the only thing which made sense — religion meant nothing any more."

It was in 1946 during a stay at a guest-house in Perthshire that Avril met and was befriended by Ann Harris, who was then designing radio sets in Glasgow. On June 1, 1947, after a prolonged illness, including the time of her twenty-first birthday, Avril went for a week's visit to Ann Harris, who was then working in Murtle House. For the first time "she felt as if she had come home and found people who talked sense." Shortly after a long talk with Dr König on June 6, she made a "firm and definite decision to remain in Camphill."

For almost 45 years Avril devoted herself to serving the work, life and ideals of Camphill in many of our centres, including Heathcot, Camphill, Newton Dee, Ringwood and Thornbury. Then in 1959 she joined the pioneer group in USA, first at Downingtown and Donegal Springs in Pennsylvania, and finally remained eight years in Camphill Village, Copake, New York.

In June 1973 Avril returned to Murtle Estate and became one of three who formed the first Camphill nurses' training course under the leadership of Gisela Schlegel. In summer 1987 she joined the work at Corbenic, to the great satisfaction of Anke Weihs, who welcomed this step because of the wealth of gifts Avril brought with her as community member, service holder, nurse and experienced co-worker.

Avril's path to anthroposophy and Camphill was a long one, fraught with many forging strokes of destiny, not all of them by any means easy to bear. Nevertheless, in her nearly 45 years of Camphill life, her contribution was graced with a spirit of unselfishness, of joy and great gratitude, which inescapably radiated to all those with whom she came into contact. This touched us also during our farewell moments with Avril at the Perth Royal Infirmary on February 8, 1992, the day before she crossed the threshold into the spiritual world.

PAUL M. AND JOAN DERIS ALLEN
From Camphill Correspondence, *1992/3.*

Ilse von der Heide

February 16, 1920 – November 19, 2003

Shortly after sunset of November 19, 2003, Ilse breathed her last. It was the day of St Elizabeth of Thuringia, the king's daughter who died young, having given her life in the service of the poor and ill. When she was christened in 1920, Ilse received the modest, short version of the name Elizabeth: Ilse. Her parents must have had an intuition that she would have much in common with St Elizabeth.

Ilse had made a good choice of her parents, looking upon them with deep gratitude. In her mother and father she had the best representatives of the world of the spirit and the world of the soul. Her father was a solicitor and businessman. He came from Westphalia and was a seeker in the realm of the spiritual and of religion. His search led him to anthroposophy while Rudolf Steiner was still alive and also to the Christian Community in its early days. Her mother came from Hamburg and in her sunny way she shared her husband's searching.

Her elder brother, Paul, came to her parents in 1918, and then in 1923 her younger brother Henning. All the children were born in Berlin.

Ilse's physical constitution was delicate. It was difficult for her digestive system to cope. All through her long and full life she showed that man does not live by bread alone. Like St Elizabeth she gave people red roses without thorns.

Ilse experienced her first move when she was four years old, to the countryside of Stettin (now Szczecin in Poland) with a hundred cows and a wide starry horizon. She had a happy childhood, a village school, friends and a love for nature. The high point was in her ninth year when she met Friedrich Rittelmeyer. In a book where she collected poems — one can feel with what devotion the little girl handed it to him — he wrote words that became a leitmotif through her life: "For those who love God everything works towards goodness."

In the same way that the star of Rudolf Steiner rose for her while she was still in the cradle, a second radiant star now rose in her sky. She was deeply impressed with the way Rittelmeyer stroked her hair: with this a sign was given by this great carer of souls, a sheltering, blessing gesture that entered Ilse's life through the Christian Community.

Another move came in her tenth year through her father's profession. She came to St Polten near Vienna. From a village school she now came to a convent school and grew especially fond of her French teacher. But she also greatly enjoyed the Protestant religion lessons, and joined many holiday camps. The Christian Community was being founded in Vienna and Rudolf Köhler came twice a month to give religion lessons in her house. He spoke about Parsifal, but what made a deep impression on Ilse, which she never forgot, was when he once pulled out the twelve stones of the Apocalypse from his pocket.

It would, however, be a mistake to imagine Ilse as a convent pupil, a stranger to the world. She painted, did gymnastics, danced and sang and went skiing, falling again and again. She lived completely in an ever-darkening world. The shadows of National Socialism were spreading, but Ilse, as always, saw the sunny side of events; community life was not touched, to begin with.

Her life and home were so rich, so filled with spiritual treasures, it shone brighter than all the rest. When she was fifteen years old, Ilse had a part in the opera for the first time — was it by chance that it was *Tannhäuser* in which the hero stands before St Elizabeth?

Ilse had two meetings which left a deep impression when she was sixteen and seventeen. The first was with a small man with dark eyes — a doctor and a Jew — who would become a further star in her sky: Dr Karl König. For two years he had an enormous practice in Vienna. Ilse already felt good in the waiting room with all the children's toys

and the aquarium. And as she went to see him, she saw a familiar picture on his desk of the Risen Christ, *Il Redentore*. The significance of this moment for Ilse, albeit unconsciously, is described in Karl König's biography by Hans Müller-Wiedemann. Later Ilse got to know what he experienced in her, but first the dark times of the Second World War had to be endured.

A year later, 35000 people gathered at Berchtesgaden in front of the Führer. Ilse was there. Some of them were greeted personally by the Führer and Ilse was one of them. Suddenly he stood in front of her, stroked her hair and asked where she had come from. This shows one difference in these two meetings: Hitler looked to the past, his light was doomed; Karl König looked to the future, to the healing of the world.

After finishing school, Ilse went to Hamburg in 1938 to learn housekeeping. There she played an active part in the Christian Community youth group with Johannes Hemleben. After this she learned to be an assistant in a doctor's practice.

When the war started, Ilse was called up for "work in the service of the Reich." She did this first on a farm in Waldviertel, the area north of Vienna from where Rudolf Steiner's parents came, and later in Wiener Neustadt where he had spent his youth. The Anthroposophical Society was forbidden in the German Reich. Ilse's father had been denounced and his firm was forced to dismiss him. He used this sad situation to take up new studies. Throughout the war he always gave his children spiritual nourishment, introducing Ilse to the poet Christian Morgenstern who meant very much to her. At the age of 22 she had the responsibility for forty eighteen-year-old girls. This was a great burden on a person who had her own anxieties. She claimed that she was not very courageous, but somehow it worked.

When the Russian army were closing on Vienna German lorries came with orders to remove valuable materials. She had the courage to disobey the orders, and instead loaded her girls onto the lorries, saving them from the Russians by sending them to the French-occupied area. As she left her father gave her the verse that Rudolf Steiner had written for people in danger.

A few days later her father was run over by a Russian lorry and died that night in their flat. The following two days Vienna was plundered by the Russians. Two Russian soldiers forced themselves into the Von der Heide's flat where her father's body was laid out. The soldiers sank to their knees, crossed themselves and left the house untouched. Ilse only heard of these events about a year later.

When the work service dissolved, she was at the end of her strength and had stomach ulcers. Like all young girls immediately after the war she had to find a place to hide. One of her grateful girls found her a place in Tyrol. Later she looked after the children of a classmate at Innsbruck.

It is characteristic of Ilse that she had bright memories from these hard times. Once when she went to fetch milk under the starry sky, the words from Michael Bauer, "Christ is the homeliest there is," became an existential experience. Also the words from the Easter service lived her in her heart again and again: "Christ walks in the spirit before you."

During those dreadful times she experienced that the love of her parents had been like a protecting shield for her. She learned of the death of her beloved father in 1946 and came home, undernourished. She was able to stay at home running the household. She took courses in eurythmy and speech and this helped her to regain her strength.

The first International Youth Conference of the Christian Community took place in Shropshire, England in 1947. Ilse was asked to represent Austria with two other youngsters. Her elder brother, who was studying medicine, asked her to find out about Dr König who was then devoting himself to building up Camphill in Scotland. She wrote and Karl König replied, sending a single ticket to Aberdeen where Mrs König met her. Everything made an enormous impression on Ilse: the noble landscape with the huge beech trees through which the wind whispered; the crystal clear starry night: the many very handicapped children around her, whose higher being was addressed so impressively at the Sunday service in the chapel.

The ring of iron which had fastened itself around her chest throughout the war and which made it impossible for her to weep, as she had so often done before, started to dissolve. She was almost 28 years old. In her characteristic way she said to Karl König, "I think I must remain here!" To which he replied, "That is what I think too!"

Thus started half a century of service to the Camphill Community and humanity, on many levels and in many areas.

WALTER WILD

Leonie van der Stok

February 19, 1921 – January 8, 2005

Leonie always loved to talk to us about her childhood. When, in later life, her movements became ever more restricted, memories were always there, surrounding her like old friends. Nevertheless, her childhood had not been easy. She was born in Berlin into a well-to-do family, the second of three girls. Her father, a lawyer, was involved in the political life of the Weimar Republic, having Gustav Stresemann, the German Chancellor, and his private secretary Henry Bernhard among his clients. There was a lot of high society entertaining at home; the girls saw little of their parents and spent their time with nannies. Leonie and her older sister were only a year apart in age and grew up a bit like twins, but they were very different in character. Evelyn, a gentle child, was the favourite daughter, while Leonie presented problems and was considered unteachable! She was a tomboy who climbed trees and could never sit still for long. The fact that she was dyslexic was not understood nor accepted in those days.

Leonie must have been about seven when the parents divorced. The mother married Stresemann's private secretary, who must have been more of a family man. It was he who searched out the Steiner School for Leonie. Other schools had not coped with her but here she felt accepted. Leonie often referred to the moment of entering the school; she heard children singing and laughing and told her stepfather that this was "her" school and here she wanted to be. It was an important day in her life.

She had a fine perception for everything spiritual and this estranged her even more from her mother. As she was often naughty she had to spend times locked in the toilet. Here were quiet moments in which she started contemplating and developing her own technique for looking back over her day and her life. So she began to realize that she must have lived before. The concept of reincarnation was firmly established in her but she

learnt to keep her convictions to herself as they were not understood at home.

The coming of the Nazi regime changed life drastically for the family. Amidst all the turbulence the parents divorced again and the stepfather, of whom they had become fond, went out of their life. The children went to live with the grandparents for a while. As they were of very mixed nationality — English, German, Czech, Polish as well as Jewish, life became difficult. Leonie, at thirteen, was conscious and aware of all that was going on. She was a very outspoken child who did not keep her opinions to herself which was extremely dangerous then. This may have contributed to a hasty departure. The girls were sent to England, ostensibly to live with their father and his new wife, but this was not to be. When they arrived they were immediately sent to boarding school. The youngest girl was nine or ten at the time.

Boarding school was the junior hostel for the pupils of Michael Hall School. Leonie integrated happily into school life. The damp conditions in the poorly heated hostel were a different matter. Leonie became ill with rheumatic fever, an illness that was to recur several times in her life.

Holidays were spent with an uninterested father and a hostile stepmother. The girls must have felt quite abandoned which the kind and well-meaning house-mother of the hostel could barely compensate for.

Eventually Evelyn started to work in the Sunfield Home in Clent. Leonie and Beatrice (the third daughter) were able to spend part of their holidays there and loved it! Soon Leonie decided that she was not returning to school but would remain in Clent instead. This brought about a severe confrontation with the parents but she managed to get her way. Some years later Beatrice joined her sisters. The father and stepmother moved to America without consulting the girls, leaving them to fend for themselves. Clent became a real home for them. Here they also found a lifelong friend in David Clement, whose family home always stood open to them.

Now Leonie could begin to unfold her real gifts. She was not a scholar but was good with her hands. She was excellent at woodwork and made beautiful carvings throughout her life. She was also introduced to gardening and the work with the children. Leonie had found her place at last. Memories of Clent played a great role in her life; we heard a lot about the festivals, the artistic approach and rich culture of those years.

In 1947 Leonie discovered Camphill. She lived and worked in several Camphill places in Scotland and England. During these years she married Hans van der Stok and had her son Francis. Later she divorced.

In 1961 she moved with Francis to Christophorus in Holland. This is where we met and shared twelve years of working together. Conflicts in the community finally resulted in our departure. Leonie went to Botton. Then in 1979 the call came to help start a new village in the south of England; Hapstead came about.

Leonie invited her eighty-year-old mother to live with her. Her mother, who had not greatly involved herself in Leonie's childhood and upbringing, was now cared for by her daughter for fifteen years until her death!

In 1985, after yet another attack of rheumatic fever, Leonie's time had come to retire. She had built up the biodynamic garden at Hapstead while at the same time running a challenging household of ten villagers and caring for her mother. She had never had a home of her own and now wished to "live out." A bungalow was purchased in Paignton, her choice of place. Here she moved with her mother and began a life she had never known. After her mother's death she enjoyed a few more years there, tending her beloved garden and making new friends. Then the time came to move closer to Hapstead once more. Leonie settled in a bungalow in Buckfastleigh, with friends as neighbours and the family nearby.

In these years Leonie's strength diminished. She had to let go of her great interests in active gardening and woodwork. If this was frustrating for her, she did not show it. Her remarkable sense of humour remained. She had always been a passionate biodynamic gardener and continued to attend biodynamic meetings as long as it was possible for her. Conversations with her son in this realm were a continuous highlight for her.

Maybe even more difficult for her was having to rely on ever more help in daily living. Having always given help rather than receive it, she was very reluctant to ask, yet ever so grateful for the smallest thing one did for her. Leonie's strong, choleric personality did not always make it easy to live with her. Having had to cope with illness and hardship alone, especially early on in life, she was not sentimental, nor impressed with minor complaints, her own or other people's. This may have come across to others as her being a bit hard on them. Yet there was always warmth, that redeeming humour and a great generosity.

Many people were helped by her strong, positive convictions, be it villagers, co-workers or later neighbours. She often saw potential where others did not and helped to bring it about.

Leonie died peacefully in the night of January 7/8, 2005.

ARDIE THIEME
From Camphill Correspondence, *2005/3.*

Anne Gairdner-Trier

December 10, 1913 – July 12, 2003

Anne was born on December 10, 1913 at the very end of the age of European glory. In many ways, Anne's long life has echoed the trials and successes that the world has gone through in the twentieth century. Anne was a person of her time.

Anne had an extremely happy childhood. The family lived in an old manor house with a large walled garden, an orchard and surrounding fields in the rolling countryside around Glastonbury in Somerset. Anne's mother was an artist and the family home was run with love, devotion and beauty. Her father was a barrister and town clerk of Taunton.

Anne was the second child and had three brothers. They were close and happily played together, in fact Anne never played with girls until the age of 12! The family had two ponies and Anne's love of horses developed early. Anne had a governess and so all her early education was at home. Although her family was upper middle class she had a natural disregard for class distinction. When the village boys came to raid her garden and to steal raspberries, she helped them, saying, "Why shouldn't they have raspberries as well?" This openness to people and treating them as they were, was a quality that went through her life.

At twelve, Anne went to a girl's school that was very strict and which she didn't like. But at fourteen, she went to another school in Berkshire, which she loved. The headmistress was a special woman who had a conversation with each girl every term. She encouraged each of her pupils to become well-rounded human beings. This left a lasting impression on Anne.

Anne left school at eighteen to take part in the usual social life of her time: dancing, tennis, riding and hunting. Her brothers had all joined the Navy and so she was more alone. One of her brothers brought home a friend who became a special friend of Anne's. They felt that they had known each other before and that they would always be friends, but Anne knew she couldn't marry Dick and was sad about this. Dick once wrote to her: "Do you believe in Christ? I think that is what life is all about." Dick died on Anne's birthday in 1941 when his ship was sunk by the Japanese. This shows two other characteristics in Anne's life. She was always close to the Christ impulse, and throughout life formed many close relationships and didn't always know how to place them.

At nineteen Anne went to the Somerset Farm Institute, which was a very happy year for her. She felt that she overcame her intolerable shyness there. She then left to go home to help in the gardens and to ride and hunt. Edward was the gardener there and he was young, handsome and well read. He was a bit of a self-made philosopher and he helped Anne to see the wider world and to see that her own life was limited and selfish. Of course they fell in love and had to court in secret. It was a great shock for her family when they found out. This was another trait in her life: she loved her family deeply, yet gave them many shocks.

Anne then went to London to study nursing. Edward followed a year later and they continued to meet and remained close friends. Edward eventually married one of Anne's friends. In the first year of the war, before Dunkirk, Anne became depressed. She wanted to marry and couldn't. She wanted to become a nurse but felt she wasn't learning enough. She described that she just wanted to lie in the sun and leave this earth. One day, doing this, she almost stopped breathing and it was a blissful experience. This is another signature of Anne's life. Although she was always involved in a down-to-earth task such as weaving, gardening or working with horses, there was always something about her that almost didn't belong on the earth. She always felt like a citizen of two worlds.

Because of the danger in London, Anne then went home for a holiday. There she decided to enrol in a VAD training for nursing and went to Weston-super- Mare to do this. While waiting at the station she saw a sign saying "Famous Psychologist Palmist." She went in to find out her future. He told her: within six months you will marry a well-to-do man from the north with blond hair and blue eyes. Anne said that she did not know him. The palmist went on to say that she was not immune to air raids.

At home, her brother Tony invited the officers of an artillery regiment to a tennis party, and there Anne met Robin Gairdner. She thought: blue eyes and blond hair, and then promptly forgot about it. They were married that year, on December 3, 1940. These were the war years and they were often separated.

Sally was born on September 26, 1942. At Christmas 1943 Anne went home to Somerset for the birth of he son, Charles, who was born on February 9, 1944. Robin was able to come for the christening and they had a special week together. During these years they often lived near Camphill and Newton Dee, but Anne never saw either.

On March 14, 1944 Robin died in an air raid in London. He was working for the War Office at the time and staying with his brother. While his brother was out on fire watch, the house with him and his sister-in-law in it, suffered a direct hit. Anne felt that Robin carried her during this time of sorrow. When picking a posy of primroses for his coffin Anne felt she was in paradise. Before the interment service she looked at herself in a mirror and thought: this is the most difficult moment in my life, how can I go through with it? Suddenly this mood was lifted and she was full of joy. After the funeral her mother said to her that Robin was there, and Anne agreed. The family then had a joyous meal together. During that year Anne felt very close to Robin. She also found in her mother's Bible the readings from the Bible Reading Fellowship. Every evening she read these and they were her mainstay.

A year after Robin's death, Anne was in Weston-Super-Mare and stayed in a rooming-house. There she met an atheist who was very depressed. Anne told her it didn't have to be that way and that it all depended on your philosophy of life. Another guest, who overheard this and was impressed by Anne, and told her of anthroposophy. Anne felt as if a window to the spiritual world had been opened and was overjoyed. This was the first anniversary of Robin's death and Anne felt that anthroposophy was a gift for them both. Anne once said to me that Robin had led her to anthroposophy.

Anne joined the biodynamic work and moved near Glasgow to be nearer to Robin's family. Carl Alexander Mier came for a visit and told her about Camphill. When she heard about this community it was as if a bell rang out for her. Out of this interest she went to lectures in Glasgow by Carlo Pietzner and Karl König. She found that the lectures were like magic and she had supper with Dr König. He then invited her to come to Camphill. Anne did go for a weekend beginning on the first Advent Sunday in 1946. While there, Dr König said: "You belong to us." Anne did decide to return to Camphill and this caused a big battle with her family. Anne had to fight for the right to take the children with her. She arrived in Camphill on March 13, 1947, the day before the third anniversary of Robin's death. She was 33 at the time, and she came recognizing a call of destiny.

At Camphill she made a life for herself. She was drawn to the adolescents and she had a gift with them. In her busy life she even had time to look towards the future. She and Donald Perkins, a priest in the Christian Community, longed to do prison work, though this never happened. Anne was able to pick up her work with horses. She acquired two ponies and started teaching riding to both the handicapped and staff children. She always felt privileged as a child and longed to share the joy of riding with others. She continued to do this until her late seventies.

On May 29, 1949 she married Hans Jürgen Trier, a refugee from Germany. A year later she had a son, Christopher John. Her life with Hans was not easy. He suffered from severe mental problems which necessitated a move for the family and much uncertainty. Hans died tragically in December 1956.

Anne had to find her way once again. In 1955 Botton Village was started for adults with special needs and she had a longing to go there. She had to plead with Dr König to be allowed to go , and as with many of her battles, she won, moving to Botton in summer 1957.

Anne was in Botton until 1973. She started the weaving workshop and did much work with plant dyes. The products produced were sold all over the country to help provide the income the Village needed. Anne was very happy in Botton and created a home with her three children and her beloved horse. Village life was very much where she belonged. An illustration of how she was is an incident told by Sally. Sally came back to Botton once after staying with a normal family and complained that she would like a real home like them. Anne looked at her and said: Home is where I am!

Once again, a change of life was heralded by tragedy. On May 15, 1971 her son Chris was killed in a car accident. This was a terrible time for her. She seemed to be making her peace with this and settling back into Botton life, when in November 1972 another accident happened in which two girls died. This was a testing time for Botton, but for Anne it was just too much and she became very ill. She was invited to go to Hermanus in South Africa, but first she stayed with Sally and Terry to recover her health. She then went to Hermanus for fourteen months where she managed to come to terms with her grief. She loved Africa and was asked to stay on, but decided to come home, as she wanted to be near her family.

When she returned to Britain she moved to Bristol and helped with the founding of the Bristol Waldorf School kindergarten. She first was house-mother for people who needed sheltered accommodation, in a house belonging to the Christian Community. She then moved to cherry Orchards, a Camphill Community, and again did riding and opened up a weaving workshop.

In January 1981 Sally and Terry moved to Botton from Bristol. Anne missed them terribly and soon followed them up north. She moved to the Croft (Camphill Community) in Malton and reopened their weaving workshop. After a year she became very ill and it was suggested to her that she should take life easier. So she moved to Castleton, a village near Botton and became involved in local life. After her eightieth birthday she moved back into Botton to retire. This she found difficult, as she always needed to be involved and have a task. But this time, she really came to be with her family, and her involvement with Botton could not be the same. Nevertheless, many of us thought she had come home to die. But Anne still held many surprises in store for us.

In 1997 Sally and Terry decided to move to Scotland and Anne insisted on moving up with them. There was a new project, Pishwanton, up there that she wished to be part of. Anne has a great love for nature and for the elements and Pishwanton spoke to her deep feelings for the future. Her Camphill commitments never ceased and she longed to take them further into the world. It was hard for her, as her capabilities were declining and Pishwanton was a pioneering place without the buildings and facilities that she needed. But she remained true to this impulse and did what she could. Now the new Craft Building is completed and houses Anne's craft equipment and her dye-plants are planted around. So her involvement will be continued there. It was fitting that the first part of Anne's funeral could be in this building.

Anne's wish to increase the relationship between man and the horse grew stronger in her last years. She spent her last years compiling a booklet about the subject which is available in a photocopied form. Anne always possessed a very strong will, was incredibly positive, loved people and had a real sense of humour, all of which sustained her over the years of a life with many challenges. She overcame many hardships and lived her life to the full. Anne died on Saturday, July 12, 2003 during Bible Evening time — a weekly event that was so important to her.

DAVID ADAMS
From Camphill Correspondence, *2004/1.*

Nina De Marez Oyens

August 25, 1916 – April 11, 2005

Nina came to us from Aigues Vertes in 1988 on what she described was a "mission." Twice, she recounted, she experienced receiving a supersensible directive naming Solborg explicitly and describing how she would have a cultural task there. That all this happened at a time when Solborg was sorely in need of cultural reinforcements is beside the point. What is important is that Nina packed her things and headed north.

She must have been rather lonely at the beginning. I remember how she was always looking forward to visiting the dentist Dr Gulevik who had his training in France and the two of them could speak French together. However, she was too busy to be lonely. First of all there was the language; the step from her native Dutch to Norwegian proved to be little more than a matter of months. Before long, she was holding the Offering Service in presentable Norwegian, as well as teaching the cultural epochs to the seminarists.

Aleksandra, one of her pupils eight years ago, who has been building Camphill's Wójtówka Village in Poland, on her first visit since then, recounts: "I'll never forget the time spent with Nina on *The Philosophy of Freedom* and the metamorphosis of the soul. She seemed fascinated by my coming from the land of 'Communist apartheid', and she gave me many extra sessions." Aleksandra, in turn, was equally fascinated by what she described as Nina's "patchwork nationality": born in Holland, grew up in Germany, lived, worked and got her passport in Britain, moved to French-speaking Switzerland and finally settled in Norway. She speaks five languages fluently, is thoroughly Camphill and completely homeless!

So Nina was indeed an asset when she settled in tiny, struggling Solborg at the age of 74. But of all the talents she brought with her, one of the most appreciated was the capacity to find something humorous in

nearly every situation. Although nearly two years have passed since she left for Vidaråsen, her hearty laughter still rings. For it was in February 1995, that everyone felt that Vidaråsen would be a better place for a lady of her age. There, a care arrangement for older co-workers was functioning, and although we all found it hard to say adieu, we agreed that the move would be the right thing.

So in August of last year (1996) when Nina's eightieth birthday rolled around, a sizeable delegation from Solborg was on hand. The event was a joyous one — a double occasion — at which Arne Krom Nilsen, another Vidaråsen co-worker who had turned eighty, shared the dais with her.

Nina, a word of congratulation and appreciation resounds herewith in recognition of the cultural mission you've fulfilled so effectively here in Camphill in Norway.

IVAN JACOBSEN
"Nina's Eightieth Birthday," from Camphill Correspondence, *2005/5.*

I would like to share a little glimpse into Nina's rich and long life which I was privileged to get while living in Ita Wegman House, Vidaråsen, where she spent her last years.

Although I scarcely met Nina before then, perhaps these years were after all of great importance and significance for her and for her surroundings, both far and near. For in much the same way that up until around the age of three, a child prepares for its life on earth, so do older people, as they draw nearer, prepare for another life in another world.

An encounter with Nina always made one immediately aware of the fact that one was in the presence of a strong personality. She was full of interesting anecdotes from life, of her experiences of growing up in Holland, Germany (she loved Berlin especially) and of course, of Camphill. Her brothers once related to me on a visit how her path led her to Camphill. At the age of 24, Nina contracted consumption in Holland, and her father was strongly advised by the doctors that Nina would need to be in a sanatorium in the mountain air in order to make a recovery. She was the first of the four siblings, and being the only girl, her father was especially devoted to her and she to him. But she was also part Jewish. And this was not a good time to be travelling in Europe. However, her father was distantly related, on the mother's side to the German ambassador at the Vatican, to whom he wrote for help. A short while afterwards, much to everyone's consternation, two S.S. officers arrived at the school where he taught Greek and Latin. Their orders? To authorise and arrange for the young lady to travel to Switzerland and its healing mountain air!

While at the Dutch sanatorium in Davos, she got to know someone connected to the work of curative education, and from the moment of that first meeting with anthroposophy, her destiny was sealed and she resolved to take up this task. When she made a full recovery she began work at Brissago on Lago Maggiore which Ita Wegman had founded.

Although her three brothers are all from entirely different walks of life, they respected their sister implicitly in her more unusual vocation as curative teacher and matron in Camphill. Nina also became Karl König's secretary and wrote all his German correspondence.

Nina was extremely well-educated and cultured and one had the impression that through her interest, enthusiasm and her positive approach to her surroundings, she lived life to the full. This surely contributed to her skill and popularity as a teacher and educator of children, and in the various seminars in which she taught. She spoke at least five languages and went on to learn Norwegian in her seventies. Nina had an immense knowledge and appreciation of music, and once told me how she had really wished to be a conductor in her youth. Her lyre playing was accomplished as was her extraordinary repertoire of songs, arias and choral works. It was not unusual for the carers in Ita Wegman House to be regaled with a recital from Handel's *Messiah* or Mozart's *Die Zauberflöte* when they knocked at the door in the morning, or went to say "good night" late in the evening!

When Nina began to lose her orientation in time and space, she expressed how she came "to herself" when singing the old Camphill songs, of which she still remembered all three or four voices and most of the verses. Equally, the classics of German literature, the recital of poetry, and her appreciation of art — especially Italian and Dutch, sustained her enjoyment of life when she became less mobile.

The breadth and scope of her knowledge included the natural world of plants and trees as well as of the animal kingdom. The house cats became her favourite companions, while the occasional visit of the nurse's dog would brighten up her whole day. To accompany Nina on a little walk in the garden was to share through and with her the sheer childlike wonderment of nature's beauty.

It was not always easy for a person of Nina's stature to find herself more and more of need of daily help, and yet she learnt to bear this too, with dignity, and gratefulness towards her carers. I am sure I am not alone in remembering with a chuckle, her special wit and humour. She could play with words with the same abandonment as a child plays with its toys, yet a brilliant intellect shone through her jokes and witticisms. When I would roar with laughter, she would say, "Oh well, if I can make you laugh, it's still worth being here!"

Nina showed tremendous courage in her unhesitating acceptance of the most demanding children in the biggest houses in Camphill. But at the same time, she became wise and knew that it is never too late to learn from life. It seemed as if Nina's engagement with the present, her characteristic spontaneity and her "presence of mind" became transformed into "presence of the spirit" or "spirit mindfulness."

I have often pondered over the late blossoming of friendships in life, and of their possible significance for the future. Of one thing I am sure though, that those of us who lived with Nina during her later years feel warmed and enriched through our encounter with her.

With this tribute I would like to express my heartfelt thanks to her, and to her brothers for their support and care.

JUDITH INGRAM
From Camphill Correspondence, *2006/1.*

Richard Poole

July 27, 1911 – June 16, 1994

On July 27, 1991 our friend Richard celebrated his eightieth birthday; this after a long service to the ideals of Camphill.

I was only a greenhorn when I first became aware that across the field that separated Murtle from Newton Dee, amazing things were happening

thanks to Richard. I remember particularly the performance of Macbeth in the theatre in Aberdeen, which was done by the upper school pupils from Newton Dee. A wonderful glow came from that part of the school — drama, literature, music and related activities constantly enriched our life thanks to Richard and Mary.

Who else but Richard could sing with such passion (and such a straight face!) about the woes of Old Mother Hubbard and her Cupboard, set to a solemn tear-jerking aria in the style of Handel? How could Camphill's Carnival celebrations have survived beyond 1951 without Richard and his cast?

Despite my youth I was aware that frequently during those most wonderful of Camphill institutions, the Schools community meetings, it was not only Dr König who stood up to give voice to a view or impulse, but that Richard would also do the same. Richard's views did not always seem to coincide with what Dr König had in mind and yet Richard would rise again, extemporizing on his ideas with greater fervour. While bathing in the sweetness of Richard's superbly spoken English I remember having the experience: yes, this is the stuff of which free spiritual life is made in a social organism. That is, when out of common social striving, we can have the courage to put forward new insights, questions or impulses that can continually bring new life to the landscape of our common search.

Richard has continued to do this, I know, and it was out of this that one of his greatest inspirations was born, the weekly gardening on Thursdays as an ever-renewing homage to Corpus Christi. We also owe him the King Arthur pageants, for so long the centre of our Whitsun celebrations. My deep gratitude goes to him for what he has brought to Camphill over these many years and that he will continue to rouse our ageing hearts with his enthusiasm for many years to come.

NORA BOCK
From Camphill Correspondence, *1995/3.*

Britain's task to prepare the spiritual soul has its most noble representation in the works of William Shakespeare. My first meeting with Richard was in connection with his great love for this poet and for his plays. Richard was probably the first person to introduce Shakespeare to Camphill. I will not forget when *Twelfth Night* was performed in Newton Dee in one of the old classrooms: there, from behind a sheltering contraption, rose up a shining bald head, like the full moon, sending shrieks of delight among the audience; it was Richard as Malvolio!

Together with Mary, Richard must have been among the first British people in Camphill. Richard recognized the impulse, the work of Karl König, with his heart. He left behind his career as an Anglican priest to join Camphill, to start work in Thornbury; Richard's heart was entirely in tune with the "Middle European" impulse, yet he himself was, and stayed, British. Thus he met only too often the many challenges, with which he was prepared to struggle!

Richard's love for Dr König and Camphill, as well as for anthroposophy, was very deep. He also felt himself alone and true to the task of his country, to develop the spiritual soul. Richard did not travel out of Britain, not even for Camphill meetings, or holidays!

Ralph Waldo Emerson wrote essays on both Shakespeare and on Goethe. Rudolf Steiner said of these essays that "the Shakespeare essay ends in words of resignation, the Goethe essay in words of confidence and hope."

Richard's life had to do with bridging these two worlds, Shakespeare's and Goethe's, through the meeting with Camphill and anthroposophy. So it seems to me. When he became ill, knowing the seriousness of his condition, his warm interest in social developments, within and beyond Camphill, was outstanding. It seemed like a deep longing from his heart, for the future, for "confidence and hope."

GERDA BLOK
From Camphill Correspondence, *1995/3.*

Mary Poole

June 20, 1912 – January 22, 2003

The advent of Beatrice Mary Poole (née Wildig) over ninety years ago on June 20, 1912, occurred in what seems to us now a distant age more ordered and secure than our own, but it stood on the cusp of change. With the sinking of the *Titanic* the first cracks began to appear in Britain's unshakeable confidence in its primacy, its sense of world destiny and the duties of empire, yet the distant rumblings of approaching conflict went unheeded. Like an eyeless dancer on the crumbling heights of Dover, life pursued its accustomed course until the deluge of the First World War swept away the old familiar certainties. Mary was born into this starched and servanted world.

Her home was just outside Harrow-on-the-Hill, at that time a rural village north of London encircled by open fields and woodland. Although she grew up surrounded by nature, in which she delighted, and the simple rhythms of country life — the parson still visited on horseback, the doctor owned one of those new-fangled horseless carriages — her childhood was anything but tranquil. Her elder brother died tragically. This experience affected her mother so deeply that she rejected her two younger children. Thus Mary was the second child but took on the destiny of a first-born.

From her widely gifted father, a director of the London Press Exchange, she inherited many talents, both athletic and artistic. She learned to play the piano at five, and from an early age music provided a world of solace into which at times she could retreat when family tensions became unbearable. Often she found herself caught up in the frictions of her parents, standing between an unhappy father, whose musical and literary gifts went unrecognized in his marriage, and a mother whose simple goodness, charm and unworldly innocence was not his intellectual equal. Mary carried this childhood legacy throughout her life but spoke little about the hurt this must have caused her. In later life she said of her mother with deep feeling: "Poor, poor woman; how she suffered!" Of her father, whose nervous collapse she witnessed in her twenties, she said only that for someone of his refined and cultural temperament the competitive stress of the business world was utterly alien. Nevertheless, she reflected that her childhood was blessed in many ways. Despite the turmoil which periodically engulfed her she was always dimly aware of a "hidden presence" that lived behind everything — "something alive and beautiful which made itself felt from time to time," as she put it. This unseen presence cast its protecting cloak about her in many difficult

moments and sustained in her a life-long conviction in the absolute reality of a spiritual dimension. She called it "one of the most treasured bless-
ings of my life."

The family tensions obviously affected her school days, but her gifts
were apparent and she gained a place at the Royal Academy of Music
where her professors expected her to become a concert performer —
which she did. But before beginning her studies she had rather inexplicably become engaged (after the usual heavily chaperoned courtship) to an
officer training at Sandhurst for the Indian army. Within the space of a
week she took and passed her L.R.A.M. exams, broke off her engagement
and left home precipitately to live temporarily with an aunt. This proved
to be anything but the haven she needed, and she found herself in London,
young and very bewildered, where she took a secretarial training and
worked in the music department of the BBC. She described this period as
a rather "grey" existence, nevertheless her debut on the concert platform
was the prestigious Wigmore Hall, and thereafter she broadcast many
piano recitals for the BBC's Third Programme. But her life's direction
remained unclear for a number of years.

Eventually, in her late twenties, through a close friend from her
Academy days, she met her future husband, Richard, at a London concert
in which he was singing. After Oxford, he had been ordained in the
Anglican Church and was then a curate in St George's, Bloomsbury, at
that time a congregation with strongly pacifist leanings which echoed his

own radical idealism. The wedding was planned for September 2, 1939, (a High Anglican Nuptial Mass filled with glorious music performed by their many friends) but the gathering storms of war finally burst and at the eleventh hour they had to abandon everything — well, not quite: the wedding cake arrived as they scrambled to catch the last train out of London to Richard's new parish in Sussex. Communication was impossible (many guests arrived to find an empty church), and all transport was in chaos. With extraordinary ingenuity, Richard's elder brother, the Precentor at Winchester Cathedral, managed to smuggle out its costly vestments and commandeered a taxi, driving across country through the blackout.

Arriving in Sussex, makeshift arrangements were hurriedly made; flowers gathered from local gardens, guests invited from the highways and byways (none of whom were known to either of them), and the local vicar gave the bride away. Curious onlookers remarked wryly, "The bride arrived with a cake and no parents," but the wedding was furnished with guests. A nearby hotel welcomed the honeymoon pair, but the following morning (September 3), the outbreak of hostilities was broadcast to a nation united in patriotic fervour — with the exception of two of its citizens who declined to stand for the National Anthem! Consequently they found themselves summarily ejected. The incident typified a non-conformist trait in Richard's character that over the years made for numerous confrontations; situations made doubly painful for Mary whose sensitivity to tension remained from her troubled childhood. Yet, for all her dislike of frictions and disagreement, she never wavered in her support of her husband whose ideals she largely shared. Hers was a softer, more intuitive way, and her graceful charm very often saved the day.

During the dark and uncertain war years there were inevitably many tense moments occasioned by this radical priest whose pacifist views were so starkly opposed to the outlook of the time. Mary's constitution was frail and gradually it all wore her down until eventually she became unwell.

Richard's pastoral work often took him into hospitals where he observed the inadequacies of conventional medicine, and this prompted them to search for an alternative approach to healing. Homeopathy was embraced, as were the ideas of Jungian psychology, but as yet no clear way forward was apparent to them. Richard's uncompromising views brought him increasingly into conflict with his church, while Mary needed peace to find the inner certainty of a life-direction she sensed but could not yet name. By 1944 they had moved to Hove on the Sussex coast, and Mary was expecting her first child. One day, Richard burst in brandishing a pamphlet, saying, "You must read this!"

"This" turned out to be an article written by one Dr Karl König on the place of faith, hope and charity in medicine, published in a newsletter of the Iona Community in Scotland. It was the turning point which would lead them eventually to anthroposophy (she joined the Society in 1948), and Camphill.

Because the army had requisitioned all the local hospitals Mary had to go to an alternative maternity home in Somerset for her confinement. Returning to Hove with her baby son, the sombre realities of wartime closed around her again and weighed ever more heavily, but slowly a new light began to dawn. Richard had attended a lecture by Alfred Heidenreich of the Christian Community, a religious movement based on the teachings of an Austrian philosopher whose name they had heard but whose ideas they had never explored. As their interest kindled and the profound implications of this philosophy began to sink in, both felt an urgent need for a period of undisturbed peace to grapple with inner questions. Fortuitously, or so it seemed, the sympathetic Bishop of Salisbury (like Richard, a pacifist) offered a tiny parish in rural Oxfordshire, to which they initially agreed to go. However, it felt to them just too perfect — the after-image of a motionless pool whose mirror-still surface concealed lifeless waters appeared in a disquieting dream — in short, a *cul-de-sac*. For Mary, who went to see it after the birth of her daughter, there was something unreal, almost surreal, about its idyllic beauty that deeply depressed her. They declined the post.

The decision was momentous, for with it grew the certainty that Richard should withdraw from the Anglican clergy, which he eventually did. Although this left them almost rudderless, the prospect of training for the priesthood of the Christian Community, embracing the spiritual landscape of anthroposophy with its selfless, divine conception of religious compassion, offered a possible new direction which they began to explore. In a visit to Albrighton Hall, then the centre of the Christian Community in Britain, Mary experienced a strange, unsettling haunting which, among other considerations, in the end decided them not to follow that path.

Before this, however, they had met Dr König and discussed the possible joining of Camphill, but at the time the idea seemed premature and was abandoned. Richard had attended the first British anthroposophical medical conference in Clent and was deeply impressed by the work being done there with handicapped children. While in the throes of extricating himself from the Anglican Church and exploring future options, he had worked for a period in Towerlease, a well-known nature-cure clinic in Bristol, and had become friends with Miss Irene Groves, a founder of Michael Hall School, who was then engaged in helping Catherine Grace establish a school for handicapped children (St Christopher's) in her own home in Bristol. One day, musing on the urgent need for a residential hostel to help the fledgling venture, Miss Groves turned to Richard and said, "Why don't *you* do it?" With that almost casual remark the die was cast; their future destiny was glimpsed and gradually began to take shape.

During this time Mary remained alone in Sussex with the two children, expecting her third child in the winter of 1947, which turned out to be one of the coldest on record. Life was very hard at times — in the seventh month she succumbed to an epidemic of dysentery — since distance only partly spared her the worry of her husband's frenzied escapades, which she accompanied vicariously through news received from time to time. And the news must have seemed improbable indeed! Despite his obviously empty pockets and less than watertight pledges of finance, Richard's boundless optimism persuaded lawyers and estate agents — never easily convinced — to allow the purchase of an old, rambling Georgian pile in an endearing state of disrepair which he had discovered in the village of Thornbury, some fifteen miles from Bristol.

This was Thornbury House, the intended hostel for St Christopher's School whose governors were understandably appalled to learn what had been purchased in their name during the summer recess! (Although too distant from Bristol for practical purposes it began nevertheless, a daily run in an old, borrowed car that would periodically grind to a halt with clouds of steam from an overheated radiator, or whose door would fall off at whim.) They moved in one dark November day in 1948, to make everything ready to receive the first children, but it was an inauspicious welcome. The chilly damp seeped downstairs and through walls to wrap them in its clammy embrace, and their first attempt to kindle a fire almost brought the venture to an abrupt halt: with an ominous roar the chimney caught, belching smoke and flames into the room. As a local crowd gathered to watch the fire brigade, one was heard to remark, "Them folk be just moving in; they'll soon be moving out." But they did not! This began a long, almost single-handed struggle which might have come to nought had not Dr König (at that time the visiting consultant for St Christopher's), been aware of their predicament and began to send experienced co-workers down from Camphill in Scotland to assist the beleaguered pair. However, as a hostel serving St Christopher's it was not to last, and Thornbury House eventually became part of the Camphill movement.

In 1952 the family moved to Scotland to join Camphill proper, first in Newton Dee Cottage for a period, then to the Lodge for many happy years spent alongside Dr König's elderly parents — so inseparable that they were referred to as a single entity: "Grandmother-and-grandfather" — who lived downstairs. But those were straightened times. One cold water tap and a tiny "Baby Belling" electric cooker with a single hotplate provided for the family plus four maladjusted teenage boys! The laundry was a lean-to outbuilding with just a boiler and cold rinsing sink; the only lavatory an earth-closet in a timbered outdoor shed whose noisome interior remains a pungent memory! But Mary weathered all these trials with grace and competence. Orderliness spread around her as if impelled from within, and her children thrived in the atmosphere created from the well-spring of her artistic nature. Music filled the house, often accompanying Richard's madrigals with her exquisitely light playing, and spilled into the community at festival times. She brought a natural refinement to everything she did, and the best aspects of her English cultural heritage contributed in some measure to a slow Anglicizing of a community, which at that time still had a distinct European flavour.

In 1961, she and Richard were asked to take on Kidbrooke Mansion, the hostel for Michael Hall School, a task they accepted in response to Dr König's call for Camphill to assist the Waldorf movement in every way possible. This lasted but a year before they were on the move again: to 122 Harley Street, the London centre at which Dr König held his clinics. As its leasehold was then under compulsory purchase for development, the search began for alternative premises, and thus Delrow House near Watford was bought and became their harbour for a while. However, the demanding work of a new venture in its pioneering stages took its toll on Mary's health, always delicate, and she needed relief. So she returned to Scotland, leaving Richard in Delrow to follow his single-minded vision for a new form of training college, and moved to Camphill House where she cooked for a while, enchanting Dr König's Viennese soul with her culinary arts.

Cooking was very close to Mary's heart. In this she possessed an almost "musical" gift, conjuring exquisitely subtle flavours from a wide palette of herbs and spices. Her reputation in this field soon grew and she gave occasional courses, although these were never theoretical, being very much a hands-on experience for the participants. Over the years she was often encouraged to develop this into a full course on nutrition, but to the disappointment of many — and, one suspects, perhaps also to herself — she did not find the time to do so; indeed, it would have been a Herculean labour to convey her largely intuitive knowledge in written form.

Mary then lived for a time in the Grange in Gloucestershire, after which she and Richard moved to Botton Village in Yorkshire in 1966. Once again they were a united force, contributing richly to the cultural fabric of a vibrant and rapidly evolving experiment in community living. Many former pupils of Botton School remember Mary for the love of music she instilled in them, and her delicate playing of piano and harpsichord embellished the festivals of the community for many years. But her own playing of keyboard instruments gradually diminished as arthritis reduced the dexterity of her hands. Instead she taught herself the recorders, and with these, too, she achieved an extraordinarily sensitive, expressive way of playing; the tonal purity and quiet beauty of her phrasing remain an abiding memory. Having mastered these, she then turned to the strings, specifically to the medieval viols, forerunners of our modern-day strings.

Eventually, these also became too much for her hands and she had per-
force to give up playing.

After leaving the harsh weather of North Yorkshire behind in 1979 —
ostensibly for softer climes, but in reality "so as not to be a burden to our
children," two of whom had just joined Botton — she and Richard
"retired" to the Sheiling School near Ringwood in Hampshire. Since
"retirement" is a word hardly recognized in the Camphill lexicon, it was
still a pretty active time for them both until Richard's death in 1994. But
during the years in Ringwood an unexpected tributary began to flow into
the wide river of her gifts as Mary took on illustrating nursery rhymes and
fairy tales for her grandchildren.

As the years drew on, living alone became less tenable, and so in 1998
her daughter Celia felt she should bring her back to Botton.

Her ninetieth birthday was a glorious occasion among family and
friends on a radiantly beautiful summers day.

From childhood on Mary was steadfast in her trust in the spiritual
world and its guidance of her life towards Camphill and anthroposophy.
Now it seemed as though her gaze rested upon it, asking to be fully
embraced in its reality at last. She died before the sun rose on the morning of January 22, 2003.

NICHOLAS POOLE
From Camphill Correspondence, *2003/6.*

Irma Roehling

April 27, 1923

*The following a story confirming Irma's conviction of guidance. She has
been a co-worker, teacher and house-mother in Camphill in Scotland,
England, the USA, South Africa and Botswana. Since 1984 she lives in
Camphill Farm Community, Hermanus, South Africa.*

Who has helped us? There are moments in life when one is helped, when
one can achieve something that seems impossible, when one is guided to
do the right thing and receives help even when feeling utterly helpless.

In 1940 children were sent from the West to the East of Germany to
escape the bombing of the big cities such as Düsseldorf. There I was with
children and teachers from a Düsseldorf high-school in a small spa called
Oybin near the city of Zittau in Saxony. Bad Oybin was a lovely place surrounded by mountains and forests. Up the hill was the Czech border,

which at that time was open and we could cross any time. Here was peace and beauty as well as tranquillity. We soon grew together in our camp. Children and teachers had a full and ordered life of school. I was responsible for everything else: leisure-time and cultural activities, sports, swimming and hiking. All of us worked harmoniously together.

The war seemed far away until the news arrived that the Russians had moved into Czechoslovakia. For two years we had lived in peace. The girls were now twelve to sixteen years old when the warning came that soon we would have to leave. Christmas was our last festival with a traditional Christmas play behind locked doors, because one no longer celebrated Christmas in this way in Germany.

Soon the day of departure came. Each of us carried a rucksack. All other belongings were packed into a cattle truck. Sadly the time had come for us to return to the West. It was in 1945 when we boarded the train from Zittau to Dresden. It was a cold, dark night and we sat as close together as we could because the train was unheated. We had travelled all night when we arrived at the huge Dresden station; we were stiff with cold and could hardly walk. There were many refugees from the East, sitting on their last possessions: bundles, suitcases, baskets, prams, children big and small watched over mainly by women, young and old. They were all waiting for the next train going west, in search for a new home. They looked tired and hopeless, united in their common need. Many must have come a long way and here they were waiting, trying to escape from the advancing Russian army!

Looking at the timetable, I discovered that our train to Plauen was to leave in half an hour. I ran to the other platform. We were expected in Plauen and the following train would be too late! I looked for help. The train was full! I found the station master and asked him to find places for 48 children and nine adults. "Look at the train," he said in despair. People were sitting on the roof and the doors did not shut properly because of the press from inside. The windows were half open and people were trying to climb in.

I knew we had to get into this train and my plea became more urgent. Suddenly he said: "Fetch the children immediately, I will unlock the doors of the postal carriage!" I ran and returned with all of them; not one was missing. The doors of the carriage were opened and we climbed in. The station master was almost engaged in a fight with another man who argued that no one should be allowed into the postal van. But he answered, "This time I do not go along with the law, I'd rather save lives!"

Did he know of what was coming? Dresden and the whole of Saxony had never before experienced an air raid. We were in the dark postal carriage, heard the whistle and the train pulled out of Dresden station. We were on our way!

It was not very long before the train stopped and we had to go into an air raid shelter and wait for the all clear. While we continued our journey to Plauen we did not know that Dresden station (and most of Dresden) was being destroyed by incendiary-bombs.*

Who was this man who had saved us, who had listened to our plea? Had he survived? Who had made my plea so urgent at a time when hundreds, even thousands of people were waiting to go on their way? Who helped us to escape?

AUTOBIOGRAPHICAL

Friedwart Bock

September 18, 1928

Friedwart Bock has been house-parent, together with his wife Nora, in three estates of the Camphill Rudolf Steiner Schools, a co-founder of St John's School and long-standing class-teacher and a much-travelled tutor on Camphill training courses in several countries. Friedwart had been appointed to be one of three joint Principals by Thomas and Anke Weihs to succeed them. He was central in the anthroposophical work, was a holder of the lay Christian services and is active in the Karl König Archives.

---

* Freddy Heimsch escaped Dresden on the same train. See p.257

During my childhood I "knew" of my parents' relationship to anthroposophy; I experienced this as a clear and strong attitude to life and things
spiritual. My father, Emil Bock, was a priest of the Christian Community.
The Priests' Seminary was on the same floor of the house as our family;
the chapel was downstairs as well as the publishing area of the Christian
Community. Each night I would be settled with the prayer, "From my head
to my feet I am the image of God," and I met the would-be priests as well
as the older ones like Friedrich Rittelmeyer, Hermann Beckh, and Kurt
von Wistinghausen. The kindergarten of the Waldorf School was where
my friends went, I visited a few times but we could not afford it. My three
years at the Waldorf School with our teacher Martin Tittmann were also
the last ones for the school itself as it had to close on March 30, 1938.
Religion lessons in the Christian Community were a lifeline and so were
the weekly eurythmy classes after this date.

     During adolescence I could still draw on my experience of the Waldorf
School and this sustained me in state schools and the armed services.

     The search and conscious meeting with anthroposophy came after the
end of the Second World War and was like a glowing fire wanting to burn
brightly. The Waldorf teachers cautioned us and wisely advised this had
better be pursued after completing school. I joined the Anthroposophical
Society in June 1951.

Adulthood had begun and I set out to find my direction and potential vocation. This led me to Camphill (my father and Karl König were good friends) for six months to begin with. The work with children "in need of special care" and the life within a community were clearly on my life's path, so I joined the Camphill Community in September 1950. This has continued to be my path in close partnership with Nora, my wife, and the friendships with the founders, with my contemporaries and the rising generation.

AUTOBIOGRAPHICAL

Henning Hansmann

February 2, 1927 – February 2, 2001

The destiny of every individual is part of the destiny of the times in which he lives. Those of us who were teenagers during the Second World War were not only physically undernourished; we were also starved of spiritual food and of the motherly love we still would have needed.

I vividly remember one night in 1943. It was after an air raid. Although we were schoolboys we had to man anti-aircraft guns, and stood by them, gazing at Berlin in flames. The whole horizon was burning. This was the town in which we spent our childhood. What I felt then was that the true German spirit, which once had been open to the world was no longer with us. Instead a demon of destruction was now at work, enwrapping us with flames of hell. Even those who recognized the demon could not escape him. What was then the meaning of life? How could we escape complete destruction?

Some of us escaped with our lives, but what happened then? In 1945 a friend of mine knocked at our door and asked for help. I gave him some old clothes so that he could take off his army uniform, but he could not take off the habits into which he had fallen. His mother had lost her life in an air raid and his father, a professor of philosophy, in an accident; now his attitude towards life was nothing short of criminal. He said to me, "You must help me." But I could not do so; I did not know how.

Who knew how to help? At university we learned almost everything except how to help another human being. No one taught us how to open the eyes of the soul of which Plato spoke. Consequently, the great amount of enthusiasm that was felt by many a young student just after the war soon withered away completely. The same demon of destruction had again appeared; it only showed a different face, working now within the souls.

Were not the ruins around us a mirror of our own inner chaos? Would we learn a lesson from the war? And who would heal the wounds?

Many new plays were performed at that time and many novels were written. In all of them the "dead" appeared, those whose lives had been unfulfilled. They spoke to our conscience, entreating us to complete the work that would have been theirs — but how was that to be done?

A student friend of mine drew my attention to Rudolf Steiner and I found some of his books in old editions in the university library. Reading them gave me the kind of joy no one could take away again; it was the joy of seeing the way to truth.

A year later I went to Stuttgart, a town where many pupils and followers of Rudolf Steiner lived. There I met Dr Karl Schubert at work with the special class entrusted to him by Rudolf Steiner a few years after the inauguration of the Waldorf School. Dr Schubert was just rehearsing a Nativity play with his children and like every visitor to his class I was taken in with warmth and openness of heart.

For the first time in my life, I saw children in need of special care and realized how in each of them was manifest in the extreme, the weaknesses or handicaps present to a lesser degree in any of us.

I was hardly able to formulate the longing which made itself felt in my soul as I watched, but soon after this I wanted to ask Dr Schubert if I could be of any use in the work with handicapped children. Before I did so Dr Schubert died. When I heard this, I remembered his last words to me as he stood, shaking my hand at the door of his classroom: "If you want to help, you can always come."

AUTOBIOGRAPHICAL
"Being Helped to Help Others," from The Cresset, *1962.*

Henning had two brothers who died young. His eldest brother, a poet and playwright, died at only 24 years of age. When Henning arrived in Camphill in 1949 he was greeted with the news that Peter, a gifted actor, the brother he was closest to, had died of pneumonia while Henning was en route to Camphill. Henning's relationship to those who had died was renewed in Aberdeen.

Most of all it was the death of his school friends and playmates that left Henning with a sense of moral duty towards the dead that was to stay with him for the rest of his life. It was perhaps this that led him to abandon his childhood ambitions and to seek a life of service to humanity. His searching led him to discover the works of Rudolf Steiner. It was due to his meeting Karl Schubert on completing his studies that Henning made his way to Camphill.

PETER HANSMANN

During his last illness, the nights were often very difficult and painful. His left side gave him a lot of discomfort, in fact he was never comfortable in his body; he restrained himself from complaining. In the night he was often visited by souls who had died long ago and this sometimes became very burdensome: people who had died in concentration camps, people who had committed suicide, sought his help and he would work with this during the day. We often spoke about death and it became more and more of a gateway to life and lost its terror. I had the feeling that in all this suffering there was already the promise of a future, a preparation for future tasks.

SIGRID HANSMANN

Sigrid Hansmann

April 23, 1926 – May 15, 2004

Sigrid was house-mother in England, Ireland and Scotland, much engaged in the social art. She developed play therapy in the Camphill Rudolf Steiner Schools.

After the war Sigrid fulfilled her wish to study anthroposophy and joined the (Waldorf) Teacher training seminar in Stuttgart. It was here that she first met her future husband Henning, though they had grown up in surprisingly close proximity in Berlin. In 1948 Sigrid received in the same post an offer to study medicine in Tübingen and a letter from Karl König with a single ticket to Aberdeen. She chose the train ticket. In coming to Camphill she felt that she had at last found the spiritual home for which she had so long been searching.

Of their time in Camphill, Sigrid and Henning often said that they were blessed to be allowed to live a life they loved, and to do work they found so fulfilling.

Following the Twin Towers terrorist attack Sigrid startled the members of the anthroposophical study group in Simeon Houses, where she was living at the time, by suggesting that they should pray not only for the victims of the terrible crime but also for the perpetrators. Sigrid understood the deep karmic link that lies between perpetrator and victim. She saw forgiveness as the most essential of Christian tasks. She had reason to know about forgiveness, having spent her life working on it.

PETER HANSMANN
From Camphill Correspondence, *2005/3.*

Wolfgang Beverley

September 20, 1930 – April 3, 1964

Wolfgang is one of us wherever Camphill lives. He should not be forgotten or overlooked; he will then become an active entity of great force and a tower of strength.

Wolfgang belonged to the stream of curative education long before he was born. His father was a teacher at the Sonnenhof in Arlesheim and Ita Wegman, the head of the curative and medical work there, expected the child to grow up in Arlesheim. She had a room prepared for him and his mother. But things did not happen as expected. The child was born in Germany: he bore the burden of illegitimacy and spent his childhood in various places. First he lived with his grandparents and later was pushed from pillar to post.

His was the destiny of a homeless and parentless boy. His heart was filled with loneliness. He found friends and threw them off again. Until at last, when he was sixteen years of age, a good lady — a widow — gave him shelter and care. It was there that he heard of Camphill and immediately joined. His destiny was waiting for this decision.

I remember his arrival: rough and unkempt, boisterous, self-assured and yet so tender that anything could make him weep. He was a typical mixture of a youngster who had to educate himself: a rough and unkempt surface with far too tender a core beneath; a maladjusted boy coming from a defeated country.

Wolfgang adjusted to a life of regular work and study with great difficulty. But his heart — full of fire and warmth — helped him to overcome many obstacles. He learned with great zeal and was ready to do any kind of work. He began to love the handicapped children and they taught him to express his own tenderness in meeting others. He managed the training course rather well and became one of the group of teachers.

For a time he left Camphill, Aberdeen, and worked in The Sheiling Schools, but later returned. Finally he decided in about 1958 to join Botton Village. There a number of hidden abilities came to light. He made the first attempt to open a village store. He bought and sold with great understanding for sellers and buyers. His shop made great strides and he established many new connections between the village and a number of firms and tradesmen. He was so successful that he took over the general management of wholesaling articles made in the village.

At the same time he achieved the greatest aim of his life; he started his own family. Solveig became his beloved wife and they had two children; a boy and a girl. He was a devoted husband and a loving father, trying to give his children what he himself missed as a child.

Then destiny struck. A severe kidney disease set in with high blood pressure. He suffered a great deal of headache, nausea and pain all over his body. He did not believe that death was near. And he had one great wish, should he recover — and he was convinced that he would — to become a priest. He was eager to preach the Gospel and distribute the holy sacraments to those in need.

With this longing Wolfgang parted from the Earth. These are the wings which carry him upwards to live in the service of Christ on the other side.

KARL KÖNIG
From The Cresset, 1964.

Eva Sachs

May 18, 1929 – September 13, 2002

Eva was born May 18, 1929, in Weissenfels/Saale in eastern Germany. Our mother's parents lived there and we spent some happy vacations in the house of these dear grandparents. Eva's birth horoscope was very harmonious; it said she would be a joy-filled person, especially in her actions.

Eva grew up in a boarding school where our parents were teachers and from 1934 to 1945, our father was headmaster. This Odenwaldschule, at the edge of the Odenwald between Darmstadt and Heidelberg was, and still is, an internationally known co-educational school, situated in beautiful, undulating countryside of woods, fields and farms.

Eva was a tender child, easily frightened by insects or other horrible creatures. Early on, when she was about two years old, she had two severe ear operations due to a middle ear infection, which nearly cost her life.

Probably this was the cause for her hearing disability, which gave her pain and trouble in later life.

Her childhood and youth were surrounded by warmth and protection, beauty of nature, the seasonal festivals, the clear structure of school life, and the stable rhythm of a loving family life. She was very close to her parents and sisters. She was not particularly interested in academic subjects, but always in people, their joys and sorrows and needs. She was able to feel herself into the soul of others.

The most important aspect of all these years was music. Music was all around. Our mother was a violin teacher and our aunt, who was also the school nurse, was a cello and piano teacher. Eva learned to play the violin in the school orchestra and a chamber orchestra.

The war years of 1940–45 were dramatic. Teachers and older classmates were drafted, some died in battle. Nightly air-raids on the big cities not too far away made the night skies glow with fire. Air raid sirens often forced us into the cellar at night, or by day into the woods where we had dug ditches. Food was scarce and we were always hungry. But school went on, music sounded, festivals were celebrated. Our houses and school remained unharmed. The very difficult time of the war's end was made harder as Eva suffered deeply when her beloved father died in 1946.

Eva lived in one of the large houses at the school, sharing a room with another girl. She belonged to a family of ten to twelve girls, with a "mother." Being older, she had moved out of our family's apartment. With some of these room-mates Eva kept up contact all her life.

One of them wrote and shared the following: "For me Ev [her nickname] in the Odenwald School, was a very, very important friend. She was tall and strong and sporty. Through her I learned to climb trees, which was difficult because of my stiffness. Ev had much patience and helped me to overcome fear, so we often sat up in the oak trees. By night and moonshine she taught me bicycling on the sports field, which was about 150 metres up in the woods. She also taught me swimming. Friendship with her meant for me physical and soul strengthening, and a help in my incarnation. She was also my protector in class as she was the strongest and all boys respected her greatly.

"In our house much went on by night. We went on excursions to a woody outcrop of rock about a mile away when one of us had received a packet of sweets. If the air raids howled, we had to run back very fast, via the cellar door, in order to be back in the house before your father noticed. Ev was always fully with us and often had the most daring ideas, which none of the adults would have thought came from her. It was our adolescent time, full of tricks.

"Ev and I had also serious talks, for instance about reincarnation, in the evening in bed. I had a deep relationship to Ev. She was my first friend in life.

"It is important for me to describe this side of her childhood, because she was many-sided and later her liveliness maybe did not come so much to the fore. Her physical strength, her winning at the sports festivals, her baseball hit further than fifty metres, were impressive. And besides this, her tender, loving devotion to nature, plants and animals. But also her sense of humour!"

We also had one important family friend in common: Robert Killian had been a Waldorf teacher in Stuttgart, and with the closing of that school at the beginning of the war, his family joined our school. Mrs Killian became like a second mother to us; she introduced us to anthroposophy, and she played the piano. Young Christof learned to play the cello, and many Camphill places have heard him and his playing partner giving concerts during the last twenty years. He was a special friend of Eva since childhood.

URSEL PIETZNER
From Camphill Correspondence, *2003/1.*

Margarete von Freeden

August 2, 1928 – November 7, 2006

In the early afternoon of November 7, 2006, Margarete crossed the threshold and set out on her path in spirit realms. It was a great moment of wonderful peace, fulfilment and release, after an active life, rich with experiences; the last 25 years of which she was afflicted with Parkinson's disease.

Margarete was born about halfway between the two world wars, in a time of great political and economic change and instability in Germany. She was the third child of Paul Galle, an orthopaedic surgeon, and his wife Ilse, a paediatric nurse. They lived in the village of Gehlsdorf on the banks of the river Warne, opposite Rostock. Here Margarete had a protected and conventional childhood in a rural setting.

The family spent holidays at the Baltic Sea and Margarete cannot remember not being able to swim. Water, especially the sea, was her joy and love all of her life. From early on, Margarete was an independent child with plenty of original ideas and a good measure of stubbornness. The parents introduced the two-year-old Margarete to the three-year-old Gerda and a wonderful, devoted and lifelong friendship developed between the two.

When she was eight years old the family moved from Gehlsdorf to the

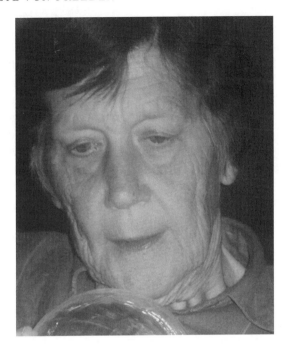

city of Hanover. Margarete found it hard to adjust to the new life. She was a bright child but found school uninteresting and was moved up a class in order to challenge her. Margarete was eleven when the Second World War broke out. Her father was called up and became supervisor for four military hospitals, and was rarely at home. In 1942 while Margarete was on holiday with Gerda's family in Gehlsdorf, the Galle's house in Hanover was destroyed in an air raid, and she stayed on with Gerda's family. One night in autumn 1943 Rostock was bombed and burned down. It was a terrible experience and Margarete discovered that by thinking about the children's service (which she got to know in Hanover) she felt safe.

Margarete was sent back to her parents who were now living with friends in primitive conditions. She was the only child at home: her older sister worked in a chemist shop in Lüneburg, her brother had been called up and was missing on the Eastern front, never to return, and her younger sister lived with an aunt in the Harz Mountains. In this situation Margarete began to take initiative and responsibility for herself as well as for others, which was much appreciated by those around her. In spring 1944 the boys in her class were called up and school stopped for the girls as well. In order to avoid working in a munitions factory or serving with the air defences, Margarete, now fifteen, chose to an agricultural apprenticeship on a large farm in Mecklenburg. It was a courageous step into the unknown. Her stubborn perseverance and independent nature coupled with an open heart and a clear mind helped her through this time of increasing chaos towards the end of the war and its aftermath.

In April 1945 Margarete led three horse-drawn carts filled with the women and children fleeing from the advancing Russian invasion. They travelled by night to avoid the strafing by enemy planes. They made it to the British zone where she found herself to be a refugee on a strange farm, not knowing if her family had survived. Margarete felt fortunate to be alive and was able to complete her apprenticeship by Easter 1946, after which she returned to her family in Hanover and attended the Waldorf School for three years, finishing with the Abitur. Margarete experienced this time back at school as a positive breathing out for the soul, but also as a real challenge as she was more intellectually than artistically gifted.

Before Margarete had finished school, Gerda had joined the Galle family because life in the Russian zone had become too dangerous for her. In school Margarete saw a notice from the Rev Richard Poole in England who was looking for an au pair girl to help with the family and suggested to Gerda to apply. Little did they know then into what a new and fulfilling future was awaiting them both.

After finishing school, Margarete had hoped to study medicine, but could not immediately get a place to study because preference was given to returning young soldiers, refugees and Jews. Although medicine was not to become her profession, Margarete kept an active interest in it for all of her life.

In Easter 1948 Margarete, at the age of twenty, came to England as house help for the Heatheringtons at Michael Hall School in Forest Row. After a year, Gerda persuaded Margarete to join her with the Pooles, who by now were in Thornbury House near Bristol, running a hostel for children with learning disabilities. Here Margarete met special needs children for the first time in her life, and soon loved them and felt fulfilled and happy working with them.

In summer 1951 she went for six months to Heathcot House near Aberdeen, and then on to Murtle House. With this move a whole new world opened up for Margarete and a new phase of life began for her. There was much to learn and plenty of opportunity to use her skills and experience. In the autumn of 1952 when Margarete was expecting Klaus, her first son, Tilla König invited her to Thornbury Park.

In the autumn of 1954 Margarete and Klaus returned to Scotland where she first worked in Newton Dee house and later in the Cottage, again with the Pooles. Margarete had by then completed the Camphill Seminar. In the summer of 1955 Margarete's dear friend Gerda (who by now was married to Hartmut von Jeetze) asked her to join them on Newton Dee Farm. It was here that Margarete and I met.

For Camphill these were wonderful years of pioneering and expanding the work, at home and abroad. It was exiting and invigorating for her and this encouraged her to deepen her understanding and commitment to the ideas of Camphill. We married in the summer of 1957 and Arend her second son was born in spring the following year.

In 1958 we moved to the Hatch in Thornbury, where Margarete's main concern was for the well-being of the house community. After the Hatch followed 3 years in the Grange helping to build up this newly started training centre. It was also here in 1960 that she experienced the great joy of becoming the mother of twins Andreas and Brigitte.

Then followed nine years in Botton Village on Falcon Farm, and later Honey Bee Nest Farm. With the move to Botton Village Margarete's activities and responsibilities, beside the farm household, included some of the administrative tasks and groups in Botton and the Camphill Village Trust. Margarete joined the first Class and became a member of the Camphill Community. In Botton we experienced the death of four-year-old Andreas, and in 1967 the birth of Martin, our youngest child.

In 1970 we moved to Newton Dee. Here her task was foremost to help strengthen the work of the community generally by joining the carrying group. Margarete brought her great enthusiasm for the village impulse and contributed with her common sense, experience, initiative and commitment for the outer and inner well-being of the community. During this time Margarete became a Class reader.

In 1979 we moved to Oaklands Park, which had been purchased to allow the expansion of the Grange Village. Margarete was now fifty years old. It was soon apparent that new experiences and tasks awaited her. Her body began to show signs of ageing. In 1981 she was diagnosed with Parkinson's disease, and in 1984 she had both her hips replaced. Except for Martin, all the children had flown the nest and in autumn 1980 her farmer husband started a priest's training. Margarete, with her enormous zest for life, took all these things in her stride.

During the later years in Oaklands, Margarete was able despite her growing physical disabilities to remain an active member of the community supported by those around her. After this followed three years where we were warmly taken in by Camphill Houses Stourbridge. Here as a couple we faced the many challenges that Margarete's failing health presented. The last two years of her life were spent in Thomas Weihs House in Botton Village where the increasing nursing needs were taken care of in a wonderful way. This gave us a chance to round off our many years of life together without the strain of my being the carer.

Reflecting on Margarete's life, one is left with the impression of a Michaelic being, deeply connected with those who strive to be active for the future.

THAMMO VON FREEDEN

Charlotte Baumert

June 23, 1916 – August 2, 2003

A great star with a humble soul has returned to her rightful home. The spiritual world was ever present in and around Charlotte. For most of her life she lived close to the gate of death, gaining deep insight into life after death and into life on earth. This made her very wise and enabled her to help the dead and the living alike. Many a person would receive advice from her; she helped to disentangle many destinies.

Often enough it needed some scratching of the surface — a rough shell enclosing a tender and warm kernel. Having reached the inner core, steadfast friendship and never wavering loyalty would meet you.

Born in Konstanz, Germany, in the middle of the First World War to an English mother and a German father, she was the eldest of five children.

Early school years were uneventful; she had faithful friends and a happy home. Still she often felt lonely. Her friends would often shake their heads and say: "Charlotte you are funny." When entering high school with her practical mind she decided to learn as much as possible in the least time.

Charlotte left school at sixteen going for a year to relations in England. Back in Germany, she worked for three years as a receptionist for a doctor. Once during this time she had a strange experience, when "out of the blue" the following words were imparted to her: "It is not easy to be completely silent, to forego one's own wishes, and only to will what destiny wills." These words remained with her for life.

She took up a course in chemistry that enabled her to take up a post in a laboratory of a steel works. When the laboratory was bombed she lost her job and then was employed by the Hitler Youth. There she befriended a young woman who was her superior and very active and idealistic, but also someone who could see the negative sides of the Nazi regime. This woman knew a young man with quite a high position in the Hitler Youth. Through this he gained sight of the black list, the list of Jews who were to be taken to concentration camps. They wrote letters to these people, warning them. Charlotte had the task to distribute the letters and the families could try to flee. Although it was a very dangerous job it never occurred to Charlotte to refuse.

Once, during a conversation with other Hitler Youth members, a girl spoke great words about patriotism, the war and so on when Charlotte found herself saying: "Hate is death, love is life. If we want to be alive we must love." Having said this, she was sure she would be put into a concentration camp, but within six weeks the war had come to an end.

In 1946, already 30 years old, Charlotte decided to matriculate and

become a Waldorf teacher. Konstanz was in the French military zone, and she had to obtain a permit to stay in the American zone to study at the Waldorf Teachers' College in Stuttgart. There she heard about Camphill. Meanwhile she went to England to stay with her grandmother who lived just outside London. From there, on her days off, she went by train to London and listened to lectures at Rudolf Steiner House or the Christian Community. At the Christian Community she met Peter Roth who invited her to come to Camphill. She accepted and went to Newton Dee, working in the same house with Peter and Kate Roth. Later she went with Tilla König to Wraxall House near Bristol; from there to Ringwood with Ann Harris, and finally to Thornbury as teacher and house-mother.

Here her wonderful inner qualities came more and more to the fore: selflessness, humility and sacrifice, which had their roots in the words she had heard so many years previously. Her ever-increasing artistic activity of painting with watercolours helped her overcome her grumpy tendency.

In 1966 she became a godmother and an important part of a small family, and no longer felt lonely. Charlotte had achieved what as a young person she had hoped for: she had become loving, understanding, selfless and wise.

LISA STEUCK
From Camphill Correspondence, *2003/6.*

Susanne Müller-Wiedemann

November 11, 1916

It is well nigh impossible to imagine the life of a person, still active, yet linked to a time when Rudolf Steiner held the great East-West congress in Vienna: the five-year old Susi Lissau then sat on his knee! Susanne Müller-Wiedemann has now given a course to a large number of medical staff and therapists in Herdecke. Indeed, a rich life lies between those two events 74 years apart. At five she began playing the piano and received eurythmy lessons: her life is one of bringing music and eurythmy together. At five she experienced Rudolf Steiner visiting her father, a personal pupil: her whole life is an unfailing service to anthroposophy. With the one fructifying the other, her outstanding musical gift uniting with her growing anthroposophical insights and applications, the long life's balance is a fruit in curative tone eurythmy from which countless people benefit. To be able to imagine Susanne's life I will attempt to fill out a picture. When looking back one sees first the more recent events; so I shall go backwards in steps of eleven or twelve years, taking occasional glimpses.

In June 1995 at Brachenreuthe, Germany, the eleventh course in curative (tone) eurythmy celebrated its conclusion in the presence of some sixty friends connected to curative education, those graduating plus others who had gone through previous courses; that moment also marked the ending of the training with Susanne, except for the possibility of some "polishing-up" courses. Seven medical doctors participated during these twelve years.

In August 1983 the inauguration of the Curative Eurythmy Course, upon the urging of Dr Friedrich Lorenz, then leader of the Medical Section, took place at Brachenreuthe in the newly-erected Johannes-Erigena Bau, a building well suited for eurythmy, therapy work and coloured shadow treatment. His encouraging words of greeting for Susanne's new course described it as, "a path which can carry this impulse into the future."

From 1971 important talks of some lyre teachers at a gathering in the Goetheanum led to the founding of the Independent Music School of which Brachenreuthe became one of eight "stations." During the time when the travelling students stayed there extra courses had to be conducted in a totally new way. In addition to the work with the music school carried by Susanne she had begun to pursue research into tone eurythmy with invited friends. So the newly built Sylvester Hall became home to both courses and the research work where tone-eurythmy exercises were worked out for individual children or for group therapies. Two special

therapies were newly developed by Susanne in those years: the listening-space therapy and trumpet-therapy.

These group therapies were taken up in other places of the Camphill movement. Their basis was described by Susanne in various papers published between 1979 and 1989.

In June 1959 Hans and Susanne Müller-Wiedemann arrived at Dawn Farm, the Camphill School in Hermanus, South Africa, to help establish the Camphill Training Course. At first intended as a visit of a few months, it became an involvement of almost seven years during which they worked in many realms of anthroposophical endeavours. Hans particularly helped to formulate Camphill's aims for co-operation with state authorities.

With Dr König having moved to Germany, the Müller-Wiedemanns wished to involve themselves there as well, and moved to the Home School Bruckfelden at Lake Constance. Their strong connection to the Middle-European spiritual striving found expression in their naming of the main house after Adalbert Stifter. Three years after Dr König's death they moved to his little house in Brachenreuthe. The Birken Häusle maintained its character as a centre for intimate conversations among friends. An all-round community began to be built up in Brachenreuthe around the therapeutic impulse.

On February 1, 1948 Susi Lissau arrived at Camphill from La Motta, Brissago, Switzerland. Full of joy Dr König wrote in the Superintendent's

Report on Camphill (1947–49): "Miss Lissau, an expert musician and curative eurythmist has joined the schools. Miss Lissau has trained for ten years in Switzerland and is now devoting her great and genuine gifts to our children, and her work has become one of the outstanding features in the curative education which we now provide."

Susanne established the Camphill Choir on September 2, 1948; having myself joined the choir in 1950 I can vouch for the earnestness with which Susanne conducted the practising sessions, with very rewarding results.

Karl König wrote the Second Community Memorandum, and under that call Susanne soon entered the Camphill Community. Coming from intensive work with Dr Ita Wegman and the musician Edmund Pracht, what must have given Susanne great joy were two events that occurred soon after her arrival at Camphill. At Michaelmas was the founding of the Ita Wegman Anthroposophical Group, and then, at the end of the year, the long visit of Edmund Pracht.

The ensuing eleven years were of greatest importance. Susanne was able to work with deaf and mute children, creating new methods of therapy. The therapy, helped by the keen interest of Karl König, was immediately practised and later documented and published. At that time Susanne also gave several two-year curative eurythmy courses for co-workers, a precursor for her later work at Brachenreuthe.

One delightful aspect we could experience was when, on rare occasions, she and Karl König played four-hand reductions of Bruckner and Mahler symphonies together, especially memorable at Dr König's fiftieth birthday party. A little later in those Camphill Estate years came the happy event of the wedding of Hans and Susanne. Next to being a curative eurythmist and therapist Susi (as we still called her) became house-mother and mother, while little Stella acquired the first skills of life.

Now let us make another twelve-year leap back. Susi Lissau had been advised by Werner Pache, the eminent curative teacher, to come to the Sonnenhof. She did so at St John's Tide 1936 at the age of nineteen and a half. There was no seminar in those days. What was offered, however, was an accompanying course in curative eurythmy with a diploma, for which Susi was well prepared after doing eurythmy in her childhood. There were many good teachers and Susanne also had the good fortune to work with Dr Ita Wegman for many years.

Another meaningful encounter was that with Edmund Pracht who worked at the Sonnenhof writing music to many *Kalevala* runes and Novalis poems. Sometimes he would put his new compositions for lyre in front of Susi, not far from the moment of performance, saying, "Can you please play this music, the notes are too difficult for me to play!" Pracht also became a guide in Susanne's search and study of anthroposophy. It was decades later, in 1968, that Susanne could give due honour to Edmund

Pracht when collecting and editing with Gotthard Starke, a volume of his songs for his seventieth birthday.

The last phase of these twelve years in Switzerland was spent in La Motta, Brissago, with the incredible view over the Lago Maggiore, where Susanne could find fulfilment in practising her art in the work with the children.

Finally, coming to the early years of Susanne's life, we see her growing up in Vienna where her father worked at a bank. He was an enthusiastic mountaineer and so the parents often went with the three children for long excursions into the mountains.

Susanne told how in her early school-days she loved singing in a choir, and that her favourite school subjects were history and gym. In the mid-1920s the recession hit the family quite hard, and there followed years of manual work, sewing clothes with her mother. Her music teacher recognized her skill on the piano and strongly encouraged her to take up a concert career. But Susi declined, realizing the sacrifice needed in the many hours of practising.

After the annexation of Austria, the Jewish family experienced the stress of discrimination. Rudi Lissau, her elder brother, managed to flee in good time via Paris to Britain, while Susanne's older sister eventually perished having been captured by the Nazis. The parents emigrated to Britain. Since her fifth year Susanne was led by her angel along a different path and so was by then in safe hands pursuing eurythmy, curative education and music in Switzerland.

Susanne's life shows a remarkable relation to the twelve-year rhythm of Jupiter; perhaps one can discern the influence of the planet of wisdom.

CHRISTOF-ANDREAS LINDENBERG
"Congratulations for her Eightieth Birthday," from Camphill Correspondence, *1996/4.*

Hans Müller-Wiedemann

November 11, 1924 – December 12, 1997

Hans Müller-Wiedemann was born at Karlsruhe, Germany. As a child he experienced the loss of both parents: his father died when he was two years old and when he was fourteen his mother died after a long illness. He grew up in his grandparents' home, his grandfather being a physician.

After leaving school he studied medicine at Freiburg, Berlin and Prague. During university holidays he did military service. At the end of the war he was in service at a military hospital near Prague when the

medical officer was shot by partisans. The twenty-one-year-old medical
student had to take full responsibility for a hundred seriously injured soldiers.

After a period as a prisoner of war he continued his studies at
Tübingen, Germany, graduating in 1949. His years as houseman and junior doctor were at Tübingen and Heidelberg. There he met the psychoan-
alyst, Felix Schottlander, who advised him against pursuing theoretical
psychoanalysis as he would not really require it. As an academic scientific
career seemed certain this advice was of importance.

Instead, the encounter with Heten Wilkens and Johannes Lenz led to
the decisive step towards anthroposophy. From the background of his
recent war experiences, the burning question was about the world of the
angels. Wilkens wrote: "Our first conversation turned to the question of
one's angel. How, in this 'time of openness,' does the human being attain
a relationship to the world of angels." This question proceeded from
Rilke's *Duinese Elegies*. These led directly to Rudolf Steiner and anthroposophy which he studied intensively.

In his twenty-eighth year there was a further decisive event in his life.
On a journey to Scotland with Johannes Lenz he visited the Camphill
community at Aberdeen. This encounter with the world of Camphill, and
particularly with Thomas Weihs (Karl König was away at that time)

whose wide scientific knowledge impressed greatly, became the decisive reason for burning his bridges to an academic career and turning his life in quite another direction. Thus in 1953 he came to Camphill.

At this time a whole group of young doctors had gathered around Dr König in order to find a way into curative education under his guidance. König would combine scientific knowledge of anthroposophy with concrete examples from the field of curative education, particularly when observing children in clinics, and in the multi-disciplinary discussions about individual children. In these clinics, "König combined the observation of a scientific trained person with the intuitive, artistic side of his nature. The physician and the curative educational teacher were simultaneously present in his person, in an intimate and significant relationship."

Thus Hans Müller-Wiedemann characterized this time. König's curative educational activity had become a model and standard in Hans' life. He described König as expecting a re-casting, even complete change of outlook from all his co-workers, and the doctors were in no way excepted. No one could rest on his gifts or acquired abilities; in Camphill he became part of a community of people whose bond not only rested on common goals, but also included the experience of everyday life with all its imperfections. Hans Müller-Wiedemann was not only active as a doctor but also in many other areas of the community as teacher, therapist, and, after his marriage to Susanne Lissau and the birth of their daughter Stella, also as a house-father.

After Dr König's long visit to South Africa where he gave many lectures and saw many children, there was a need to found some Camphill work there. So the young Müller-Wiedemann family found itself aboard ship, bound for South Africa. Three years later when Dr König visited again, the Camphill work in South Africa was firmly established. Hans Müller-Wiedemann had been intensely building up curative educational work which would soon expand to cover social therapy. A curative educational training course had been started and the work of Camphill was now widely recognized. Following Dr König's suggestion Hans completed a further doctorate at the University of Cape Town with a thesis on "Psychological Aspects of the Post-Encephalitic Syndrome." At this time too his interest in developmental-psychological themes began.

Following Dr König's death Hans and Susanne returned to Middle Europe with their daughter, to help with the building up of the Camphill movement in Germany. Together with Dr Georg von Arnim he carried the responsibility for the growing and gradually expanding work in the Middle European region. At first the family lived in a small special home-school, the Adalbert Stifter House at Bruckfelden, near Lake Constance. Here, for the first time in Germany, was an institution for children with early childhood autism (then still known as "contact disturbance").

As well as the work at Bruckfelden, Hans Müller Wiedemann took on the medical responsibility for the Lehenhof, the first village community in Germany created on the model of Botton Village in Yorkshire. His attention was drawn more strongly to the question raised by work with handicapped adults. The "Model Village Community" occupied him quite intensively, particularly with regard to the social challenges of integrating many varied initiatives.

Towards the end of the 1960s Hans moved to Brachenreuthe which became his home through the seventies and eighties. Karl König had spent his last years there. Now a very productive period of inner and outer work set in for Hans. Within a few years a curative educational village settlement grew out of the old home farm and the number of children trebled. The idea of a "curative educational province or domain" hovered before his mind in the sense of Goethe's "Pedagogical Province" (in *Wilhelm Meister),* a kind of community organism with curative educational tasks in the centre, accompanied by social and spiritual concerns of equal value.

The enigma of the autistic child formed the centre of Hans Müller-Wiedemann's researches, in particular finding a curative educational approach to try to unlock the soul of the autistic child while freeing him from his inner anxieties and compulsions. The centre of the curative educational work was in the collegial discussions about the children led by Hans. He had an affectionate relationship to the children, and someone remarked that he made his speech available to those who could not speak or only spoke poorly. In this way the real nature of the child came to light.

Many parents found comfort and courage in the way he was able to speak about their child, clearly, not glossing over the difficulties but taking their destiny into consideration and looking towards the future.

Although focused on the needs of the children and adults cared for, he was aware that community life depended to an equal degree on the formation of community among the co-workers. Out of this a rich anthroposophical life came about, for example the annual work around Christmas. The celebration of festivals with plays, pageants, lectures and much else created an atmosphere in which curative education was always seen in relation to the life-spring of anthroposophy.

Hans Müller-Wiedemann was known widely and highly regarded as a researcher, teacher, author and lecturer. Especially because of his research into autism he was often invited to speak at professional conferences. In contrast to many other scientists at such conferences, he spoke freely with few notes achieving an immediate and direct rapport with his audience. He did much for anthroposophical curative and medical work to receive public and professional recognition.

Within the anthroposophical movement his lectures were also highly valued. He always spoke out of the moment, if necessary putting aside his prepared notes, in order to relate directly to the audience. The same sort of liveliness and clarity was evident in the teachers' meeting of the Camphill Seminar, where he worked particularly to deepen our understanding of Rudolf Steiner's Curative Education Course.

Socially, Hans Müller-Wiedemann was aware that his work depended on many people. Mindful of this he always spoke of a "we." He had a great ability to reconcile. Of course life at Brachenreuthe was by no means free of mistakes and muddles, just as he was himself not without weaknesses and faults. Nonetheless no quarrels and conflicts existed around him, and solutions, often surprising, were found from a more elevated viewpoint.

One of his greatest strengths lay in his ability to listen and understand. When he repeated in his own words what another person had just said, the person not only felt understood, but understood himself better.

At the beginning of the 1980s Hans Müller-Wiedemann began to see the need for a handover of responsibilities to younger hands. A number of young doctors assisted him and relieved him of daily chores and a circle of responsible co-workers grew into the experience of management.

The appearance of his volume of poetry, *Nahe dem Engel* (Close to the Angel) in 1987 gave a glimpse of his gift for poetry and marked the start of a new period in his life. It was marked by illness and the three serious operations. These catapulted him out of everyday life, perhaps preventing a more natural maturing into a life free of everyday responsibilities. Instead the extended periods of hospitalization were experienced as exile and isolation, and estranged him too soon from everyday life. Thus in his last years he became inwardly homeless, as he had been as a child.

He worked at the biography of Karl König, which appeared in 1992. It was born out of the pain and psychological distress of illness and yet the essential spirit of the author sounds clearly through the book, allowing the being of König to arise.

Outwardly and inwardly his situation in life became ever more difficult. He suffered from the loss of the ability to work and to set things in motion. It seemed to me that during this time he would have liked the "father" quality to become more that of a "brother." This was not easy, for just as it is difficult to transform the paternal aura, so it is just as difficult to take up a father into a fraternal circle.

In December 1996 Hans moved to Nikolas Cusanus Haus in Stuttgart. Weak and ill, depression cast its shadow and he struggled with the question of what was the task now put to him in this situation of life. In 1997 his second volume of poetry *Unterwegs* (On the Way) was published with a foreword by his friend, Johannes Lenz. During his final months he immersed himself, through his poetry, in the time of his youth. He prepared a third volume of poems, *Sternenfahrten* (Star-Paths), before suffering a stroke, in October. He was admitted to the Filder Klinik. Seriously ill, he could be experienced as if freed from burdens and surrounded by a light. He needed further surgery, after which in the early morning of the December 12, 1997, he died.

RÜDIGER GRIMM
From Camphill Correspondence, *1998/3.*

Christiane Lauppe

December 11, 1926

I was born a twin. It was a difficult Caesarean birth. My twin sister was the expected child; I was just a little extra, tiny and the odd one out! I was a late developer, managing at school thanks to my strong and clever sister. We needed each other and the teachers were kind enough to keep us together. At the age of thirteen to fourteen we went to a boarding school — my sister fell ill and had to go home and that was when I finally "woke up" and became myself. In later life we each went our own way. My sister Barbara died in May 2002.

I was born into what now is called an upper middle class family in East Thuringia, Germany. Most of the family members were involved in running a weaving mill with a thousand looms, large farms and forests. We built houses for our working families and a home for the elderly.

My parents divorced when we were six years old. Mother brought us twins up and our older sister lived on her own. Mother was strict and had a no-nonsense approach; although we had servants we had to make our own beds and help in the kitchen, etc. We had a car and travelled widely through Germany: to Dresden (where the Sistine Madonna could be seen), to Leipzig (for classical concerts) thereby absorbing Middle European culture. We visited old churches and museums but attended church only at Christmas.

Above the altar in our very Protestant church there was written in large golden letters, "I am the Way, the Truth and the Life." This imprinted itself on my mind during the long sermons and only later, in Camphill's Bible Evening, did I discover the origin of these words. Before arriving in Camphill I never held a Bible in my hands!

One of my aunts was an anthroposophist and she converted one of her big gardens to the biodynamic method. Some pre-war biodynamic conferences were held there.

As with many of our generation, the war and its end brought about enormous changes. Our part of Germany was occupied by the Russian army. I had to leave boarding school early and could not finish with the leaving certificate. There was my mother with three teenage daughters! We were saved from the worst because the Russian commander of the town moved into our house. Within an hour we had to move with several of our friends and relatives who had found refuge with us and had to live in our big loft. The few items of value that we could take were exchanged for food in due course to save us from starving.

My aunt, her husband and head-gardener fled to the Black Forest after first having been imprisoned by the Russians. We had to find work or else would have been transported to Russia. I therefore began a gardener's training. A young girl, also working in this nursery, had trained under my aunt and her head-gardener. One day, sitting under a tree she said: "Do you know about reincarnation?" We talked and talked — and from then on my true path of life began. I know now that from that time on I was being led in a remarkable way through dangerous, often impossible situations. When I finished my training (also a school for applying one's will), being able to dig for eight hours, a letter arrived from my aunt asking me to join her former head-gardener on a biodynamic farm in the south of the Black Forest. My angel got me there without any papers or money. I worked there for one year and during this time in 1948 a youth conference took place in Stuttgart. I was allowed to attend and I remember someone saying: "Why don't you go to Dr König in Scotland?"

Back on the farm they thought it would be all right and I was helped to obtain identity papers, passport, etc. by bribing the local official with butter!

To me these turbulent post-war years were filled with a strong feeling of joy and light, gaining freedom from old restricting ties. I never longed to go back to look for a lost home.

I arrived at London Harley Street on November 11, 1949 and two days later at Aberdeen. Reg Bould met me at the station and took me to Newton Dee House. I remember Maria Selinger trying to teach Mark Gartner and me how to cook porridge. Kate Elderton (later Roth) and Beatie Warburton ruled as matrons supreme! Annemarie Kresse and I lived for some time in a shed in the back yard next to the coal heap. I looked after a group of five boys and also took on Newton Dee garden.

For me there was one sure feeling: "I had come home!" There were no days off, only rest hours. Twice a week after lunch we would drive to Camphill House for Seminar sessions with Dr König on embryology, the twelve senses and more; with Peter Roth we turned to world evolution.

For the Youth Group Dr König wrote the Advent Play in which, I think, I played Hermoine. In early 1950, I was admitted to the Community, together with Gisela Schlegel and Henning Hansmann. This event took place in the entrance hall of Murtle House, followed by a large Bible Evening prepared in the Big Room. The three of us stood there in the middle of the entrance hall — all the other members wore suits and long grey dresses. It was overwhelming! Dr König spoke to us full of warmth with very earnest words about Middle Europe, having been sent three young representatives from the North, the Middle and the South. Later on I became a full member during a festival of offering held in Camphill chapel.

In 1951 or 1952 Gisela Schlegel and I moved to Thornbury Park which had been bought. We worked there under the guidance of Tilla König, a wonderful experience! After three years I followed the call to join the pioneering group at Dawn Farm, Hermanus, South Africa. I left in autumn 1958 from Southampton on the Union Castle ship *Stirling Castle*. At Dawn Farm I met Eva Marie Knipping, Renate and Julian Sleigh, Margit Metraux and others. Michael Lauppe arrived in May 1959, and later Susanne and Hans Müller-Wiedemann.

In 1960 came the call to start Cresset House at Johannesburg Dr König and Alix Roth stayed with us for one week, interviewing parents and children prior to admission. This was a special time. Hans and Ella van der Stok soon joined us, as did Irmgard Lazarus.

Michael and I got married in August 1961 and our two daughters were born in Cresset House.

AUTOBIOGRAPHICAL

Michael Lauppe

May 23, 1933

My childhood and youth appears chaotic. However, in looking back, there seemed to be a guiding spirit that led me steadily to the work I was destined to do.

My mother was just twenty when I was born in Berlin. She had been a troublesome teenager, leaving home at nineteen. She was not interested in a conventional marriage and refused a liaison with my father. I remained her only child, growing up with friends and in other families for most of my first sixteen years, before I left "home."

At one point I was a foster child with Christof-Andreas Lindenberg's

Christiane and Michael Lauppe

family in Munich. My first teacher impressed me by bringing an ice-cream making machine to school. Dresden Waldorf School I remember because we all wrote letters to the Führer to keep our school open, and because the teachers all cried on the day the school had to close. I loved my teacher Mr Rutz at the Stuttgart Waldorf School, but I was restless and unsure of going to the upper classes. I was a loner and sometimes went with Andreas Suchantke catching butterflies. He too was a loner. I left school and my mother in summer 1949 and went to Switzerland.

I became a farm apprentice in the Emmenthal and completed the training after two years with good marks. I loved Switzerland, learned fluent *Berndütch* and later French in Canton Vaud. Although I would probably not have made a good farmer, the relationship to the soil, the world of plants and animals has never left me.

Following a visit to the Institute Pedagogic Curative in St Prex, I decided to join there in June 1953. Due to a shortage in the children's unit, Mlle Schroeder called on me to help. At first I was quite hopeless. The group consisted of French-speaking children between five and eight, many of them with Down's syndrome. They were delightful but I lacked the ability of enjoying them and of being with them! Fun and humour had not featured in my formative years, nor had I learned to adapt and use imagination! However, I soon began to love these children and I knew that the work with them was my calling. I needed them as much as they needed me!

Some time earlier I had already heard about Camphill from Christof-Andreas Lindenberg (St Prex was not part of it at that stage). Then a small man with a large head visited and gave a series of lectures. I knew at once that I should go to "his" Camphill in Scotland in order to train there. I put this to Dr König after the talks and received his invitation.

I arrived in Newton Dee in September 1955 just as the weekly anthroposophical group meeting was about to begin. Someone stood at the entrance and, as I approached; I practised my English by asking the lady for "someone responsible" in the house. She gave me a lovely smile and beckoned me to follow her: she then led me to the kitchen and handed me over to Rhoswitha Volkamer, one of the co-workers. It had been Anke Weihs who met me! I was to share a bedroom with John Bryan. It was past 11 pm and I hoped to be able to go to sleep. Finally John came in close to midnight, but instead of going to bed he sat down and studied the Bible for some time! Wow! I thought — whatever next?

Another event stands out: a holiday tour to Finland with Karin von Schilling. Karin, too had been a foster child at the Lindenberg's in the 1940s. The idea to visit Finland came from Anke; we were naturally surprised — but took to the idea. We got a little money, hitch-hiked on our journey and stayed in youth hostels. When our money was almost spent we spoke to a young man who answered in fluent English. He took us to friends of his at the nearby lake who invited us to stay with them for a week. Then another young man came for a visit and on leaving entreated us to visit his family and sister. And so we did. The Koistinen family lived in a house at the edge of forest and lake, like so many Finns do. Their daughter Kaarina (later married to Freddy Heimsch) was not well but promised to be up the next day.

A walk through the woods with Kaarina next day was very special, and prepared her own destiny. She told me of her awareness of gnomes and other elemental beings and of her growing up in this elemental nature. I persuaded her to come to Camphill in Scotland if her application to become an air-hostess would fail. Unexpectedly she came to Camphill the next year.

Thomas Weihs addressed me at the completion of my two years Camphill Seminar: I had been a good student, but had lacked imaginative and independent thoughts. I know, I am a good plodder! After working in Newton Dee House, in spring 1959 Dr König invited me to his room and asked if I would be prepared to go to South Africa and join the pioneers in Hermanus? He gave me one week to decide.

I sailed in April 1959 in a one-class ship bound for Cape Town, Australia and New Zealand. It was full of grandmothers and aunts going to visit relatives. Cape Town appeared in the very early morning after fifteen days at sea. First just the lights, then Table Mountain and Table Bay; what a glorious way to arrive!

At the valley of Hemel-en-Aarde near Hermanus the Onrus River was in spate, so I had to carry my cases across the ford to the waiting car. Dawn Farm Rudolf Steiner School was still small at that time. A forest of big trees: gums and pines and behind them rising steeply, the mountain. Everything was so new to me, the vegetation, the black people and the wild sea and mountains. Only the children were familiar, but a tough lot they were!

I spent eighteen months in the school, teaching a class and becoming involved in the life of the little community. Hans and Susanne Müller-Wiedemann arrived in 1960 and with them came eurythmy, lyre-playing, choir singing and the children's clinics.

During the early months of the year 1961 Cresset House near Johannesburg was purchased by the parents group there. Christiane Hansen was chosen to become the matron and a small team was formed around her. I was drafted into this group, with some regret by the friends at Hermanus who would have preferred to keep me. In retrospect I feel that this our work at Cresset as pioneers laid the foundation for several more steps of pioneering into which I was placed in the following years.

Dr König, Hans Müller-Wiedemann and Alix Roth saw the children and applicants for the start of Cresset House. Christiane and I were present in the background. It gave us the privilege to be close to Dr König for a few very special days.

I enjoyed my new tasks and freedom enormously. Besides teaching the children, the estate needed to be developed and this brought me into contact with the Zulu people whom we employed for the work on the land. In those days we followed the tradition of giving out weekly food-rations to all families living on the estate. Christiane helped with medical and hygiene questions and I had occasions to seek the release of one or more of our Zulus from police cells. This occurred mostly on weekends when a worker was found drunk in a prohibited area.

Christiane and I worked well in tandem and in the southern summer we went together on holiday exploring Lesotho. Back at Cresset we were soon joined by Hans van der Stok, and later Ella Snoek (who became his wife). We were also sent a "grandmother": Irmgard Lazarus! She however would have none of the duties of a grandmother and proceeded to teach eurythmy to the children! Thomas and Anke Weihs visited us from Scotland and it was then that Christiane and I announced our engagement. We tied the knot on August 12, 1962. In September 1962 we were able to fly (!) to Europe and attended the Opening of Camphill Hall in Scotland as part of our honeymoon.

In 1969 we moved to Natal to start a school. Camphill's expansion in South Africa had gone from one to five places in just a few years. When a number of key members of Camphill in the Cape Province decided to return to Europe a crisis ensued. In the end shrinkage was the only solution. With a heavy heart in December 1967 we handed our fledgling work in Natal to the Parents Committee (who were none too pleased!) and headed back to Hermanus where we were needed.

The tasks facing me in Dawn Farm (re-named Camphill School in the 1970s) were taxing. The "Mother-place" was having a low period: many friends were returning to Europe; two pupils were lost on the mountain, there was very little money, and five households had to be managed with insufficient co-workers. As time went on, I had to admit to myself that I was not managing well. A visit to Camphill/Scotland resulted in an offer of relief by Ingrid Röder (later Adler) enabling a six month sabbatical for us in Europe. So in January 1970 we sailed with our children, now aged five and six from Cape Town to Southampton.

Subsequently after more meetings and reflections, Christiane and I concluded that we would remain in Europe. It was hard that we did not return to Hermanus to bring nearly twelve years to a conclusion. We were offered a place in Murtle Estate (Camphill). I taught a class, Christiane ran the big vegetable garden and the children began their schooling. It was a hard "home coming!" I felt out of my depth, misunderstood, and two efforts to be allowed to come into my own came to nothing. I could not reconnect. The result was that we left in 1973 and began a homeless period until "our star" reappeared.

Four years later in September 1977 we found our home and task in the abandoned "Workhouse" near Stroud, Gloucestershire, now William Morris House. By that time I was very low, also my dear wife who, however, never showed it. We began to wonder whether we would be "left out in the cold." We had moved nine times (twice within a community) and it was also showing on our children. However, all the hard lessons learned stood me in good stead when it came to building up the work in Gloucestershire. In time we had the joy of being visited by many of our Camphill colleagues and of becoming a thriving Camphill Community for students, trainees (15 to 25), and the many volunteers and co-workers, who still come every year.

AUTOBIOGRAPHICAL

Those who Arrived in the Fifties

Gisela Schlegel

January 16, 1924

Visiting Gisela in hospital not so long ago was a revelation. So enthusiastic was the life-long nurse at seeing hospital from the patient's point of view, so interested in each single nurse, each fellow patient and every experience, that the healthy visitor left inspired, uplifted and "better." Even as a patient, Gisela was able to be a healer.

Gisela devoted her life to the art of healing. Her confidence in the healing forces of life and destiny, her *joie de vivre* and interest, have created a home for countless children, carried generations of co-workers through illness or crisis and been a beacon of consolation and hope for many approaching the threshold of death.

Taking a young child with a badly grazed knee for treatment, the nervous parent is assured that the healing forces are in the body itself — one can support them but should allow them to work: a little calendula perhaps, but most importantly water, also the circulation of air, and time, confidence in life, the forces of life, and destiny.

Gisela has spent a lifetime making so many others feel younger, more energetic, and whole. We had an example of leadership through devotion to others. Devotion, not through denial, but — like some of her close friends, our founder members, and like her grandfather's well-known friend, Rudolf Steiner — devotion with a sense of fun, with style, and a love of life.

PETER HOWE
"Gisela at 75," from Camphill Correspondence, *1999/1.*

I was born on January 16, 1924, in the house of my grandfather Emil Schlegel, a well known homeopathic doctor. He had a very spacious house with a large garden and this is where our family lived during my first seven years. I was the second child with an older brother and a younger sister. I had a very free and harmonious childhood. My grandfather had an enormous practice, so he had to ask my father and uncle, both also homeopathic doctors, to help with his growing stream of patients. Young as I was, this made a great impression on me. I still remember the thought: it must be beautiful to help these poor people. My grandfather, who was Marie Steiner's doctor, had quite some contact with Rudolf Steiner who visited him on various occasions. Rudolf Steiner respected my grandfather and had most of his books in his library. My mother was an anthroposophist and a member of the Christian Community.

In 1931 we moved to Pforzheim and two years later Hitler came to

power. My grandfather called together his large family to warn them of what lay ahead for Germany through Hitler's leadership. This proved only too true.

The famous industrialist, Robert Bosch, built a large hospital in Stuttgart to further homeopathy and as a friend of my father's called him to teach and work in this hospital. So in 1937 we moved to Stuttgart. I was confirmed in the Christian Community in 1938.

After a very deep meeting with a young doctor, a friend of our family who died in 1941, I knew that I wanted to become a nurse, to make his ideals to help and heal into my own ideals.

The war years were not easy, my father being often endangered by the Nazi regime as he knew too much of what was going on. In 1942 I became a trainee nurse in the Robert Bosch Homeopathic Hospital. I lived through many bomb attacks and as ever more hospitals were destroyed in Stuttgart we took in more and more badly injured and dying patients. Yet I loved my profession and loved to look after the very ill and dying. In 1945 I took my examination with excellent results.

I had a very strong premonition that I would not marry but rather look after other peoples' children. I had the longing to live with others and not to work for money but work freely where I saw a need. I stayed on as a staff nurse for another two years.

Then I had another experience through a lecture by Herbert Hahn (a Waldorf teacher), which inspired me. He had spoken of St Michael who has overcome the dragon, the evil forces in heaven and how it is now up to us to fight the battle here on earth, a battle which can only be fought if we find each other in Michael's service. I felt called and wanted to inspire others, but nobody understood me. So I decided to leave the hospital, which was difficult but I knew I could not continue there.

I applied to the London Homeopathic Hospital as a staff nurse. They would have gladly accepted me if I had sufficient knowledge of English, but I did not. My sister who worked as a nurse in Brissago, Switzerland, wrote to me, "Why don't you go to Camphill to Dr König?" So I wrote to Dr König who replied: "We will gladly accept you as a nurse. We have a small hospital and nurse's school. Yes, bring your uniform, but I am not interested in your examination results, only in you as a person."

So I arrived in my nurses' uniform and was highly surprised: I was put in charge, with another person, of a big group of difficult children. The "hospital" — two sick rooms and a nurse — were in a house on another estate.

Although I had made many friends in Camphill and loved my work I was clear about leaving after a year to work in hospital again. Dr König was always very kind to me and supported me in my work as a nurse. He did not try to influence my decision to leave at Easter 1951. In my last talk with him before leaving he said: "I will describe a picture of Camphill for you: Camphill is like a large house. Many people can go in and out. The house is fashioned by many grey stones, and each of you is such a grey stone on whom the work rests. You can see the house but what you can't see is how far into the depths and how high into the heights this house reaches."

Back in Germany I took up nursing, this time in a state hospital. I felt fulfilled again in my work and was happy. However I missed my friends in Camphill, the way we lived and worked together and the sense of striving for something higher.

After only four months back in Germany I decided to return to Camphill. Dr König seemed to known I would and wrote a welcoming letter.

At the beginning of 1952 Dr König had a new impulse for the profession of nursing. It was to begin in conjunction with the work with spastic children and we were to start a structured nurses' training in the mansion house of Thornbury Park, near Bristol. Our work was extremely demanding, physically but also spiritually, striving for high ideals. Within the year this training ended, mainly I think out of the recognition that spastic children needed not only skill in their physical care but also a great deal of education which demanded a different attitude. However, the work with spastic children continued.

Dr König called me back to Camphill in 1958. I was now to be house-mother and nurse for more than forty years, initially in Camphill House, which was home also for Dr König, then in St Andrew's House and later for many years in Murtle House.

At the beginning of 1962 there was a special meeting of the Camphill nurses with Dr König. Later he wrote: "We came together because of the wish to make another attempt at a meaningful understanding of the direction of nursing. This became a good conversation in which we tried to kindle a new nurse impulse." That summer Dr König asked me to call together all nurses from the Camphill movement. Eight of us came. It was wonderful gathering around this deep impulse. We met for two days, including a Bible Evening. Dr König wrote: "It was strong and solemn and one could experience that the seed of a new nurses' impulse was given birth." We were given new inner guidance out of Dr König's deep insight with which we started to work in our nurses' group.

In 1970 the question came up to establish a place where people could be nursed through a severe illness and convalesce, and where elderly people could find a home when no longer able to live in a house with lively children. To begin with, it was not easy for me to respond positively to Anke Weihs' invitation to take on this task, as I loved to be house-mother in Murtle House with thirty-five children. We had become so much of a family. However, I knew that my real task was nursing and to this call I should again say, "Yes." So in 1971 St Devenicks in Murtle estate became this house for ill and older people. My mother, then 79, and physically frail could also find a home there and was grateful to spend the last phase of her life in Camphill.

It was in 1972 that the Camphill Nurses Course started. It became a two-year course with three to six students who were fully integrated into the life of a house-community. These courses continued (with a year's interruption) until 2002, ending with a one-year course. It had to stop because of new demands and regulations imposed on the nursing profession. However, I believe that the Camphill nurses' impulse will never die, and it is encouraging to know of Erika Nauck, a Camphill nurse, responding to invitations from two Camphill Villages, who will share this impulse with interested students in the USA.

AUTOBIOGRAPHICAL

Eva Maria Glück

July 4, 1925 – January 3, 2000

Eva was born in Geislingen, Germany, the fourth of five children. Her parents were anthroposophists but could never speak about this during the Third Reich. As well as the tumultuous world events, two personal tragedies cut into an otherwise happy and secure family life, and would become leading motifs in Eva's life.

When she was nine, her older sister developed multiple sclerosis at the age of sixteen, dying just six years later. And in 1943, when Eva was eighteen, her brother, a pilot in the Luftwaffe, was shot down on a reconnaissance flight over Scotland. He was 23.

During and after the war, Eva worked and trained as a nurse, experiencing in her youth the full horror of a military hospital.

Later, looking for work in anthroposophical children's homes, she heard of Karl König's work in Scotland and followed the trail of her brother to that country.

Eva arrived in Camphill on January 5, 1950. On her first holiday she explored the area where her brother had died; a photo of the handsome young pilot stood on her desk for the rest of her life.

There followed many years of life and work as a children's nurse and house-mother. Generations of pupils, co-workers and their children experienced the warm-hearted and motherly Eva, unstinting in her response to other's needs, a no-nonsense approach, but always a twinkle in her eye. I doubt if she had a single enemy in her long life, yet was unbending in her convictions.

In Camphill and especially through the Bible Evening, Eva gained an access to Christianity. She also said that through reading Rudolf Steiner's lectures, *The Fifth Gospel,* she "understood the Gospels." An active member of the Christian Community, a Class member and a service holder, Eva had a refreshingly non-intellectual approach. She expressed her convictions through clear-hearted actions and through her quality of being, notably her way of greeting and of taking an interest in others.

PETER HOWE
From Camphill Correspondence, *2000/5.*

Christof-Andreas Lindenberg

August 20, 1932

Born in Berlin in 1932 I spent the first years of my life in the city where, as a boy, my father, Horst Lindenberg, had listened to many a lecture by Rudolf Steiner. In his early youth, especially between the ages of thirteen to sixteen, he was free to roam Berlin, his home city, after school hours. He had read books on philosophy, and, noticing posters advertising lectures by Rudolf Steiner, was attracted to attend these lectures in the years from 1916 to 1920. At the end of this time he received religion lessons from Friedrich Rittelmeyer, then still a Protestant minister. Seven years later, in 1926 Friedrich Rittelmeyer ordained him to be a priest of the Christian Community. Tilla Maasberg (later König) was also studying in Berlin in the twenties, and she once told me that she knew and liked my father very much then.

My mother had also been, like Tilla, in Berlin training to become a nurse, and she later founded a nursing home in the Erzgebirge where my father first met her. A little later, in spring 1932, Mother, who was already acquainted with Karl König, went to one of the conferences for nurses and social workers at Eisenach, arranged by him and Emil Bock. Dr König saw her pregnant state and told her: "He whom you carry under your heart will one day be my co-worker." These prophetic words came true eight-

een and a half years later when, after arriving at Heathcot, Dr König greeted me: "Good, here you are!"

I tell this story here as it is an unusual way into Camphill, having been guided more according to a heavenly plan than my own doing. In fact, my mother who had built up a children's home during the war thought it a good idea I should train with Dr König for a year in Scotland and then help her run the home. My parents also heard of a positive letter Friedwart Bock had written from his work with children in Camphill, and so, after finishing school in Munich I was "sent" to Camphill.

My upbringing in a Christian Community household, latterly with many children beyond our own family of six, and with a very free-thinking and energetic mother, as well as my own hard wartime-experiences in the Hitler Youth movement, had brought me to a point where I thought that at eighteen I was grown up enough to prove my independence to work with children in need. Thus I was convinced that it was I who had decided to come to Camphill. Only later did I realize that this "I" was embedded in a preordained interweaving of karma. This realization was given weight when I recalled a special moment which occurred in Stuttgart, where I was attending the Waldorf School after the war: I had a clear vision of the houses and children I was to meet at Heathcot. I saw it in such detail that when I finally came to that place I recognized some of the individual children.

My father was a musician, and we grew up with anthroposophical and Wandervögel songs, playing many instruments and improvising in old musical cadences and keys, four-hand on the piano. Through my father we also had the good fortune of preparing for any concerts by going over the themes of the respective symphony or concerto we were to hear. It sometimes felt a little embarrassing when in the overcrowded tram, Father, who happened to have jumped onto the front section would whistle the unrehearsed motif over the heads of passengers towards the back of the carriage where we had squeezed in. Not only this, but Father expected us to whistle back, for instance, the completion of a half quoted tune, again over all the heads that separated us from him.

After completing school I began to prepare for entry into the Munich Music College in the belief that it is easy to become a conductor, and I was conceited enough to think there was nothing I did not know about music. Yet, the second seminar group with Dr König was about to begin, and the abruptness of my going to Camphill left behind my academic ambitions.

On my arrival (I think on October 5, 1950) the matron, Janet McGavin, handed me a lyre saying: "As this is a rest-day we sing *When I hold Him ever** for the children in the afternoon, you should join us!" Astonished that I should play on what looked like a plinky-plonky and rather flimsy instrument I tried it anyway. A little later I was once again playing on my beloved piano, it was early on a Saturday afternoon, when Janet came by, speaking sternly: "Who in this place plays piano on a Saturday afternoon when all preparations go towards the Bible Evening, inwardly and outwardly!" I closed the piano lid never to open it again! That, however, was the making of a Camphill lyre player, not least with Janet's ongoing help.

Added to the two inclinations of the religious attitude and of the music, both of which came largely through my father, I had two other characteristics which my mother had implanted. One: the all-round handyman; the other: to recall events of the past. After Father was taken away by the Gestapo in June 1941 (when the Christian Community was forbidden and many of its priests were rounded up) Mother lost no time bringing in other children, among them some with Jewish background, and some even with special needs, and soon went about renovating a house in the country away from the threatened city of Munich. Getting any building materials was a feat in those days of the war. We children helped, and later I was for a short time engaged by a local joiner who gave me a crash-course in carpentry. This must have caused my mother to state in my application to Camphill that I had a joiner's training. Subsequently soon after my arrival at Heathcot, Hubert Zipperlen opened the big door of the garage full of broken furniture awaiting the "joiner," who was, however, blissfully unaware of his required profession. Well, I did my best, and whatever I

* A three part chorus by Edmund Pracht with words by Novalis.

had learned as a youngster came to good use in my life in Camphill. The building of the first houses in Glencraig required every ounce of experience I ever had acquired in that realm.

What a gift I received from Carlo Pietzner! He showed me, over and again, the importance of form, both in outer application as well as in inner pursuit. That helped the earlier perhaps sanguine nature to mature and ultimately to give meaning beyond mere utility. Form represents a Rosicrucian element both in work and service. Outwardly I have since kept a workbench in my house, mainly for mending chairs and making shelves or picture frames, while inwardly this form element helped me structure musical compositions and the creation of Camphill festivals. This form element has brought me real happiness up to the present.

The preoccupation with the past at first made me keep records of events and people who had died including their obituaries. Through that another world was opened. Fleeting communication with those who have died became possible. Here I struggle, as these contacts are sporadic and often more like a dream. It is rare that I get a clear image or message, but when it comes I am deeply grateful to have been led to this doorway. Hans-Heinrich Engel helps me steadily from the other side.

In these last 55 Camphill years I have a growing notion that I am not a teacher, nor a home-maker, nor really a community-builder, though I tried all of these; I am not a lecturer, nor a writer, nor a counsellor; I am not gifted at public relations, nor in contributing to association meetings, and I am no longer a musical performer. With all that notion there is a dawning sureness of becoming a therapist that wants to link in therapeutic endeavour to the Being that stands behind our Camphill community, serving the Raphael-impulse. And thus the path to Camphill is ever leading on, perhaps more self-determined, more Michaelic.

AUTOBIOGRAPHICAL

Muriel Valentien, née Thomson

August 31, 1925

In Toronto, six hours behind Central European Time, the date of the invasion of Poland in 1939 was August 31, the late evening of my fourteenth birthday. From this day on I recorded in my diary many events of the conflict, as reported by radio and newspapers, right until the end. Nearer to the war, in my personal life, I didn't come. Many Canadian soldiers, sailors and airmen died in Europe, friends of ours lost fathers, sons,

brothers, but the war was drawing to a close by the time my own brother was ready to go overseas as a flying officer.

We had no bombing, none of the unspeakable suffering of the Europeans. But I couldn't forget the war. After university, as a journalist in Montreal, I welcomed every opportunity to meet Europeans or returning Canadians at the harbour (one still crossed the ocean by ship then) or the airport, to write about their experiences, also to find life-stories within the varied ethnic groups in Montreal itself. And all the time some strong underground (or underwater) current seemed to be tugging me across the ocean. I hadn't suffered personally through the war, but maybe I could still do something to help those who had. So I thought then.

I was particularly concerned with *children* who had suffered, those deprived of home and parents. And this went along with something else. Journalism was an interesting, sometimes even exciting profession, but more and more I experienced it as a looking-on at life, not as life itself. I needed to get *into life*. And to this came persistent questions. What *is* life, its purpose, its end? What is my own goal within it, my *raison d'être?* So it was with a twofold purpose that I finally crossed the ocean in a former troopship in the summer 1950.

I started with the International Voluntary Service, helping to convert a city dump into a playground in war-damaged Leeds, then helping refugees from Eastern Germany build houses in the West. Next, a school for deprived, war-damaged children in the south of France. Feeling ill-equipped for this, still too inexperienced to begin with such extremely difficult destinies, I moved on to Switzerland, looking for further work with refugees. Walking the streets of Geneva for three days, I applied at eleven different social agencies, each time being told that Switzerland wasn't taking on "outside help" then, it needed work for its own citizens. The twelfth attempt would be my last. If nothing was there I would go back where I came from, feeling that my "mission" in Europe had failed.

But at this agency for International Voluntary Service, the young woman in charge listened for two hours to my "life-story" of 25 years. I marvelled then (and now) at her patience! Then she said "I know where you belong, a curative home for handicapped children on Lake Geneva is looking for help. If you want to accept." Oh yes, I did want to. She made the arrangements by phone, then told me, "Get off the train at Morges. You will be met by a *monsieur* in a white smock and glasses."

This *monsieur* was Hans Spalinger, the white smock was because he and his co-workers were painting the house at St Prex, into which they had recently moved. And the moment I walked in the front door of this house I felt in the right place: it was a home-coming. Here I could combine my two goals, one of them slightly adjusted: to help children who — if not directly victims of war — carried other imprints of the twentieth century in their disturbed constitutions. And through anthroposophy, on which the life and work of this house was based, I would learn, little by little, about what I was calling the *what-for* of our earthly existence.

How many helpers do we have along our way who remain unrecognized and unnamed! One of them was the young woman in Geneva who took the trouble to listen at such length to this unknown foreigner who had just drifted in! I was very happy at St Prex. Life took on ever deeper and richer dimensions. I could speak French with the children, but German was the language for the seminar in curative education and for the evening study sessions of the co-workers. Although I knew almost no German, I did consider returning after a summer holiday to attempt the seminar. But back in Britain, and on my way to visit my ancestral origins in Dornoch, Sutherland. I stopped off to visit Camphill, of which I had heard. It was Michaelmas time, September 28. The whole community was enjoying the harvest meal in the Newton Dee barn. I was invited to join, and sat up in the loft, warmly welcomed by the same kind of children — though individually different of course — whom I regretfully had left behind in St Prex. Again came that intense sense of being at home, belonging to the same "stream" as there. But here the work, the seminar, were in the English language. That was decisive for me.

In those days applicants sometimes had to wait to be accepted, it was a question of having enough room. I waited three days in Aberdeen on pins and needles, so to speak. Would there be room? To my unspeakable relief, there was! I could go back to collect my luggage and begin at once!

Only three years later did I get to Dornoch in Sutherland to visit the graves of my ancestors, when escorting one of our children to his home in the area. In between I was introduced to a Dorn*ach,* in Switzerland.

AUTOBIOGRAPHICAL

Hans Christof Valentien

March 13, 1927 – April 19, 2003

On Easter Saturday 2003, in the stillness of dawn, the silken thread of Hans Christof's life was severed. Hans Christof had left Camphill in 1971 to become a teacher of mathematics at the Engelberg Waldorf School near Stuttgart, an important step in his destiny. But inwardly, I have always felt, he never left Camphill. During the years of his illness he wandered through his past, meeting again the "old" Camphillers, remembering many of the children in the class he had taught for ten years. Once, when moving uncertainly through the house with the help of his stick, he said, "Now I know how it was for Trevor Pullman [a partially sighted boy in his class]. He also couldn't be sure of the distance between his eye and the floor!"

He had two great loves: anthroposophy and mathematics. To anthroposophy he came at the age of eighteen, after his return from the war. He then took part in anthroposophical study weeks in Stuttgart, a source of inspiration for hundreds of enthusiastic young people at that time. Here he met Gottwalt Hahn and Suso Vetter, who were to become his colleagues later at the Engelberg. His interest in mathematics had been kindled in high school through one of his teachers. In his own later studies he worked intensively on projective geometry, two of his mentors being George Adams and Louis Locher-Ernst.

At the age of fourteen he took glider lessons, receiving his pilot's license three years later. He would have loved to take up flying as a career, had it been allowed by Occupation Powers after the war. At age sixteen, together with his classmates, he was assigned to anti-aircraft duty in defence of Stuttgart airport. Some of his companions did not survive the nights of bombing. In January 1945, recruited into the Air Force, he trained as a radio operator.

During the last days of the war, he and members of his unit were taken prisoner by Allied forces. They were to be held in a French prisoner-of-

war camp. A French officer stood at the gate of the camp letting the prisoners through in single file. As Hans Christof approached him the officer gave a quick nod with his head, indicating that he should not go in, but walk away. This he did, but in the course of the day was caught again by the Americans. Here, too, he was further protected. Roll call had not yet been established in the American camp and he managed to hide himself in a shed. In his shoe he had hidden a pair of pliers. When the night came he crept to the perimeter fence and between the flashes of the searchlight cut through the fence and escaped.

This experience called up questions of destiny, especially when he later heard that the prisoners in the French camp were taken to France, from where the survivors returned home only years later.

Then came the meeting with anthroposophy, the resumption of his education and the decision to study mathematics. While attending the first wedding of his friend, Freddy Heimsch in Ringwood, he met Renate, his future wife, and became acquainted with and drawn to the ideals of Camphill. In the next weeks he had to make an important decision. He had been offered a teaching post at the Tübingen Waldorf School. But the meeting with Camphill had convinced him that the study and practice of curative education would give him the necessary basis for all future teaching. He decided for Camphill, where he remained for fifteen years.

MURIEL VALENTIEN

Hans van der Stok

January 24, 1912 – April 24, 1986

Born in Germany of a German father and Dutch mother, Hans van der Stok grew up in Dornach, Switzerland where as a child he met Rudolf Steiner. After a few years teaching at the Amsterdam Waldorf School he moved to Camphill, teaching at St John's School. He worked for ten years in South Africa before leading the Camphill Seminar at Thornbury, England.

I was born in Oberhambach in the Odenwald in Germany. Though both my parents were thoroughly Dutch, I was born there, because at that time they both worked as teachers in the Odenwaldschule. Moeke (Frisian for mother) taught Dalcroze eurhythmics and my father was art teacher. I was, however, only a few months old when my parents left the Odenwaldschule and returned to Holland. My father wanted to make money and therefore, after his divorce from Moeke, he gave up his painting career, went back to Indonesia (where he was born) and became administrator of a coffee and rubber plantation.

It was I who actually told Moeke that she should marry Atti (Paul Bay)! This happened in Dornach in 1921. Moeke and I had moved there, because she wanted to be near Rudolf Steiner whose teachings she had come to cherish.

My education was very erratic. After having started primary school in two places in Holland, I went to Dornach, first to a lovely, if somewhat Bohemian school for children of Anthroposophists, until one day the Swiss police came and said that all the children below 14 would have to go to an approved State school. So I went for a while to a Catholic primary school. In 1923 we moved to Stuttgart, but as the Waldorf School was so full (classes of 55 or more children), they could not take me, but put me on the waiting list. For about two years I had to go to a state school where the teachers were both sadistic and sentimental. Once, when I was beaten for something of which I was innocent, I knocked the teacher down by hitting him over the head with a big ink bottle. After my glorious exit from the state school the Waldorf School opened its portals to me.

However, I needed three years to outgrow a little bit of the damage done to me in the state school. I left the Waldorf School after ninth grade, because Atti and Moeke thought that I should become and artist. This was the greatest mistake they ever made regarding me. For although I was definitely gifted in drawing, painting and carving, I was no less gifted in lit-

erature, poetry and history, and my premature removal from the Waldorf school resulted in definite symptoms of deprivation.

When, in 1929, we moved with the whole family to Beatenberg, I immersed myself into training as a designer-woodcarver and sculptor. My main teacher was Atti himself. We grew so close together in our work that it would often happen that Atti carved designs, which I had made. By this time Atti had started an studio in Beatenberg for woodcarving, furniture, gravestones, and so on. We ran this studio under our joint names, Bay & van der Stok.

Elisabeth and I married in Beatenberg itself, where we also lived in the house built by Atti. I had already fallen in love with your mother in the Waldorf School, where we were in the same class. A friend of mine brought some of my love sonnets "to Elisabeth" to our teacher, Dr Hahn, who was wise enough to judge them on their own merit and who stimulated me to try my hand at play-writing. When I was fourteen years old I wrote quite an impressive historical tragedy in 5 acts on Henry IV, the medieval German Emperor, which Dr Hahn praised highly. Elisabeth, however, was not at all pleased at being teased over my love poems to her. For the rest of our school time together she did not even talk to me any more, so that I was known as the unrequited lover! We came to know each other better in later years through letter-writing, which I initiated.

In the early thirties Atti was offered a designer's job by an anthroposophical button and buckle factory in Stuttgart. During this time mother and I carried on in Beatenberg. When the Bay family returned to Beatenberg, we moved to Stuttgart, where I stepped into Atti's office and became designer of the Aurora button factory. We stayed there from 1935 to 1938. I earned a good amount of money, but felt myself increasingly as a kind of traitor to my artistic and spiritual conscience, as a result of the compromises I was forced to make in my design work.

The advent of the Nazis started to make life in Germany ever more unbearable, and so we happily returned to a much poorer life in Beatenberg. During the main years of the war, mother and I had the Beatenberg "empire" more or less to ourselves, as Atti was called up to the Swiss army and put in command of refugee camps. At the end of 1944 the opportunity arose for Dutch men living in Switzerland to join the allied forces in France. I joined up and spent some unforgettable four months in Paris, and then three months at the Belgian border in a military hospital in Lille with a collapsed lung. This put an end to my artistic career. When I returned to Switzerland I was not permitted to do any manual work (such as carving) for about one year. So I fell in to Moeke's enterprise of designing "children's villages" for war-orphans.

AUTOBIOGRAPHICAL
Edited from notes for his children

I would like to share a few impressions of Hans van der Stok as I experienced my father shortly before he died and then again as he lay in his coffin. In very early spring 1986, we were all made aware of the dimming of his earthly light. One by one, friends and relatives came to bid Hans a farewell. Each one was made well aware of the nature of their visit, for he himself prepared those around him for his death.

Only three weeks before he died, Roswitha (his second eldest daughter) and myself (the fourth and youngest) flew over from America to spend a short week with our father. From the moment we arrived until we left we lost all sense of time; it became immaterial in the face of this important and precious meeting. As the door opened and we walked in to greet Hans, a wave of love and gratitude enveloped us — a love and gratitude totally devoid of the usual sentiment typical of such occasions. Here was an individual so actively preparing for his death, so ready to pass on everything, that he was no longer "burdened" by major concerns and issues, but could be utterly free, open and giving. And governing his mood of soul was this all-pervading gesture of gratitude. He expressed this gratitude verbally too, giving thanks to the nursing staff in the hospital for their care and concern, giving thanks to all those who were making the effort to come and visit him and, above all, expressing gratitude for the illness and what it could teach him. "Now I know something about the physical body," he said, "and without this illness, that would not have been possible."

During our visit he had again to be hospitalized. So, for the rest of our short stay we visited him in the hospital. It was very touching but also impressive to experience this serene old man, hooked up to a nasal drip, lying in his bed in a ward full with approximately twenty other ill men and women. Not much peace, you could say, certainly no seclusion; and yet he was grateful and in his mood buoyant. On one such visit, he spoke to me of the importance of the cultivation of *trust,* the trust that never wavers even when faced with error. He gave personal examples to that effect, and it was moving to hear him tell of his struggles.

And so our visit drew to a close and we had to leave. Before we parted from him, I allowed my eyes to rest a while on a part of his body that had remained visibly untouched by the ravishes of illness — his hands; beautiful hands, exquisitely sculptured and so expressive. These I took with me, as it were, and flew home to my family and community.

Two weeks later, and exactly one week after Carlo Pietzner had died, Hans bid his final farewell to us all. One of the last thoughts he had shared with me was his concern that one should always strive for greater, deeper friendship, brotherhood. When I received the news of his passing, I was just involved in a workshop on Brotherhood, and had been struggling to put into eurythmical interpretation words from St Paul to the Romans (12:9f). "Love in all sincerity, loathing evil and clinging to the good. Let love for our brotherhood breed warmth of mutual affection. Give pride of place to one another in esteem."

On the day after his death, Alona (his eldest daughter, later Paula) and myself, accompanied by two of his grandchildren, Colum Lindenberg and Ikenna Imegwu, made the journey to Thornbury. There were those hands again, folded serenely and resting peacefully, and now they spoke to me not only of the great artistic gifts of this individual in his life on earth, but of a future life. And I could remember so recently having felt those hands gently caressing my cheek, stroking my hand; but more than that, the message that flowed through them then was now apparent again as they reposed there, and the message spoke of "Healing." Yes, on reflection I could say that already before he died, when the constant stream of farewell visits were underway, he radiated this *healing* attitude; and though he died through illness, he was already beginning to develop the sense of healing.

He lay for three days in the coffin in his own room. The birds sang unceasingly outside the open window and there was such a serene, uplifting mood about him. On the fourth day, his funeral was celebrated in

Thorn Hall. Above his head, hanging in the place of the altar picture, was a portrait of Rudolf Steiner which he had made from memory, and we were all reminded of the fact that he had been able to meet and experience this great teacher in person. This special day was one of celebration as we were able to hear his biography and share our experiences of Hans. Thus the pain of parting very soon gave way to joy of new finding and I left with his new song in my heart.

RAYMONDE VAN DER STOK FRIED
From Camphill Correspondence, *2000/2.*

Elisabeth van der Stok

October 21, 1912 – October 22, 1999

Elisabeth Karoline Berner was born in Stuttgart, Germany, the eldest of three children. She was not particularly robust in health or physical strength, but made up for this with her zest for life and her interest in the world and the people around her. Indeed, she was a tomboy during her childhood, preferring to play boys' games.

At the age of six, when she should have been starting school, Elisabeth was pushed down a staircase by a rowdy boy and fractured her spine, which necessitated that she spend a whole year lying flat on her back in a body cast. Elisabeth thereby missed the first year of the first class of the first Waldorf School, but was carried to the school for the opening ceremony.

While she was thus restricted in her movements, Elisabeth's imagination travelled far. She also had a very special grandfather who would carry her out into the garden and introduce her to the wonders of nature. He was also a great storyteller and entertained her with many wonderful tales.

Both Elisabeth's love of nature and her love for story telling were nurtured in this year. This time of confinement was also made more bearable by the presence of a neighbour who played the piano. For Elisabeth this sounded like heavenly music and it helped awaken a lifelong love of music. She loved to sing and was later to take up the violin, and much later, the lyre.

After her convalescence, Elisabeth was finally able to join her class in the Waldorf School, which was one of the great joys of her life. Elisabeth felt blessed in her teachers and treasured the visits of Rudolf Steiner to the classroom.

Her love of learning and of her teachers instilled in her a great love of language, literature, history, geography and the arts and this came to expression years later in her love of teaching. She was also able to maintain contact with her former classmates and teachers, and corresponded with some of them throughout her life. It was also in the Waldorf School that Elisabeth developed her love of eurythmy, a life-long passion for her. Indeed, one of her last outings to the Duffcarrig Hall was for a eurythmy performance less than a month before she died. Elisabeth excelled in the arts and handwork, and her schoolbooks were meticulously and beautifully written and illustrated.

When Elisabeth was in sixth grade a Dutch boy named Hans van der Stok joined the class. Little did Elisabeth know that he would one day be her husband — indeed, she would have laughed at the very idea! Hans took a liking to her and wrote sonnets to Elisabeth, but she was definitely not interested!

In High School Elisabeth had her sights set on eurythmy training, but when she had finished school she was too young to begin this training and in the interim went to Switzerland for one year to help in the household of the Bay family. This turned into a very long year, because Hans van der Stok was the eldest of this family (Paul Bay was his stepfather) and as destiny would have it, Hans and Elisabeth became engaged and were married shortly before Elisabeth's twentieth birthday. Eleven months later their first child, Alona (later known as Paula), was born.

In 1934 the family moved to Stuttgart where Olaf, their only son, was born the following year. By 1938, with the Nazi regime sweeping Germany towards war, it became too uncomfortable to remain in Germany so the family returned to Switzerland where, during the early years of the war, they lived in considerable poverty. However, Elisabeth's creativity and resourcefulness enabled her to turn the simplest food into a meal beautifully garnished with fresh herbs, while donated clothes were transformed into beautifully embroidered clothes for the children. Elisabeth's sense of colour and attention to detail served the family well in those hard war years. Another daughter, Roswitha, was born during this time.

In 1944 Hans joined the Allied forces on the French front, but a serious illness led to his discharge with a good army pension — a great help to the family. When Hans came home to convalesce there followed one of the happiest periods of their married life. Hans began work on a set of hand-carved marionettes for a production of *Faust,* for which Elisabeth made beautiful garments.

In 1947 Hans, wishing to return to his native Holland, sold the marionettes and so enabled the family to move to Haarlem and later to Amsterdam where Hans became a teacher at the Geert Groote (Waldorf) School. Their daughter Johanna was born that year in Holland.

Once again Elisabeth supported Hans in his (teaching) work by providing him with ideas and inspiration for subject matter (she was always

an avid reader and had a wealth of material in her memory). She also helped him correct the students' school-work and taught handwork in the school.

After one year in Holland in the summer of 1948, Elisabeth and Hans experienced the loss of her only son who drowned in the estuary of the river Rhine at the age of thirteen. Hans had planned a beach vacation with the two eldest children, and for some mysterious reason Elisabeth decided to wash her son's feet before he left. She did this with love and her usual attention to detail and it was this deed that enabled her, many days later, to identify Olaf by his feet when he was finally washed up on the shore! Throughout this time she was unbelievably brave.

In 1950 the family Bay invited Hans to visit them in Camphill Scotland where they had settled. Hans was so enthused by his encounter with Camphill that he returned to Holland and convinced Elisabeth that the family should move to Scotland. A dream in which Olaf appeared to her convinced Elisabeth of the rightness of the move to Camphill. She was expecting her fifth child, when she travelled to Newton Dee in January 1951 and Raymonde was born that March. Two weeks later Hans and the three other daughters made the move to Scotland, and so began a life-long commitment to Camphill for Hans as well as Elisabeth.

In the autumn of that year, 1951, Elisabeth entered the main vocation of her life — curative education. Those who knew her in those days would know what a dedicated and inspired teacher she was. And just as she maintained contact with her teachers and classmates, she maintained contact with several of her former pupils.

Elisabeth's dedication to her teaching work often meant that she had little or no time for her own children, who suffered from a certain degree of "benevolent neglect" and ran pretty wild. However, she had a marvellous way of supporting us in our interests and we were sure of her love for us and of her devotion to her ideals and vocation, and this we could respect.

During the midpoint of her life, in 1954, Elisabeth and Hans' marriage was dissolved. Elisabeth had resisted granting Hans a divorce until she had a dream that a child wanted to be born that would not be her child. She did not want to stand in the way of this child, so she agreed to the divorce. There followed a very painful time for Elisabeth, yet she never allowed us to harbor any ill feelings towards our father, and it was obvious that a part of her always continued to love him.

In 1958 Elisabeth was invited to move south and teach in Thornbury, England, where she continued her work as a teacher for the next twelve years. Her willingness to serve where she was needed was demonstrated again in 1970 when she returned to Camphill, Scotland to take care of her two African grandchildren (refugees from the Biafra civil war in Nigeria) and thereby enable Roswitha, their mother, to complete her university education. Elisabeth proved to be the perfect granny and took care of these two boys in a selfless and loving way for three years.

At the end of this period, in the summer of 1973, Elisabeth was invited to Duffcarrig in Ireland to teach the Elsholtz children as well as some local children (including the son of the undertaker who recently took care of Elisabeth when she died). Later she ran a lively little kindergarten and also did music, storytelling and finishing work for the weavery. It has also been said that she kept many people from walking about in rags by mending their clothes for them! Elisabeth again came into her own as a grandmother, not just to her own grandchildren, but to the Duffcarrig community and its children. She maintained her strong sense of hospitality and was always welcoming to visitors. She did not speak ill of people and had a way of seeing the positive in every person.

In the last year Elisabeth increasingly expressed the feeling that she had completed what she needed to do in this life, and more recently it was obvious that she was withdrawing from life. When it became clear that she was approaching the threshold, her four daughters were all able to come together for the first time in 31 years. She received the Last Anointing on October 20, and the following day family members and friends gathered to celebrate her 87th birthday with her. The next day, Friday, October 22, Elisabeth crossed peacefully over the threshold.

ROSWITHA IMEGWU
From Camphill Correspondence, *2000/2.*

Erika Opitz

March 28, 1919 – March 19, 2005

For some time I had the longing to combine pottery (in which I had a master's diploma) with some other activity. In talks with the leader of the Stuttgart Waldorf School I heard that there might be a chance, once some building was completed. So I started the Teachers' Training Course. In the second year we were scheduled to visit classes. Dr Schwebsch had told me earlier on that once in Stuttgart I should not miss meeting Dr Schubert. This I did, and the encounter was most surprising. When I entered the classroom I met children with learning difficulties for the first time. The experience of how Dr Schubert worked with them was unforgettable.

After completing the course there was a vacancy at a children's village in Wahlwies at Lake Constance. I joined in order to establish a pottery and to work with some adolescents. This was my first experience of working within a community. Following a breakdown in management, I was forced to accept a change, and took up a position in a school for arts and crafts. Though I received a professor's salary, everything was running counter to my liking.

I had already corresponded with Camphill and in September 1950 decided to join. After sightseeing in London and a long journey to Aberdeen I was met at the station and taken to Newton Dee. In my memory the feeling is imprinted: "I have come home!" I was flooded by new impressions. My introductory visit to Dr König and later his Sunday evening lectures were unforgettable. The seasonal festivals and the Seminar were occasions for learning from every aspect.

For the second time I established a pottery and worked with disabled adolescents. What a rich field of learning. The participation in the treatment of blind and deaf children was a wonderful experience.

AUTOBIOGRAPHICAL
Translated by Johannes Surkamp

Erika developed her craft into therapy and helped hundreds of children and adults in Scotland and England and spent her later years in Norway.

Hans-Heinrich Engel

June 29, 1921 – October 30, 1973

Hans-Heinrich Engel belongs to the second generation of carrying curative educators of the anthroposophical movement. During his 22 years working in Camphill establishments he has made excellent and fruitful contributions, especially in the field of music therapy through his original approach. Engel's courage as a medical doctor lay in following his own path of developing therapies.

Hans-Heinrich was born as the second son of a homeopathic doctor on June 29, 1921 at Greifswald, Germany. His older brother, Kurt, who served in the German Air Force and fell in 1939, was close to him all his life. Hans-Heinrich also had a younger sister and brother.

After completing his school, he studied medicine at Greifswald and Tübingen which he concluded in 1945. During the war he was active as an officer in the German Navy and was a prisoner of war for a short time. On returning he graduated in Tübingen. Through his first wife, Margit, whom he had married in 1944 and with whom he had a daughter, Birgit, he was introduced to anthroposophy and became a member of the Anthroposophical Society in 1949.

After graduation Hans-Heinrich took up work with Friedrich Husemann in Wiesneck, Germany. However, he remained only a short while before taking over his father's practice in the rural district of Lindau

where he was accessible for his patients at any time of day and night, sometimes even tending to a cow or horse. In 1951 he and his wife became members of the Christian Community in Lindau. During a visit to Camphill, Scotland, Karl König invited him to join the work there. Upon return to Lindau he was able to pass back the practice to his father and move to Camphill. His wife Margit, a medical doctor as well, followed a short while later with their daughter, Birgit.

Hans-Heinrich's activity was devoted to curative education and the Seminar. As Karl König's personal physician he attended to his medical needs. During the following years he joined Thomas and Anke Weihs in the leadership of Camphill, Aberdeen.

After parting from his first wife, Hans-Heinrich married Turid Nielsen, with whom he had a son, Finnolaf, in 1968. In 1960 he worked at Glencraig home-school, founded by Carlo Pietzner. From there, as a much sought-after physician, he supported the expansion of Camphill in Scandinavia, Holland and Switzerland. Following his intuition and creative ideas he found new therapeutic approaches. During his twelve-year period in Northern Ireland, he worked together with Hermann Pfrogner to further develop music therapy. He developed a musical anthropology for an understanding of the organs and the therapeutic effects of music upon them. Hans-Heinrich Engel was a good organizer and inspiring teacher. As a lecturer he was also valued and much sought after, speaking on musical themes as well as mythology and general anthroposophy.

He supported the foundations of two village communities in Ireland: Mourne Grange in the North and Duffcarrig in the South. In the midst of an active life, greatly valued by many co-workers in the Camphill movement, he suffered a severe accident resulting in his death on October 30, 1973 in Bern.

FRIEDWART BOCK

Margit Engel

January 19, 1921

Conceived in Tana near the North Cape of Norway (today close to the Russian border), I was born January 19, 1921 in Oslo. My father had a medical practice first in Tana, later in the south of Norway, in Fossnes. There I was miraculously saved from drowning, walking on a frozen river.

My father was German and after some time he felt he should move to the south of Germany. From there they made journeys to South Georgia, the remote whaling station in the South Atlantic. Later they travelled to East Africa where they collected fairy tales from different African tribes who still lived in their wonderful old African culture.

In 1938 I revisited my school friends in Norway and participated in a Christian Girl Guide Whitsun retreat near Larvik in the south of Norway. Sitting during a long break outside on a stony little hill pondering, suddenly there was a strong light within which a figure like Christ appeared. On seeing it, a certainty arose within me: "Christ *is.*" I had not had any special Christian education, and later no church could satisfy me, but the certainty of "Christ *is"* remained. Later anthroposophy confirmed the way I had experienced Him.

My father had made some prehistoric discoveries and only came back from Africa shortly before the Second World War. During my parents' expeditions I changed my home between Norway, Africa and Germany and consequently went to five different schools. In Norway I met a deeply Christian leader of the Girl Guide group who impressed me, helping me to a deeper grasp of Christianity.

In 1939 I started to study philosophy and medicine in Germany and took my medical exams in 1945. In 1944 I married a fellow medical student, Hans-Heinrich Engel, and our daughter was born in June 1945.

Again in 1947 my life was miraculously saved during the Easter days

from an acute blood disease. I had lost my second child in January, a fully mature boy with the umbilical cord around his neck. I noticed the moment of his death as I carried the stillborn child for about ten days within my womb, I contracted septic fever, which, for some weeks after the birth caused severe bleeding; the doctors declared it fatal. While saying farewell to my husband and my parents during the Easter week, the bleeding lessened during the night following Good Friday and stopped completely on Easter Sunday! The professor for internal medicine could only explain it as a miracle, and so did I. I felt as if a new life had been handed to me.

Then for a long time I searched for a task corresponding to this experience: first in a clinic, then I considered going to the seminary of the Christian Community. At that time I met Dr Karl König lecturing in Stuttgart, telling about the work in which he was engaged with children in need of special care in Scotland. After his talk I went to him, asking whether I could join him in Camphill. He agreed and I arrived with my daughter Birgit in August 1950.

Thus I had left our safe little house and a very dedicated husband. He later joined me in Camphill. In 1953 I went back to Norway, but my first efforts there failed. But in 1964 I was asked back to Norway again to work as a deputy director of a large institute, Emma Hjorts Hjem, and as an assistant doctor at the psychiatric university clinic of Oslo. At this time we looked for a possibility to start a Camphill village. Together with an American couple, Phyllis and Ivan Jacobsen, and a Norwegian technician, Trygve Thornæs, I started Vidaråsen, the first Camphill village community in Norway. Students from Oslo and surrounding towns enthusiastically collected money. For fourteen years around Christmas-time they sold small candles which the village produced. This made it possible for us to build a new house every year. Some years later the call came from the west coast of Norway. Again through miraculous coincidences, a second village, Hogganvik was founded. In 1977 a third, Solborg, and then a fourth and fifth village, Jössåsen and Vallersund, could be started. During all those years both professionals and enthusiastic young people came to work.

The first visit to Russia began in 1977. When travelling became easier in 1992 we helped to found a village near Tallinn in Estonia, at that time a part of the Soviet Union.

Through being introduced to a Russian journalist who came to Vidaråsen, our first village, a few of us were invited to a conference in Moscow. There we met a professor interested in new ideas, and Nicolai Anikin who helped us with a gift of 48 hectares of land. In this way Svetlana started. The Norwegian Camphill villages were able to help to finance the first buildings both in Pahkla in Estonia as well as in Svetlana, Russia.

Through a meeting with two teachers who visited Vidaråsen, I was invited together with Arild Smeby, a Norwegian social worker to Irkutsk in Siberia in 1998. There we met the local authorities, who, to my big surprise told us of two nearby villages, both more than twenty years old — one for criminals, one for mentally retarded people — started by Nicolai Belov, a psychiatrist. After his experience of Vidaråsen, he instituted a wood-workshop, which now has a hundred villagers and has become economically viable.

Looking back, I am immensely grateful for fifty-five years of living and working with people whom society has diagnosed as abnormal. I found them understanding with their hearts and with a deeper ability of recognition than many "normal" people. They love their work and the cultural and social life.

AUTOBIOGRAPHICAL

Joan Watt

April 4, 1903 – August 22, 1980

Joan was born near Gloucester on the April 4, 1903. She was the third of six daughters, the second and sixth dying in infancy. Her parents were gentle and cultured people who valued the arts, and at an early age the children were introduced to music, literature and art. There was a strong bond between the sisters and they were educated at home until the age of fourteen; Joan was considered delicate but resented any special attention. At fourteen she was sent to a boarding school which she disliked and her sisters remembered her as being unhappy and withdrawn at this time. As she grew older she became an idealistic person who searched for the true values of life; it was a lonely way.

In her late twenties Joan travelled to different countries. She married and lived in Africa for ten years. These were years of suffering and hardship for her and she seldom spoke of them. After separating from her husband she was able to spend six fulfilling years with a friend at Cape Town. It was during this time that she did her speech training. It was in Cape Town that she heard an anthroposophical lecture and on returning to England went first to Michael Hall.

Joan met Dr König in 1957 and spent a Christmas week in Camphill. In 1958 on her birthday, April 4, she joined Camphill, Aberdeen, where she joined the seminar and started to work with children who needed remedial speech.

Anthroposophy changed Joan's life; through it she found guidance and a way of relating to life. Her sisters say she became a different person.

Whatever the occasion, Joan was always present. No festival, service or gathering of any kind went by without her being there. She was not one to play a prominent role, but was always intensely awake, never late, always prepared. A figure who could easily escape one's notice — walking slowly, a bag on her arm, her appearance modest and unassuming. You had to go towards her if you wanted to be met.

In 1974 Joan moved from Camphill to Ringwood after a severe illness, which had led her to the conviction that she had to find a person to whom she could pass on her vast knowledge and experience in her work with speech therapy. However, that person did nor appear and years of intensive work passed by. Only in the very last year did Joan reduce the number of children who streamed all day into her tiny room. To have met Joan working with an individual child was an inspiration and a revelation. The vigour, yet tenderness, liveliness and joy with which she worked gave to each lesson with a child the quality of a sacrament. Day after day she worked with this genuine youthfulness and unfailing interest in the person she encountered. Many children were not only helped to make use of their ability to communicate, but also found full recognition.

Joan was modest in all her needs, as long as she had a small room and a corner for the toys and books she used for her lessons, she was content. The furnishings were made of everything others did not want and in no time she would create her own homely corner. Joan never wasted time, her hands were always busy sewing, knitting or crocheting and in the last years all her work went to help Folly Farm School.

Joan's strength was failing in the last months, and it was with anticipation and great joy that she looked forward to the arrival, at last, of a successor. Andrea Flack was completing her speech training in London and had experience in curative education.

Joan's sisters spoke of her earlier years of extreme loneliness and struggle, her deep searching and infinite courage. In later years her faithfulness to the community, her ability to actively listen, her interest and concern not only in the people around her but also in world events, and her humility are the qualities that shine out in her life.

PENELOPE GUY

Renate Reich

August 25, 1928 – October 6, 1999

Renate's life was time and again a deeply testing one, from early childhood onward. Her parents had known the young Dr König, so Renate came to Camphill, a young talented person full of energy and good humour, but sensitive and ready to take on any task, of which there were many! With her musicality and love for the lyre, singing and composing, she soon helped with the treatment of the deaf and mute. Later on she took over the choir from Susanne Müller-Wiedemann. Renate's way led her to the Sheiling in the early years of its existence. There she met her husband Hans Christoph Valentien. Back in Scotland, Christoph and Gotwalt were born to them. Later the marriage broke up. Around that time Renate answered a desperate call for help from Bremen, Germany, where two young children needed mothering, as their mother had died and their father was unable to look after them. Eventually Ingo and Renate married, and the family stabilized. There were Ingo's two children, Renate's two boys and little David who was born to them. Time permitting, Renate worked again with the lyre and recorders. She had pupils as well as offering her gifts to the Christian Community and others.

Renate seemed to have a disposition to ill-health and her later life was often testing and a great strain. She endured countless operations and much pain, and mastered depression. Her husband Ingo stood by her side with infinite love and patience. Whenever better spells surfaced, Renate was back in life, active and planning.

A wonderful fruit of her suffering became her deeply rooted connection and faith in the Christ-being and her total acceptance of her destiny. Her faithfulness and love for Camphill, the Community and her friends never faltered. They remained an anchor in her life.

EVA SACHS
From Camphill Correspondence, *2000/2.*

Marianne Lehr

March 16, 1923 – July 10, 1982

It was the loss of their first child — a child so different from other children — and the subsequent meeting with Dr König that led the artists Günther and Marianne Lehr from Germany to Camphill, Scotland. They settled first in Cairnlee Cottage, at that time a primitive abode, creating a very modest home and workshop. Cairnlee in the early fifties had a house community which, one could sense, had profound bonds of destiny. Günther and Marianne contributed strong elements within this community setting.

None of us knew much of anthroposophy and only gradually did we grasp how it had to be lived. It was a daily struggle but we knew it was worthwhile. We wanted to understand Rudolf Steiner's message and, more than anything, we wanted Camphill. This common path of early striving forged lifelong friendships among us.

Somehow the atmosphere around this special couple brought back to us qualities of times long past and now lost. Many a burdened soul came to find refuge and comfort in this little cottage. It was a place of giving and sharing. Marianne was to be seen everywhere in those days, actively helping, enriching daily life with her warmth of heart, beautifying our surroundings with her artistic touch.

Later we were called to different working centres. The Lehrs moved to Murtle and then to Newton Dee where finally the Croft, transformed by their artistic craftsmanship, became their home. Here all could come, and were welcomed. After a stormy period of life it felt like coming home into a sheltered haven of peace. Healing talks of friendship warmed our hearts and the words and times of Goethe and Novalis often coloured the mood of these nightly conversations where past and present seemed to mingle in a wondrous way.

Then came the move to Botton, that bustling village, with new demands and responsibilities until Marianne's strength seemed no longer to be sufficient for what life asked of her. The three sons who were born in Cairnlee and Newton Dee had demanded their share of time and energy. What would now restore Marianne's strength? Was it perhaps Middle-Europe, which she so strongly carried in her heart that would bring healing? Hans-Heinrich Engel, the friend and brother since Cairnlee days, thought so.

When I came to Beitenwil in Switzerland in 1973, Marianne and Günther were there in the Turmhaus. Again, wherever these two wonderful people lived, every corner of the house and garden was penetrated

with loving care. Furthermore everyday life and its surroundings received a festive expression. On my arrival a poem written by Günther greeted me, and a picture from the brush of Marianne decorated the room.

By now the children had outgrown their parents' home. There was a space in Günther and Marianne's life as artists to undergo a renewal. Once more they moved and became students of Margarethe Hauschka in Bad Boll.

Afterwards, at the Lehenhof, I especially remember Marianne's joy when she told me of the work she had achieved and showed me her new pictures, where the step from the formal naturalistic to an etherically free expression of contour had been taken. It was as if a new world had opened up for Marianne, which she could now express in contemporary creative activity and which, in the time that now followed, bore fruit in therapeutic and other painting lessons with villagers and seminarists.

Our last encounter was in October 1981. One after the other several old Cairnlee friends came to visit Marianne and Günther. Before leaving, the three of us had an early breakfast together. We spoke of the hopes for the future developments of our work and community and how ever and again we have to step down from the peak of our wider view into the valley of practical possibilities. Marianne mentioned a verse of Schiller's *(Immer strebe zum Ganzen* / Always strive for wholeness) which she gave to me as a farewell greeting. She said the words had been a guiding star to her for a number of years. They seem to echo her lifelong striving spirit.

Then, on a Saturday morning July 10, 1982, her life ebbed away, quietly, undramatically, as had been her way in life.

On the evening before, she and Günther had eagerly shared plans and ideas for the new coloured windows of the crypt of the Lehenhof Hall. There on the following days we could bid her farewell.

MARGIT ENGEL
From Camphill Correspondence, *1982/10.*

Günther Lehr

February 17, 1925

The most important events in the lives of Marianne and myself are the meetings with Karl König and our way to Camphill. Especially the first encounters in 1949/50 in Stuttgart and the last one in Botton Village in 1965, shortly before his death.

Karl König's greatness was his fatherly stimulating and healing relationship to countless people. At the first meeting both of us found in him our teacher when we looked into each other's eyes and had a decisive conversation.

Soon after the war he came to Germany and held lectures in the hall of the Stuttgart Waldorf School. We were made aware of these by a friend. After the third lecture, the "Art of Healing," in which he featured Hippocrates, Paracelsus and Hahnemann, the decisive meeting came about.

At that time we had planned to emigrate to Brazil, but friends in Camphill who had heard about this plan, asked us to come to Camphill, "because we need you there." The lecture had moved us very deeply. König's description of these physicians spanned a wide arc from the past into the present. Many aspects had come together in this special hour culminating in a clear awareness of our search for new ideals, for finding a dignified human task where our abilities could be of service to others in need. We carried all these questions, wishes, plans and uncertainties into

the overcrowded hall.

Before us was the empty lectern on the stage. Into the stillness König entered with sure and measured steps; dressed in black, small in stature, but with a remarkable head and serious expression. Then he spoke with a sonorous voice, reaching the last seats without amplification. Like the arc of a rainbow spanned between him and his audience and he touched us, yet leaving us quite free.

Marianne and I exchanged foot-signs, speechless within the chorus of applause. We stood in a long queue and a friend introduced us to the speaker. His greeting was warm and knowing, as we looked into each other's eyes. What followed in all brevity was pure human and spiritual presence finding open hearts, "Yes, you are the Lehrs; are you not booked to leave for South America?"

"No, not any more."

"Since when?"

"Since this evening."

"Oh, before or after the lecture?"

"After your lecture."

"Excellent! We'll have to speak together."

"When may we come to see you?"

"Come tomorrow to the house of my host."

With this our decision was taken to turn 180 degrees. The details were worked out later. Our belongings were shipped to Aberdeen, and we arrived at London by boat and train, in May 1951. London was celebrating the Festival of Britain with full illumination, "for our reception." The next day we arrived with Nina Oyens at Aberdeen and were taken by Hartmut von Jeetze to Heathcot. Later we lived in Garden Cottage with Hubert and Anna Zipperlen, and after that in Cairnlee.

To enter into the community all the new circumstances had to be mastered: the foreign country, a different language, the many new people, the children in need, the five estates and many houses, the workshops, the seminar, the festivals and plays with all the other events including lectures, gatherings, conferences, clinics for the children, and the house-evenings. All this was overwhelming for the newcomer. On top of it there was my project to create a printing workshop, the Camphill Press, and with it a photo studio for medical photos.

Two and a half years had passed when a severe crisis gripped me in 1953 and tore open again old wounds of soul inflicted by the war and the period following 1945. It is hard to describe what led me to desert Camphill quietly in darkness of soul and spirit, leaving behind the family with a small son and all the community. No one knew about it, nor did I know where to turn. In vain I tried to find a job aboard ship in Hamburg, and after some futile attempts to find a job I landed at my parental home for a sad and woeful Christmas. In the new year I could still not find a job, not even in my profession in the printing trade.

Once again, after searching in vain for a job in other towns, I took shelter in an inn from the bitter cold and blizzards, I sat down over a cup of tea in a dark corner, when I noticed a guest at the bar with a drink; the door opened and with a blast of snow another man entered, walking with measured steps to the bar. My eyes gazed spell-bound: he was small, wore a black suit, had a large head — in hairstyle and gestures and every detail that of Karl König! But how could he be here, drinking beer? I remained as if paralysed. Before long he was gone again. Who was this man? Upon enquiring I heard that it was the local dentist.

On reaching home I found a letter sent by Dr König in answer to my letter to him, asking for a prolonged leave of absence. The content was fatherly and strict, reprimanding my conduct and ending with the words, "First of all, what concerns the own self does not matter, but what I have to do (and what I owe others), that matters; I hope this is sufficient to bring you to your senses!"

Some days had passed when I felt the strong urge to return to Camphill in Scotland; I felt a strong pull. Having listened to my story, the official in the British Consulate entered into my passport "see special circumstances." Years after my return as a "prodigal son," I got to know that during my absence the house-community, made up of members of five different nations, had gathered every evening for a short prayer to reach out to me in my misery.

The experience of gladness of being received back again kindled a new sense of community and a new faithfulness.

Günther now lives in Austria; he is the author of Verdichtete Geschichte *(a history in poetry) and* Heimatlose Grenzgänger *(Homeless Wanderers across Borders). He also edited Karl König's artistic work with Steiner's* Calendar of the Soul.
AUTOBIOGRAPHICAL

Baruch Urieli

October 24, 1923

Baruch Urieli grew up in a Jewish artist family in Vienna. At fourteen he was helped to flee Vienna with a group of young people, leaving his parents.

Having fled from Vienna to Czechoslovakia after the Anschluss in 1938, the Nazis had invaded my new country. Where we lived they confiscated the sports centre and its grounds, but demanded that it be handed over "in good order." The grass on the sports lawn had grown too high. Since there was no lawnmower available, about a dozen of us had to form a line and mow the lawn by hand while two soldiers watched our work. After two hours or so the lawn was perfectly "mown" and we could leave.

On our summer camp in the country one of our activities was to weed a carrot field for a farmer. Since I am of a pedantic constitution my weeding was somewhat slower but there were no weeds left in the rows I was weeding. This drew the attention of our instructor and led eventually to my being nominated for a group of youngsters, which was to go to Denmark in order to work there in agriculture as a stepping-stone to joining a kibbutz in Israel. I was informed about this decision by a Jewish dignitary who stressed that this was a great kindness done by the organization, since my family was known in the Jewish circles of Moravia not to be proper Jews, but rather German assimilants. In this way it was weeding that saved my life.

After a time in Denmark the idyllic life in Kjelstrup came to an abrupt end in early 1940 when the man who was our teacher and guide told us that as a first step of our journey to Palestine our two groups in North

Jutland would move to a youth hostel near Odense. Within two days we
had to pack our belongings, have a little farewell party at the pastor's
house in Hillerslev and travel to Odense. On December 3, 1940 we left
the youth hostel and went to Copenhagen where we still had a lovely
farewell party managed by the Women's League who had cared for us
and then we travelled to Stockholm. (It was only in Stockholm or later
that we got to know that our precipitated departure from Jutland was due
to the fact that the Danish Underground had informed our organization
that in four days the region of Jutland in which we lived would become
a German military district. That would have meant our deportation and
annihilation.)

From Stockholm our route led via Turku and Helsinki to Leningrad
(now St Petersburg) and from there, I believe, via Moscow to Odessa.
Then we crossed the Black Sea to Istanbul from where we travelled via
Aleppo and Beirut to Haifa. We arrived on Christmas Eve, and when we
had our evening meal in the receiving centre we could light the candle
which each of us had received at the farewell party in Copenhagen with
the instruction to light it on our safe arrival in Palestine. It was a remarkable coincidence that this happened to be Christmas Eve.

In Palestine we had a full programme of training, which took place in
the afternoons and evenings. As to our daytime we could choose into
which branch of the work we would like to enter. I chose to go into vegetable gardening. We learned to work hard, to speak fluent Hebrew and we
had a full training course lasting two years. It was in the year 1942 that I
became friends with a girl called Tamar Schönfeld who was to become my
wife six years later. She was given the work to help a lady who was in
charge of the flower garden, called Lotte Marcusi.

Lotte was a kind of outsider in the settlement because she was of
German origin while the main bulk of the members came from Poland and
Russia and could usually only speak Yiddish but no proper German. She
was an anthroposophist. When this good lady heard that I was the friend
of Tamar she invited me for some tea because she wanted to know what
kind of a fellow I was. After tea I asked if I could look at her large German
Library.

There I found a book by Manfred Kyber about occultism and I asked if
I could borrow it. Kyber writes in the book about a certain Rudolf Steiner
and he says that he is not sure if he was the greatest initiate or the greatest charlatan of his time. A week later I returned that book and asked if I
could borrow a book by Steiner for I had seen that in this lady's library
there were a large amount of books by this man. And so it came that I read
myself gradually through the anthroposophical library and became a convinced anthroposophist.

When my youth group left the place in order to start a new kibbutz

Baruch and Tamar Urieli

together with another youth group, I was asked to stay and become a tutor
to the younger group of which Tamar was a member. And when this group
was sent to strengthen another kibbutz I followed in Tamar's footsteps, but
soon made another move in order to complete my own education. I had
received a small inheritance which made it possible for me to go to
Jerusalem in August 1945 and study for a year at the Teacher's College
which was part of the Hebrew University of Jerusalem, and then I was
able to do the two years of teacher training.

Tamar too had moved to Jerusalem to train as a nurse. This was possible for her because her father lived in Jerusalem. After hearing that his
wife, Tamar's mother, had died in a German concentration camp in
Yugoslavia, he had remarried and had his business there.

War had broken out after the declaration of independence and the foundation of the state of Israel, and both Tamar and I had to go through a
short period of military training during our studies. I finished my
teacher's training in 1948 on April 9; April 10 was sabbath, and on April
11 Tamar and I got married in the city of Jerusalem, which was besieged
by the Arabs. As a Jewish wedding has to take place under the open sky
we had to go to that part of the flat roof of the Jewish administration of
Jerusalem which was not in the firing field of Arab snipers. After the wedding we had a meal in the house of Tamar's father together with our wit-
nesses and guests. After the reception Tamar's father gave to us a special

wedding gift, a loaf of white bread. This was an incredible gift in a besieged town where the bread rations became smaller and smaller from week to week.

After a short period the Israeli forces broke the siege of Jerusalem and soon Tamar and I could leave the army. In 1949 we moved to the kibbutz Ramath Yohanan. There I became a teacher for a class of children, many of whom were disturbed or handicapped because they had reached Palestine in difficult circumstances or did not know what had become of their parents. After a while I realized that I was not really equipped for such a task of teaching and I heard about the Camphill Schools near Aberdeen where one could train in curative education without paying fees. So I wrote to Dr König and asked if we could both come and do the two years' training course in curative education. Dr König invited us on condition that we would bring with us our return tickets to Israel since Camphill would not have the means for this extra expense. So we left Israel in August 1951. On our journey we still visited relatives and friends who had survived the holocaust and the war and finally arrived at Aberdeen on September 10 to settle down in Camphill Cottage.

On the following day we were introduced to Dr König and started our work in Camphill. Our two years' stay extended to three years because in 1952 our first son, Doron John, was born. When three years had passed it became clear to us that we would stay on for good and not return to Israel. Thus our life in Camphill began. It led us to many places and to many tasks, which enriched our life more and more. Full of gratitude we can now look back onto our life. It still gave us a second son, David (born in 1957), and six grand children and many more gifts as well as trials, which in hindsight were valuable experiences leading to new steps and new faculties. Thus I can say now that in retrospect my life looks like a fairy tale.

AUTOBIOGRAPHICAL
From his unpublished autobiography.

Baruch and Tamar made valuable contributions to the development of Camphill in Scotland, Norway, England and Ireland. Baruch became a priest of the Christian Community and a beacon of the spiritual life as a lecturer, tutor, counsellor and author.

Tamar Urieli

December 25, 1925

Directly after the annexation of Austria, in March 1938, Jews were rounded up streetwise, to be sent to the concentration camps from which very few returned. Men were taken first, the very first being those who had been denounced. To be denounced had nothing to do with having done anything wrong, but if a Nazi wished to get a Jew's house or business all he had to do was to go to the authorities and tell them the Jewish owner's name and address.

My father had a clerk who became a Nazi very early on, and he knew that this man wished to become the owner of the business. Father knew that the only way to save his life was to flee immediately. However, it was not possible for a Jew without connections abroad, to leave Austria legally.

So one night my father said a hasty goodbye to his wife and children and walked off, with a well-paid guide. After a gruelling trek he arrived in Czechoslovakia but could not go to his brothers or Father because a new law had just been issued which forbade Jewish refugees to stay anywhere except in the town of Brno. He made the acquaintance of a Jewish man who owned a wine cellar in Brno. There he was relatively safe from the police, working literally underground for many hours of the day.

I joined him in Brno beginning of August 1938 and lived with Father. I was a dreamy child of twelve and a half when I joined him, totally unused to looking after myself. Mother wanted to stay with her elderly mother and older daughter. All three perished in concentration camps.

Life became less and less secure. After a month in Czechoslovakia, Father received a police notice that he had to leave the country within 24 hours. There was nowhere to go. Naturally Father had left no leaf unturned in trying to find a country which might still give a visa to a Jew, but he was unsuccessful. After much searching and much sorrow, he decided to take the only way still open and joined a paramilitary Zionist movement, which organized transports to Israel. This meant leaving Czechoslovakia legally but arriving in Palestine illegally, with the aim of building up an underground army which would drive out the British and conquer land from the Arabs. In order to be admitted Father dyed his greying hair back to brown. For me, he found an old-fashioned long dress which made me look older than my just thirteen years and I had to tell everybody that I was sixteen.

Eventually, we got on to the list of transports to Israel. Father had to beg among relatives and acquaintances for the very large sum of money that was asked for the transport. He also had to find the equipment which everyone had to take with them in a rucksack: food for one month (mainly ship's biscuits), a blanket, warm clothing, for we would go by boat down the Danube, which was still partly frozen.

At last we were given a date of departure, March 10, 1939. However, two days before travelling I fell ill with a severe bout of mumps. There was no question of staying in bed or of staying behind. Father found for me a scarf which I had to wrap around my swollen face and neck and which I was not to take off, so my contagious illness would not be discovered and we be rejected at the last moment. Thus, in spite of my high temperature, we got to the assembly place.

The journey down the Danube took three weeks. When we arrived at the Black Sea we left the steamer and got on to a coal freighter, which was to take us to Israel. The hull of the ship had been emptied. Along the sides, two rows of wide shelves had been constructed. This was our accommodation. All around the shelves the hull was coal black and damp. Everyone used their rucksack for a pillow and wrapped themselves in a blanket. We had to lie sideways so as to save space, body against body, and could not move at night. This did not bother me much as I could snuggle against my father's back. I slept well in all conditions. By day, it was possible to climb up the narrow passage which ran along the side of the ship. There was only one supply of water through which water trickled at certain times.

There was one exciting moment, when we heard that a baby was being born among us. A young pregnant woman had managed to get herself into the transport.

The Black Sea was very rough. Soon most people were seasick. I felt very unwell but not actually sick. Most of the day I stood on the deck in the icy wind, looking at the huge dark waves. It took seven days to get from Constanta in Romania to the Bosphorus. After the rough voyage the sight of land was welcome.

We sailed onwards through the Aegean Sea with its innumerable islands. A few days later we had sailed through the Mediterranean and had entered the waters belonging to Palestine. And that was as far as we got. We drew near the shore by night. British coastal patrols spied the boat and gave a warning signal. This was not heeded, and they shot. Two of the Greek crew were wounded. The captain turned the boat and hurried back out of reach of danger and headed for Greece; but we were not permitted to land anywhere. We would stay there for ten weeks. Eventually, I found out that among the seven hundred passengers there was a girl of my age; we became inseparable.

Although there was no food, I don't remember ever having felt hungry. We must have been given some water to drink, which the ship's crew got for us from the freshwater wells on the shore. I did not mind not washing for weeks on end. The adults, of course, worried about food. Later I realized that I had loved living in the midst of the sea, beneath hot sunshine by day and under the starry sky by night.

Eventually, the Jewish community at Athens came to our rescue. They bought a yacht and hired sailors. When the time came to transfer to the yacht, the sea was rough. The yacht was designed for twenty passengers, but all seven hundred had to find space in it and on it. Those people who were too ill to sit were laid into the hull of the yacht. The others were made to sit on the deck with their legs apart, every person sitting between the legs of the one behind him. Two hundred of the younger people volunteered to be tied to the outside of the yacht. When everybody was on board we moved towards Palestine. But the sea was rough and the yacht overweight; this voyage took another 48 hours, during which, of course, no one could move.

Then the yacht started to leak. SOS calls were sent out and heard by the Palestine coastal patrols who came to our rescue from Haifa.

Tamar's brother lived in Jerusalem, father and daughter were united with him. Father established a small spaghetti factory; Tamar worked in a kibbutz, later trained as a children's nurse, living on and off with her father. When she got her own flat she met Baruch. They married, but she still had to serve in the army during the War of Independence. Later news reached her in Camphill, Scotland, of her father's death in April 1952.

AUTOBIOGRAPHICAL
From her unpublished autobiography.

Elisabeth Löwe

June 26, 1902 – May 11, 1985

Few people were as youthful as Elisabeth. I enjoyed meeting her whenever I could visit the Lehenhof. Her interest in all that was going on, her concern for world-events, her knowledge of recent books, made it valuable to talk to her.

What was so lovely about Elisabeth was the way she related to the villagers. They were real people for her, important, to be corrected where necessary, no doubt, but to be esteemed and loved.

One can hardly think of Elisabeth without calling to mind Timmy Nassau. Among my early impressions when I first came to Camphill in

Scotland was the way Elisabeth cared for this small blind boy. Timmy grew up to be a man and ended his days at the Lehenhof, for he had accompanied Elisabeth and Ilse Rascher when they moved from Scotland to Germany.

Remembering Elisabeth also means paying tribute to one of the most beautiful friendships that we have been able to know: the working together and mutual support of Ilse and Elisabeth. While one can say that Elisabeth followed Ilse, it was not a "following" of being a step behind, but of being a facilitator, an enabler; one who makes it possible to achieve the aims both hold dear.

If any of us, as we grow older, begin to feel sorry for ourselves, we need only to think of Elisabeth, and thus be inspired by the gentle but ever-courageous Lion.

JULIAN SLEIGH
From Camphill Correspondence, *1985/7.*

Ilse Rascher

March 10, 1906 – April 1, 1988

Ilse came from Vienna where she met anthroposophy at the age of fifteen and joined the Anthroposophical Society a year later. In 1924 Karl König came to join the same anthroposophical youth group to which Ilse belonged. Ilse moved to Pilgramshain in 1929 and it was there that she found her vocation: curative education. After the war, Karl König invited Ilse to Camphill where she arrived in 1951 together with her three children and her friend and colleague Elisabeth. Both women built up the work with blind and partially sighted children. Ilse inspired many young people in our life and work with children. She moved to the Lehenhof Village in Germany in 1966.

FRIEDWART BOCK
From Camphill Correspondence, *1995/1.*

Karin von Schilling

March 18, 1933

I came to Camphill in Scotland in September 1951; the Michael festival was the first one I experienced there. I was then eighteen years of age. What has led me there?

Apart from the first four years of my life which I spent on a Canadian homestead under the wide-open sky, and four days on horseback from the next town, I spent my childhood in post-war Berlin. This childhood and youth was dominated by the situation of the defeat of Germany which resulted in homelessness and uncertainty. Berlin after the war was a city largely in ruins, with widespread poverty and the experience of death all around. Yet it was also a city in which cultural life blossomed, probably just because of the hopeless outer situation. A person like Emil Bock gave lectures to audiences of a thousand and more. Yehudi Menuhin played there soon after the end of war as a deed of reconciliation, with many others to follow. There was not enough money for food but one queued overnight for cheap tickets.

These two elements lived in my soul at that time. The war had left its scars, but the enthusiasm to rebuild a better world was alive. My mother had met anthroposophy and also the Christian Community and so I was blessed from early adolescence to meet these cultural and religious streams and appreciate their message.

Herr Löffler, one of the founders of anthroposophical curative education suggested that I go for a year to Camphill in Scotland in order, as he put it, "to learn to become social." Well, this I have tried to learn for well over fifty years! Whether I have to some degree succeeded, I leave others to judge.

I entered Camphill at a time when it was a far-away place. In my experience it was similar to a religious order in the spirit of anthroposophy. One encountered in the leading personalities totally devoted "knights" of a modern kind. One felt honoured to be a kitchen maid in their castle! It was exceptionally hard work on a practical level and accompanied by an intensely strong spiritual life.

When I had finished the training course I was twenty and intent on going to America; but Alix Roth suggested to me that I first learn about teaching. This I did with much enthusiasm for the following eighteen years, mainly in Scotland, but also in Ireland and England.

My family originated from Baltic aristocracy. While heredity is less important today, looking back over my life I know that this aristocratic background gave a certain colouring to my soul. The ideal of living a

monastic life demanding the qualities of a devoted nun, often caused inner conflicts. Again and again I had to balance these two qualities, both equally real and strong. Anke Weihs, one of the founders of Camphill, once told me that she was "a rebellious servant." On a much less prominent scale I experienced such a nature time and again in myself.

In *Candle on the Hill* I wrote that we co-workers were the building stones for a "mighty cathedral." We did what was necessary and what was considered best in the situation of a growing community living with children with special needs; we were serving a higher order.

The inspiration of my life was and is anthroposophy and its Christian heart. It kindled the necessary fire and light, and even endurance. I think it was always the primary goal. An older friend once told me that much as we fully enjoyed our work with the children with special needs, it was a kind of tribute we gave for the gift of receiving anthroposophy. However, I also recall that we were made to feel responsible for all kinds of problems the world is suffering from, due to a lack of earnestness in our inner work. There is no doubt that the Camphill impulse has made a significant contribution to the working of anthroposophy in the world, particularly into forms and practice of social life.

After twenty years in Camphill in Britain, mainly Scotland, I left for South Africa with my six-year-old daughter, Saskia. There was a need to carry and develop the work of Camphill in Johannesburg. Many had advised against my going; someone even said: "You will be back in two years without having succeeded!" But there was no going back, quite apart from the fact that I had neither a return ticket nor any money. It was a question of "making or breaking."

I helped to rebuild the new Cresset (the original work at Cresset had to relocate to a larger, purpose-built site) and put all my strength into this effort. Although supported by many younger co-workers, I stood alone "like a tree against the open horizon." I loved this task and situation.

In 1979 my thirteen-year-old daughter died instantly in a head-on car crash. Very few of my many good friends from near and far were able to give me any real help. Lots of love and sympathy, and many kind thoughts reached me, but they helped little. No one seemed able to really grasp or *feel* what had happened. The finality was overwhelming.*

And what remains of this work in the end? Ralph Waldo Emerson put it thus: "The reward of having completed a work well, is to have done it." This thought has often been a solace. I still try to make a contribution if asked for, by leading weekend retreats and giving talks to teachers for the Johannesburg and Pretoria Waldorf Schools. I am also caring for a former young South African co-worker volunteer, who suffered severe encephalitis fifteen years ago and consequently lost his short-term memory. After staying in Cresset for some years, he is now committed to a state hospital and needs support more than ever.

I also feel sure that what remains and endures beyond our own life is what we were able to ignite as enthusiasm and support towards the fulfilment of other people's aims and tasks. Our own failures and mistakes (and there are plenty of them) we take along to be sorted later. But during our lifetime lived it was not so much the question of how to deal with those, but rather what we manage to do beyond them!

AUTOBIOGRAPHICAL

---

* Karin wrote about coming to terms with the death of her daughter in *Where Are You Now?* (Anthroposophic Press, New York 1988)

Inge Chambers

April 27, 1929 – January 10, 1993

Ingeborg Marie Louise was born in pre-war Berlin. She was the first and only child for five and a half years until her sister Karin joined her. Inge's mother came from a large, well-to-do Prussian family; she was a violinist in her own right, and she was also a very gifted visual artist although she left all this behind when she married. Inge's father was well known and employed by the German government: he cast the great Olympic bell and many of the German golden eagles. He also worked as a sculptor and carried out restoration work in churches and other ancient buildings. He was able to continue as an artist during the war and was never drafted into the army.

Inge's childhood was not easy. She was a very sensitive, good, but shy child. School was very difficult: her teachers were hard on her, and her learning difficulties (dyslexia) soon became apparent. When teachers and parents tried to force her to read, write or do maths, she would withdraw. She became unhappy at school. At home she soon realized that her much younger sister was the favourite.

As a very young child Inge displayed some amazing faculties. At the age of three years she was once listening to some Japanese dance-tunes: she got up and began to dance to the music, doing the appropriate Japanese hand-movements to it. This early association with Japan appeared again much later, when she went to Japan with a group of potters, having studied and learned the language. She had some very significant meetings there and was able to take part in some of the Japanese tea ceremonies. She learned the Japanese brush-strokes and decorated many of her pots with them.

Inge was also very musical; at an early age she would sit down at the piano and start composing. At the age of five she began to write down these compositions: we were able to listen to two of them on her memorial evening; they were filled with a light, butterfly quality.

During the war years the family house was bombed and severely damaged three times. Because of this the family decided to move to southern Germany; there they escaped some of the worst atrocities of the end of the war. In her early teens Inge helped in a nearby pottery in her spare time. She was very gifted and would often bring clay home with her and continue to create figures and ornaments. This did not help the relationship to her father who perhaps felt threatened by her artistic skills. She was not allowed to take up art and craft training and was not allowed to go out with friends at night. This led to her leaving home at the age of sixteen.

Inge then began nursery class training with Protestant nuns. This was again difficult for Inge, for they too were strict for her light artistic and sensitive nature. After this training she decided to work in a large hospital in Düsseldorf as a nurses' aide; there she met a young medical student who introduced her to the work of Rudolf Steiner and curative education.

Inge found her way to La Motta, a curative-educational home in the Ticino, Switzerland. There she met Johannes Surkamp and they worked together for one year. She got engaged to him and they decided to take up the training offered at Camphill in Scotland. They arrived on September 2, 1952 and took up the training course in curative education. Inge had a flair for this work: her artistic and imaginative nature helped her to be creative and change difficult situations into fun and humour.

When the engagement with Johannes broke off, Inge returned to Germany for some time where she met a young man who was severely war-damaged and with whom she had a child. She returned to Camphill in Ireland where her son, Edgar, was born. Inge, coping with single motherhood, remained in Ireland for some years and became a teacher until she decided to join Jack Walker in a new Camphill centre in Port Elizabeth, South Africa. She went there with her four-year-old son in 1961. From there she went to work in Cresset House, which had recently opened, and later came to the Camphill School at Hermanus. She always worked as house-mother and teacher. At Hermanus she met Bill Chambers, a South African forester; they married and Sonja was born.

In 1972 Bill and Inge joined Camphill Village near Cape Town. Here a new phase started for Inge: she became a potter. Her amazing imagination enabled her to create ever-new forms. Pottery was very important for Inge: it grounded her very sanguine nature, while expressing it in art. She was interested in so many new discoveries and yet had very conservative attitudes. Perhaps her deepest interest during her last years was sacred dancing; this filled her soul with awe. She began to introduce these dances at our festivals, and the great Sunflower Dance accompanied us at one of our retreats.

Her last illness went on for nearly a year. As death drew near she became more and more serene; her vision began to span two worlds. She saw her angel; she saw her mother who had died many years ago. She could relate all these experiences to the many friends who surrounded and visited her.

Then on Sunday evening of January 10, 1993, we had sung and prayed for her; with lyre playing, her family surrounded the bedside. Her difficult breathing stopped and a great calm spread over the room, the little cottage, and over the whole village. Inge was free; she could spread her wings and soar into the heights.

RENATE SLEIGH
From Camphill Correspondence, *1993/3.*

Johannes Michael Surkamp

March 16, 1928

I was born in Stuttgart to a couple who had found each other through anthroposophy. My father was fifty when I was born, and I grew up with a sister in happy circumstances. My father, from Westphalia, a scholar of literature and languages, was by profession a book-dealer and publisher. My mother came from a Swabian family of forestry officials.

We spent happy holidays in the Alps or at the North Sea but mostly in the same farm house in the Black Forest, joining in with all the farm work and exploring the beautiful surroundings.

I went to the Waldorf Kindergarten and for three years to the Waldorf School up to its closure by the Nazis in 1938. Both at the Waldorf School and in the state school I met Friedwart Bock whom I would met again later in Scotland. During the war, when following events on the map, my

attention strangely focused on the triangle Aberdeen, Edinburgh and Glasgow, where the longer part of my life was to unfold.

I was called up to the air-defence where in night watches I studied the constellations in the sky. After a severe raid, I saw from the hill-top our home district in flames and got leave to help my parents rescue valuables from the burning house, especially books by Rudolf Steiner. I was able to arrange the move for my elderly parents to Tübingen, south of Stuttgart.

In 1945 followed a spell in the Labour Service, with guns instead of spades, marching by night towards the "Fortress Tyrol." On the way I landed up in a hotel-turned-military-hospital, with blisters!

Dismissed as under-age, but threatened with forced labour in France, an agricultural training was a way out. This enabled me to help my starving parents. After concluding this training I attended an evening school in Stuttgart for my school-leaving certificate, and worked during the day in a bookbindery. During this time I made many contacts and attended many lectures including one by Karl König.

Aged 21, I attended the seminary of the Christian Community for a semester. It was suggested I work in a curative home for a time and so I went for a year to La Motta, near Locarno, in Switzerland, a home founded by Ita Wegman. The year, however, extended to 45 years in curative education.

In September 1952 together with Inge Lemcke, I arrived at Camphill for the two years of training, which were to become the beginning of a life's task and commitment. I lived and worked in Camphill Estate, Murtle, Newton Dee and for two periods at Thornbury near Bristol.

After seven years I married Jean Chambers and after another seven years we adopted three baby girls who were a great joy, as well as in later years our five grandchildren.

In 1971 there was a request to take over a small residential school, Ochil Tower, in the middle of Auchterarder, Perthshire, run by the elderly couple, Bob and Ann Lewers. After visiting, it became clear that this was a call of destiny. A private sale was agreed and we arrived in January 1972 from Thornbury, with gifts of some furniture, paint and brushes. As well as making it a Camphill place, an expansion began, doubling the number of children and adding other buildings and enlarging the estate. In 1979, Three-Kings-Hall and some classrooms were built, replacing two Nissen huts. Before long there were 36 children in three classes, two of them in the new Three-Shepherds-Building. Children and co-workers alike enjoyed a rich social life, and made many friends. Ochil Tower School was joined during the following years by two Camphill neighbours, Blair Drummond and Corbenic and became the host for the next seven years of the Scottish Neighbourhood Meetings. Active involvement with Camphill neighbours continued well into the new century, including the earlier co-founding of Camphill Scotland and the Association of Camphill Communities. In 1995 I was awarded an MBE by the Queen.

After handing over the responsibility for the School to Ueli and Hilary Ruprecht in January 1996, I continued caring for the trees and flower borders. I took up new tasks in the anthroposophical field, including the labour of love of editing this book. As a thank-you to the town of Auchterarder, I served for six years as Secretary and Vice Chair of Auchterarder and District Community Council.

AUTOBIOGRAPHICAL

Jean Surkamp

November 24, 1925

Born in 1925 near Wolverhampton I spent my childhood with my hard-working grandparents. My father died before I was born and my mother worked, always away from home. I saw her early mornings and evenings and Sundays. I often played nanny to my (what became twelve) cousins. I lost my grandparents around eleven years old and spent the next few years with my mother, very much filled with the impressions of war.

I was the youngest air raid warden at sixteen, leaving school and becoming a "technical computer" as war work. I was using a slide rule and climbing over a wind tunnel in the designing of heat-exchangers for air-craft. It was exciting and meaningful work. There was no time to think.

My mother and I were busy day and night. Then she became ill, and I was told she would have to go to bed and never get up. She died within the year. During that dreadful time I continued work.

I moved from the flat we had shared to Wolverhampton closer to my place of work. I earned only just enough to live on alone, but now I could turn to art — next to maths my best subject in school. I enrolled in evenings classes at the Art School. It was still war, but when it ended I was able to get a full-time grant on reaching twenty-one.

This was a brighter side to those troublesome years. I met quite differ-ent friends and among them my life-long friend, Jean Bowerman, a painter and farmer's wife. During this time I also became involved in Moral Rearmament, a group of young people who believed they could change the world by changing themselves.

For four years I studied sculpture day and night with the same intensity as I had worked during the war years. After the graduation our large group of fine-art students wanted to round off our time together in a festive way before going on our own ways. So about thirty of us planned a week away at Attingham Park, centred around the other arts: poetry, music, literature, etc, calling it "Universe, Earth and Man." We invited speakers to join us. Unknown to us, some were anthroposophists: George Trevelyan and Dr Ernst Lehrs, a scientist. It was the concept of reincarnation that made the greatest impact on several of us and when we accompanied Ernst Lehrs to his taxi we knew that we would follow it up.

I did this a few weeks later at Wynstones School where he was leading a youth conference. I was very much the odd one out — the other participants were all old Steiner school pupils and quite familiar with all that was so entirely new to me. Nevertheless, during that week I joined a group of young people to visit a children's home in Clent, (I learned later that they were people from Camphill). I saw a class of Down's syndrome children having a painting lesson and I knew in that very moment that this was to be my life's work.

I had just won a three-years' scholarship to the Royal College of Art in London. What was I to do? I did go to London and contacted Rudolf Steiner House and four months later I walked there into a room where Ernst Lehrs was about to give a lecture. He came towards me, hands outstretched: "Where have you been, I have been searching for you all day!"

On completing my three years in South Kensington and often cycling across Regent Park to Steiner House, I eventually joined Camphill in Scotland. Within four days, although I was then only a seminar student of the two-year course in curative education, I was given a class to teach. I have had one ever since, right to my seventieth year, with a short interruption while our three children were still very young.

AUTOBIOGRAPHICAL

Marianne Sander

January 25, 1930

I was born in Breslau in Silesia, then in the east of Germany; today it is part of Poland and Breslau has become Wroclaw.

My father, who by profession was a sales representative in the textile industry, had been active in the Wandervögel, an idealistic youth movement that had sprung up after the First World War. Here he met and befriended Hermann Kirchner, who later became a well-known painter and the originator of dynamic drawing, a method of therapy much used in anthroposophical curative educational homes. Kirchner, who was an earnest pupil of anthroposophy, one day took my father along to a lecture by Rudolf Steiner in Breslau. The theme, I was told later, was about

Atlantean times. My father, to whom what was spoken sounded totally incomprehensible and rather fantastical, left midway through the lecture and later declared that, although he could not enter in to the spirit of this world-view, he admired and endorsed the practical applications in agriculture, medicine, education, etc.

Being rather large-headed, I had still not learned to walk at eighteen months and was taken to be seen by a doctor who practised once a week at the surgery of Dr Ludwig Engel (Peter Engel's father) in Breslau. This doctor was Dr Karl König, who at the time lived and worked in nearby Pilgramshain. Needless to say, soon afterwards I could walk.

In 1933, my father being of Jewish descent, saw the writing on the wall; my mother, though, had come from a Roman Catholic family. Hitler had risen to power, the pogroms and humiliation of the Jews had begun and my parents decided to move to Holland. Like so many others, they too, were not allowed to take any savings with them. We settled in Amsterdam, and after a long uphill struggle they managed, with the help of a partner in Canada who provided the initial capital, to build up a small factory producing machine-knitted pullovers and cardigans.

I had a brother called Ulrich, two years my senior, who had to start school in 1934, the year the first Waldorf School in Amsterdam opened its doors. This was a natural choice for my parents and so I, and my younger sister in turn, joined this growing school with its wonderful teachers.

My sister Ilse was born in 1935, and now the family was complete. Family life was good while we were still young, but without doubt our father was the dominant figure. It was impressive to see how he, as an agnostic, created each year the most delightful Christmas festival with the gospel readings and everything that belongs to it.

We grew up bilingually — our parents spoke to us mainly in German and we responded in Dutch, although gradually they too used the Dutch language.

I was a shy and somewhat over-sensitive child but got on well in school and was eager to learn. As soon as I could read I became an avid reader which has continued to the present day.

Wartime in Holland brought its own problems. My father had to do forced labour, to wear the star of David and sometimes, when the pogroms were frequent, had to go into hiding. In autumn 1944 my brother was sent to Germany by the Nazis. He managed to flee back to Holland, very ill and weak, and died a month after the end of the war without having seen his family again.

Ulrich had been an extremely talented and promising person. His loss had a profound impact on each of us. In a sense, he had been the centre of the family, which now seemed unable to hold together and each one

became isolated. As well as this, like so many parents who provided a good family life while the children were young, as soon as the children became adolescent, they were at a loss how to understand or guide us.

This affected me too, and I looked increasingly for understanding and life elsewhere. My four years at the Amsterdam Lyceum, which I attended after eight years at the Waldorf School came to an abrupt end, because from having hitherto been one of the best in class I now fell almost to the bottom of the class. I no longer felt able to do my homework and for some years the death of Ulrich cast its shadow over my existence.

When I was eighteen, I read *Man and Animal* by Hermann Poppelbaum. This book inspired me to turn more seriously to anthroposophy. Back in Amsterdam I joined a vibrant anthroposophical student group and recognized from then on that anthroposophy would be my way to find the way back, as well as forward, to the source and the meaning of life.

I then began four years at the School of Arts and Crafts which proved to be a road leading up again. It was both constructive and enjoyable, making new friends and meeting many new experiences.

Then, in 1949, I decided to spend the summer holidays "somewhere" in Britain to learn better English. Lily Herz, who had been my curative teacher in the Waldorf School, advised me to go to Camphill in Scotland. There I went and this became an eye-opener.

Here were genuine people with genuine work to be done. There was at certain times total seriousness in what was being done and at other times lively enjoyment and wonderful humour with an unerring sense of occasion. The work with the children was demanding, yet at the same time immensely rewarding. One could not hide behind a "mask," one was known and supported and in turn gradually learned to know and support others.

In Camphill it was obvious that everyday life and the life of ideals and ideas could be fully merged. I loved this place from the first moment and after two months of being there I knew that I had to come back after finishing the School of Arts and Crafts.

It was unexpectedly difficult to convince my parents that this would be the right decision. No wages, no career opportunity, and so on, seemed to them to be insurmountable obstacles. It needed two visits by Hans van der Stok, my sister's class teacher at the Waldorf School, who himself planned to go and live in Camphill, to give them some understanding of what Camphill was like.

And finally, in 1952, I arrived in Camphill on Michaelmas day and a new chapter of my life began.

AUTOBIOGRAPHICAL

Michael Schmundt

June 10, 1930

On the June 17, 1953, just after my 23rd birthday, I walked down Newton Dee drive, with my suitcase in my hand and great anticipation in my soul. It was still early in the morning and all was quiet, yet it did not feel empty: The trees flanking the drive, the cattle in the field, the hills in the distance to the West and the glistening of the River Dee at one of its bends. Everything breathed confidence, even the air in the early midsummer sun. The birds seemed to twitter, "Yes, this is right." I began to relax into the whole atmosphere, which so welcomed me.

I had crossed the North Sea on a German cargo boat from Hamburg to Newcastle and had stayed the night at the YMCA hostel in Aberdeen. News of a worker's rising in Berlin and other places in East Germany was anxiously discussed by a group of young men from different parts of Britain. All this was still echoing in me as I was walking down the drive. It is a short distance — yet in these few minutes much went on in me as if I was crossing a threshold. Behind me were great questions of human and social disintegration, and before me something I did not know as yet.

I had heard the most diverse opinions about Camphill and I was hoping for real answers to those questions. At this moment something streamed into my soul like warm light: This is the place!

I walked into the farm and was warmly welcomed by Lucy Kühn. She took me into the house and I was greeted by Gerda von Jeetze and Michael Cohen. The men and boys were out in the fields; they came in at lunchtime: Hartmut, Hank, John, Gordon and Stuart, Colin and James. This was going to be my new family with whom I was to share life for two and a quarter years. This time would become the wellspring of everything I have managed to do in my life ever since. It even seems that the years prior to entering Newton Dee were predominantly a preparation towards this meeting with the Camphill Impulse.

Four years before I was born, my parents had moved from Berlin to Königsberg (now Kaliningrad) because my father, an engineer, was asked to carry out the electrification of the then undeveloped German province of East Prussia. They had met anthroposophy during their student years in Berlin and it was alive in our family, still young and full of enthusiasm. My parents were actively helping to introduce anthroposophy and the Christian Community in the city and province. To me it seemed as if there were always guests staying. I remember, for instance, sitting on Emil Bock's knees while he was translating the Bible at my father's desk.

In 1938, Klaus my older brother, died of diphtheria. This, although a sad event, connected our family strongly to a real and living world of the spirit. Mother said later: "Without Klaus' help from the other side I would not have survived the difficult years at the end of the war and its aftermath." Mother had as a young girl contracted tuberculosis for which reason she had spent several years in the Austrian Alps where she also trained as a wood carver. She was very practical and artistic, and filled our lives with warmth of soul. I also had a brother, Christof, and a sister, Maria, three and eleven years younger than me.

Death, which during the war was happening all around us, was never a desperate event for us children but a positive pointer to a spiritual world and the future, thanks to the attitude of my parents.

From 1938 onwards I became aware that the world around us began to grow dark and threatening: the Christian Community was forbidden, the friends who visited regularly became fewer, sounding worried and bewildered. We children were advised not to talk to people about certain things which had always been dear to us. Sometimes strange men came to talk with my parents, and we children had to be out of the way. I began to live two lives, one at home and another at school and the twice weekly compulsory Hitler Jugend meetings.

In 1941 my father was called up to the army as an engineer to help keep the industries of the Ukraine going, which had just been occupied by the German army.

When I was ten I decided to become a farmer. I spent every holiday during the remaining four summers in East Prussia on a farm, either on a biodynamic farm near Königsberg or on a farm belonging to my Aunt Lotte near the Polish border. This saved my life. When in June 1944 the front had almost reached the border, the German authorities desperately recruited even fourteen-year-old boys to dig trenches at the Eastern Front. While queuing for bread my mother heard from a neighbour that her son had just been taken for "the digging." My mother ran home and packed me up to travel to Aunt Lotte. Minutes later the men came to collect me, and Mother said: "Oh, he is on land service." They were satisfied and left. The boys who had gone digging never came back.

At Aunt Lotte's I witnessed the endless treks of Lithuanians with their horses and carts fleeing from the fighting. We heard the noise of battle and felt the ground shaking with explosions. A few days after I had returned home, there were two terrible air raids on Königsberg. The second damaged our house badly. Mother decided we should leave with the next train. The only train leaving from the badly hit station was full. People were even clinging to its outside. Mother pushed us through a window and promised to find us later. And she did find us. When night fell the train started off. Mother, as always in chaotic situations, preserved her presence of mind: "Look once more at Königsberg now burning to ashes, was it not a wonderful home?"

As I stood jammed between many hundreds of people in that train, in a flash I was aware that an old world had come to a sudden end and a new era opened with vast new possibilities. I wanted to meet it! That train journey seemed like an endless tormented night of disturbed sleep and bad dreams. But finally we arrived at good friends of my parents at Lake Constance. The family of Dr Alexander Rust (who had been assistant to Dr König in Pilgramshain) had invited us in case of need. This need had now come.

Only when I came to Camphill I began to guess why I had to spend my first fourteen years in Königsberg. Königsberg had been a wonderful home! There I grew up in the atmosphere of the Teutonic knights and their patron saint, Elizabeth. It was also the birthplace of Herder and the city of Immanuel Kant, two philosophers. At Lake Constance I entered the atmosphere of Celtic Christianity, for the area had been settled by Irish and Scottish monks. The sternness of the vast Prussian East was replaced by the vivacity of nature. I was allowed to work with local farmers in the little fields, orchards and vineyards, sharing the farmer's life still full of devoted piety. The interruption of schooling during the few months at the end of the war did not bother me. It was more satisfying to bring home some extra butter, milk, eggs, bread and more.

I should have been confirmed at Easter 1945. Father had sent me some preparatory notes for this event from wherever he had been posted. These were most wonderful commentaries on the Creed of the Christian Community relating it to the turbulent events in the world. This was food out of anthroposophy for my unsettled soul. Also, as a preparation, Mother had read *Parsifal* with me. With some other refugee friends my mother arranged the Confirmation for me and another boy in a simple, but deeply moving way. Four weeks later French troops arrived. After a ban of seven years the Christian Community began again, and I took part in the first Act of Consecration. I was even allowed to travel to Stuttgart to attend the first postwar Christian Community conference, probably being the youngest participant, not yet fifteen.

In 1946 Father arrived back from a prisoner-of-war camp sick with dropsy. Mother, too, was very often unwell. She said later that it was the good food I brought home from the farms that made them both better. In spite of his illness, Father applied for a post as a mathematics and physics teacher in a Waldorf school, and was immediately offered a post at the Hanover Waldorf School which had just re-opened. His family soon followed, though for a time we could not live together and he joined us at weekends until a flat with two rooms could be found in the devastated city. Now we children were allowed to attend the Waldorf School! For me this meant three and a half years of school which I enjoyed very much. It was a wonderful co-operation between teachers who had gone through much suffering and pupils starved and hungry for education: each lesson was an exciting event! I found a world-view and ideals, which grounded me and gave me trust in life amid all the insecurities around.

Partly to alleviate the shortage of food and fuel, but mainly because of my inclination towards farming I spent most of my holidays helping on one farm or other. In return I was given precious food and once even a whole truck-load of firewood, which saw the family through the bad winter of 1947/48.

When I was eighteen I was chosen to join the first post-war school exchange with England. I spent four months at Michael Hall School in Sussex as well as half term visiting a children's home at Clent where I was deeply moved by the encounter with the children and adolescents with their handicaps. There I also met Ernst Lehrs and Fried Geuter who were very important to me.

On returning to Hanover I decided not to sit for the Abitur exams, but to start three years of farming apprenticeship; two of which I did with Immanuel Vögele who had attended Rudolf Steiner's Agricultural Course, and was one of the most important pioneers of biodynamics. He had been the assistant manager of the estate of the von Jeetze family at Pilgramshain in Silesia during the time Karl König had been there. As well as the technical skills and perseverance I learned to feel a deep reverence for the living world: earth, plant and animal.

Before I would have a farm, marry and settle, I decided I should experience something of the world. I wrote to Carl Alexander Mier who at that time was secretary of the Biodynamic Agricultural Association in Britain asking him where I could find work. He suggested the only fitting one was Newton Dee near Aberdeen, belonging to Camphill. I did not really want to go to Camphill as I had heard that there was little possibility to practice proper biodynamic farming. But as there was no other opportunity open in Britain, I applied and arrived in Camphill on June 17, 1953.

Now in my seventies, after a lifetime of working socially and in biodynamics, I feel deeply connected to the innermost mission of the Camphill movement, and feel a certainty that I belong to it even beyond this earthly life. This links up with the "dreams" I had as a teenager, when I imagined myself on a farm, healing the earth and a community of all sorts of people around who want to serve the good.

AUTOBIOGRAPHICAL

Lisa Steuck

July 7, 1926

Being half Jewish, I was forced to leave Germany in 1940. My aunt, who had looked after me since the age of four after my parents' death, was invited to emigrate to Sweden. Leaving school at sixteen, I wanted to train either as a nurse or work with children. Being too young for a nurse's training I decided to work as an auxiliary nurse meantime. After about two and a half years at a private hospital run by Methodist sisters, it turned out that a nurse's profession was not for me. I had to have an operation on both feet which made it necessary to change. The Methodist environment had a great influence on me. I became a member of the church and very active within the youth movement and was very happy to have become a Christian. My Jewish aunt, being very open-minded, accepted my way of life. Still there were many questions in my mind and heart which nobody seemed able to answer. "Blind faith" was not for me; I knew there was more to life, more about heaven and earth. Already as a child I asked questions that nobody could answer. I was then regarded as "the stupid Liz" and learned to keep my questions to myself.

Eventually I went through a kindergarten training. During the second year I had the opportunity of working with handicapped, severely spastic children. I had an immediate rapport with them. For the subject of my thesis I chose the "Cerebral Palsied Child." Having done my observations at the main institutions in Stockholm I was offered a position as a kindergarten teacher following my examination. The destiny of these children posed many questions, but these had to wait.

For personal reasons I decided to leave Sweden for one or two years to learn more especially about cerebral palsy. I turned to my former teacher who told me about Camphill. She had just visited and was full of it. I knew instantly that this was the place for me. I was only one of two young people in the whole of Sweden who had gone through this special kindergarten training. My teacher had planned that we should take on a brand new kindergarten; there would be ample funds available and we would have complete freedom to arrange the place — simply ideal! The other one took up the position offered, but I refused; I knew I had to go to Camphill.

A few months later, in June 1953, I arrived in Camphill. I was met by Dr Hans-Heinrich Engel and was taken to Cairnlee House. The following time was very hard and Hans-Heinrich became my mentor and salvation. We had great discussions and I heard for the first time about reincarnation and karma, subjects that made me very thoughtful and gradually answered many questions I had carried with me through life. Also Dr König's Seminar sessions were incredible to listen to and completely changed my attitude towards life. I then moved to Heathcot House for spastic children. The caring for these children was a profound experience compared to what I had been doing in Sweden. Suddenly I could see a full human being behind the outer appearance. At the hand of these children karma and rein-carnation became meaningful to me. I found meaning in anthroposophy of which I had never heard before, and I became acquainted with the Christian Community. It was only a small step to become a member, and I also joined the Anthroposophical Society.

Barbara Lipsker, always a shining example in daily life, introduced me to the Camphill Community. In her and Hans-Heinrich Engel I had found my "guiding stars."

AUTOBIOGRAPHICAL

Udo Steuck

May 18, 1928

As a young teacher I had my first placement in a village on the German island of Rügen. In this little God-forsaken place there lived two anthro-posophists, as well as a headmistress who knew about Waldorf education and whose best friend was one of the earliest members of the Christian Community. Furthermore, there was a retired teacher with a fair number of books by Rudolf Steiner which he had inherited from his sister.

It turned out that the one anthroposophist was a teacher like myself. She had lost a son of my age during the last year of the war. We shared teaching 125 school-beginners in three classes. Our flats were in the schoolhouse just above the classrooms. We met frequently to review our work with the children and soon became good friends. I had dozens of questions for her.

The end of the war and my adventurous journey through part of Austria and the whole length of Germany had stirred presentiments in me, with warnings and helpful guidance coming from an invisible world which later I connected with the tragic death of my twenty-two-month-old sister. My colleague's answers made sense to me. They came from a life lived with and out of anthroposophy. Anthroposophy did not seem strange to me. It was like meeting a long-lost friend again. I joined the little circle where Emil Bock's contemplations on the four gospels as well as books by Rudolf Steiner were read on a weekly basis.

Udo and Lisa Steuck

One day the headmistress' friend came for a visit. She was the first member of the Christian Community I met. She told me of the very beginnings of this movement of religious renewal. She had met the young men and women in Breitbrunn in Bavaria, preparing for the founding. From there they had travelled to Dornach, Switzerland, where they received their final preparations and were then ordained. However, it took another year before in 1949 I could experience my first Act of Consecration of Man.

Not long afterwards I went to Stuttgart to study at the Waldorf Teachers' Seminar. During this time I became a member of both the Anthroposophical Society and the Christian Community. I also heard two lectures by Dr Karl König. I was impressed, but did not seek to meet him.

After the completion of my studies I first helped out at the Reutlingen Waldorf School and then worked as a teacher in a curative home in the Black Forest. As there was no resident doctor it became my task to take a pupil to see Dr König who was visiting the institution Eckwälden. I experienced first hand Dr König's deep understanding of the boy's condition. Dr König radiated warmth and humanity, and it was there and then that I asked him whether I could join the work in Camphill. Not long after this I received an invitation and arrived at Aberdeen. I was placed in Murtle with Anke and Thomas Weihs and had my first talk with Anke about the Camphill Community and its aims and membership commitment. During the following half year I had many talks with some of the founding members of Camphill. I felt deeply connected with them. The step towards membership seemed natural and in time Camphill became my spiritual home.

In 1985 I was ordained as priest of the Christian Community and in 1986 my wife, Lisa, and I took up residence in Mourne Grange, Northern Ireland where I serve as a priest.

AUTOBIOGRAPHICAL

Birthe Hougaard

July 14, 1922 – April 11, 1990

Birthe came to Camphill about 1952/53 and was in Cairnlee, Ringwood and Thornbury. In 1973 she started Coleg Elidyr, a place for further education for sixteen- to nineteen -year-old youngsters with special needs. She died peacefully in her sleep at Coleg Elidyr after many months of illness and pain.

We first met Birthe six years ago when our daughter became a student at Coleg Elidyr and from the start we were impressed. We felt that Birthe knew, she understood, and was right.

About three years ago, when my husband retired, he offered to help with the adult education programme for the apprentices at Coleg, which he knew Birthe was keen to start. I would do mending and make curtains. We both went to discuss all this with Birthe. She was very enthusiastic about the adult education, but then she turned that look upon me and said, "But you have been working with old people."

I found it hard to understand the relevance of this comment, but I did not know Birthe quite so well then. She went on to suggest that I might help with the Care Course, "just the practical part."

But then six months later, when a teacher left Coleg Elidyr, Birthe in her inimitable way, managed to persuade me that I could teach. I was extremely reluctant and doubtful of the outcome, but we all know how persuasive she could be. So I taught, and I felt that she found a sort of impish pleasure in proving that she was right.

One day I was talking to her about the difficulties our Care Course students were having in working in homes for the elderly on their work experience. Birthe took up pen and paper and started to draw, saying "This is how it can be."

She drew a house which she said would be our old people's home where our youngsters could care for the elderly residents, but with special staff who understood our students' difficulties. The young people could work with the elderly, their pace matching that of the youngsters, and each might learn from and help the other.

Birthe went on to draw flowers around the house. "Some of our youngsters would want to grow flowers for the old people," she said. She drew cabbages. "There will be those youngsters who want to grow vegetables for the old people." Not, "there may be," but "there will be!"

"It will be a dream House," she said, "because anything is possible in dreams."

And so the plans were laid, and the last weeks of he life, a few of us were privileged to hear her talk about her "dream house" and how she wanted it to be. Even when she was really too weak to talk, she would invite us to share with her what were very special Bible suppers as we sat around her bed and listened. Amazingly she summoned up her strength for half an hour on one occasion — with that urgency in her voice even then — and we came away inspired. It was as we left Coleg after the last of these Bible suppers that my husband said to me, "Even when it comes to dying, Birthe sets a very high standard."

We were fortunate in being able to take part in Parents' Seminar weekends which Birthe organized for us over the past two years. She was a superb teacher and a delight to listen to. At the very last seminar, when she was barely able to stand at the blackboard for more than a minute or so, Birthe was still able to hold and inspire her audience.

During the last weeks when Birthe came home from hospital I was able to play a small part in helping to care for her — and those were very special times. She would ask eagerly about her Care Course students, and be so delighted to hear about their progress that they were making. Even when she was so weak and tired, it was not easy to persuade her to rest, and she would still try to help and guide my teaching. I shall always remember those times with Birthe as having been one of the greatest privileges in my life. It is not easy for a nurse to sit still, not to talk, and not to be "doing." But with Birthe it was a unique experience and pleasure. She opened our eyes, our hearts, and our minds to so much, and no doubt with her continuing help, we shall be able to carry forward so much of what she taught us into the creation of her Dream House. We trust that it will be a fitting memorial to a much loved and truly special person.

STEPHANIE HOLDEN
From Camphill Correspondence, *1990/3.*

Martha Hönig

June 10, 1921 – September 25, 2005

When Martha Hönig came to Camphill in 1952 she had a conversation with Dr König who asked her, "Was it your father, or your mother?" Martha said it was her mother, and they spoke no more about it. From that moment Martha experienced that Karl König understood her and felt a closeness to him for the rest of her life. Because of the traumatic experiences in childhood, her mother never accepting her, there were very few people Martha could trust. But she knew Karl König understood her struggles.

Martha was born in Basel, Switzerland on June 10, 1921. It was in June 12–16, 1921 that Rudolf Steiner first met with a group of young people in Stuttgart and held six lectures which led to the founding of the Christian Community in September the next year. The Christian Community and anthroposophy were central in Martha's life.

Martha was born out of wedlock, and in Switzerland in 1921 that was difficult. Her mother was not good to her and tried to prevent her having contact with her father, whom she loved dearly. Martha's first memory was from New Years Eve 1922, when she was just $1^1/_2$ years old. She remembered her uncle coming in and saying that the Goetheanum was on fire. Martha's mother later married. Martha's two half-sisters were cared for much better.

When she was in her teens, Martha walked on her own initiative from where she lived in Basel to Arlesheim. She walked towards her future. In Arlesheim she felt at home and soon began to work at the Sonnenhof with children in need of special care. Of the personalities who were active in Dornach in the 1930s she was especially impressed meeting Ita Wegman. It may well be that Martha met Kate Elderton, later Kate Roth, at the Sonnenhof before the war. (Later, Martha was asked by Kate and Peter to be godmother for their son, Simon.)

Martha worked in curative education throughout the late 1930s and the war. In the 1940s she worked with Madame Vachadze in a castle in Switzerland where the children in need of special care were the princes and princesses. Children in need of special care were always Martha's princes and princesses.

Martha came to England in the early fifties and worked for a time at Sunfield, the curative home in the Midlands. There she met Elisabeth Knottenbelt, who became her friend and who was instrumental in Martha later moving to Norway.

In 1952 Martha came to Camphill, and came home. Outwardly Martha

was a homeless soul, inwardly Camphill was her home, also during the many later years she lived elsewhere. Martha loved children. She often had five or six children in her nursery, including the most difficult ones. In order to manage, she had children sleeping in her room. Her contact with adults was more difficult, often her temperament getting in the way. Martha's frequent moves within Camphill, and in life generally, may have been a result of those difficulties.

There was one little boy whom she cared for, who could barely speak. One day he got lost. This little boy wandered away, and in the hustle and bustle of looking after all the children, disappeared. Many began searching the slopes of Murtle and the fields leading to the river. Late that night Martha was still outside searching, when she heard a little voice say, "Martha," and she found him. If she had not been so very close to the bush he lay in, she would not have heard him.

When Karl König was no longer in Scotland to hold his protecting hand over Martha, human difficulties led to her moving from house to house in Camphill and to her leaving Camphill for a while. Her friend Elisabeth had left England earlier. On the train Elisabeth met a person who advised her to travel to Norway and not home to Holland. She took this advice from the complete stranger and bought a smallholding on an island in the far south in Norway. She later married the neighbouring farmer, Leonard Kleppe. Now Elisabeth Kleppe invited Martha to Norway, where she lived for the second half of her life.

Martha began working in Emma Hjorts home near Oslo. She was active in the Christian Community and was one of those who wrote to Margit Engel asking her to help bring Camphill to Norway. She took part in the preparatory meetings before Vidaråsen was founded.

Martha moved to Vidaråsen in the late 1960s. She lived in the flat adjoining the bakery and ran the doll workshop. Martha was very gifted with her hands, with sewing and all kinds of handwork. The Vidaråsen dolls received their round, healthy goodness from Martha!

As so many times before, Martha needed to move and worked again at Emma Hjorts near Oslo. There she had her workshop, the leadership was grateful for her good work and she did not need to struggle with others. Martha worked there until she retired in 1988.

Martha moved to Nøtterøy soon after retiring, also at the suggestion of a friend, and lived close to the Rudolf Steiner school. Life was not easy for her in retirement. Her good friend Elisabeth invited Martha to Hidra. Martha packed up for the last big move and sold her flat. In the far south of Norway she rented, first a flat in Flekkesfjord, but after quarrelling with her neighbour, moved to a little house on the island of Hidra. Shortly after Martha had moved near to her, Elisabeth slipped when out walking, fell down a cliff and died on April 29, 1994. Her friend, the reason for moving to the far south, was no longer living. But Martha could no longer move. Instead she began moving from her physical body. Her mind began wandering. She began to lose her memory and was moved to a nursing home after a time. The last years she lived there, peacefully, without recognizing people.

Looking back it seems that Martha wanted to be born just there and just then. The difficulty was that her mother didn't understand this. She didn't want Martha and made her life difficult as a child, and her childhood experiences made life difficult for her as an adult. But many, many children can be grateful that, through her own trials, Martha could understand their problems. Karl König understood her struggles and it was perhaps not just by chance that she died on Karl König's birthday, September 25.

JOHN BAUM
From Camphill Correspondence, *2006/1.*

Eva-Marie Knipping

January 27, 1915 – November 8, 1993

Although I knew Eva-Marie only in the last seven years of her life, such was her impact that knowing and befriending her counts as one of the richest experiences of my lifetime. When I first came to help her in the Coffee Bar in Newton Dee, she appeared to me as a lady of great honesty and dedication, performing her tasks, however mundane, to the best of her ability. Her standards, which she set herself, were high, and she expected these same high standards from everyone else. She could express herself quite trenchantly if she encountered carelessness or shoddy work! Her customers were more like guests, especially on Saturday mornings, when old customers of long standing would come.

In the course of time we were to become firm friends. But not at once — one had to win her respect first. Once you had won it, however, you found her a friend in a thousand. There was no one more loyal and trustworthy than Eva-Marie. It was my great pleasure to sit and have coffee with her in her room, and listen to her reminiscences of the old days. A feeling of peace and well-being filled these times; I remember them with gratitude. She would talk of her home, her doctor father, her sisters and her brother. She would talk of the Odenwaldschule, and her years there. She would remember, too, her experiences in South Africa. All of these memories, some bright, some dark, were fresh and green to Eva-Marie; the faraway people would become alive in the telling of the stories for me as well as for her. So many threads, from so many different places — how lucky that they should join with mine when they did.

Some of the happiest memories of Eva-Marie arise when I think of the holidays we took together. Prague! The colour of that holiday was gold, gold because the sun shone throughout our entire stay. There was gold, too, in the lime trees, which were in full flower then; their fragrance would drift into our hotel and on the balcony where we had our al fresco breakfast. The day we first saw the Karlstein was gold, too, the castle walls suffused with sunlight and outlined against deep blue of a cloudless sky. "Ach, but that is beautiful!" she would exclaim, as a view of mountain or river revealed itself.

Engraved on the memory, too, is a much frailer Eva-Marie, as recently as last year, sitting on the twenty-second floor in the hotel restaurant in Tallinn, with the red rooftops of the old city below us, and the sky growing redder and redder in the glory of the Baltic sunset. Tired though she was, she would not leave until the last streak of red had disappeared, and the first stars twinkled out.

Though she is gone, what remains in my heart is her honesty, her courage and her selflessness. I think I can say that Eva-Marie was one of the most honest people I have known. This often meant that she had to speak the brutal truth on occasions when it would have been more palatable to the listener for her to prevaricate. But she could never prevaricate; there was no atom of pretence in her nature. And this to me was her "spice," her "Eva-Marieness." It was one of the things that made her such an interesting and valuable friend. She was a courageous little person in every way. She deserves to be remembered with love and gratitude.

MAUREEN RAMSAY
From Camphill Correspondence, *1994/2.*

The Rudolf Steiner School at Hermanus near to Cape Town was started under the wings of Dr König in about 1948 and was guided through the first years by a young man whom Dr König had sent to South Africa. This young man was followed by Eva-Marie Knipping in the early 1950s and with her arrival at Hermanus the small school began to grow and find its place.

My husband and I had been loosely connected to the School since its inception but our connection deepened with the coming of Eva-Marie. Full of enthusiasm she set about establishing the school as an offshoot of Camphill. Eva-Marie captivated my daughter who thereafter would insist on frequent visits to Dawn House, to the saying of graces at all meals and, in so far as she could manage it, the institution of some Camphill ways in our own home.

At the time when we were starting the first very small seedlings, which were to grow into the Anthroposophical Society in South Africa, we had the support of Eva-Marie. With her enthusiasm the first performance of the Oberufer Paradise Play was held in our garden.

I remember very vividly the Eva-Marie of those early years in Hermanus. She was always busy, always bustling about in the house, in the garden, in meetings, establishing the work of Camphill — and in her office, though I never understood how with her vagueness she ever managed to deal with the work of administration!

To remember Eva-Marie at Dawn House in Hermanus is to remember this woman of such great warmth and social ability caring for this new venture in a new land. By the time Renate and Julian Sleigh and Margaret Metraux came in 1958 Eva-Marie had laid strong foundations on which the work in Camphill could grow. South Africa indeed owes much to Eva-Marie Knipping.

JOAN TALLO
From Camphill Correspondence, *1994/2.*

Julian Sleigh

October 6, 1927

When I was twelve or thirteen years old I was at a Scout Camp and I remember that my Scout Master, a man I greatly respected, said that he would like to give up his job and work for handicapped children. At the time, I thought little of this remark but later it returned to me.

Years after, as a student of Social Science, I became concerned at the way in which the pressure of industrial and commercial life had, in modern society, destroyed the quality of community in the relationship of people. I longed to find a way in which the social and political order could assure each person of the possibility to develop and express his personality and through this, to allow his more inner life to unfold. As a Catholic, I found inspiration in Jacques Maritain and, as a youthful socialist, I turned to the Fabian Society. But when I was in the army I was forced to realize that no ideal social pattern could succeed in giving content to the empty soul life of so many young people of all classes unless it was based upon a profound insight into the nature of man, the purpose of life and the working of the spiritual life into man. The years I then spent in industry further convinced me of this. I met and joined many noble schemes for improving working conditions, relations between management and worker, welfare schemes and "community centres" but I could see that the work in the factory could hardly offer a place for the dignity of man to unfold and develop. All one's optimism was so rudely shattered when watching the rush to the factory gates the moment the hooter sounded at the end of the working day — a stampede to get out, to reach the bus first, to return to a little council house until the next day.

I was working in a factory built on the site of a former Franciscan Monastery in Anglesey, opposite Penmaenmawr, when a new worker came for a time into the next department to mine. He made a deep impression on me and we became friends. He often joined me at my lodgings and we spent many hours talking together — or rather I listened and he talked. He told me of Rudolf Steiner and anthroposophy and about the Camphill Schools and handicapped children. He left the factory and I lost track of him but I began to read lectures by Rudolf Steiner. I found them not easy to grasp and I decided to spend the following Christmas at Camphill. I had so often felt how the decay of spiritual values seemed to show itself so especially at Christmas time — but at Murtle I found the spirit of Christmas alive, serving worthwhile work. I found there also the attempt at community life which yet left the individual free; I found the purposeful cultivation of beauty, of traditions

brought from many lands and I found an earnest search for the understanding of the being of man through the encounter with handicapped
children — the handicapped children of whom I had first heard at a
Scout Camp fourteen years before.

After I had worked in Camphill for some time, Dr König went on a visit
to South Africa. Before he left, Renate asked him to see if there would be
a place of work for her in South Africa. Soon after he arrived and became
acquainted with the home in Hermanus, Dr König wrote to her to say,
"Yes," help was urgently needed there. So she and Margaret Metraux
announced at the next Thursday Group meeting that they would be emigrating to South Africa to take up work at Hermanus. Some days later
Renate came to me in the office and asked if I would help them with the
quite complicated immigration procedures. My response was, "Yes, I'll do

this gladly, provided I can also come." Whereupon she replied "Well, why don't you?" So my interest in going to South Africa was given life, so, also my interest in Renate König.

AUTOBIOGRAPHICAL
"How I met Camphill," from A Walk through my Life.

The National Council for Mental Health in South Africa had a special subdivision for the mentally handicapped and it was in that section that my friend and colleague Julian Sleigh was fighting a lone battle on behalf of the Camphill movement. This movement had been given a very low rating in the first Parliamentary Report in 1967 the reason being given that it did not measure up to "Christian National Education." Despite this, Julian was not easily brushed aside. During the following years, he radically changed the negative perception some people had of the Camphill movement. In the process he made life-long friends with some of the leading people, academics and doctors who worked in this field. As the ultimate reward and proof of his success, he was appointed as National Chairman of the Division for the Mentally Handicapped in 1980. It was in this role that he rallied the small burgeoning organizations that were working privately in this field, to join hands in Forums and take initiative for the future of curative education. Those Forums could make representations to the government. The first Forum convened by Julian Sleigh was aptly called the "Forum for the Mentally Handicapped in the Western Cape," Other forums subsequently began in Johannesburg and in the Eastern Cape.

MELVILLE SEGAL
From the book, Turn Right at Magnolia Street.

Manfred Seyfert-Landgraf

June 14, 1924

I was born in Baden-Baden, in the south-west of Germany, although our family home was in Berlin. Before I was born my mother suffered from a severe kidney inflammation and the doctors in Berlin doubted that we would both survive and recommended an abortion. My father, a staunch Darwinist, supported them wholeheartedly. My mother was adamant that one should not interfere with nature. In order to be left in peace for the remaining pregnancy she took her two-year-old daughter and moved to her own mother, who at that time lived in Baden-Baden. In the end we

both not only survived the birth but also a severe bout of diphtheria immediately afterwards.

When I was about three years old, the differences between my parents,
in their world conception and temperament became so untenable that a
divorce was inevitable. By that time my father had moved to Dessau while
we two children stayed, to begin with, with our mother in Berlin. About
two years after the divorce a man came into our family to whom I had,
from the first moment of meeting him, a great affection; to be honest, I
loved this man more than my father. His name was Hugo Landgraf; several years later he married our mother and became our stepfather. Hugo
Landgraf, too, was a Goetheanist and at the time he came into our family
he had been a founding member and lecturer at the Goethe Institute for
Foreign Students in Berlin. Later on, after Hitler came to power in
Germany, this institute was closed and he then worked as a freelance
reporter for both radio and a first experimental television station at the
Berlin Broadcasting Company. Much later my mother told me that after
the First World War Hugo Landgraf was an enthusiastic member of
Friedrich Rittelmeyer's Lutheran congregation in Berlin. As a young student he was also a friend of Dr Hellmut Vermehren, who later became a
priest in the Christian Community and who admitted my mother to the
Christian Community in November 1948.

When my mother and Hugo Landgraf married I was nearly ten years
old and no longer lived with her in Berlin, but in a children's home in
Braunlage in the Harz Mountains. My greatest regret was that I could
not attend their wedding. Nevertheless, I was so happy about it, that I
immediately deleted the name Seyfert, proclaiming that my new name
was Landgraf. This resulted in a severe reprimand from my father.
Though my connections to mother and stepfather were much greater
than to my natural father, the courts gave the guardianship to my father.
So from my eighth year I lived for a short while with him in Dessau,
being looked after by a governess, and later in the children's home in
Braunlage. During that time my interest for music began to awaken and
for a short while I had piano lessons. It was hard to give up these lessons; but later, when I became a drummer in the Hitler Jugend, I was
happy again.

Not long after the wedding of my mother and Hugo Landgraf, my
father, who had moved to Munich by now, took me away from this children's home and placed me in a small residential school south of Munich.
There I stayed for the next five years until my father died a few weeks
before the war started. This was, in a way, the most difficult time of my
childhood and youth, and yet it proved to be also very important for my
inner development. The director at this school was a great admirer of King
Ludwig II of Bavaria and of his friendship with Richard Wagner. He was

able to convey his great enthusiasm for these personalities to his pupils. This became important for me in later life, after I had moved to the British Isles, and it helped me to gain a deeper understanding of the karmic background of their friendship which goes back to the events connected with the legends of Merlin and King Arthur, and to the transformation of the task of the Celtic folk spirit, when it became the guiding spirit of the esoteric or Grail Christianity. Several years later, when I had decided that my future was in anthroposophy, I met Margarethe Hauschka who told me that this director was, at the end of his life, her patient in a homeopathic hospital near Munich, and that he had studied Rudolf Steiner's educational lectures with great interest, regretting that he did not know about this approach to education earlier and could now no longer put this into practice.

After the death of my father I lived with my mother and stepfather again in Berlin but, due to the Second World War, this was only short lived. Hugo Landgraf was soon called up as war reporter and, because of the continuous air raids over Berlin, my mother decided at Easter 1940 to send me out of the city. So I went again to a small private boarding school some sixty km north of Berlin. However, now I was near my mother and I could sometimes go home for the weekend. My stepfather considered adopting me but due to the war this had to be postponed. However, he permitted my sister and me to use his name as a second surname. Later, adoption was no longer possible as my stepfather died in 1946 in a Russian prisoner of war camp.

While attending boarding school, I took part in school performances with great enthusiasm, but when in Berlin I saw performances by the great actor, Will Quadflieg (who, I found out later, was an anthroposophist), I decided that this was the profession for me. In preparation for the necessary exam, I took some acting lessons during school holidays with my mother's cousin who was chief producer at the Munich Chamber Theatre. Then, shortly after my eighteenth birthday, I passed this exam.

Seven months later, in February 1943, I was called up to the army and left the school with an emergency matriculation. At that time it was impossible to be a conscientious objector. Luckily, I was serving in an infantry communications unit as telephone operator; our main task was to lay and to repair telephone lines. At least I was not in the front line.

On November 26, 1943, during active service in the Ukraine, I was severely wounded on the right side of my head and my right leg. To begin with the doctors gave me no more than a five per cent chance of survival; but in German there is a saying "Weeds are indestructible!" It was nearly $3^1/_2$ years before I was finally discharged from the various hospital treatments. Even then I was left with a paralysis on the right side of my face and frequent headaches. To begin with, I also suffered complete blackouts when I was under mental or physical stress; fortunately, these became gradually less and eventually ceased altogether.

During the last half year of my hospital treatments I saw there an advertisement from an organization called the Christian Community, for some lectures about the "Miracle of Birth and Death." This theme interested me greatly. During these lectures by Kurt von Wistinghausen and Wilhelm Kelber, I heard for the first time about the idea of reincarnation and karma from a Christian point of view. If this idea about repeated earthly lives is true, I thought to myself, then I must work through whatever difficulties might still come towards me, otherwise things would become more difficult in my next life.

Due to the facial paralysis I was now no longer able to become an actor, so I studied science of stagecraft for a career as director and stage producer. However, in May 1948, after two semesters of study and nine months as a trainee stage assistant the currency devalued leading to the closure of more than half the theatres. Not knowing how quickly the situation would recover, I decided to change my plans and train as a librarian in Stuttgart instead. In retrospect it seems to me that my wish to train as librarian was only the outer reason for the move to Stuttgart; the real reason was that now, at the age of twenty-four, I was ready to meet anthroposophy, and within weeks of my arrival I made my first contact with it. Herbert Hahn, a Waldorf teacher, gave a sequence of public lectures, "Europe, as a Spiritual Unity," which was about some of the European folk souls. (I wonder if he could have imagined that the country in which he had grown up, Estonia, would after some fifty years become part of a European Union.) Herbert Hahn lived only five houses down the road from my student quarters and we usually went home together by tram. Soon we were absorbed in conversations about anthroposophical subjects.

Due to my disabilities at the time it was more difficult to find the right professional activity; there were only very few anthroposophical libraries in Germany. I wondered whether there would be a chance for me to work with children in need of special care, and approached the Seminar for Curative Education in Eckwälden. I was admitted to the course, which was theoretical in the mornings and the afternoons were filled with various artistic activities including an hour of eurythmy; additionally I was given curative eurythmy for my war injuries. However, after a year, Dr Geraths in Eckwälden told me bluntly that I was not suitable for working with children with special needs. I had to do something else.

As I had always a deep connection to the religious life, I thought of turning to the priesthood in the Christian Community. But upon discussing this with the relevant priests, and realizing that it was impossible for me to stand for a whole hour, this was obviously not the right solution.

Eventually I found my way to Hofgut Ehrenberg, in the Neckar valley where I was able to work for the next fifteen months. Yet again, some of the heavier farm work proved to be too much for me; I was therefore entrusted with making and applying the biodynamic preparations. However interesting this work was, I could not see myself doing this for the rest of my life.

Thus, when I saw an advertisement from the curative educational home St Prex on the Lake of Geneva, for somebody who could care for the sheep and also help either in a dormitory or the garden, I applied for it and was accepted. At that time St Prex was a private home of the Spalinger family and did not belong to Camphill, but there were already close connections. Dr Hans-Heinrich Engel, for instance, came from time to time to hold clinics. When he visited in November 1953 and spoke about Camphill, its social and religious life and the seminar, I became very interested and gave him a letter to Dr König expressing my wish to work in Camphill the next spring.

I arrived in Camphill on the April 1, 1954, and was asked to take over the garden in Camphill Estate. Soon it became obvious that it was far too much to carry the responsibility for this garden on my own and, consequently, I became ill. With the arrival of the Hellström family I worked under Ivar's guidance, who was a trained gardener.

Soon it became clear to me that here in Camphill I had found at long last what for many years I had been searching for. This experience was reinforced by a dream which I had a few weeks after arriving in Camphill and which I remember as vividly today as it was then. In this dream I saw myself standing in front of Murtle House, chatting with friends, when suddenly a German broadcasting van arrived. Out stepped Hugo Landgraf. I ran to him asking him, "How have you come here? I thought you had died?" Whereupon he waved at me saying, "I will speak with you later. First I must see Dr König; I want to become a teacher at St John's School." This dream showed me clearly that it was, in fact, the spirit of my stepfather who had led me through these years. He brought me to anthroposophy, and finally to Camphill, as he had led my mother to the Christian Community. For this reason it is important to me that I am known as Manfred Seyfert-*Landgraf,* even if the second name is not in my passport. I strongly feel the presence of his spirit as the source of my inspiration.

AUTOBIOGRAPHICAL

Charles Campbell McWilliam

June 1, 1924 – January 25, 2001

Charles was born at Towie Manse, Aberdeenshire, very close to Kirkton House. His first landscape must have been like the landscape surrounding those who ten years later lived at Kirkton House and gave birth to Camphill. His father was a minister in the Church of Scotland and his mother a teacher. It has always been important to Charles that the Christmas Foundation Meeting of the Anthroposophical Society in 1923/24 took place as he was on his way into incarnation. He was a second child. An older sister, he and a younger brother formed a trio, close together in years and soul. His youngest sister was born nine years later. She bore the brunt of difficult family circumstances, thus setting Charles free to devote himself to his work in Camphill.

As a young school child Charles suffered long and painful illnesses, spending months in hospital. One day the family was gathered around his bed; he wondered why, when a little bird alighted on the windowsill and began to sing. He suddenly understood why they were there but he also knew that he would live. Charles told me that coping with the considerable physical pain that the doctors had to inflict upon him daily helped him in later life to handle his extremely thin-skinned constitution.

By this time the family had moved to Cowdenbeath in Fife, an active mining area. The miners' sons with whom he went to school were intellectually brilliant. Charles had not only to compete with them but had to make up for lost time. Fighting was forbidden in the school yet the toughest bully engaged him in a fight and through some strange quirk Charles won, thus winning the respect of his classmates and the bully. Charles developed a strong and disciplined will which stayed with him for the rest of his life. He always set himself tasks, never out of ambition but out of interest and motivation.

Early in life Charles showed a mechanical aptitude, and a gift for improving on designs. His father decided he should become an engineer, which he did with flying colours: probably the first and last time that he submitted his own will and initiative to another's.

As an engineering apprentice, Charles got along well with work in the metal foundry. One day a huge sledgehammer went out of control, making straight for him; wearing earmuffs and goggles he could neither see nor hear, but he bent down to pick something up and the heavy metal block zoomed past him. Everyone was in shock and turned pale except Charles. About fifty men lined up and shook his hand.

During college in Glasgow Charles' world widened out. He came into contact with music, art and theatre. He took piano lessons from a Viennese lady, a pianist who had to flee the Nazis. She had a profound impact on

Charles. He joined an acting company and his love for speech and drama were born. His love for nature found expression in sailing and rock-climbing.

While working for De Haviland's aircraft factory in London, Charles started out on his spiritual quest He became a member of the Rosicrucian Order, Amok. This was the first contact with meditation and spiritual practice; he had started on his path. At one of the Amok gatherings Charles met three Camphill co-workers who told him about the light and colour treatment. Charles said to himself, "This is not natural science." He visited Camphill and decided to join, burning all his boats behind him, spiritual and physical. Charles' father did not forgive him until he was ninety years of age.

He arrived in Newton Dee House, where Anke Weihs was housemother, in autumn 1954. The idea of a Scottish engineer determined to join Camphill was seen with amazement.

A very full life of learning and experience, with two dormitories, now began. Overlapping timetables forced him temporarily to compromise with his innate punctuality, but despite all the outer demands he found time to read one or two Rudolf Steiner lectures a night. Through reading, attending seminar and lectures, mainly by Dr König and conversations with König, Thomas Weihs, Hans-Heinrich Engel and many others, came the realization that his special charges were windows into anthroposophy, of which he became a serious and devoted student and researcher until the end of his life. Putting himself into the surroundings of mid-European culture, he found himself a foreigner in his own country. This position was a lonely one, often misunderstood and misjudged.

Charles was not a strict disciplinarian towards others, only towards himself. He never allowed the slightest sentimentality to enter his soul or his actions. A choleric and a melancholic, he considered that tempers would have been self-indulgence, and bouts of sadness too. He took Rudolf Steiner's advice seriously: three steps in morality for every step in knowledge.

ADOLA MCWILLIAM
From Camphill Correspondence, *2001/4.*

Gerda Seifriz-Blok

December 31, 1931

I was born on the very last day of 1931. I was the second of six children, all girls. My parents had moved from South to Central Germany to look for a large farm. In the south there were only smallholdings. Jüterbog, a small old town south of Berlin, became their new home. All the children

were born there and we lived there until the end of the war. Hitler had come to power while the family lived in Jüterbog and Germany had a new lease of life with work for everyone; the inflation years had ended. The Autobahns were build and military activities were everywhere. Next to the old town of Jüterbog, a new Jüterbog became the living quarters for increased military personnel. My father was offered a position on a large training-farm for rehabilitating soldiers. With hindsight it is obvious that Hitler's mind was on expanding Germany, and my father, too, hoped for a farm in the East.

I think back with great happiness to my childhood years. I was eight years old when the war started, and had little understanding but I felt a change in my hitherto harmonious life. I was enrolled in primary school but all around me was military activity. At ten I moved on to secondary school in the old town. I did not like school especially, but enjoyed the social life around. I hardly remember school, we were always playing, playing families. In spring the girls brought their dolls out and we played hospital. I was always the doctor and we had surgery hours in the back-yard. Life was dominated with play, school was boring.

A month before the war ended we had to flee as the Russians were pressing forwards. For us children the flight with horse and cart was a great adventure though not so for our parents. I was thirteen years old at the time, and still remember the adventures we had. After three months we arrived all intact at our grandparents at Konstanz in the south of Germany. There was no way of returning, so life began to unfold in these new surroundings. After a year I was confirmed in the Christian Community. For the first time I learned about Christianity; I treasured this experience and ever since stayed connected with the Christian Community.

A year later, when I was fifteen, I heard about Camphill and I had an instant feeling, "That's what I want," and I secretly carried this in my heart. Everything from that time onwards was a preparation for going to Camphill. My parents were not happy with this wish, as they had experienced two world wars and had lost their money again and again, and in Camphill you got no wages! I felt different, left school at seventeen and started a practical craft-training.

Those three years were wonderful; I made many friends and was successful in all I did. I still lived at home for two more years hoping to get my parents good-will. But they were afraid, and so at 21 I found a good job at a couture in Zurich, designing and making clothes for rich ladies. The two years were wonderful with a sense of freedom. Then I received an invitation from Dr König to come to Scotland and join the seminar. I was 23 when I left Germany and Switzerland for Cairnlee House in Scotland.

From the first moment I knew I had found my second home. Soon I met Piet who came with children from Heathcot for folk-dancing and games. Life was truly wonderful but different from anything I had known before. After completing the seminar I committed myself to two years in Botton village. There I started a workshop making toys for children. When Piet returned from his year in Camphill in America, we got married in Botton, staying there for nearly thirty years helping and building this first village community. After our children grew up we accepted an invitation to join Delrow Community staying for six years before moving to the Mount Camphill Community. Now, fifteen years after leaving Botton, we find ourselves as "grandparents" to Gannicox Community in Stroud, living just ten minutes away.

My parents have now died, but they visited us in Botton and we saw how happy it made them. They spoke highly of biodynamics and Waldorf education, saying, "You are working for the future." I think it is what they themselves would have wanted to do, when they were young. I am deeply grateful to my angel, pointing me towards Dr König and Camphill.

Autobiographical

Piet Blok

June 19, 1936

I was born in Holland, the oldest of three children who later all spent some time in Camphill. My Father and mother were very idealistic. Mother was the youngest daughter of a cobbler from the small town of Apeldoorn. After school she went into psychiatric nursing, which was linked with the church, long before the whole revolution in health-care and medicine started. Father was the son of a diamond cutter in Amsterdam. As a young man he decided to become a vegetarian, because he was concerned about the effect of diet on health long before it became fashionable. He too tried psychiatric nursing where he met my mother whom he took out, against all convention, on the back of a Dutch bicycle. They married and in about 1931 started a health-food shop, the second in the Netherlands.

It was a very good and caring family; Mother, though always busy, made time for the many friends who came to the shop and knew each other from outdoor activities. This searching and striving family sent their second child to the Waldorf School which started up again after the end of the war. I did not manage to go to the Waldorf School as there was no class for my age group. I did, however, accompany my sister at times to social activities at the school, which was such a contrast to mine. Father loved English and used every opportunity to practice on visitors. We children imitated and pretended to speak English; I also had six years of a correspondence course in English but was very shy of speaking.

After school I trained as an electrician, but discovered that I came from a very different world from the ordinary workman and dreamed of other things. After finishing school my sister went to Camphill. That came about because Hans van der Stok had been a teacher at the Amsterdam Waldorf School and had gone to Camphill in the late forties, so there was a connection. She thoroughly enjoyed working with some quite difficult children and wrote enthusiastic letters home, awaking in me a desire to try this life for, say, three months. I corresponded with Peter Roth who then lived at Ringwood and who invited me in 1955. I never looked back, but lost my heart to the children, the life and the striving in the Camphill communities. I probably caused my family grief as my parents had hoped I would take over the business, but my destiny lay in England. After only three weeks at Ringwood I was invited to join Thornbury. After Thornbury I spent three years doing the seminar in Aberdeen, where I met Gerda Seifriz. After spending a year in America at Dr König's suggestion and thoroughly enjoying the challenge, I married Gerda and we spent thirty years at Botton raising our three daughters, supporting the Botton Waldorf

School with a little teaching, supporting the budding Eurythmy School, doing a thousand other things alongside maintenance and general repairs.

After thirty years in Botton we were invited to join the Delrow community. Six years at Delrow, were followed by six years at the Mount, a youth-guidance centre. And now, since 2004, we have become part of Gannicox Camphill Community in Stroud.

AUTOBIOGRAPHICAL

Margaret Mentzel

June 15, 1933

After a childhood in Germany during the Second World War, in 1952 I found myself in Haus Hohenfried, an anthroposophical institution for children in need of special care. My parents, Maria and Johannes Halder had moved there as my father could not find work. In Hohenfried we lived in the gardener's cottage. This was a wooden hut with three rooms, one for my parents, one for my sister Michaela and myself, and the third was occupied by a group of four teenagers, whom my parents cared for. During the holidays we were joined by our younger brother who at other times was with a foster-family. I found a dressmakers workshop nearby where I could finish my apprenticeship. In my spare time I enjoyed helping in the nursery of Ruth-Hildegard Strohschein. I loved children in need of special care; during the war one of my friends was a woman with Down's syndrome.

My greatest wish for my future was to leave Germany as soon as I was twenty-one years of age. Rudolf Schweiker, whose mother was matron of Hohenfried, returned from Scotland having finished the Seminar in Camphill. Through him I heard about Camphill and Karl König. One day Rudolf told me that a co-worker from Camphill, Irmgard Lazarus, was to collect a pupil who had stayed with us for his holidays. Spontaneously I said, "I must see her!"

In the evening, when returning from my work, she was sitting in my parents' room. She told about herself and her eurythmy courses in Thornbury. I said to her that I would like to come in summer to stay for two years in order to enter this course.

In spring 1954, after the final examination as a dressmaker, I knew that my time in Germany would soon come to an end as I had already received the invitation to Thornbury. Whilst waiting for my visa I planned to use the time hitch-hiking through southern Germany, to say goodbye to friends "for ever." I headed south to Basel and then by tram to Dornach. My seventeen-year-old sister Michaela was at that time at the Sonnenhof in neighbouring Arlesheim for a "practical year." I was able to stay with her for a few days. My intention was to become a member of the Anthroposophical Society. The next day I walked up the hill to the Goetheanum, knocking at the door of the secretariat. On entering I asked to become a member. The secretary asked if I had read the statutes and any introductory books by Rudolf Steiner. I answered that it was my intention to do so on turning twenty-one. This seemed to satisfy her.

At the Sonnenhof I met Herr Pache, the principal, who asked who I was and so on. When he heard that I was about to go to Camphill, he just turned his back on me. However, I was convinced that I was on the right track.

Finally, having received my visa, I set off by train and boat via Ostend and arrived at the Camphill office in Harley Street in London. I was met by Donald Perkins who spoke no German, and I did not speak much English. Soon I met others with whom I could communicate in German. After three days in London, I took the train to Bristol. At the station Irmgard Lazarus had come to meet me. On Saturday July the 6, 1954, I arrived at Thornbury House, and it felt like coming home.

Trude Amann was the matron (a term used in those days), assisted by

Jens Holbek. To begin with I helped in her nursery and by mending clothes. As I was a dressmaker I was very soon asked to sew dresses for Tilla König and others. After the holidays the eurythmy course took place every afternoon on weekdays. The three participants were Irmgard Röhling, Rosemarie Herberg and myself.

From Jens Holbek I learned to turn to the inner path of self-development. I noticed that there must be something more to curative education than just the outer work. The first book by Rudolf Steiner I read was on the Gospel of St Luke. I read these lectures like an exciting novel while preparing for the Bible Evenings held every Saturday.

Around Michealmas I began to grasp what made the community tick. I had a talk with Trude who told me about the inner community. A month later I asked to be admitted to it, which took place on December 14, 1954.

In summer 1955 Irmgard Lazarus was asked by Dr König to return to Camphill, Scotland. I had to decide to either take up the Seminar in Scotland, or to stay caring for a dormitory of children on my own. The latter being a great honour, I decided to look after the children. I had often written to my parents and enthused them with my experiences. They showed interest in joining the work, Father as a gardener and Mother as a cook. They were able to move to Thornbury Park in November 1955.

At the beginning of the autumn term 1956 a first year Seminar was started in Thornbury in which I participated. At that time quite a number of young people came to Thornbury. Life was wonderful, as we all enjoyed living and working together. Some of them are still living in one of the many places of Camphill around the world.

Having finished the first year Seminar, I moved to Scotland in summer 1957 to continue with the second and third years. I joined Camphill Cottage, a unit for mainly deaf and mute children. Hans and Susanne Müller-Wiedemann were in charge. Under Dr König's guidance Susanne had developed a special treatment for these children.

I was entrusted with five girls aged between nine and fourteen years of age. Unfortunately I soon fell critically ill and had to be hospitalized for over three weeks. Thereafter I had to learn to walk again. For recuperation I stayed in the sickroom, at that time situated next to Dr König's quarters. He helped me a great deal in regaining my health. After my convalescence I returned to Camphill Cottage to help in the house generally and to cook for the house community.

After finishing my second year Seminar, I moved to Camphill Lodge. There I was in charge of a group of six children in need of special care who suffered from partial — or full blindness. Piet Blok lived in the same house, caring for four boys with the same handicap. Ilse Rascher was our matron. I was allowed to assist her with the treatment for the blind, which

Karl König had introduced and developed together with Ilse Rascher and Elisabeth Löwe. There were amazing results to be experienced: when for instance a spastic boy started to gain some degree of sight, although the diagnosis was that he was never to see again as the particular nerves had been destroyed.

At the beginning of that term, Manfred Mentzel returned from Germany to take up the second Seminar year. He came to Camphill Cottage to work with some of the children I had been living with, and we became good friends. After I had finished my third year training, I decided to take a course in painting in Stuttgart. He followed me there, and we married. Together we came back to Camphill. It is now 53 years since my joining Camphill, and I have never regretted it.

AUTOBIOGRAPHICAL

Manfred Mentzel

September 2, 1938

I was born 1938 as the second son, my brother being seven years older. My parents were anthroposophists and my father had met Rudolf Steiner and visited the first Goetheanum.

A year later the Second World War was to erupt and in 1941 our family moved to Berlin where my father found an adequate position. Meanwhile the Anthroposophical Society, the Waldorf Schools and later the Christian Community were forbidden, and my father had to hide most of Rudolf Steiner's books on the hayloft of relatives of my mother's family near Stuttgart. From 1942 to 1945 bombs were dropped over Berlin almost daily. Though we lived in the outskirts of the city, houses near to us suffered direct hits. However, we were lucky, only the roof of our house was blasted away.

I remember my father opening the big atlas looking at southern England, as we had heard that Penzance in Cornwall had been hit by German bombers. My mother's sister had married an Englishman and had moved to Newlyn close to Penzance. We were worried, praying that they had not become victims of the bombs. Later we heard that this family had prayed for us to survive the bombings on Berlin.

At the beginning of September 1944, around my sixth birthday, I started primary school. This day is still in my memory, not so much because of the customary first-day school excitement, but for having to stand to attention and keeping our right arms raised while singing to the

Margareta and Manfred Mentzel

Nazi flag. We eventually had to support our outstretched right arms with our left hands as this event seemed to go on forever. Whenever the air-raid sirens sounded we had to descend into a dark cellar. However, I usually managed to run off to our house.

After the war Berlin was divided into four occupied areas and we found ourselves in the Russian sector. This became part of East Germany with the ever increasing pressure of the ruling Communist party. My father had a leading position in the centralized state-run schools supplier. He was asked to join the ruling party, but was able to avoid this, just as he had refused to become a member of the Nazi party. However, apart from the increasing pressure to join the Communist party, his firm also had to supply schoolbooks which of course were all full of the socialist propaganda. He left this firm as his conscience did not allow him to be responsible for the distorted teaching material. We applied to leave East Berlin in order to move to West Berlin, succeeding in November 1954.

I left school intending to becoming a management trainee with Siemens. I was asked to sit an exam, which was successful. However, I felt I needed to first learn some English, which in East Germany was not considered to be important.

From a priest of the Christian Community my father heard about Camphill and told me of the possibility to work there for a year to learn English. I had always felt the strong inclination to assist the less able, as well as older people and younger children. My father had heard Karl König as lecturer and wrote to Camphill in Aberdeen. I was told to send my application to the Sheiling Schools in Thornbury, as Camphill Scotland was concentrating on the second and third year of the Seminar. Within a short time I received an invitation from the School and a visa to stay in England for one year. I arrived at Thornbury on February 25, 1957. The Hatch, an adjacent building, was to become my home for the next few months. Christiane Hansen (later Lauppe) was the house-mother; the house-father, Alan Cais, was "borrowed" from nearby Thornbury Park.

With only minimal instruction I was to look after a group of older boys. I remember one in particular, Michael, a little older than me. When playing the piano (I was only a beginner), he showed interest and I discovered that he had the gift of perfect pitch. When I asked him about it he agreed, but continued to tease my apparent inability to learn. Many years later I met him again in Botton Village. With glee he remembered our time at the piano and his making fun of me.

My main task was to work with some of the boys in the large vegetable garden. Eventually I learnt how to cope. Having to plant many hundreds of leeks was quite challenging, giving me backache. But after about six weeks I adjusted to the work and the long hours. The very dry summer of 1957 was a special challenge: there was a hose-pipe ban. Following the rule we began to water the precious vegetables with watering cans between sunset and midnight.

On one occasion I wanted to light a bonfire. The wind was gusty and my match would not light it. I remembered a petrol canister. When I tried again to light the fire, there was an explosion which threw me backwards and my face was burnt. Fortunately I was wearing my glasses which protected my eyes. Gisela Schlegel, our nurse at Thornbury House, gave me first aid with Combudoron lotion. An ambulance was called but a long time to arrive. In hospital my whole face was covered, leaving only two holes for my nose and a small hole for sucking liquids. I recovered, and much to the amazement of the doctors at the hospital, no scars remained.

I had a more subtle experience at my first Bible Evening in the Hatch. The Bible Evening started with waiting in silence for quarter of an hour. We sat in a small circle outside the room in which it was to take place. Suddenly I began to experience the warm presence of a person I could not see. From behind me I felt a gentle confirming touch on my shoulders and I knew this was my grandmother. For years I did not tell anyone what I had experienced. Later I heard that Karl König experienced the Bible Evening as an event to which the souls from the other side of the threshold were attracted. Years later I told my father about this experience. He did not seem surprised as he had asked his mother before she died to keep a guiding hand over her grandchildren.

After half a year in the Hatch working in the large garden I was asked to move to Thornbury Park, where Janet MacGavin was matron. Now I was to work with spastic children. I grew to admire Dr Lotte Sahlmann who, as well as her medical work in Thornbury and at St Christopher's School in Bristol, gave all the physiotherapy needed. She was also a very good teacher in our Seminar.

Later I moved into the Park where I was entrusted with a group of very young children of both sexes. This was a very rewarding and important experience for me. I learnt to do plaits and to "iron" the ribbons each night by winding them, soaked in water, around the warm pipes in the bathroom. Eventually I began to realize that my activity was part of an effort to allow anthroposophy become a living quality, which is more than merely acquiring knowledge.

However, my visa ran out, and I returned to Germany to train at Siemens. As my train arrived in Berlin I looked out of the window and saw my tall father in the distance. Back in my compartment I had a kind of vision. I saw two pathways: one led to a comfortable situation, the other was a stony path into the future. In a moment I decided for the "stony pathway." When I greeted my parents and told them that I would be going back to Camphill they were astonished, but much to my relief accepted my sudden change of mind. Later I wondered how it had been possible for me to decide for the seemingly less favourable situation. I became convinced that my angel had helped me to find the "right path."

I corresponded with Camphill, Aberdeen. As I had completed a full year of the Seminar I was allowed to continue with the second year at Camphill starting September 1958. I joined the children's holiday-train from London to Aberdeen. In Camphill Cottage the house-parents were Hans Christoph and Renate Valentien. In Camphill Estate I was to meet Margaret Halder again who had been in Thornbury House since July 1954 and had started the Seminar a year before me. We had a friendly correspondence after she had left Thornbury in the summer of 1957 to join the second year in Camphill Estate. I had admired her for her hard work and creativity in anything practical, and for the love and devotion she gave the group of children in her charge. She could laugh, and at the same time be very serious when it came to essentials. I saw her artistic flair when she made me a present of the book, *Occult Science,* bound in leather with a fine engraving. In the course of the following months we saw more of each other and began a serious relationship.

Meanwhile I became class helper to Karin von Schilling and I grew to appreciate this work, and when Karin fell ill I was allowed to replace her. The Seminar itself was a great experience and gave us a solid foundation not only in working with the children but also for life in general. We received an all-round education, performed plays, learned about art, mythology and much else which considerably widened our horizon. The children's meetings and the regular clinics, in which the doctors saw individual children, were of great help in understanding their needs and how therapeutic measures were developed. The physicians working at that time in Camphill, Aberdeen were, next to Karl König, Thomas Weihs, Hans-Heinrich Engel, Margit Engel, Hans Müller-Wiedemann and Peter Engel.

In Camphill Cottage we had some younger children suffering from autistic and pre-psychotic disorders. One little girl in particular posed a challenge: even experienced co-workers did not manage to contain her tempers. Eventually I was entrusted with looking after her as well as another young girl. I played with them a lot, gently singing nursery rhymes, and sitting together with them on a large swing. To the astonishment of my house-mother the girls soon calmed down and their behaviour improved.

When my second year of seminar had finished in summer 1959, Margaret Halder had successfully completed her third year and set off to participate in a painting course in Stuttgart. She had the intention to return to Camphill but did so earlier than originally anticipated, because we got married in November 1959.

To begin with we stayed in a quaint wooden hut next to Newton Dee House and later moved on to Murtle House. Here I looked after a group of boys and became a class helper to Veronica Bay. After our daughter Gabriela was born and I finished the Seminar, we set off to Glencraig in Northern Ireland. Twelve wonderful years of strenuous work were to follow.

In 1972 we were asked by Hans Müller-Wiedemann to join the work at the Brachenreuthe school at Lake Constance. We moved there with our three daughters who did not speak any German. Here we stayed for fifteen years. For thirteen of these years we were teachers as well as house-parents. When the second Camphill Village Community in Germany, the Hermannsberg, needed experienced Camphill co-workers, we were asked to move there.

Now we have become old enough to step back, having worked and lived in Hermannsberg for over twenty years out of our total time of over fifty years in Camphill. We are grateful for all those years which gave us the opportunity to work and learn, to meet the most wonderful children and partners in community life.

AUTOBIOGRAPHICAL

Peter Engel

May 19, 1922 – March 26, 1976

Peter Engel was born in Breslau (now Wroclaw in Poland), into an anthroposophical family and was baptized into the Christian Community. He
came to London in 1935, at the age of thirteen years. He attended both
Michael Hall and Wynstones schools. During the war he was interned as
an alien, first on the Isle of Man, and later in Canada. The convoy in which
he returned to Britain was attacked, but he arrived safely. He became a
student in the Royal College of Surgeons, Edinburgh, and was invited by
Dr Karl König to work in Camphill during his vacations. Upon qualifying
he served as house-surgeon in hospitals in Dundee and Glasgow. It was
during this period that he met his wife Muriel. He performed his military
service, holding the rank of Captain in the R.A.M.C. Peter and Muriel
lived in Canterbury and while there formed and led an anthroposophical
group.

Peter became the Medical Officer in the Camphill Schools, Aberdeen,
in 1955 (and later for Newton Dee Village), which position he held until
January 1971, when he suffered a severe heart attack. It was as a doctor in
Camphill that he found his life-task. Although there are many people who
have reason to be grateful for Peter's help and friendship, his service to
the children was his true vocation, and in his service he excelled both as
doctor and friend.

Peter was an unassuming man. Perhaps humility was his greatest
virtue, but he inspired his patients, both children and adults, with confidence. He brought to the sick bed the qualities of a family doctor: warmth,
understanding and the true gift of healing.

Peter had a deep interest in the medical herbs which grew in the vicin-
ity of Camphill. These he gathered and made into some of his homoeo-
pathic medicines.

The nature of his long illness made it impossible for him to continue
his full and busy life, but he faced his deprivation with courage. He was
still able to make important contributions through his research writing and
translations, and to attend certain children's clinics.

We shall remember Peter with love and gratitude, as a good friend and
a wise and true physician.

DONALD M. PERKINS
From Camphill Correspondence, *1976/7*

The earliest memory I have of Peter Engel is of an evening spent at
Heathcot Lodge where he and Muriel lived when they first came to

Camphill. At that time I had just finished the first year at University and was spending the summer holidays helping at Murtle House.

Peter and Muriel invited me for supper along with another medical student, and I know we went away quite inspired after a most fascinating and wonderful evening. I cannot now remember the details of all that Peter shared and told us, but the impression which remained was of his immense and active interest in all phenomena of nature. Looking back now over the years, I feel that this living devotion to all natural phenomena was characteristic of him and shone through all he was and did. Whether he was turning to a child in clinic or college meeting; whether he was discovering or describing a new syndrome, or teaching sense physiology and diagnostics in Seminar; whether he was proving or making a new remedy, there was always the same enthusiasm and accurate attention to the details of the phenomenon.

He had an immense knowledge of mineral substances, plants and animals, and loved to go in search of stones, gather plants and make them into remedies, ointments and natural dyes.

He gathered together a wonderful collection of paintings and drawings by psychotic children, and also made it his task every year to take a photograph of each child in the schools for inclusion in the child's care records. It often proved very revealing to be able to look back and follow a child's progress as depicted in his changing appearance over the years.

Peter was interested in research and always seemed to know where to find any piece of information, often using Dr König's library, or the University Library in Aberdeen.

It was due to his initiative that the third year Seminar projects were started, and he seemed to have an inexhaustible wealth of ideas for subjects which could be taken up by the students.

He was an active member and supporter of the Therapy College and was especially keen that the whole realm of light therapy should find a place in Camphill. In fact, the very evening before his final illness, he came to tell me about his ideas and designs for the new light treatment to be developed.

Peter had a wonderful sense of humour but was very shy, humble and self-effacing. It was difficult to really meet him, but on the few occasions when this was possible, I was struck by his almost childlike trust, innocence and vulnerability. It was a great sorrow to him that he was unable to continue with active medical work following his illness, but his enthusiasm for research found expression in his scholarly investigations into the early history of Murtle Estate, and his interest in the mediaeval School of Chartres.

I was most impressed by his knowledge of Latin, and full of admiration for his ability to translate ancient documents as well as medieval Latin poetry. He translated some of the works of Alanus ab Insulis, one of the teachers of the School of Chartres, and I feel that perhaps some of the wisdom and the devotion to the Golden Natura, which once lived within the School of Chartres, found reflection and continuation in Peter's deepest aims and being.

SUSAN MECHIE
From Camphill Correspondence, *1976/7.*

Johannes Halder

June 25, 1911 – August 5, 1996

Johannes was an orphan. He grew up with his paternal aunt and left school at fourteen to begin a three-year apprenticeship as a decorator, a hard and harsh experience. He continued to be a journeyman for several years thereafter. It was a time of great political and industrial unrest in Germany and Johannes travelled the breadth of the country, often covering long distances by bicycle in search of work. Many a night on his travels in summer was spent in the open. Youth movements of many political colours were abundant at the time and after a very fleeting association with a Communist-backed movement, he joined a youth movement of workers connected with the Christian Community in the industrial heartland of the Ruhr. It was here that he met his future wife, Maria. It was also his introduction to anthroposophy. At the age of twenty-one they married in the Christian Community, a marriage that was to last 64 years. They were looking for new social forms of working with other people in a land-based environment of biodynamic agriculture and horticulture. Soon after their first daughter was born they moved to the south of Germany Four years later their second daughter was born.

It was obvious that Johannes's grasp of many anthroposophical concepts were as real to him then as they were to him in the final year of his life, indeed, in his final hours. He was to become a very faithful member of the Anthroposophical Society in his early twenties, and a stalwart of the local group.

By this time it was 1937 and the Nazi dictatorship was well established. There were repeated attempts to force him to join the political party, which he opposed, making no effort to conceal his reasons. This placed the whole family in a dangerous position. Not long after the war broke out he was called up at the age of 28. This saved his family from the increasing

harassment by the Gestapo (who had no jurisdiction over the armed forces) and possibly from the fate of the concentration camps.

He briefly saw service in France and was posted to the Eastern Front when Germany attacked the Soviet Union in June 1941. For the next four years Johannes witnessed the full horror of war with its immeasurable suffering of cataclysmic dimensions. In spite of the many occasions when he found himself in a dangerous situation he never knowingly fired a shot at anyone. He was forever prepared to help others, irrespective of whether they were friend or foe. He loved the Russian people and their country and had an inkling that he would survive. He was to volunteer to rescue his comrades from besieged and encircled positions against overwhelming odds. At one stage he was nicknamed, "the black devil of Rzhev" (a small town on the Volga) because of his black hair, dark complexion and singular courage in rescuing the remnants of a platoon hopelessly trapped in a valley where access was blocked by heavy artillery fire. He embarked on this particular mission in which all predecessors had lost their lives, completely calm and collected.

Many years later when asked how he plucked up the immense courage to go through these life-threatening experiences he would say that in order to survive one had to rise above any intellectual activity, never *think,* but have total trust in the powers that be. He recounted innumerable anecdotes, many humorous, but often depicting the appalling and gruesome reality of this violent war and of the rescue of injured fellow men.

In summer 1944 Johannes had a strong premonition that something untoward would happen to him. When asked by his companions why he was packing up his few possessions, he replied: "I don't think I'll be with you tomorrow."

The following day he sustained severe injuries from a shell that landed beneath him. He was transported to a field hospital. In and out of consciousness, peppered with shrapnel from head to foot and soaked in blood, he distinctly recalled the doctor giving him up as hopelessly injured. In one of his more defiant moments of consciousness, Johannes is reported to have risen to his feet, stuck his pistol to the doctor's chest and threatened to shoot him if he was not operated on. At this point he must have lost consciousness again and collapsed. The doctor relented. He underwent an operation of several hours followed by a nightmare journey to a hospital farther behind the lines, and was given leave of several months to recover. He was prematurely posted back to the carnage and mayhem of the retreating front in November 1944.

Throughout the war he carried three artefacts with him: a photograph of his wife, the *Soul Calendar* by Rudolf Steiner and a small print of *Angel in Prayer* by Fillipo Lippi. Johannes wrote to Maria almost every day without fail. Miraculously, most of the letters arrived.

He returned home in the summer of 1945 after a difficult and adventurous journey through the chaos of a country laid waste by the ravages of war; his only son was born shortly thereafter.

After the war, unemployment was high and food was scarce. In 1952 destiny led him to take his family to a curative home in the south-eastern corner of Bavaria, twenty-one years after the first attempt to work on the land in a new social context. He took over the farm and garden of the estate and shortly afterwards heard of Camphill through Rudolf Schweiker. In 1955 with his wife and son, he followed his eldest daughter, Margaret, to the Sheiling Schools, Thornbury. Later they moved to Cairnlee where he lived for the next 35 years.

In his later years when he was no longer able to tend the community garden he continued to take a great interest in the land and tended his own garden with devotion and care. His interest and support for the weavery his wife ran was unfailing. He developed and used methods of dying wool from plant materials, often collected from far afield. Johannes exercised his artistic ability by drawing and painting innumerable pictures throughout his life. He was surprisingly musical and appreciated music to great depth; his favourite composers were Mahler, Bruckner, Beethoven, Mozart and Tchaikovsky.

His fervent resolve was to serve his fellow human beings in all circumstances. His life could be described as one where he recognized the true humanity in every person.

MARGARET MENTZEL, FRIEDWARTH HALDER
From Camphill Correspondence, *1997/1.*

Maria Christine Halder

February 26, 1911 – March 26, 1999

Maria was born as the youngest of five children into the family of a tailor in Essen in the heart of industrialized Germany. She was a frail child, often ill and at the age of fourteen had to spend time in the countryside in order to get well.

This red-haired fairy-like girl, however, possessed a strong will and determined to seek other shores than those provided by her own family background, Her elder brother had come into contact with anthroposophy and this led her at the age of sixteen to Dornach where she helped families with small children, as well as cooking for the actors and eurythmists of the Goetheanum stage. She learned to know all the important people of the Anthroposophical Society and treasured their memory, displaying the photographs of the first Vorstand of the Society on the shelf above her bed until her death in 1999.

Later she met Johannes Halder, her husband to be, at the Arbeiterschule in Essen which had been founded by the Christian Community to offer further education for unemployed young people. They married when they were both twenty-one years old, and within a year their first daughter

Margaret was born — to be followed by Michaela and Friedwarth. Maria was determined to learn a trade, while her husband had to serve in the war. She attended night classes and within a few years managed to qualify with distinction as a dressmaker. She also acquired basic skills in weaving and craft work which were a foundation for her future work as a weaver in Camphill.

After the war the family hoped to find their social impulses fulfilled in gaining work at a curative home in Germany. When their eldest daughter Margaret found her way in 1954 to Camphill, Thornbury, it did not take long for her parents, upon hearing of the work done there, to move to Thornbury themselves. Here Maria took up the task of running Thornbury Park's large kitchen, while Johannes grew the vegetables. Then there came the call to the Grange where a village community was founded.

Maria began a weaving workshop and Johannes continued gardening while sharing their life with five villagers. In the early sixties they were asked to move to Camphill, Aberdeen, where Maria took over the weaving workshop at Cairnlee which was later substantially enlarged so that about ten youngsters could find therapeutic training under her able and firm guidance.

Maria was constantly seeking ways of integrating difficult youngsters into her work programme. As a result of diligence and high standards, the weavery products were exceptionally artistic and of a high standard. She was appreciated by her many customers who bought woven fabrics ranging from fine silk to heavy linens, and was also held in high esteem by fellow weavers, becoming a member of the Weavers' Guild.

Maria, however, found it difficult to integrate into the social life and preferred to live at her workshop where she was happy to receive guests. She was greatly helped by her husband who, as time went on, contributed to the artistic quality of the work done.

With increasing age Maria was no longer able to meet her own exacting standards and was frustrated that her work could not continue in the way she envisaged. On the other hand she could not let go and with her increasing disabilities she and Johannes, by then wheelchair bound, had to be cared for. She and her husband supported each other in a harmonious way and after his death she always seemed to be waiting — waiting to be called into the spiritual world. After a short illness she passed away a month after her eighty-eighth birthday. She not only longed to find her husband but as she said the day before she died, "to meet the Christ."

MANFRED MENTZEL
From Camphill Correspondence, *1999/4.*

Nina Rowley

August 25, 1916 – August 15, 2006

It began one day when I had been to the dentist and was waiting for a bus to take me home. The bus stop was just in front of an old bookshop and I could look at the "sixpence each" stand on the pavement while I was waiting. I found a book by someone called Rudolf Steiner. I'd belonged to the Theosophical Society for the last year, and I'd seen his photo at the TS headquarters. But I was puzzled. The title was *Christianity as a Mystical Fact* — and that didn't sound like Theosophy.

I wasn't yet ready to read the book: but its title intrigued me and I bought it. The Liberal Catholic Church was leading me to a Christ-centred life. Theosophy wasn't: it put Christianity on par with all other religions. And its focus was on the ancient wisdom: Was that good enough for the time we lived in now?

My doubts intensified and a year later I left the TS. I was adrift again. Then I saw an advertisement at the station: the Wimbledon branch of the Workers Educational Association was starting a once-a-week Literature course. It drew me. But when it came to the opening lecture, I couldn't get moving: I just wanted a quiet evening at home. I lit my coal fire — almost defiantly. Yet inexplicably (it wasn't even stormy) the chimney started smoking, and the room was soon smoke-laden. No choice now. I opened the window wide, and went to the Literature course. When I got home the room was smoke-free, and the next evening I lit the fire without trouble: the chimney didn't need clearing.

The Literature course indeed proved its value. My reading had focussed on the nineteenth century — Dickens and Jane Austen. Now I was in the twentieth century. With T.S. Eliot and Christopher Fry. They could not have written in the nineteenth century: something new had come about in these last decades. What was it?

The answer came through Anthony. He had met up with an old school-friend called James Garton. Julia had met James, and now phoned me about him. She said that he talked like me, and asked if I would come for supper on a Wednesday (which was his only free evening). But my Literature course was on Wednesdays, so I said, "sorry — that means I can't meet him." So she said, "Well, you must." So I rang off. But the next Wednesday our Literature tutor asked us a great favour: could we excuse him from his lecture the following Wednesday because he had to attend a special meeting? So I phoned Julia: that one Wednesday I could manage after all. She forgave me for my rude ring-off, and the supper meeting came about on January 19, 1955. I had always remembered Daddy's death-day, and this was the twentieth anniversary.

In no time James and I were in deep conversation. I asked how I could hear more and he told me about a lecture at Rudolf Steiner House a few days later. The lecturer was Walter Johannes Stein, one of Rudolf Steiner's pupils, so I would be listening to someone who had personal memories. As yet I didn't know that the Anthroposophical Society had its centre in Switzerland. When Dr Stein now spoke about this centre, something suddenly clicked. It was called "Goetheanum" — after Goethe. Daddy might never have heard of anthroposophy, but the name Goethe meant something to him. He had shown me Goethe's portrait at the Malkasten in Düsseldorf. No doubt Steiner would have known this building and the portrait, as he gave several lectures in Düsseldorf.

I had a friend named Frieda. She knew that I was working on a novel called *Rain Before Noon,* which was somewhat autobiographical. My next letter began, "I shall not write my novel now." Its main character was killed in a road accident at the age of 32 (her cycle-wheel got stuck in a disused tram-line, and there was a bus right behind her: that had actually happened to me, and I never knew how I escaped. When I met the work of Rudolf Steiner, I realized that my quasi-novel would now be quite untrue. My life could not end now: it was only just beginning.

James had explained how Steiner had first been a Theosophist, but had gone much further. We had a follow-up still-longer conversation a few days later. When I thanked him for giving up so much time, he answered, "It was necessary." Mummy had used that word "necessary" when I was six years old; now I knew what it meant. James also told me about Camphill, where I could live anthroposophy — especially Ringwood, where he himself had been. The time was ripe — as soon as I could wind things up with my job and my flat. Eight weeks later I had an appointment with Ursula Gleed in Harley Street, followed by two visits to Ringwood. And eventually landed there, on May 2, 1955. The night before, as I was emptying my bookshelf, a book of Matthew Arnold's poetry fell open on the floor. I read the words, "The homes that were not destined to be ours."

AUTOBIOGRAPHICAL
"A Wall and a Doorway," from her unpublished autobiography.

Nina worked as a group-mother with children and later as a secretary to Dr König in Scotland and to Julian Sleigh in South Africa.

Hans van Walsum

April 12, 1927 –December 16, 1996

Hans was born on the April 12, 1927 at Borgehout in Belgium. He was brought up by his Dutch mother as an only child. It was war-time during his years of Secondary School and he spent the last years in hiding with his half-brother. He ended up in the East Indies, where an illness saved him from fighting in the Indonesian Independence War.

Back in Holland, Hans studied classical languages, and the piano. It was through this that Hans met his first wife, Lies. During his studies he encountered the work of Bernard Lievegoed, which led him joining the Zonnehuis at Zeist. He spent nine years there as a class teacher, as well as being active in the anthroposophical youth movement. It was also during this period that he took up sculpture. Then he moved with his family to Camphill, Scotland where he spent several years in the sixties.

I believe Hans had just divorced when I first got to know him in 1964. From his first marriage he had four children. With Karin von Schilling he had a child. Then he met my sister Mary whom he married They had two children. He was a class teacher then and giving art classes in the seminar as well as an open art class for co-workers. I remember this time as stimulating and rich in research and reflection, not only in art but also in community and social life. Through him one learnt to know the "independent-minded Dutchman." Thomas Weihs was a close friend of Hans, especially through Hans' years of doubts and questions about Camphill and his relationship to its inner impulses as well as to anthroposophy.

Hans and Mary left Camphill for a residential school in England, rich in the experience of the work with Camphill's disturbed youngsters and the reflections that Thomas had stimulated, arising out of the work of psychiatrists like Laing and Cooper. A few years later they moved with their children to Holland. There Hans took up a teaching post at Amsterdam University in the Special Education Department, until taking early retirement after a serious illness. A third marriage and divorce followed. Single once more, he lived in Amsterdam and took up sculpture again as well as painting. During this period he also spent several years on the island of Milos in Greece. It was during another relapse that Hans died in Amsterdam on December 16, 1996.

Some among us will remember Hans as an artist, others as a teacher or co-worker. In all fields he put pointed questions and would not be content with easy answers. More important he was an active searcher and researcher. A questioner who took nothing for granted, he was not exactly a stabilizing factor in institutional life. I always had the impression that intellectual honesty and acting with integrity were key values to him, often determining the changes in his life situations. Now, beyond the threshold, perhaps Hans will meet the only one of his children he knew so little on this side: Saskia, whose early death inspired her mother, Karin von Schilling, to write the book, *Where Are You?*

JOHN BYRDE
From Camphill Correspondence, *1997/3.*

Turid Engel

December 7, 1933

I was born in Norway into a loving and harmonious family as the second child. My sister was only $1\frac{1}{2}$ years older and we grew up almost like twins in identical beautiful clothes. Six years later a little brother joined us. There was lots of laughter and our happiness was complete, but not for long.

The war came to Norway in 1940 and a year after, my father was betrayed and arrested as a leader of the resistance and condemned to death. He was deported to Germany but was only executed by the Nazis in 1945 as the Allied forces were advancing.

For us it was not easy to survive the war. Our family was punished by not being allowed to receive wages. We had to be very inventive and produce things for sale. My sister and I did the household so that mother could work. In Norway at the time we were praised as "heroes," but that we were close to starvation worried no one. Here a seed for cynicism was laid: lots of empty words and no deeds to match them. However, we managed to survive; mother was a great woman, never complaining and having a wide circle of friends.

My childhood was followed by a wonderful youth with enjoyable school, girl-guides, Red Cross Mountain Rescue training, dancing and lots of friends. On the other hand I had more and more the question about the meaning of life. I experienced myself living in two different worlds. Bridging both was my early work with children. I took up a nurses training and intended to become a nursery-class teacher.

In the summer prior to starting college I replied to an advert: "nurse sought for seven-year-old boy," was accepted and moved to Bergen to meet Lillebror, an autistic boy (the syndrome was not yet identified) who was severely retarded, wore nappies and had to be spoon-fed. I took him in hand and achieved a little, but the family thought I was a miracle worker. This task was taken up again during the next holidays.

The following summer I had to do a work placement for the college. Lillebror was going to a children's home, and they asked me to take my placement there, so that he might have someone familiar to relate to. At that time, life had no meaning for me — I was indifferent to everything, so I went to this institution, called Helgeseter. It was a school and home for children with special needs whose patron was an anthroposophist and a supporter of the Rudolf Steiner School in Bergen. This lady, having heard Dr König speak about Camphill, wanted Camphill in Bergen. At Helgeseter I met Margit Engel, Jacoba Holle, Marianne Sander, Baruch and Tamar Urieli with little Doron, Molly and Reg Bould with their family, and a few Norwegians.

While there the college discovered that they had admitted me without a health certificate, as I had been nursing in Denmark at that time. This had to be rectified; so I went off to the doctor in Helgeseter. He took only one look at me and said, "No way." It surprised me no end that here was someone who saw right through me and found that I was not really alive, just functioning. He insisted that I should go to a sanatorium, but I insisted on staying in Helgeseter. Anthroposophy, which I met there for the first time, did not really interest me much, but the way these "strange" people lived together made sense to me.

As well as having three difficult children to look after, I was given a group of four staff children. It surprised me that the parents did not care for their own children, but as we got on very well together, it seemed all right. One day when walking they told me that they once saw a huge troll, but he went the other way and they were not afraid. Being a pedagogue I did not argue with them, but at coffee spoke about this to the other co-workers. Baruch Urieli merely said: "I am sure they did see a troll." This was yet another oddity of these strange Camphill people!

After half a year I returned to college for full-time study and could only occasionally visit Helgeseter which had become a kind of lifeline for me, especially Margit Engel.

Then Helgeseter "collapsed." The Norwegian coworkers, in deep disagreement with Camphill, had staged a coup. They had taken great care not to take me into their plans, knowing that I would not have kept quiet. Following this I saw my new Camphill friends off on the ship for England. As they sailed away something of myself sailed away with them. However, I finished college and another half year at Helgeseter.

Then I went to Oslo to a large institution in order to earn enough money to pay back my loans. The head doctor, also responsible for all the work with disabled children in the country, knew of Camphill, had visited Camphill in Scotland and spoken to Dr König whom he greatly admired. Recognizing from my papers that I had been in Helgeseter, he used to say: "Yes, Dr König; yes, Camphill; but ..." and then he tapped his forehead in a gesture of madness. Nevertheless, he asked me if I would be willing to take on a little house with autistic children and live together with them and two nurses whom he had trained especially for these children.

After some time I decided to visit Camphill, to find out what it was all about. I was invited by Dr Engel to the Sheiling School at Ringwood, England, where I was very "special," as the only Norwegian who had not gone against Camphill and was allowed to join the training course mid-term. As the half year drew to an end Margit Engel did not *tell* me what I should do, but suggested that — as I was going to return to Norway — I might like to go to Camphill, Aberdeen, just to see where it all started. That made sense, and I arrived at Murtle where I was not a bit special, just one of those students from the south.

Turid attended and finished the Seminar in Camphill, Aberdeen, and worked in the schools. She was asked by Hans-Heinrich Engel to work at Glencraig in Northern Ireland. She and Hans-Heinrich Engel, former husband of Margit Engel, were married there. In 1968, Turid and Saralies van der Briel became joint principals, and from 1975 Turid had this responsibility on her own. In 1979 she handed over her task to others and accepted an invitation to join Humanus Haus in Switzerland, where her husband had died in 1973.
AUTOBIOGRAPHICAL

Alice Schwabe

September 11, 1931 – December 21, 2005

Ever since I knew Alice after my arrival in 1966 in Camphill Beaver Run, North America, I experienced her great longing for improvement. Improving herself, others, conditions of poverty and suffering. In short, to make life a better place. It brought results. The children, now adults whom she taught in school will surely not forget her.

During the last few years Alice painted many pictures. For several months Joan Allen hung a collection of these paintings on the walls of the foyer in Kepler House, Kimberton Hills Village. I always looked at them when I came to the Village, two or three times a week. Gradually the colours of these paintings became, for me, worthy of an inner celebration.

We do not always meet another person's soul through words. It was as if now Alice's had begun to fulfil her longing to make life a better place. Not so much through conversation but through her loving connection to the colours of her paintings. I feel that from here on it gives a new meaning to her life.

CHRISTL BENDER
From Camphill Correspondence, *2006/3.*

Erika von Arnim

July 8, 1918 – July 17, 2007

Born in 1918 as the first of four siblings to parents who did everything they could for their children, I had a special task in the family. As my parents had difficulties with each other, time and again I tried to mediate.

When I experienced something difficult at home or elsewhere I had, as a child the inner experience: "What happens in the day is not the real truth; what happens in the night when the stars are shining in the heavens and our angel comes — that is the truth, that is real."

After my Protestant confirmation I taught younger children in Sunday school. My time of adolescence was free of outer pressures, and I enjoyed parties and dancing. After completing the dancing lessons my partner and I went in for competitions and won prizes.

My father owned a factory in Pforzheim, Germany, producing jewellery; he travelled much and looked to me to continue his work later on.

I enjoyed my time in primary school and secondary school for girls, which was followed by a commercial school. After completing school I worked in my father's business. When of age I went on business trips throughout Germany and Austria on my own. These were interesting but sometimes difficult.

Throughout my school days I had many friends, in particular one girlfriend who tragically lost her life in the ruins of her house when shot by a low-flying aircraft. I also lost my only brother at Stalingrad and a younger sister in childbirth.

None of my family supported the Nazi regime, although I briefly attended the Hitler Jugend. We were all shocked by the Nazi policies and the disappearances of Jewish friends.

At the beginning of the Second World War, I offered myself for nurses service and was trained and placed in different military hospitals. I eventually took a course for staff nurses and was placed as charge nurse in a hospital for officers. It was there that I experienced the end of the war.

My parents had lost their home and factory in an air raid and moved into the country. On joining them I became a village teacher and was later transferred to a town. The trained teachers had been obliged to join the Nazi party and were now dismissed by the occupying forces. I received in-service training at weekends.

The parental business and dwelling house was rebuilt and I could live at home again. Many new friendships developed. I was searching for inner certainties. One teacher insisted that everything in man is biologically determined. Another teacher gave me a book on yoga of which I only remember a concluding sentence: "I am and will be for ever!" A teacher of the rebuilt Pforzheim Waldorf School told me of Pilgramshain (one of the first anthroposophical curative-educational homes) where he had worked together with Dr Karl König.

Some time earlier, at my sister's wedding I had heard for the first time very briefly from our host something about anthroposophy. My family had no knowledge or interest in it.

I had become motivated to attend the introductory course held in the Waldorf School in Stuttgart and also bought and read with great interest the basic books by Rudolf Steiner. This brought about a real new beginning.

In 1950 I became a member of the Anthroposophical Society and hosted anthroposophical group meetings in my home. I had the deeply stirring experience: "I have to change my life!"

On a visit to the Sonnenhof curative home at Arlesheim, Switzerland, I had talks with the director, Mr Pache, about joining his curative educational work. He offered me a place and looked forward to my coming.

In a suburb of Pforzheim I walked on a pavement (I still remember the spot) when a bright ray of light entered and surrounded me, a very real experience, when again with inner certainty I became conscious: "I have to change my life," but this time accompanied almost audibly by: "Karl König!"

After this experience I wrote to him and asked to be accepted to Camphill. His positive answer came promptly. I arrived by plane in Aberdeen in September 1951.

Although my decision was a disappointment to the Sonnenhof, in retrospect I knew that it was the right and necessary decision I had taken. I had an experience of grace in this real experience of light.

My first task in Scotland was caring for many spastic children in Heathcot house. It was truly a new life. I slept together with a group of Down's syndrome children in the same room. Carlo Pietzner and Janet McGavin were responsible for the house and children. Among the co-workers were Taco Bay and his wife-to-be, Ita. Several of the seminarists whom I met at that time helped later on to build up the work in Brachenreuthe and Föhrenbühl.

Later on I worked in Murtle and Newton Dee and for the last two years I was responsible for Camphill House. I had many new and valuable experiences, including the Bible Evenings and gatherings of the Community: a new Christian path. At Whitsun 1954 I held my first children's service. I had also joined the First Class.

Karl König and I had several talks about the future of Camphill. He expressed how important it would be for Middle Europe if Camphill could be established there. In the West much had been established and formed. Middle Europe, whence the founders of Camphill had come was of great importance for what was still in the lap of the future in the East. Several times he addressed me personally: "Erika, that will be a task for you to start our work there!"

In spring 1958 a former German co-worker of Camphill made Karl König aware of a property for rent close to Lake Constance — Brachenreuthe. Karl König arranged for a visit and was impressed by what he saw and later asked me, together with others trained in Camphill centres, to return to Germany and start the work there. In 1964 he and Alix Roth moved to Brachenreuthe, for what became the last phase of his life. I drove Karl König to many venues for lectures and meetings. This gave the opportunity for lengthy and meaningful talks.

After some years Föhrenbühl came on the market. On our visit we found it very suitable. In June 1963 I was able to sign the contract and move into the house with the first children and co-workers. We were soon joined by teachers, therapists and artists.

The title of Karl König's first lecture at Föhrenbühl was "Mankind at the Threshold." An extraordinary time had begun of establishing home-life, school, seminar, the celebration of festivals and arranging for events with large numbers of visitors. It was special to have Karl König and Alix living so close by.

A year later Georg von Arnim joined us as a doctor from Camphill, Scotland, where he had stayed for two years with his family. With him a very intensive time of development began in many spheres.

On March 28, 1965 important talks took place between Karl König and the leadership of the Anthroposophical Society. He noted: "This indeed was a blessed day. An open and full conversation took place."

In the night of March 27, 1966 Georg was called to Karl König's bedside; he had suffered a stroke. He died the following morning just during the time when the Sunday services were being held.

The time surrounding Karl König's funeral was very special. A priest of the Christian Community, Rudolf Meyer, who was deeply befriended with Karl König referred to him at the memorial evening, saying: "He was a brother to all men!" These words were spoken out of the hearts of everyone present and beyond. His passing had an impact on all our lives.

Georg and I carried on working closely together, also with our co-workers and friends on the further development of Föhrenbühl. New houses and the Hall of Childhood were built and the garden enlarged. Georg and I went on several journeys to Camphill places in South Africa, Scandinavia and USA. These were intensive years of working and learning together. We married in 1968.

Georg's oncoming illness brought for me — and others — new tasks. His death on November 7, 2000 was a deep shock.

My responsibilities included involvement in many Camphill-regional councils and liaison with the curative-educational movement and the Medical Section at the Goetheanum as well as meetings for religious teaching and services.

I can look back on a long biography rich in events, but learning about the love for truth, beauty and goodness never comes to an end.

AUTOBIOGRAPHICAL
Translated by Johannes Surkamp.

Georg Ehrenfried von Arnim

September 26, 1920 – November 7, 2000

Georg von Arnim started his life on the family farm Gross-Marschwitz in Silesia, not far from Breslau. His father Ehrenfried died soon after in 1921 from war wounds. The following years were then rather tumultuous. For instance, his mother's second marriage to Albrecht, Count Keyserlingk, took him for some years to a coffee farm in Angola and then to a number

of different places in Germany. In the Second World War Georg von
Arnim became an army officer leading troops into Russia, where he was
wounded several times and taken prisoner. After the war he studied elec-
tronics but due to ill health he had to stop. After 1947 he began studying
medicine, and as a student found his way to anthroposophy.

Georg worked as a paediatrician in various hospitals and built up his
own practice in Stuttgart before moving to Scotland in 1962 to work with
the circle of doctors around Dr König. There it was that he could extend
his healing impulse into education, community building and questions of
destiny. Camphill became his home.

At the end of 1964 Karl König asked him to move to Lake Constance
to help Erika Sautter, who later became his wife. She had been instrumental in the founding of Camphill work in Germany, with Brachenreuthe in
1958 and then from 1963 in Föhrenbühl. It was a deep wish of Karl König
that the Camphill impulse should take root in geographical middle
Europe.

For Georg a time of intensive pioneering, medical work and research
began as the middle European region expanded, the community in
Föhrenbühl became the biggest school of the Camphill movement and the
curative seminar developed. At the same time he was continuously
involved in the social process of the whole Camphill movement, active in
the creation of the movement group, for instance; and was one of the small

group that prepared and founded in 1979 the International Conference for Curative Education and Social Therapy. This, and his intensive involvement with the leaders at the Goetheanum, can also be seen as a direct continuation of tasks that lay close to Karl König's heart.

Only recently have we realized how much activity Georg actually engendered, particularly in the 1960s and seventies, in seeing children and in lecturing, not just at Lake Constance but also in many other places and countries. He continued working with doctors, therapists, eurythmists and teachers in Berlin and South Africa. One should especially mention the courses for speech therapists that started in Dornach and then took place regularly in Föhrenbühl.

Georg had little time to devote to writing, and his modest manner did not lead him to write books. It has become clear that so much potential in many fields relating to our work had not found its way into publication. It was decided to gather what material could be found in order to publish it for Georg's eightieth birthday.*

Although Georg had been so ill for many years his death took friends and family by surprise. It was not planned that his son from his first marriage, Christian, who lives in Scotland, should have been there at the time, but he was one of those able to be at the bedside. November 7, 2000, was an unusually radiant day and from the moment of Georg's passing, golden evening light grew in the room. Once more one could experience the pertinence of the situation, which arises at the gate of death. That mood which Georg had often brought to experience for others and sometimes expressed in consultative conversations was something which he had carried through the years of illness: confidence in the wisdom of destiny.

Georg was an individual who always prepared his steps carefully — every word and deed was thoughtfully chosen. One was often struck and inspired by the modesty and at the same time certainty. Often neither deed nor word was necessary — his very presence could sometimes solve problems, calm emotions or part the essential from the inessential. The quality of light and warmth that he brought into each encounter was mirrored in the elements during those three days. Before the funeral took place a calm, shining rainbow appeared in the sky.

RICHARD STEEL
From Camphill Correspondence, *2001/2.*

---

* Bewegung, Sprache, Denkkraft. Der geistige Impuls der Heilpädagogik, *(Movement, speech, strength of thought: the spiritual impulse of curative education) edited by Richard Steel.*

Louisa van der Meulen

October 14, 1934 – January 13, 2004

Louisa had a way of turning challenges into creative projects, throwing herself utterly into things and producing a work of art, be it aesthetic or social. In a way, that was how she approached her illness and her death. When in Park Attwood Clinic she befriended a fellow nurse convalescing there and spoke to her about Copake and our nursing needs. A few years later, sure enough, Anke Smeele came to Copake. Louisa had handpicked her successor. Anke had a year or so to settle in the village, and then Louisa fell ill again and Anke began to take on the nursing tasks. For the next year, the friendship developed and deepened as the torch of the Camphill nursing stream was passed on. As Louisa weakened, Anke was more and more involved with her care. And it was Anke who made it possible for Louisa to spend her last weeks on earth at home in the village, through her devoted nursing care.

When Louisa knew that the end was nigh, she knew exactly how she wanted to proceed. She got a group together to work through all sorts of practical details. When she no longer could take in any nutrients or even hold down water, she went into hospital but stayed there only long enough to be stabilized and strengthened. She spoke to the doctors and hospice people explaining that she could have a good quality of life at home for her last few weeks, and then she came home in time for Christmas. She saw so many people, engaging in deep and inspiring conversations. She gave things away as Christmas gifts to some of her dear former pupils, house-mates and friends. She made little paintings for others. She heard music, had an evening of jokes and laughter, an afternoon of poetry, a daily reading of a lecture from a cycle by Rudolf Steiner. For three weeks she lived solely on a saline drip and morphine. From where did her strength and energy come? And she talked so fearlessly of the future — without an ounce of sentimentality — that her bearing called that forth in others. I have never seen such a dry-eyed passing for someone so utterly beloved. And so the Muse continues her task, inspiring others by her example to do what we have to do with beauty and enthusiasm, inviting us to come closer to the threshold, with certainty and joy.

WANDA ROOT
From Camphill Correspondence, *2004/3.*

Gabor Tallo

February 11, 1910 – December 26, 1978

Born of Jewish parents in Brezno, then in Hungary but now part of the Slovakia, Gabor grew up and was educated in Budapest. After leaving school at a rather early age he went to Gent, Belgium and started studying architecture, but after a year moved to Vienna where he added art to his studies. During this time in Vienna he met anthroposophy through Professor Wannemaker and his daughter. In 1931 at the age of 21, having completed his studies, he went to Dornach where he worked for several years, and where he also became interested in sculpture, working both with stone and wood. During this time it was found that he had severe type 1 diabetes (a disease from which his younger brother had died when Gabor was ten years old) and was admitted to Arlesheim Clinic where he was given insulin injections. After Dornach he went to Genoa, Italy, where he practised for two years in partnership with a local architect.

Always somewhat of a wanderer, but also very sensitive to the atmosphere which was then building up in Europe, he emigrated to South Africa in 1936, taking a re-qualifying exam in Architecture and working in both Johannesburg and Pretoria. During the war, unable to join the army due to

his illness, he became a government censor. These early years in South Africa also saw him developing as an artist, holding many exhibitions of his charcoal and pastel studies of Africans, landscapes and later oils. He was fascinated by the variety and vastness of the South African land-scapes, the barrenness of the Karroo and the ever-changing lights and colours. In 1943 he moved to Cape Town where he found employment as an architect with Cape Town City Council. Such employment totally frus-trated his creative abilities and it was during this time that he built up his reputation as an artist. On his marriage in 1945 to Joan Thompson, a law student at the University of Cape Town, he started his own practice in architecture, and then almost entirely gave up his painting and drawing, as he felt unable to carry both art and architecture.

Always very conscious of his allegiance to anthroposophy, he was a founder member of the Anthroposophical Society of South Africa.

In 1957 Gabor met Dr Karl König who was on his first visit to South Africa. From the very first telephone conversation between these two, the deep connection which they had became apparent. Together with Dr König, Gabor designed the first of his Camphill houses at Dawn Farm, Hermanus. But his severe diabetes had begun to take its toll and from that year he began to suffer from diabetic gangrene and circulation trouble. His left foot was badly affected and at Easter 1958 he was admitted to Groote Schuur hospital where a young and enterprising surgeon "worked on him" for three months in order to save the foot and leg. It was obvious during this time that the whole pattern of Gabor's life would have to change, as he could no longer continue his architectural work with a very real split between his idealism and the demands of commercial architecture. He spoke then about devoting his life to art and living away from the stresses and strains of city life and moving to Basutoland (now Lesotho), but a letter from Dr König arrived almost on the day he left hospital inviting him to join Camphill in Great Britain as its architect, and within a few months, on November 1, 1958, he joined Camphill in Scotland with his wife and two children.

Gabor's fight against ill health continued throughout the remaining years of his life; gangrenous infection in his left leg resulted in the loss of a large part of his foot. And in 1968 the infection started in the right foot resulting in amputation at the end of the year. He always lived in fear of further infection and of blindness as he suffered for many years from haemorrhages in both eyes, but he was spared the loss of his sight. His whole life was devoted to his architecture and during the last three years the greatest pain of all he suffered when he was no longer able to work. In some manner he coped with his physical condition, but not with the loss of his ability to work.

JOAN TALLO
From Camphill Correspondence, *1979/3.*

Gabor Tallo meant a tremendous amount for the life and development of Camphill. Numerous houses were designed for Camphill in Britain, first by him alone, then in co-operation with Joan Allen. The peak of his life were the years he and his wife worked in Camphill in Scotland, while Dr König was still alive, and the culmination of this was the designing with Dr König of the Hall in Murtle in 1962. This hall was at the same time the Camphill movement hall which inspired the designs of all the other Camphill halls.

PETER ROTH
From Camphill Correspondence, *1979/3.*

Joan Elizabeth Tallo

September 19, 1922 – June 6, 2004

On the evening of the June 6, 2004, Joan Tallo slipped peacefully over the threshold. She was in Aberdeen Royal Infirmary having been admitted with a stomach ulcer just a couple of days before. She was 81 years old.

Born on September 19, 1922, in Johannesburg, South Africa, Joan was the younger of two sisters. Pamela, two years her elder, was never really close, although they remained in periodic contact right until Joan's death. Joan's father, Arthur Clement Thompson, was born in England but brought up in South Africa. He studied law at Cambridge, where he also met his future wife, Phyllis Truman. He qualified as a barrister, becoming Attorney General for the British Protectorate areas of Southern Africa (now Botswana, Lesotho and Swaziland). For this work, he was made a Q.C. and knighted.

Joan and Pam grew up as fairly privileged among the elite of South Africa. She attended Kingsmead School for Girls, a school modelled after the English public schools (private schools primarily intended for children of the upper classes) founded by her grandfather in Johannesburg. By this time, her aunt Doris had become headmistress, something which Joan always found difficult, being the granddaughter of the founder and the niece of the headmistress! She had a carefree childhood and youth, looked after by a nanny and protected from much of the hardship around her at the time. At the same time, her family held quite liberal views regarding Apartheid; this was to follow Joan all her years. She went to parties, went riding and played sports such as lacrosse and tennis. By all accounts she was a popular girl, well aware of her beauty and with many friends of both sexes. She learnt early to get what she wanted from her father, always maintaining a certain coolness and distance from her mother. She spoke many times in later life how she wished that she had had better contact with her mother.

After her matriculation, Joan quickly decided to follow in her father's footsteps and studied law at the University of Cape Town. At that time, it was not the career choice for women; only once before in South African history had a woman qualified as a barrister. In the fifty or so years since then, women were encouraged to take their place primarily as a wife and mother. After her much publicized graduation in 1946, Joan found the male dominance overwhelming, and she stopped practising shortly after 1950. Although admitted to the Bar of the South African High Court, she was only offered divorce cases! She felt for the rest of her life that she had become a victim of male prejudice.

In 1943, on her twenty-first birthday, she met her future husband Gabor Tallo. A mutual friend arranged a blind date, thinking that they would be good for each other. How right he was! Gabor was every-thing that was foreign to Joan: he was a struggling artist and architect, penniless, and what was perhaps even harder for her family to accept, he was a Jewish Hungarian refugee! After living together for a year or so, they married on the January 24, 1945. Their daughter, Michèle, was born at the end of October 1945. After a short break, Joan went back to university to complete her degree. On her graduation, the press in Cape Town made much of the young mother receiving her degree with

a daughter on her arm! Her second child, John Peter, was born in January 1950.

It was after this that she decided to stop practising law. She now turned her energies to various projects; growing flowers for the Cape Malay women to sell in the market in Cape Town; a chicken farm producing oven-ready birds for the best hotels and restaurants. From this time, her love of gardening developed to follow her all through her life. Between 1945 and 1958, Joan and Gabor built no less than three houses, often doing much of the work themselves. In the last house, in the affluent Cape Town suburb of Constantia, they lived for less than six years. While struggling with little money, they led a life with a rich social interchange with friends. Life seemed, during the 1950s, to be full of promise. On the other hand, their marriage was always a stormy one, rows often resulting in Gabor walking out for a day or two. But they always made up in the end, remaining together right up to Gabor's death in 1978.

Gabor had met anthroposophy in the early 1930s, studying sculpture and architecture in Dornach, Switzerland. So it was through him that Joan first came into contact with the work of Rudolf Steiner. For Joan, it was especially the lectures on world economy and social structure that caught her attention. All through her life she returned to these questions time and again.

The contact with Camphill came about in the mid-fifties when Dr Karl König was invited to South Africa to visit the small newly started curative school at Dawn Farm, Hermanus, in the Cape. Gabor had designed their first house, Roberts House, and Dr König asked if he would not be willing to move to Camphill in Aberdeen to help with the design of a new Hall for the growing Camphill movement. In October 1958, after selling up their home and most of their possessions, the family set sail for Europe and Camphill. For Joan, this was a major step as she had hardly been out of South Africa, and certainly not to Europe. It was on a damp and dreary day in November that the family arrived in Aberdeen to be met at the railway station by Thomas Weihs.

Gabor quickly became involved in design and building work, while Joan joined the Seminar for Curative Education as well as working in the weavery in Cairnlee. The family lived at that time in just two rooms in the old Cairnlee Cottage. During those first months in Cairnlee, Joan and the children experienced a snowy Scottish winter for the first time.

In 1960, Dr König asked Joan to take on legal and financial advisory work for the young Camphill Village Trust, so the family moved to 122 Harley Street in the centre of London, where the Camphill Village Trust had its registered office at the time. She was soon joined by Ann Harris with whom she had a close working relationship and friendship for much of her active life in Camphill. By 1964 it became clear that a larger property would be needed not far from London, and Delrow House, 21 miles north of London was purchased. Until 1969 this was to be the Tallo family's home. After these five pioneer years in Delrow, Joan and Gabor moved to Botton Village, where they lived for another seven years. In many ways, these were happy years, with Joan running a house, while Gabor established the Camphill Architects office in what had been a garage.

With Gabor's worsening health in 1976, it became a necessity to move to a milder climate, so the Grange became home for Joan and Gabor until Gabor's death in the early hours of Boxing Day, 1978. Although the years had in many ways been stormy ones for Joan and Gabor, their love for each other had kept them together.

Now, with Gabor's passing over the threshold after many years of ill health, Joan found that for the first time she could go where she liked. This was not easy for her; she soon moved back to Delrow, taking on a house and continuing with her work for the Camphill Village Trust and other companies within Camphill. As the years passed she relinquished being a house-parent and started the long process of entering retirement. She moved several times within Delrow, each time living on her own accompanied by a co-worker or two.

It was only after her stroke in 1997 while on holiday in Tunisia that she was finally forced to give up all her work for the Camphill Village Trust. The last seven years of her life were increasingly difficult as she fought against increasing dependence on others for her daily needs. The stroke left her unable to read; this was probably the one disability that bothered her most. During her last five years Joan lived in Simeon Houses on Cairnlee Estate in Aberdeen. Shortly after her stroke, Joan spent some time in St Devenicks on Murtle Estate at the same time as Sigrid Hansmann. They became close friends, supporting each other through ups and downs until Sigrid's passing over the threshold just three weeks before Joan.

From early in the 1950s when she met the work of Rudolf Steiner right up to her death, Joan lived for anthroposophy. She was widely read and, as in other aspects of her life, she interpreted things for herself and was not always tolerant of others, especially when they did not speak from own experience. This often led to difficult situations, something which bothered her all her life. In later years this became a little easier for her but always played into her relationships with others. She had many friends but always felt lonely. Joan was proud of her family, especially her six grand-children and three great-grandchildren. She had high expectations for both her children, trying to support and help them always, even when this was not appreciated by them. At the same time she could be playful and open, and the family have many fond memories of joyful family occasions. Whether ruefully or joyfully, Joan will be missed by the very many peo-ple she came into contact with during her life. Even those who battled most with her will miss her. At the time of passing she was ready and wait-ing with something akin to eagerness for the event.

JOHN TALLO
From Camphill Correspondence, *2004/5.*

Agnete von Zschok

July 15, 1931 – August 21, 1978

Agnete's crossing of the threshold was a sudden one: instant death brought about by the collision of her car with a bus. The accident occurred on an outing in Scotland. One of her passengers died a fortnight later; the other survived with multiple fractures.

Agnete, the youngest of three children, was born in Germany. Her father, an army officer and writer of religious poems, was from an old aristocratic family. Her mother was of Hungarian descent from East Prussia who, before her marriage, was an active teacher and writer.

Agnete's childhood was spent in Dresden, where she also experienced the beginning of the war. The sudden death of her mother was a great shock to the twelve-year-old girl. At the time Agnete was in hospital with scarlet fever. Only on her return home did she find that her mother was no longer with them. A year later the father married again; this was not a happy situation for Agnete. When she was fourteen her father was taken prisoner at the eastern front, her brother was missing and the sister was no longer living at home. The war years were a time of loneliness and anxiety for Agnete in which she joined a voluntary corps that provided help for people who had suffered bombing.

After the war her sister had come into contact with anthroposophy and arranged for Agnete to attend the Waldorf School in Stuttgart for the last two classes. In 1949 Agnete went to England as a working student in Hawkwood College, and it was during this time that she paid her first visit to Camphill. After the completion of her nurse's training at the Royal Hospital in London, Agnete became pregnant, returned to Germany where her son, Reinhard, was born.

In 1958 Agnete came to the Sheiling School in Ringwood, where she joined the training course and decided to become a curative teacher. Her teaching was stimulated and enriched by her great enthusiasm for the subjects she taught and by her loving interest in each child in her class. Her artistic abilities, especially for craft-work, painting and drawing were a great asset.

Agnete was a very sociable person who showed a great concern for the well being of others. The marriage of her son in 1977 was one of the happiest events of her life.

Agnete has devoted twenty years to the work and aims of the Camphill movement, a work in which she found joy and fulfilment.

MARIANNE GORGE
From Camphill Correspondence, *1978/10.*

My strongest memory of Agnete relates to our first meeting; it was, as they say in the old song, "seeing her across a crowded room." Vibrant life forces were at work within her and were immediately visible, and her smile showed unreserved joy.

Agnete never tried to ease her own path; on the contrary she was constantly alert to new challenges, especially in her work with the children. In her class she always had room for one more child, provided of course that he or she was difficult. It was the same in her house; if there was one girl with an especially difficult history, Agnete's Herculean strength couldn't wait to come to grips with this destiny. She saw each new challenge as a growing point for her class or the members of her house, and the other children seemed aware of this and supported her. Under her influence the girls and the cottage bloomed, the floors shone, flowers and plants blossomed, and beautiful and well-chosen pictures appeared in all the right places.

JEAN BELL
From Camphill Correspondence, *1978/10.*

Lieven Blockhuys

April 29, 1904 – May 11, 1987

The details I know of Lieven's life are but scant and yet I feel compelled to speak of him. Lieven was Belgian, born in Ghent. He became a biodynamic gardener and came to Camphill in 1956 with an impulse to develop biodynamic gardening through community living.

I last met Lieven two years before he died when he invited me to supper in his rooms at the Hermannsberg, Germany. He had cooked supper himself, clad in an apron, standing as tall as an oak tree and full of vitality. I thought: he has the strength to outlive us all. He shared with me both a delicious supper as well as his experiences of the living Christ, delivered in a great voice at great speed — indeed a rich supper.

For those who worked with Lieven there were wonderful moments of instruction when the fullness of his insight into nature poured forth with great generosity, and there were many happy memories of his teaching. One only has to remember Lieven's titanic labour in transforming the landscape around Murtle Hall to be filled anew with awe at this man's magical strength and rapport with trees and plants.

When he came to Camphill with his wife and two children he had a powerful encounter with Dr König from whom he received a task, which became a driving force in his Camphill life. When one saw Dr König and Lieven together they seemed like two kings in communion: the one having gone through the transformation of much that he brought with him from earlier existence to make him a healer and helper of men; the other having perhaps brought too much with him, which made him a magician in the world of plants, but often proud and at variance with the human world.

When Lieven then moved to Germany and acquired the Hermannsberg, he had hoped he would have been able to realize Dr König's ideals of true land-based village life, but he became less and less able to convey the peculiar alchemy that passed between the two "kings" and his latter years were increasingly ones of disappointment, misunderstanding and friction.

In some of us there arose a concern that Lieven would leave life in the same mood of intractability and pride in which he had isolated himself in later years. But then a wonderful thing happened: returning from an examination by his doctor who pronounced him fit except for ischial pains, Lieven then went for a cure; but he returned early saying that he was ready to die, and after ten days he did, peacefully in the early hours of May 11, 1987, at the age of 83.

ANKE WEIHS
From Camphill Correspondence, *1987/5.*

Peter Elsholtz

April 22, 1932 – November 10, 2002

Peter's parents were actors in Dresden, although Berlin was their real home. Life was hard from the start. His father was a successful and renowned actor, always busy and on the move. His young mother could not carry her responsibility of bringing up a child while following the glittering life of the theatre. She died when Peter was only three months old.

His father remarried and Peter had two half-sisters. His education suffered through the war years. For ten years of his childhood he was taken in by an aunt, who was a eurythmist at the Lauenstein, an anthroposophical home for mentally handicapped children. So, early on Peter encountered children with special needs. He experienced the Children's service and the wholesome, rhythmical life of an anthroposophical institution.

His birth had been a Caesarean; he had problems with his feet and needed special boots. It was as if he had difficulties being fully on the earth. He had a dreamy childhood, protected from much that could have harmed his soul. Peter was very open to, and seemed to live very close to, the other world.

As a young man Peter worked in Hamburg and spent his spare time enjoying music and going to concerts. He took evening classes to catch up with an academic education. Then he heard of Karl König and the possibility of Camphill work without the need for formal training. He joined the community at Ringwood in England, where he met Susanne, in 1959. They later married and had four children and ten grandchildren. Peter and Susanne founded the Camphill Community Duffcarrig in 1972, a small-holding in County Wexford, Ireland, where Peter was the farmer as well as carrying much of the administration.

Later in Camphill Hermanus, South Africa, he worked with bio-dynamic principles on the land, including a herb garden. He loved music and attended concerts whenever he had the chance. In the last two years of his life a love for the composer Mahler grew. Peter once said that he would have liked to be a composer or conductor! This would fit with his all-encompassing consciousness. He was a great supporter of anthroposophical work, and was a service holder.

Peter had a big circle of friends. He was able to raise any occasion to a special level with his warmth and human interest. Personally, I especially valued Peter's help and advice, in particular in forming my decision to go into the priesthood in the Christian Community. Out of an anthroposophical perspective and out of living a Christian life that recognizes Christ as the Lord of Karma, Peter could be totally at peace with what life had brought.

PETER HOLMAN
From Camphill Correspondence, *2003/2.*

Kaarina Heimsch

October 12, 1933

I was born in Helsinki and grew up in a nearby town where my father was a teacher and principal of a big school. During the war years my two brothers and I spent the summers in different parts of Sweden. I was sent there to begin with to have treatment for tuberculosis. These years gave me an important experience of a different culture and language, as well as making me more independent and opening my eyes to seeing the world and Finland in a new light.

In 1957 I was chosen as one of twelve youngsters by the Rotary Club to receive a stipend to travel to Germany where we could attend a Steiner residential school in Bielefeld and journey around in Northern Germany.

I met Steiner pedagogy which was a revelation to me. As well as seeing the ruined cities such as Hamburg and Hanover, it was my first meeting with the name Rudolf Steiner. The way of teaching and the social life between the teachers and pupils impressed me deeply.

Back home I was asked to relate my experiences to the class in school. I did so with great enthusiasm. The teacher's response was a great shock. He more or less threw me out scornfully and accused me of arrogance: how dare I speak like that!

I did not say a word; in that moment I decided to swallow my anger and keep my experience hidden in my heart for a more receptive understanding.

During my school time I did a lot of reading of both history and literature, including Schopenhauer, Kierkegaard, Kant and Buddhism. I played the piano, and in fact wanted to study music, but I had to give up the playing because of an illness of the wrists which took years to heal. I continued my studies for two years in a teachers' college in the north of Finland. After finishing I got a good job as a class teacher in my father's school.

I lived at home with my parents. I loved the school and the children, but one morning it suddenly struck me painfully that I could not face these children and take responsibility for their destinies and unfolding development because I did not know enough about the human being. I had to do something else, find another way.

During the years of my study I had got to know a person who was a member of the Rosicrucian Brotherhood. We had long talks and in this connection he always tried to make me aware that for the sake of my future I would have to go away from home to find my own life, to prepare myself for the task I had in my destiny.

Through his advice and help I got a scholarship to go for a year to the USA to study different ways of teaching music to children.

I left in spring 1956, but my mother came with me, because my parents thought it better that I should not go alone. Thus I spent a year in Michigan, took courses in the Teachers' College of Marguette, lived a student's life and worked to earn money for my expenses. It was an interesting time with many journeys. But in May of the following year a forceful impression arose within me: "I have to leave quickly and go back to Europe!" I felt that I was being tempted, swallowed up and invaded by what was to me a strange being, called America, and I had to leave before it was too late. I felt I did not have the strength to stand up against it alone. My mother and friends tried to convince me that I should stay at least until July to the end of the term. But I felt that my life was at stake and we booked the next boat from New York to Liverpool and sailed back across an Atlantic as smooth as a sheet of glass, in contrast to the outward voyage with terrible storms and drifting icebergs.

Back home I took up my teaching post anew but the need "to do something else" grew stronger and stronger. My Rosicrucian friend wanted to meet me, but I said that I first wanted to become clear about my future. Soon after this he suddenly died.

One morning after breakfast I opened the daily newspaper and read an advertisement: "American Airlines seeking young Finnish women to train in New York as air hostesses." I applied with the result that out of four hundred applicants twelve were chosen, and I was one of them. Before I was to travel in late 1958 to enter the course, I spent the summer in the country. We received a phone-call from my brother that he had met a couple who looked "in need of special care." My brother, speaking English and always outgoing, had talked to them and it became clear that these two people had run out of money; they wanted to see Finland by hitch-hiking but got stuck and did not know what to do and where to turn. My brother invited them to our place and told them that his mother would feed and look after them and they would see real Finnish country life. They were very happy and, indeed, appeared one day at our doorsteps: Karin von Schilling and Michael Lauppe.

I was ill in bed with temperature at that moment. My mother received them, speaking Finnish and with hands and feet but called me down to help. They stayed for some days, though I don't remember much of it. Later, after their departure I began to receive post from Michael. He apologized for writing to me so directly but felt that I should come to see Camphill. He sent me Steiner's *Calender of the Soul,* written in his own hand in a beautiful book and also *How to attain Knowledge of Higher Worlds* and many descriptions of their life in Scotland.

I was very interested but I told him then that I had applied for a course in New York which would start around Christmas time but I would consider coming later on.

Christmas 1958 was coming; I had started packing and was prepared to leave when American Airlines in Helsinki called, saying that I would have to wait for the next course starting in March 1959. For me there was no way of turning back. I had arranged to leave for something new, and it flashed into my mind that instead of America, I could go for half a year to Scotland. I phoned Michael and said that I would not come for Christmas but straight after.

He tried to persuade me to spend Christmas in Scotland but I kept to my decision: Christmas at home. Later on I grasped, of course, why he would have liked me to spend Christmas in Camphill.

So in January 1959 I flew to London. Meeting some Camphill co-workers at Harley Street, I joined the children's transport, remembering nothing except Harley Street and my arrival in Camphill on January 7. I stepped out of the bus at Camphill House, saw the Highland landscape in wintry morning light, and I was convinced that I knew this place, I had been here before. In a clear dream at the age of seventeen I had been in that place. This was quite a revelation and I felt inwardly happy.

I had started on the path of incarnation into Camphill and into my own true self. I had never really met a handicapped child before, despite being a teacher. It was a journey into a new land, every day bringing new revelations on all levels. Often when I felt lost I found a firm inner or outer anchor-point in human encounters, children, nature, festivals, lectures, or daily events. All the while the conviction grew within me, "This must be my way." Dreams and soul experiences further convinced me.

The intended half year extended to a stay of $5^{1}/_{2}$ years in Scotland. Dr

König and Alix Roth also lived in Camphill House and my meetings with them were decisive. When I sat down with Dr König and looked into his eyes I "recognized" him, and then I just knew that I had come to the right place!

Here I could learn to meet my real task and to grow strong enough to answer the deepest longing of my heart: to find the Christ and put myself at the service of the Finnish folk spirit. This is how I then felt. Finally one had to divest oneself of all personal longings and wishes, "burn all bridges behind, just trust in the spirit, go forward and destiny will tell you what to do." These words of Dr König gave me courage to stay and to meet myself and my destiny.

Early on Margit Engel asked me, "How do you like anthroposophy?"

I said I did not know what it was.

She said, "It is the way we try to live."

Then the name Rudolf Steiner rose up in my memory from the experience nine years earlier in Germany, and the enthusiasm I then experienced resurrected from deep in my soul. Through the Camphill life, the Bible Evenings, lectures, seminar, the children, the services and through the Camphill library, new clarity came and new ground was conquered to stand upon. The process included, even physically, much that could be called catharsis. After two years I fell very ill, had to be sent to hospital and was then strictly ordered by Dr König to rest in bed.

In these three months I read, of course, half the library. When Alix Roth saw in my hands *The Chymical Wedding of Christian Rosenkreutz,* she said, "Now you can get up."

Rather weakened I was granted a long summer holiday in Finland, but Dr König looked into my eyes and said, "If you don't come back, I will come myself to fetch you." He knew, of course, how my heart was longing to do something in Finland. Obediently I returned on his birthday September 25, 1960 and when I shook hands with him, tears just poured out. He hugged me and said: "I am happy that you are here. I know how you feel but things will be alright."

I knew that I had crossed a bridge and freed myself to follow my true calling. I had been asked in Helsinki Steiner School to take the first class. I had been introduced to Sylvia-koti which was then in existence near Helsinki and I told Dr König of these possibilities to start the work in Finland. Much later I heard that Carita Steinbäck, the director of Sylvia-koti, wrote to Dr König and asked if he could send me to help establish the curative work in Finland.

Now another phase in my life in Camphill began. Dr König, in spite of his hectic life wanted to see me every week. This could not, of course happen quite regularly, because of his journeys, illness and workload. He and Alix Roth were for me the key people through whom I found my brothers and sisters in spirit, who are ever present to this very day in my life.

I was asked to take the first school class in Camphill. I also joined the Camphill Community. I had finished Camphill Seminar in $1^1/_2$ years (I missed a part because of my illness). Much later I understood that time was pressing. From early youth onwards I knew in my heart that I had a certain task. I knew that my coming to Camphill was to be a preparation for it. I was tempted to go back to Finland many times to start work there, but Dr König said, "You are not yet going anywhere. You must have a group which goes with you. Alone you will be crushed. The counterforces are too powerful in our time for one person to stand alone. Time will show what comes towards you."

I met Freddy Heimsch, and it was soon clear that our ways would go together into the future whatever it would be. Freddy and I moved to the blind children's unit with Ilse Rascher and Elisabeth Löwe to learn about the treatment and therapies for about a year. Our son, Juhani, was born December 30, 1962.

In summer 1963 my parents wanted to come to see what we were doing. I was always close to my father, and he said that once he was retired he would help us to start our work in Finland. He had been unwell with heart problems for some years but wanted to come to see Camphill before he retired. My parents came; they lived with us in the Swedish House while we were still busy with the summer conference. They met Dr König and took part in the closing festival. On Sunday afternoon, July 28, my father developed fever and died in my arms a few hours later. The funeral took place in Newton Dee and we decided that Freddy would take my mother back to Finland.

This gave him the possibility to meet Finland for the first time and having been there for two weeks he felt that he could come with me after a year and we would start to find out whether Camphill would find a footing in the country.

Dr König in the end accepted our decision to leave in April 1964, though he would have liked us to stay longer. We went with prayers and hopes in our hearts to start curative work in Finland. But we still had to find out if it was really wanted.

It was to become a testing three years of preparation. I was offered a teaching post to start English teaching in a primary school, and Freddy taught at a language school in Lahti. We gave courses to teachers about Waldorf education and in summers Freddy gave various courses. Thus we kept ourselves alive. Our family grew with a daughter 1964 and a son 1967. Life was hectic, but at all times we tried to find where an opening would be, and where people were interested in our intended work. Throughout this time we had felt all along the nearness of my father.

In March 1966 the news of Dr König's death shook us. The following night he came into my dream and comforted me and showed me everything that had to be done in Finland to make Camphill to become a reality. Next morning I woke up with joy and conviction that we were on the right path.

Soon after this we received a postcard from Dr Kari Krohn who told us to contact Carita Steinbäck who had become ill. She had carried Sylvia-koti, a home for very ill, handicapped children for ten years, trying her best to use Steiner methods with the help of curative teachers from Germany.

We went to Sylvia-Koti and after only fifteen minutes, Carita Steinbäck asked if she could give this place to us. We said that we could not jump in immediately because of our tasks elsewhere, but within a year we could start. Carita's trust was great. She had built Sylvia-koti out of love for the children and trusting in the spirit. She knew Dr König and Camphill. When she met us she handed over her life's work to us and after a few days she left and never came back to check how we continued. We kept in touch with her until her death and her greatest joy was to hear that Sylvia-koti was flourishing and had a future.

Our family had to move again to the town of Hyvinkää where Sylvia-koti was. For the last three years we had been living and working in Lahti where we had a close circle of friends who had important posts and who knew what we really wanted to do. Of course we had thought of starting with a small group of children and slowly grow to become a school, home, village, a cultural centre of activities inspired by anthroposophy. Again, confidence that this could come about came from a dream in which I saw the Sylvia-koti as it now stands: eighteen white houses on a hillside and the Sylvia-koti hall on top, crowning the hill. But this took thirty years to come about.

After we had taken over the home with thirty children, we soon realized that the big rented villa was unsuitable for a home-school. We did not find anything suitable, and had little money, but we had clear ideas what we wanted. We decided to go to the Ministry of Social Affairs in Helsinki to ask for help. When we explained our ideas, they listened politely but thought us to be unrealistic idealists. Yet slowly they listened with their hearts and began to grasp that we were speaking about something real and true. So in the end the state paid two thirds of the cost of building the new Sylvia-koti in Lahti, for 36 children.

Dr Hans-Heinrich Engel was the first one to visit us from Camphill, and we asked him to be godfather to our youngest son. Then came Gabor Tallo who made the first drawings and later worked with the Finnish architect. Unfortunately these designs were rejected on the grounds that they did not fit to the Finnish landscape. This refusal was a serious set-back, but Peter Roth's words on his later visit in 1970, were like healing medicine, "You have to build modern catacombs." So outwardly the buildings are not much different from the conventional style, but in the course of time we could reconstruct and fill the buildings with the right kind of life and spirit. Interestingly, we were allowed to keep the basic lay-out with a heart in the center and later added a protective ring around it.

Sylvia-koti has become a source of positive radiation into the surrounding. The 37 years of Camphill Seminar equipped many to take on responsibilities in the curative and Steiner-school movement. Other ventures and institutions have benefited by its existence and helped the foundation of other curative centres: Ristola, Juola, Karjalohja, Koinkoti and little Marjatta.

AUTOBIOGRAPHICAL

Freddy Heimsch

March 11, 1927

Freddy was born in Volos, Greece, and moved to Athens where he lived for ten years until he was twelve. His playgrounds were on the slopes and hillsides of the Acropolis. His father was a German businessman who started a factory in Athens. His mother, Anglo-Irish, was born in South Africa. Freddy's mother was a gifted piano player, giving concerts already as a young girl. At seventeen she visited Greece on a concert tour and met Freddy's father. Within a few weeks they were married and Freddy was born on March 11, 1927. As well as a sister he had a brother who died when he was half a year old. At home he learned English and German, and in the neighbourhood Greek When the war was approaching times became difficult for foreigners in Greece. The family decided to move back to Germany. Freddy was sent for a time to a boarding school but when he was fifteen he was called up to home defence.

Aged sixteen he was at Lake Constance near Friedrichshafen. There he met Hans Christof Valentien and they became good friends. In these chaotic times he was sent to many places and had several miraculous escapes. For example he had stopped in Dresden. It was a beautiful afternoon as he was walking around the city looking at the architecture, and he thought of staying overnight to visit the museums the following day. He cannot remember what made him change his mind, but he found himself at the packed train station when there was an announcement that a train to the west would be leaving shortly, and Freddy caught it. After a couple of hours the train had to stop. It was dark but in the east was the blood-red sky of the fire-storm of destruction raging over Dresden.

During the last days of the war he was in Berlin. The Russians were advancing in full force. Freddy was sitting in a hole when he felt he had to jump to another ditch. In the next moment a huge tree fell that would have crushed him.

The following night Freddy escaped with another young soldier. They fled from Berlin to the Elbe, using every possible means of hiding among the hundreds of thousands of refugees. They kept moving by foot, by horse carriage, by lorries, spending their nights in barns and the last night in an empty school. In the middle of the night they heard the sound of Russians approaching. In the chaos the boys escaped through the back door into the forest and bushes, running for their lives. They finally reached the Elbe on a truck crossing the last bridge still standing. On the other side they surrendered to the Americans and were taken prisoner with thousands of other soldiers. The camp was simply an open

empty field surrounded by barbed wire. It was spring and the nights were cold.

For three months they were kept in this camp, and then one morning lorries arrived and they were told that they would be transported to freedom. The lorries were loaded full with men standing. Going down a long hill the brakes failed and at a bend the lorry overturned flinging all men out. Many died or were injured. Freddy slid on his face on the grass between trees. He got up and recognized the place: it was not far from the village where his mother and sister lived. So he started running, leaving the scene behind and reached home in the afternoon, frightening his mother, dirty and smelly as he was.

He tried to get back to finish school, but those who had gone through the war had a difficult time adjusting to sitting in classes with children, three to four years younger. Freddy then decided to take a training as a radio technician, study literature and work alongside his studies. Hans Christof, whose help he asked with mathematics, told him about interesting lectures he had heard. Karl Schubert spoke of reincarnation. This event was the opening and Freddy wanted to know more. In Stuttgart there was a person to whom he was recommended. Freddy then studied the basics of anthroposophy for three years with Frau Thylmann, whose husband had been an architect and co-worker of Rudolf Steiner.

In the meantime he had finished his practical training and was offered a very good position in Telefunken. In discussion about the future Frau Thylmann said, "Why don't you go into curative education?"

At that moment he had earned enough to pay for his studies at the Sonnenhof for one year, but would have to break his studies to earn enough for the second year. Camphill offered a better prospect as the training as well as pocket money was offered. He was anyhow discontent with the money orientated society in Germany at that time.

He wrote to Scotland and the answer was that he could start immediately. He arrived on October 4, 1950. He initially lived next to the goats shed in Camphill and his first job was to stoke the kitchen stove. He worked in many estates, houses and had many tasks. He immediately sensed the importance of Camphill and wanted to know what was "behind" it. He applied to take part in the Bible Evening which was still closed at that time. In 1955 he gave his first lecture and soon became involved in finances, teaching in school and seminar, house-parenting, farming, gardening, and beekeeping. As a member of the building group he would liaise with the architect.

KAARINA HEIMSCH

Saralies van den Briel

July 11, 1930 – April 18, 1981

Saralies van den Briel was born in Holland on July 11, 1930. Her father was an officer in the Dutch army and her childhood was therefore marked by many moves from garrison to garrison. When the war broke out, her father was taken for four years to a prisoner-of-war camp in Germany, and the family went through a lot of suffering, especially hunger. After the war Saralies who was so weakened had to be transferred to a Quaker school, where the curriculum was less intense in order to finish her studies and complete her exams.

At the age of nineteen she married a young Swiss man. However, the marriage broke up and, pregnant, she returned to Holland and took up studies in photography and began a career in this field. When her son Johannes was born she had to give up her profession. During this time she met the work of Rudolf Steiner and became an ardent student of anthroposophy. One of her anthroposophical friends then advised her to meet Dr Hans-Heinrich Engel with the view to work with handicapped children. This led her to join the Camphill work in July 1959 under the guidance of Birthe Hougaard. A year later Saralies and Johannes moved to Glencraig and two years later she was joined by her father and mother. Saralies entered the work with gifts, determination and immense love and understanding for the handicapped child and his needs.

In 1968 she was asked by Dr Engel to become co-principal with Turid Engel of the Glencraig School and she carried this work with great energy, coping with the additional responsibilities after the death of Dr Engel. When the need arose to start a Rudolf Steiner School for normal children she offered to undertake this task for seven years and began with a small group of children in Autumn 1975. The school quickly outgrew its first home at Glencraig. It wandered through a number of temporary premises until through Saralies's great determination a suitable house was found and funds to purchase it were raised. This enabled the Holywood School to carry on its fast development. This task of bringing the school to life was Saralies's deepest concern and she followed up this development with extraordinary single-mindedness and energy until the school numbers had grown well beyond the hundred mark.

Then, in summer 1979, around the time of her forty-ninth birthday, her illness began to show itself, first as a hoarseness and loss of voice until it became gradually clear that it was a very rare, incurable and fatal disease. It became an immense battle for Saralies that her strong will for deeds could be used less and less. Step by step she withdrew her links with the world in which she could no longer act. The remaining connections were with her son and with the Holywood School. She was alert to the end and fought consciously to the last moment, refusing any ameliorating medication.

Only with deepest respect can one look at this life and especially at the heroic struggle of the last year. There is little doubt that during this time a human will was being re-forged in the fire of pain and suffering into a spirit will. Those who were near her could experience in the three days when her body lay in Glencraig Chapel how this new will turned immediately to new tasks, to spirit tasks.

And we, who are her friends, be it at Glencraig, be it at Holywood School, be it at the Camphill centres and all those places where the work of Rudolf Seiner is being continued, can be sure that her Michaelic spirit is ready and eager to help and battle at every place where men are willing to fulfill the Michaelic mission of this age.

BARUCH URIELI
From Camphill Correspondence, *1981/5.*

Those Who Arrived
in the Sixties

Nicholas Joiner

December 6, 1925 – March 8, 2001

Nicholas Joiner was born on St Nicholas Day, 1925, into a Dorset family of very humble circumstances. His father was an invalid from the First World War who was becoming increasingly ill and hospitalized, and the main influence in the boy's childhood was the maternal uncle who provided him with a home and family life, and also taught him various practical skills: gardening, woodwork, camping and so on. Being keen to learn both these and more academic subjects, he gained a place at Queen Elizabeth Grammar School in Wimborne, from where in due course he progressed further to Oriel College, Oxford.

By this time, however, it was the middle of the Second World War and in 1944, aged only eighteen, Nicholas enlisted in the RAF, training as a navigator in Canada from where he was then posted to South East Asia. In those days the nocturnal navigation of aircraft was done literally by the stars, and he thereby gained extensive first-hand knowledge of the heavenly constellations, which remained a life-long interest. One flight he navigated flew General Aung San, the creator of modern Burma, on his mission to persuade the northern Burmese tribes to join an independent union. Some forty years later this episode acquired a deep retrospective significance for Nicholas when the General's daughter Aung San Suu Kyi stepped forward to lead a democratic movement in the face of a repressive military junta governing her country and has been known ever since as a shining exemplar of moral courage in the political world.

After the end of the Second World War Nicholas returned to Oxford to resume his interrupted university studies. His tutor was C.S. Lewis who instilled in him a love for English poetry as well as leading him towards a Christian outlook. While at Oxford he also met Catherine who soon became his wife, and over the following years their five children were born.

In 1952 Nicholas started on his lengthy teaching career by taking a post at Thornbury Grammar School. Here he met anthroposophy by entering one day into casual conversation with a co-worker from the newly founded Camphill School in the neighbourhood whom he chanced to meet while on a walk. His interest quickly grew in both the work of Camphill and in Steiner's published writings which formed its background, and after listening to a lecture by Karl König he said to himself, "I could follow this man to the end of my life!"

However, it was still some years before the opportunity arose to put this into practice. In the meantime he took further teaching posts at Soham near Ely, and then at Dudley in the West Midlands so that his own

children could attend Elmfield School in nearby Stourbridge. But contact was maintained with König who, in 1960, finally asked him to join the then five-year-old village school at Botton.

This was pioneering work in every sense. Encouraged especially by Peter and Kate Roth, but only supplied with the most meagre of material resources, Nicholas had to transform himself into a Waldorf teacher for what, in regard to the ages of the children, was at first a combination of the first four separate classes. However, his love for children, his continuous creativity and his infectious enthusiasm carried him forward and laid secure foundations for the growing enterprise which Botton School slowly became. He also contributed substantially to the community both in lectures and in the many plays which he not only directed but also quite often wrote himself. During this time two more children were born and they also took in three foster children.

After fifteen years at Botton, Nicholas with his second wife, Margaret, moved out of Camphill in 1975 and joined the teachers at Elmfield. Here he became actively involved in establishing an in-service training programme and running parent workshops and study groups, serving as Chairman of the College of Teachers, helping to found the West Midlands Eurythmy School and giving numerous lectures to anthroposophical group meetings at Clent.

In 1984 there sounded a new call to found a Waldorf School in North Wales to which he decided to respond, and the Tan-yr-Allt School in

Tremadog duly came into being. Despite his firm commitment to the venture it proved a hard task to build this school in an area of strong Welsh nationalism, but nonetheless there formed in time a succession of happy children and eager parents who were inspired by his vision. For these and other members he began an anthroposophical group, to which were later added meetings of the First Class.

On his retirement in 1993 Nicholas moved down to South Wales and returned to a Camphill community at Glasallt Fawr where, as well as becoming the local Class reader, he also provided much cultural input, giving regular co-worker seminars and adult education sessions. In particular he helped to found the Towy Valley Steiner School by advising its first group of teachers in their work, acting himself as the administrator and even continued to produce school plays well into his seventies.

The twin poles between which Nicholas' whole life revolved were a dedication to children and a love for the stars. The last issue of his monthly star-notes was sent out to a circle of friends only a few days before his death. May his abundant energy now ray down from the starry heavens onto all those people who had the fortune to meet him on his earthly paths.

CRISPIAN VILLENEUVE
From Camphill Correspondence, *2001/5.*

Meg Farquhar

March 31, 1925 – April 12, 2000

Meg was born in Aberdeen as the youngest of three sisters. Her father became the last Provost of Ellon. Meg married in 1948 and Alistair was born in September 1949 with a frail constitution but with a capacity for sparkling joy and special forces of the heart. His education and care was not really met by the provisions available at the time and Meg's marriage was going through difficult times. In 1959 she followed an advertisement placed by Ann Harris to take on the laundry at Murtle House for about eighty souls. Alistair came to St John's School as a day-pupil and soon Meg found a spiritual home at Camphill. She moved in as a co-worker in April 1960; Alistair became a boarder at the Camphill Schools and his needs were met.

For the next eleven years Meg brought a unique contribution to the life and work of the community at the Camphill Rudolf Steiner Schools. She became familiar with anthroposophy and became a special and sincere

representative of this. Meg was at Camphill House, St Andrew's and Newton Dee House before taking on the task of a teacher in St John's School in 1965. She was the house-mother in a small unit and was renowned for giving guidance to the most challenging children and co-workers.

In 1972, she helped the Bay family in Edinburgh enabling Ita to follow the priest's training. Following this she spent some time at Shalesbrook (the priests' training centre in Sussex), working at Park Attwood Clinic for a period, followed by four years of teaching at the Aberdeen Waldorf School.

In 1982 Meg and Alistair moved to Newton Dee and for the following eighteen years she made her special contribution to the Village Community. In October 1998 Alistair's health failed and he died. Meg now struggled with her own health.

On April 12, 2000 Meg was released to join Alistair and the great host of those who have crossed the threshold and send their help and strength to those living on the earth.

FRIEDWART BOCK
From Camphill Correspondence, *2000/6.*

Erika von Bülow

January 19, 1909 – February 8, 1982

I stood at the doorway and knocked. The door opened and at the threshold stood Erika — leading me into new worlds of experience. How many of us could use such a picture in describing the impact Erika had on our lives. So many people have said: "How fortunate I was to have met Erika." Quiet, neat, filled with humility — but what strength! from the quiet voice flowed a power which changed us. The words so carefully chosen could turn one from despair to hope.

Having absorbed the deeply challenging, often hurtful experiences that met her during her life, having transformed these and crystallized them into wisdom, she resolutely walked the path of truth, knowledge and love, and opened the way for others.

The will to help was predominant in Erika. And help she did on countless occasions. But there were also moments when help could not be given, and these were experienced deeply and with pain. Acceptance of whatever was given to her — the grace to help on the difficult path of destiny — marked her outlook to life. Her special gift was an understanding for the struggle of the handicapped child — the struggle for the unfolding of the individuality. Out of this understanding and the necessity to earn a living, Casa do Sol, Johannesburg, a day school for mentally handicapped children was born.

To begin with Erika was the driving force, the impetus, covering the teaching and administration, becoming ever more and more the quiet, unobtrusive heart and centre of the work. The difficult children were her special protégés. She read extensively, was a deep observer and thinker and found ever new and unorthodox ways of solving the riddles the children presented. The problems of the adults found resolution through airing and discussion with her. Parents gave ear to her advice — advice she was able to give because of her personal experience in facing and overcoming just such problems as were facing them.

Not only people called for her powers, however. She would turn a room from chaos to order; change a garden from a place where a few plants straggled and stooped, to a place of beauty. She was a creator and shaper of beauty, and included in this was her task as a pruner and shaper of people.

She had an understanding that extended beyond the earthly, and therefore was able to be a bridge to the heavenly spheres. Through her we were able to glimpse the glory of that place.

PENNY GREARSON
From Camphill Correspondence, *1982/7.*

Renate Sachs

May 10, 1936 – December 27, 1993

Renate Sachs was born on a Sunday at 12 noon in Heidelberg, Germany. She was the youngest of three children, her sisters Eva and Ursel being seven and nine years her elder. Renate grew up in the Odenwaldschule, a liberal, progressive boarding school of which her father, Heinrich Sachs, was the director. Her father was a philosopher and educator, a painter and sculptor; a very wise man with a maturity beyond description. Her mother Elisabeth, gentle, loving and good, was a musician, as were her aunt and her grandparents. The Odenwaldschule was situated in a beautiful wooded valley and Renate spent her childhood surrounded by a landscape imbued with the strong, unspoiled forces of nature, in a world permeated with music.

Renate had a wonderful, radiant childhood. Although she was very much a child, with her broad forehead seeming to fill half her little face, she was wide awake, interested in the world and independent. Her very

first word was spoken in a moment of great triumph when having struggled in her playpen to pull herself up on its bars, she finally succeeded.
Her joy knew no bounds and she let out a cry of victory, "Jaaa!" Another
very early word was "by myself!" By the age of four she could carry her
own voice in a complex musical round. She was a very warm and loving
child, radiating joy; people loved to be with her, old and young alike. She
was gifted, quick with her mind, clever with her hands: she could make
and do everything. The only cloud over her childhood was her sorrow that
her sisters were too old to be her playmates.

Although growing up in wartime, it seemed hardly to disturb her happy
childhood. Her father sheltered Jewish children in his school, and also
took in anthroposophists, including the Killian family, as teachers.

Towards the end of the war ended some colleagues betrayed her father.
He was thrown out of the school he had loved and served so well. The
family then entered into a time of hardships. Renate remained at the
Odenwaldschule, living with her grandmother. The rest of the family went
to Stuttgart, where Eva and Ursel were taken in by the Killians whom
Heinrich had sheltered during the war. Meanwhile, Heinrich tried to
rebuild his broken life, but he died a year later of extreme exhaustion and
a broken heart. Renate was very much her father's child and his great
being accompanied her throughout the rest of her life.

Renate joined the family in Stuttgart when she was thirteen and
attended the Waldorf School where Herbert Hahn was her class teacher

and religion teacher. That same year, 1949, her sisters went off to Scotland to work with a Dr König in a place called Camphill. During her years in Stuttgart, Renate accompanied her mother on several trips to visit Camphill. Dr König must have loved Renate very much. She thought Camphill a nice enough place for her sisters, but it was certainly not what she wanted to do with her life! Her mother also thought that losing two daughters to Camphill was enough.

Renate graduated from the Waldorf School and went to Detmold to music school. She must have been a beautiful, elegant young woman, and an accomplished pianist. One of her teachers realized that Renate, although a gifted pianist, did not belong on the concert stage, for her greatest gift was a social one. She was someone who could open up the hearts of others through music. Upon completing her music studies Renate went to Vienna for further musical training. It was here that Renate decided what she wanted to do with her life. She would be a music therapist in a women's prison. Before starting on her new career, she went on a concert tour of Britain. She played in Botton Village and fell in love with the place. Suddenly she knew, beyond all doubt, that Camphill was her home.

Renate decided to join the Pietzners (her sister Ursel had meanwhile married Carlo Pietzner) with their pioneering work in America. So in 1961 she was one of the group of pioneers who crossed the Atlantic in fierce weather and went on to found Camphill Village, Copake. Although she had no previous background or training in Camphill, she took to it and was soon carrying all aspects of village life.

At Easter 1967 Renate became very seriously ill and was sent to Europe for treatment. Her kidneys failed and she went to hospital in Basle to be one of the very first recipients of a kidney transplant. She received one of a pair of kidneys, the other going to another patient. The other woman did not survive the transplant and Renate carried this awareness throughout her life. She spent the year in and out of hospital there, followed by a time in Brachenreuthe, so that she was in Camphill and yet not too far away from the hospital and doctors who knew her well. However, she was not so happy in Brachenreuthe: it did not give scope for her free and independent being. When she heard from Carlo of his intentions to embark on a series of Art Retreats, she returned to Copake in October 1972 and lived in the newly built studio in the centre of the village, becoming its heart and soul until her death.

The Art Retreats began in November 1972. They were a series of intensive, disciplined, and highly crafted studies on the Seven Arts. They were highly significant for the participants and inspired work in many other settings in the movement. The collaboration of Renate and Carlo in this work, the artist and the musician, was truly creative.

For the next twenty-one years Renate grew and developed, within the needs and challenges of Village life. But she was also struggling with her illness with great courage and strength. She was the longest survivor of the early kidney transplants. After nine years, that kidney failed, and she was the first person to survive a second transplant. She made medical history and was a medical miracle! Throughout the years, Renate had recurring medical crises, and often stood at death's door. Having come to the threshold in 1967, she was never far from it again. Is that why her being became ever more luminous, ever more selfless? The strong medicines she needed to avoid rejection of the transplanted kidney had serious side effects. After some time she could no longer assimilate nourishment from the food that she ate. Her bones became brittle and she had to have her hip replaced. Her skin began to break down, every bruise became a problem, and skin cancer spread mercilessly. Renate had no resistance to infection and any illness became life threatening. Her second transplanted kidney lasted nine years and then Renate went on peritoneal dialysis.

However, in between life-threatening episodes she radiated health, joy, enthusiasm and unbounded energy. Sometimes we might try to slow her down and she would always ask: "Why should I hold myself back? What should I save myself for?"

Renate loved the village and its ever changing challenges, richness and diversity. She poured her strength into the needs of the village and was constantly replenished. She was continually active in the cultural life, playing the piano at many occasions, carrying the Friday afternoon craft concerts for many years, teaching the village how to sing, recognizing and encouraging the musical talents of others, giving piano lessons to some of the children, as well as helping to organize Miha Pogacnic's music festivals (Idriat) and arranging the concerts and performances of guests.

Renate had a tremendous, childlike enthusiasm. She took delight in pleasures great and small, loved challenges, ably tackling the most practical tasks or some delicate matter of human relationships. She had an unusual faculty for selfless listening and could weave the ideas and contributions of others into a new celebration for a festival, a new insight for the community.

The autumn of 1993 was an intensely busy time for Renate. And didn't she seem to be wearing thin? And she was going to the Michaelmas Conference in Dornach. She was determined to be present at this important event. She returned deeply inspired and grateful. When she became ill in the week before Christmas she seemed to have the gastric flu that many of us had had. She rapidly became weak and dehydrated. She hoped to sleep it off, for she had to play the piano for the two Christmas plays!

Once in the hospital, Renate seemed not to have the energy to take on this latest illness. Complications arose and she was told that the only hope was surgery, with a small chance of success. She became certain. "No surgery! I want to die now, to die in peace." After this clear and resolute moment of decision, she approached her death quite consciously and knowingly, her spirit radiating a truly holy peace. Her last words, like her first, were words of affirmation: "Ja, Ja, Ja." She radiated peace, greatness and majesty.

WANDA ROOT
From Camphill Correspondence, *1994/3.*

Gustav Schramm

December 21, 1929

This story begins in the town of Freiburg in Germany. It was on a hot summer afternoon: I was waiting in a small restaurant near the cathedral. As I sat there, my thoughts wandered into my own past and it became clear to me that I would have to change the course of my life. But when I tried to picture this new life, all my courage vanished. Words of H.G. Fabre, which I had recently read came into my mind and I was comforted: "The darkness was profound ... The butterfly goes forward without hesitation; so well does it direct its tortuous flight that in spite of all the obstacles in its way, it arrives in a state of perfect freshness, its great wings intact. The darkness is light enough."

I was awakened out of my musing by the sight of a person who sat down at the next table. I was suddenly seized by longing to exchange words with a fellow human being — a longing that was so powerful that it seemed as though there was some force behind me. I had never seen this person before, nor could I make clear to myself just why I should so want to talk to her. I felt embarrassed, paid my bill quickly and left the restaurant.

As soon as I was about to cross the street, the immense longing to talk to the person in the restaurant overcame me again and I could not help but turn back. Yet I did not dare to go in again. I stood outside and studied the menu despairingly and all at once — I am not sure how it happened — I found myself going back into the restaurant.

I greeted the person who was still sitting there, excused myself for being so importunate and asked if I might talk to her. Although she obviously thought this to be a strange request, she granted me my wish.

I now sat there at the table for what seemed an eternity unable to begin. At last in despair, I began to tell my listener why I was in Freiburg, that I had only been there two days, and that on the following day I was

going to have a job interview at a big publishing company. The urge to work there was born out of the longing to take an active part in the world, and I thought my literary possibilities would find some expression if I worked in a publishing firm. But — so I said — I knew very well that in order to make the change from being a bank clerk to an editor, I would have to solve my religious problems. This seemed possible as the publishing firm was Catholic and I was a Catholic myself. When I had spread out all my past in front of the person sitting at the table with me, I felt very much relieved. She told me that she herself had only just arrived in Freiburg; through a misunderstanding she had an hour to wait for a friend she was visiting. She had come from Dornach near Basle to meet her friend and was travelling back the same night. Before she and I had parted she gave me an address of a place in Scotland — the Camphill Rudolf Steiner Schools — and said I should visit it at some time, explaining quickly what kind of work was done at Camphill, before hurrying away.

Months passed by. I began work as an apprentice in the publishing firm. In spite of my hopes, my religious problems were not solved; on the contrary it became clear to me that I would have to leave my church but I had nothing else to put in its place. The question arose: What now? My life seemed to have no purpose; it was as if I was drowning in habits and routine and was losing the ability to breathe. "The darkness was profound."

In the ensuing state of loneliness and helplessness all doors seemed closed. Then, all at once, I remembered the address I had been given — the address of Camphill. I wrote, had a reply and went there.

When I arrived in Camphill everything was very new to me and very foreign. Soon all my literary ambitions fell away like an old cloak. I found anthroposophy there which took on increasing meaning, and in the encounter with the children, reincarnation and karma became an experience.

My urge to take an active part in the world found expression. Illusion changed into truth, ambition into duty and responsibility, and pride into service. Although "the darkness was profound," my path led out of the nothingness into a new life.

AUTOBIOGRAPHICAL
"My Way to Camphill," from The Cresset, *VII/4.*

Hans Spalinger

October 15, 1915 – November 5, 2000

The active time in life at a later age is in German called *Feierabend,* literally "celebrating the evening." Occasionally a great image of my life's eighty years appears before me. I am amazed at the multitude of places, experiences, activities and encounters; I am most impressed by the many children, young people and adults whom we were allowed to help a little, but who were actually our teachers. The stages of my activity as a curative teacher appear: Sonnenhof, Herrliberg at the Lake of Zürich, the south of France at the foot of the Pyrenees, Lausanne, Bussigny near Lausanne, St Prex, Geneva, Ittigen and finally Beitenwil. Looking back I can experience my past and ongoing connection with hundreds of people: those we cared for, their parents and families, co-workers, colleagues, friends, officials and more. I can look back on lives and destinies of many who came to us fifty years ago and who lived with us for thirty, forty and some even fifty years. I am overcome with gratitude. With the help of parents, friends and co-workers it was possible to start a few places which serve the education and care of people with special needs, in which we could apply to many the manifold possibilities of help springing out of anthroposophy, and where many lives changed because of the coming together of many human beings. Without the active help of co-workers, friends, of my wife Johanna, but also of the authorities, these places could not have grown, not even Beitenwil. But the greatest help and guidance came from the

spiritual world. From there we were accompanied by all those who had left us behind on earth.

For fifty-five years I have been allowed to work with others in social therapy and curative education. A powerful stream of love, warmth and goodwill always came towards us from those we tried to help. They helped and continue to help to create such life communities in particular.

Feierabend? from our secure and well-funded places we experience in the world around us the incredible hardships and suffering of people with special needs, in particular in Eastern Europe. My "retirement" gave me the opportunity to help in Romania, to build up a home for children and young people with special needs. Again I was able to reckon with the help of many friends and sponsors. Whenever I gratefully look back on what has been possible, I truly experience the end of my life as *Feierabend.*

AUTOBIOGRAPHICAL
From Camphill Correspondence, *2001/2.*

Johanna Spalinger

October 21, 1926

Through the place of my birth, Arlesheim near Dornach, and through my parents, I had already found my first "access" to anthroposophy. They had experienced lectures by Rudolf Steiner in Dornach.

I was born on October 21, 1926, the birthday of Edmund Pracht who, in that year had just built the first lyre. The lyre was to accompany me in adult years in my profession as curative teacher and music therapist. I was baptized by Friedrich Doldinger, the Christian Community priest, and my godfather was the psychiatrist Dr Friedrich Husemann. I met both again, aged fourteen, at Wiesneck near Freiburg.

My parents, while attending courses, placed my pram under a tree at the Goetheanum, and in later years dream-images of eurythmy perform-ances given in the Goetheanum arose within me. For a year we lived in Stuttgart where my father received his training as a Waldorf teacher. In 1929, he started the Rudolf Steiner School in Dresden.

This made it possible for me and my four siblings to attend this school from 1933 to 1941 when the school was closed by the Nazis. I look back to this time with great gratitude, a time when the child's soul was formed.

The pressure of the Nazi time and the tumult of war were increasing. After finishing school I was called up to the Labour Service where my artistic and cultural "baggage" was of great help. It also accompanied me during the bombardment of Dresden when my parents and sisters remained safe. It accompanied me again when fleeing from the approach-ing war front in the east and again later fleeing, together with the Heynitz family, from the Russians before the end of the war in 1945.

Shortly after the war I studied medicine in Jena. There a group of stu-dents found themselves together studying Rudolf Steiner's *Philosophy of Spiritual Activity.* The Russian occupation and the increasing restrictions of the Communist government made me decide to flee to the west together with a fellow student. We headed for the first postwar anthroposophical youth gathering in 1947 in Dornach, where I also first met Hans Spalinger.

After this I continued my studies in Heidelberg, changing course to German language and literature, and music. I visited Friedrich Husemann in his psychiatric clinic at Wiesneck several times. There I gave violin concerts for the patients which Friedrich Doldinger accompanied on the piano. I felt very close to the patients and wanted to help them. It was the same feeling I had when visiting the curative educational home Pilgramshain as a twelve-year-old. My heart quickly embraced these chil-dren.

In 1948 Hans Spalinger asked me to help in building up a curative educational home he had just started. Following the currency devaluation in Germany, I was penniless, and it was an easy choice to follow this invitation. The work in the first small home in Bussigny near Lausanne gave me much joy. We worked together with our co-workers as a big family. Hans Spalinger and I married in 1949. In the following years, in addition to care-children, we were blessed with seven children of our own.

After two years the number of our care-children had increased to forty which made it necessary to look for another place. In 1950 we found a large villa suitable for our purposes near St Prex, on the hillside overlooking Lake Geneva, surrounded by fields, meadows and magnificent cedar and pine forests. We moved there with forty children and their carers after the building alterations had been completed. After initial financial difficulties, we were able to build up solid curative educational work with good medical support. Soon thereafter the quest for new social forms began.

Hans had to take one of the care-children to Camphill in Scotland, and this brought about the first encounter and intensive conversation with Dr König. These conversations were resumed when Dr König accepted our invitation to visit us. The college meetings and his lectures left a deep impression on us.

The following year we travelled to Ringwood, Thornbury and Aberdeen where we were made very welcome. We met very many of the co-workers with whom we had intensive talks about Camphill. Special encounters came about with Dr Hans-Heinrich Engel and Marianne and Günther Lehr. These talks led the way in the quest for the inner community.

When Karl König suffered a severe heart attack and could not continue his work with us, he asked Hans-Heinrich Engel to do this. Hans-Heinrich first arrived in 1955 and intensive work began to deepen our curative work from a medical perspective. From then on he visited us twice yearly. We conducted many children's clinics and college meetings with him, and he gave many lectures. At that time I began, together with him, to build up an intensive music-therapeutic work.

Of great significance for Hans and myself were the conversations concerning the inner aims and tasks of the Camphill Community to which we were admitted in Scotland in 1961. We also attended the annual summer conferences and meetings which led to the deepening of anthroposophical curative educational content. From this a strong friendship with Hans-Heinrich developed.

The home Perceval in St Prex developed well as a *centre de pedagogie curative*. For those in our care who had grown older we had built up different workshops in which they learned to work. Favourable circumstances allowed the village Aigues Vertes near Geneva to start in 1961, supported by the local parents' association and co-financed by the Lions Club.

St Prex became part of the Camphill movement in October 1965. Many of the older co-workers could not follow this step and left us. However, their departure was with a positive mutual respect.

Karl König formulated the special task given to us as "the metamorphosis of the artistic into a healing art in the field of curative education, music, painting, eurythmy, sculpture and singing." St Prex should become a village for children, artists and curative teachers. He also had the idea to found a music therapy academy. This only came about in 1997 with the founding of the Orpheus School for Music Therapy at the Humanus-Haus.

Shortly after our admission to the Camphill Community we started the Camphill Seminar; this was still prepared by Karl König and began at St Prex, Brachenreuthe and Föhrenbühl at the same time. In this connection, too, a joint Seminar collegium met regularly for some years for intensive and constructive study at which both Hans and I took part.

Before his death in 1966 Karl König had sent helpful people as co-workers for the transformation of Perceval. These included Sigrid and Leonardo Fulgosi, Heide and John Byrde and Brigitte Köber. In order to bring about the process of transformation more easily, it was felt to be better if we were not part of it. We therefore decided to start a new task.

To begin with we found a vacant house in Ittigen near Bern. This new beginning made it possible for us and our children, five of whom attended Rudolf Steiner Schools in Bern, Basel and Zürich (there was no Waldorf School near St Prex), to meet again as a family after many years of separation.

Some of the oldest of the villagers joined us. We still wanted to put into practice what was Karl König's concern for St Prex, as well as our own, to work ever more strongly in artistic therapy. By renting additional accommodation and erecting a workshop building and therapy rooms, a small Humanus-Haus came about in Ittigen in the course of six years, caring for forty people with special needs. There too, we worked intensively with Hans-Heinrich Engel, especially in the field of music therapy. This led to the founding of the Independent School of Music in 1970. Among the twelve founder teachers were Susanne Müller-Wiedemann, Christoph Andreas Lindenberg and myself. We were able to include some elements of Camphill into this school.

At last, after a prolonged search we found the large Humanus-Haus, a former home for the elderly, in a beautiful secluded situation with a view of the Bern Alps. Hans-Heinrich, the friend who had always given us encouragement, joined us together with his wife Turid for this new beginning. Tragically his life came to an end with an accident there. In a certain way we experienced his death as a very special consecration of Humanus-Haus.

Since then the Humanus-Haus has developed further and in 2003 it celebrated its thirty years anniversary. Now 85 adolescents and adults live in twelve house-communities and work in twelve workshops including an agricultural enterprise.

In 1990 a call led us to Romania. We responded, aware that Karl König had looked to the East of Europe as future potential for the work of Camphill. While much has happened there, an awakening for Camphill's mission is still very tentative.

Since Hans's death on November 5, 2000 there is much in transition with us, as everywhere in the world. The new millennium challenges each individual and every community to face the greatest inner tests. The Camphill Community is being tested in its mission to lead the Christian and social impulse into the future.

AUTOBIOGRAPHICAL
Translated by Johannes Surkamp

Reinhard Böhm

January 26, 1930 – December 27, 1999

Reinhard Böhm saw the light of day in Leibnitz, Silesia. He attributed great significance to this locality of birth because it was situated between Koberwitz and Pilgramshain. In Koberwitz just outside Breslau (now Wroclaw) Rudolf Steiner had given the Agricultural Course, which is the beginning of biodynamic agriculture. Pilgramshain is where Karl König started his curative educational work. Both of these streams were leitmotifs in Reinhard Böhm's biography. Both flowed together in the Lehenhof near Lake Constance.

Reinhard grew up in a small village near Schweidnitz (now Swidnica) in Silesia. He was fascinated by the ancient crafts, the village life, the surrounding landscape and nature, and the farm where he spent his free time helping. His father and mother were part of the Wandervogel movement which was searching for a new and natural trend in modern life. His father was a teacher. At home he experienced Christian piety, musicality and hospitality. All these had a profound influence on young Reinhard.

The Nazi regime and the Second World War cast a dark shadow over his youth. His father was called up; he was wounded and later was a prisoner of war of the British until 1948. Towards the end of the war the fourteen-year-old Reinhard was called up to dig trenches. In January 1945 the Red Army broke through the defensive lines, and Breslau was encircled. His mother fled to Austria with five children, the youngest being barely two years old. Later she moved to Osnabrück in northern Germany.

Reinhard as the oldest one remained behind so as not to burden his mother. Without any possessions except the clothes he wore, he made his way, finding occasional work on a number of farms. Eventually after many adventures, he managed to reach the West.

Between 1946 and 1949 Reinhard followed an apprenticeship in farming in the Osnabrück area, with great enthusiasm. In spring 1948 a mare shattered his arm; he got himself to hospital on a bicycle and had to remain there for ten weeks. During this time a brochure about biodynamic agriculture came into his hands and he was greatly impressed and took deep interest in it. He followed it up by working on a number of biodynamic farms after the completion of his apprenticeship, the last place being the Wurzerhof in Carinthia, Austria, belonging to the Bartsch family where he had the post of administrator.

Through Dr Eberhard Bartsch, Reinhard came into contact with anthroposophy. In May 1960 he met Dr Karl König who was visiting the farm. Bartsch and König planned to establish a curative educational centre at the

Wurzerhof. However, this did not happen as Eberhard Bartsch died a few months later. Reinhard, however, accepted König's invitation to come to Camphill. Here the homeless and impecunious bachelor discovered the community which was an answer to his innermost concerns. Things fell into place when he got to know Cordula Klett. They married in 1963.

Karl König had a vision to unite agriculture and social therapy and this also became Reinhard's direction. It was close to his heart to connect the interest in nature and the earth with the interest in his fellow human being.

STEFAN SIEGEL-HOLZ
From Camphill Correspondence, *2000/3.*

Werner Groth

December 14, 1929 – September 17, 2006

The story of my life has five turning points, and except for the first one they are all shared between Roswitha and myself; the last two with our children as well.

At the end of my business training I was working "outside" in sales, when I decided to visit my sister Elsbeth in Camphill Cairnlee. Two intensive weeks, during which I was allowed to attend a Seminar session with Thomas Weihs, made a deep impression on me, especially the social structure of Camphill, as it then appeared to a visitor. The final push was a talk with Dr König in 122 Harley Street. So the decision was made to join Camphill as a seminarist in the following year.

First steps into anthroposophy, helped by a friendship with Wolfgang Beverley convinced me that the threefold social order would play a part in my life. This was the second point, so after the end of seminar I left for Germany to help in the family factory and to see if the threefold social order could find a place in this setting. In a meeting with Roswitha Koehler it became immediately clear that we belonged together and that the field of curative education would be the content of our life.

After I had a very serious car accident Dr König was contacted, and the medication he suggested helped to an astonishing recovery. We then decided to join Camphill in the Sheiling School at Ringwood. It was a happy but also strenuous time there and the family grew to four children.

The fourth point was at the Camphill Conference in Scotland in 1970. Roswitha had the strong impulse that we should go to Africa to help Camphill there. A connection to Julian and Renate Sleigh helped towards this decision. But during a short visit to Botswana the great need for a curative work there became clear and so we went to start a Camphill School there in 1974.

The last turning point was the handing over of all responsibilities, due to advancing age and a serious development of cancer. It gives great satisfaction and happiness to witness that Camphill in Botswana is fully integrated into the country, especially with its people.

AUTOBIOGRAPHICAL

Apart from his work with the disabled, Werner always strove to create employment for members of the extended community. He studied, and put into practice, the concept of creating harmony and balance between the spiritual, social and economic spheres of life. Werner was a true socialist who always had time for people and tried to assist wherever possible. I remember Werner once saying, "The actual contribution I made to life started in 1974, everything else was preparation." In 1974 the work in Botswana began. What did he mean by "everything else was preparation"?

Werner was born in Dessau, Germany to Claus and Christiane Elisabeth Groth.

In 1952, having finished a thorough training in business management, Werner came for a brief visit to Camphill in Scotland, where his sister was working. On his way back to Germany he met Dr König at his Harley Street office and decided to follow his invitation to come to Camphill. He

returned to Scotland in 1953 and found himself in Heathcot House, working with severely spastic children. He was encouraged to take up the seminar in curative education, which he completed in 1954. Meeting life in a
community and experiencing anthroposophy as an inspiration for all areas
of life, Werner became acquainted with Rudolf Steiner's ideas on new
ways to order social life. He became especially interested in Steiner's indi-
cations about economic life.

After completing the seminar, Werner went back to Germany to support
his father and older brother in developing a small factory. Starting off with
next to nothing, other than ideas, skills and determination, the endeavour
began to thrive. As the factory was situated in a rural area the workers
were well known to the management and it was possible to respond
favourably to situations such as illness in a worker's family. Thus a way
of running a business based on mutual trust and loyalty was achieved.

Soon after returning to Germany, Werner met Roswitha Koehler, a
trained kindergarten teacher. They married in 1956 and two children, Icky
and Andreas, were born.

In winter 1962, Werner had a severe car accident leaving him unconscious for some days. However, he made a miraculous recovery after
which it became clear to Roswitha and Werner that they should leave
Germany and join Camphill with their family. They lived and worked in
the Sheiling Schools, Ringwood from 1963 to 1974. The experience of
embracing a wider community, and the community having to accept a

family in their midst, brought challenges and opened insights in practising social awareness, coherence and tolerance. During this time two more children were born — Melanie and Oliver.

Was all this a sufficient preparation to answer a calling that both Roswitha and Werner repeatedly felt — namely, to work with African children in a country without apartheid? Encouragement finally came from Thomas Weihs who said, "The only way to find out whether the impulse is genuine is to go to an African country and see whether doors will be opened for you."

On August 31, 1973, the family left Ringwood and sailed for Cape Town. Roswitha and the family stayed on in Camphill Village South Africa, when Werner and the oldest son went north to Botswana. Having been a British Protectorate, Botswana had become independent and the first president succeeded in making a peaceful transition and black and white population worked harmoniously side by side. Having been put in touch with a doctor of the hospital in Ramotswa, Werner discussed with him the intention to work with disabled black children. His response was, "I have the children for you, for there are some severely disabled children, both physically and mentally, who should not be in our hospital." And a place to start work? "We have at present the chief of the local tribe as a patient in the hospital, who is responsible for the tribal land of this area."

The intention was communicated to the chief and the outcome was that a deserted and dilapidated farmhouse and some tribal land were offered in Otse, south of Ramotswa, where the impulse could begin. Support seemed to come from a different realm.

When the place was put into some kind of order and made liveable, the family left the Cape and were reunited in Rankoromane, where the first handicapped children soon joined them. From the nearby village Otse a few women came to help with the children and establish a small garden. As Rankoromane slowly developed and became known to the government, more children knocked at the door to be admitted. Also, the family was completed by the arrival of the fifth child, Nicola.

This was the time when a living connection to the Camphill movement was established, as individual communities answered the request to support a child by taking up "god-parentship." Friends of Werner in Germany, who had become successful businessmen formed the Friends of Camphill Botswana Trust and raised money. The nearest Camphill neighbour, Cresset, helped with gifts in kind.

Other gestures proved that the impulse was accepted. Teachers were trained under Roswitha's guidance and the school was established, social cohesion and awareness were cared for and practised, Werner was able to carefully introduce Rudolf Steiner's ideas relating to the economic sphere when a furniture making factory was added to support the growing school, as the government could not afford to pay school fees. All this forms the story of a long uphill struggle.

Werner was inspired by Dieter Brüll, a Dutch professor who in his book, *The Anthroposophical Social Impulse,* provided detailed guidance in how to respond with insight, sensitivity and flexibility to the changing situations which occurred over the years.

Werner and Roswitha's retirement had been carefully planned. Responsibilities for the care and well-being of children and staff, as well as the children's schooling and the estate management and security, now became salaried arrangements. The government, still not paying school fees, was repeatedly urged to take on more financial responsibility for the running of the place. They have meanwhile agreed to refund a certain percentage of the running expenses.

After 32 years of work, Rankoromane (the school), Legodemo (a training centre for school leavers), Motse wa Badiri (a home with sheltered employment for adults), and the furniture factory are working as autonomous but closely associated organizations belonging to one Trust.

Werner was also a founding member of the Council for the Disabled in Botswana.

Werner, or Mmonamogolo as he was affectionately called, is survived by his wife Roswitha, five children and twelve grandchildren, among the many others who have lived in his home and respected him as their father. He will be greatly missed by all those whose lives he touched.

The immigration officials at Gaborone International Airport in Botswana were not always so friendly. This time I was welcomed with a smile, "And what is the reason for your stay?"

"Well, actually I am here for a funeral. The man who started Rankoromane in Otse, has died. Maybe you have heard about Mmonamogolo, Werner Groth?"

"Oh yes, I know about him, because I used to go to school in Otse," he said. "He was a great man."

"Yes, he was a great man."

"Mmonamogolo" means Old Man, which is a very respectable title in Botswana.

For many evenings after Werner died all the people from Camphill Motse wa Badiri, Rankoromane, Legodimo, and many from the village of Otse came together to pray and sing for him. Pastors from different denominations took it in turns to lead the prayers. Interspersed with the prayers and speeches was the singing of the local people. The prayers and speeches were sincere, heartfelt and beautiful. The singing was pure soul, strong, full of love, and very beautiful, as its substance was pure feeling without sentimentality. It was a goodbye to a loved one and a coming to terms with grief at the same time. It was the Soul of Africa encompassing all who were there.

ELSBETH GROTH
From Camphill Correspondence, *2007/1.*

In Botswana it is the custom for the community to conduct a wake during the last night before a funeral. As many people had been very busy for the last few days, it was decided that on this last evening the wake would conclude at midnight. More prayers and singing. In fact people did not stop at midnight — they went on all the way through the night.

Early the next morning was the funeral service. This took place in a large marquee, erected for that purpose. I suppose that it is only possible in Africa, to spontaneously interrupt a Christian Community priest in order to deliver an impromptu translation of Werner's life story. The priest observed how Werner had always had the gift of bringing the right people together to make things possible. That is also how it felt on this morning when all witnessed this beautiful occasion as one community. And of course, there was more singing. The local community expressing the fact that one of their own was leaving.

The crowd was surrounded by all that had been achieved: the school buildings; the furniture factory; the gardens; Motse wa Badiri, the Place of the Workers; the orange grove, the thriving garden centre and tea garden; and all the bigger and smaller buildings that make this community possible, and all the life and work they represent. Of course Werner did not do all that by himself, but I don't think any of this would have happened if he had not lived, worked and striven here for so long. All around us were flowering trees and plants of all kinds. There was that special, sweet, bready smell of African soil in early morning, or after rain. And everywhere the twittering of busy weaver-birds. The sun shone in a beautiful blue sky.

I was told that in his life he had time to talk to anybody, greet him or her in the most cheerful way in English, Setswana or German. There would be a real meeting, even if only for a few moments at a petrol station. This meeting could also be in the form of a challenge when he thought it necessary. He also lived with many questions and did not take things for granted.

He was no saint but he was a great man: courageous, independent minded, more interested in what held seeds for the future than in convention. And he stuck it through for many years in a very demanding place.

It was an honour to be a small part of this great leave-taking.

HENRIE VAN ROOIJ
From Camphill Correspondence *2007/1.*

Margaret Blomkamp

March 5, 1924 – February 6, 1984

Margaret was one of the early South Africans who joined the Camphill School at Hermanus; she was part of the first Seminar training held and established by Dr Hans and Susanne Müller-Wiedemann in the early 1960s.

Margaret was born in Cape Town. She was born with a hip problem, her legs were folded up to her shoulders at birth instead of reaching down; this gave her endless trouble. She went to school in a wheelchair and had to wear callipers. One day she was taken to a faith healer who helped her to walk freely; he also asked her to discard her callipers, which she did. However her gait was still laboured and she had to swing her legs outward with every step. This handicap helped to enhance her great empathy for the many children that were in her care. Margaret was a teacher, a house-mother, and later in the 1970s became the Principal of the Camphill School. She had a wonderful way with the young people, the children and the parent body.

During the mid-seventies work became very difficult at Hermanus; apartheid was rife, and the Camphill Movement Council advised us to pack up and return to Europe as we were working under this law of apartheid. Many co-workers left at that time to return to Europe and the Camphill School was very thinly staffed. On two occasions the School's Council advised that the place be sold and the work be given up. It was Margaret and her friend Wendy Tucker who stood firm to their commitment to the children and their parents. This was a heroic deed of Margaret's, and showed her true Michaelic spirit. She would not abandon ship, but saw her way through the difficult time and steered through its rough passage.

Margaret had a very kind and gentle nature, but with it she had great clarity of thought, that is where her Michaelic nature came to the fore and her high moral standards shone through. She was, what one might term a "heart-thinker."

In the early 1980s a new group of co-workers arrived at Camphill School. It seemed that a new time had come and many of the old carrying people left. Margaret too felt that her time had come for a change. She joined Camphill Village in 1982. At that time Margaret's health was beginning to fail, her body was beginning to become a burden. She was unwell and in a lot of pain and it took time for a diagnosis to be established. What was eventually found was cancer of the stomach. Margaret then decided not to go for an operation, neither for chemotherapy, but rather to carry her illness through into death. Margaret was a touching patient, she would laughingly say, "I do not know whether to pray to live, or pray to die?" She was peaceful and long-suffering. Her great love was the sea, and water was a healing companion. To have her feet bathed in water during the last days of her illness was a balm. The picture by her bedside was that of great seahorses in the form of strong waves riding to the shore.

The day after Margaret's passing into the next world, one of our older villagers died. It seemed as though he had waited for someone to open the gate into the next world, so that he could cross over with friendly help.

Margaret was a friend and giver to all throughout her life and into death.

RENATE SLEIGH

Ursula Schroeder

January 30, 1928

I was not quite eighteen years old when a school-friend told me about Rudolf Steiner and anthroposophy. At first, however, I had to doubt and question this new view of life and evolution. I had adored natural science, physics and mathematics. Yet I also held a deep conviction that there is an eternal core in each one of us. The war years with so much suffering and depression had strengthened an inner certainty that there is a greater being above us.

My family background had been unconventional and free regarding religion. Both parents had been "rebels" against tradition. My father came from a strict Catholic family in Aachen. He broke out and joined a lifestyle called Mazdaznan. My mother had joined the Wandervögel, a youth movement. We celebrated the seasonal festivals but Christmas and Easter were the only times we went to a Protestant church. All of us four children were baptized in a Protestant church and three of us also confirmed there. However, the life of Christ was never referred to. We were vegetarians and practised music and singing with friends.

After the First World War, my father, an aero-engineer, struggled to find jobs in the private sector. He therefore welcomed a call from Junkers in Dessau. He was a skilled mathematician and kindled a love for geometry in us children.

After the winter of 1944/45, when Dessau (including our house) was destroyed in air attacks, and when the Russian army approached, my

mother and I managed to flee further west. My sister had been evacuated from Berlin to Quedlinburg (east of the Harz) with her little daughter and there we found a temporary shelter.

Even under Russian occupation, Quedlinburg became a cultural oasis for many refugees. In one of the old houses a music professor from Berlin, Dr Johnen, was able to set up his instruments and open a music college. I got permission to practice on one of his pianos. He even offered me a grant to become a full time student, which I gratefully accepted.

During the first year of my study I got to know other students who had a connection to anthroposophy and also told me about the Christian Community. With some of them I studied one of the basic books, *Theosophy,* and then on my own *How to Attain Knowledge of Higher Worlds.* When I read Rudolf Steiner's words in this book, I became completely convinced that this was the path I wanted to follow.

On Michaelmas Day, September 29, 1948, early in the morning one of my friends took me along to a mountain in the Harz region of Germany where a member of the Christian Community was able to accommodate a small conference in her hotel. When we arrived, the service — the Act of Consecration of Man — was just beginning, celebrated by Ludwig Köhler from Berlin. The recognition then came to me, that it was the Christ-Impulse I had been longing for and wanted to serve.

My sister, ten years my senior, had also found her way to anthroposophy through an elderly lady, Ellida Wagner, who had been a pupil of Rudolf Steiner before the First World War. He had appointed her to lead the group of the Anthroposophical Society in the Harz area. During the Nazi regime her house was raided by the Gestapo. Most of her anthroposophical books were confiscated and burned in the market place. Later she managed to get many of Steiner's lectures typed or hand-copied and these were hidden behind handwork material in her crafts shop. When my sister made her acquaintance another raid was imminent — this time by the Secret Police of East Germany. Late one evening in November, my sister and I carried boxes of lectures to my sister's room and hid them under her bed!

When members of the group wanted to gather for study in Ellida Wagner's house they arrived at different times in order to avoid drawing attention to themselves. These study evenings were very inspiring. It was a rare occasion when we had a visitor from Hamburg.

When I attended the Act of Consecration again, this time in a member's house in another small town, one of the members of the Christian Community, Rosemary Oberwinter, told me about Camphill and curative education. At that time I could only admire these impulses but felt totally unsuitable.

In 1949 I graduated from Music College and could teach private pupils. My mother, however, needed my help because my father had gone to West Germany as an engineer. He managed to get permission for my mother and myself to fly from West Berlin to Hamburg in autumn 1950. It was then that I joined the Anthroposophical Society and attended study groups, eurythmy and speech-formation courses, and got to know many fine people.

My hope was to teach at the Wandsbek Waldorf School. I was accepted and started by accompanying eurythmy lessons and replacing the music teacher. It was a great shock to discover that my hearing was impaired as a result of infections and probably earlier exposure to bomb blasts. Teachers, like Heinz Müller, helped me to accept the inevitable with warm understanding. However, incidental piano accompaniment did not suffice to meet my living expenses; I had to learn some office skills and find a full-time job.

During the winter of 1955/56 I joined the Birkenhof in the Lüneburg Heath, an anthroposophical home school and learned to care for a group of very retarded children. One of the pioneers of this work at the Lauenstein was Dr Heinrich Hardt, our consultant. I received special guidance from the curative teachers Victoria and Hans Nippodt, also from the Lauenstein.

After two years the infection in my ears flared up again and I became very ill and deaf. I had to get medical help in Hamburg and Berlin and needed a long time to recover.

During this time, the Nippoldts had been called to Berlin to start a small home for children under the umbrella of the Christian Community's social work initiative. They desperately needed co-workers. As soon as I felt strong enough I joined their work with fourteen deprived and maladjusted children. There I worked from 1959 to 1963, helping to build up this work. During those years I often missed the support of a real community. The Berlin Wall was built in 1961 which cut off would-be helpers from the eastern side of Berlin.

Earlier, in my first year at the Birkenhof, during a conference on curative education in 1956, I met Dr Thomas Weihs and Dr Hans-Heinrich Engel from Camphill. Each of them gave a talk. I was deeply impressed especially by Thomas Weihs. Together with a friend we talked with him afterwards and expressed our wish to join the work of Camphill at a future time.

In Berlin I had the opportunity to listen to lectures by Dr König. After one of his lectures I was able to speak with him personally. Expressing my wish to join Camphill he warmly invited me to come as soon as I could be replaced. This was in 1962. Only a year later was I able to leave Berlin to join Camphill and with it a life leading into a real experience of community.

AUTOBIOGRAPHICAL

Hermann Gross

February 4, 1904 – January 9, 1988

Herman Gross was born in Lahr, in the south-west of Germany. At the age of six the family moved to Stuttgart where he attended school until 1919. Due to the First World War, retired teachers had to be recalled to their profession. One of them was an artist with whom Hermann had already, at the age of twelve, formed a very special relationship. When it was time to leave school it was clear that Hermann wanted to be an artist. He had already received lessons in painting and drawing from his teacher for several years.

However, Hermann's father disagreed with this plan. He was in the publishing business and knew that in order to survive as an artist, Hermann would need a practical profession. He therefore insisted that he attend a college in Stuttgart, where he learned to become a gold and silversmith. This training was to prove important and became visible in all his later art, which showed a thorough and accurate craftsmanship.

From 1925 Hermann attended Art College in Berlin, where he made many friends. From Berlin he moved to Paris where he studied sculpture

and painting. Paris and France had a great influence on Hermann and in many ways he became very French. Although Paris was artistically very stimulating, he had to endure great physical hardship. He was forced to make a living by being an artist, resulting in having to live very frugally.

In 1935 he returned to Berlin to continue as a sculptor and painter. In 1940 he was called up to the Luftwaffe, spending most of his time in France and some time in Russia. During this time he had to use his skill of accurate drawing for propaganda, and it is not hard to imagine the pain this must have caused him. Hermann returned from the war, seemingly unscarred, but a school friend who knew him well wrote: "Although Hermann Gross has survived the war physically, he is not the same man."

In 1946 he returned to Paris and from 1948–56 he had a studio in New York; he married and although America brought him material comfort, he could not thrive and develop there as an artist and returned in 1956 to Stuttgart. Soon afterwards he met Trude, his second wife. They shared a studio together; both followed their professional careers, he as a painter and sculptor, she as a children's programme-maker for the radio. Life seemed to be settled until, through a friend of Trude's who lived in Camphill, Scotland, Dr König was shown pictures of Hermann's work.

After some time a meeting was arranged in Switzerland, which must have been an extraordinary event. In Hermann's own words: "There at the shores of Lake Zürich, one afternoon, our lives were transformed." The consequences were dramatic.

In 1963, at the age of 59, to the total bewilderment of his friends, Hermann decided to leave his native Stuttgart and without security of any kind, uproot himself and move to Camphill, Scotland. Here he established a modest studio, first in Newton Dee Village and later in the Camphill Schools. He gathered some students around him and very soon Thomas Weihs became his most active pupil. A new, and probably the most important phase of Hermann's life had begun.

Hermann worked his way into the Camphill Community quietly, by degrees. He taught the students of the Seminar; he formed important and interesting relationships to the children and held a special place in the community.

His first major works were the Archangels for the Camphill Hall and the coloured windows for the altar, where he developed quite a new technique, using stained glass. His main task, however, remained painting.

Many modern artists in our time gather around themselves an extraordinary assortment of tools and have to live unusual life-styles to find stimulation. Hermann Gross never required any of this. What comes to expression in all of his art is the art of simplicity and of clarity and above all, what is visible in his sculptures and in his paintings again and again, is his impeccable craftsmanship.

BERND EHLEN
From Camphill Correspondence, *1988/6.*

Trude Gross

December 9, 1905 – June 3, 1991

Trude was born in Augsburg, Germany; her birthday fell in Advent and much of the struggle of light and darkness of this special time could be found in her life.

Trude came from a well-to-do family. She had one brother and probably more than one sister; both the father and older brother were lawyers. Trude attended the Odenwaldschule (as did Eva Marie Knipping) for about ten years.

On leaving school Trude trained as a dancer in Berlin and there she met Hermann for the first time, without either of them being particularly attracted to each other. Feeling insufficiently gifted to continue dancing, Trude then studied journalism, working for many years as a broadcaster and playwright for the Stuttgart School Radio. Life was never dull for Trude; she interviewed many professional people, visiting special farm projects and places of work. At the same time she was co-editor of a magazine for school children. Her lifelong interest in drama with school children began here and she became involved in school drama.

While still working for Radio Stuttgart in the late fifties, Trude once again met Hermann Gross who had by then become established as an artist, and with this meeting their friendship did develop. At that time, Trude's life was extremely active and she passed through it like a whirlwind, from one to another of her commitments and interviews. Friendship with Hermann helped them both. From him she learned patience, reflection and a calmer approach to life; while he could refresh himself at her fount of optimism, warmth and the vitality, something she could always rekindle, even when plagued by self-doubt.

This second meeting led to the decision to marry, and from that time the promotion and support of Hermann's artistic work was the goal nearest to Trude's heart and to which she devoted all her strength and energy. After meeting with Dr König in 1960 they decided to come to Camphill. At first to Newton Dee, later making Murtle their home.

It has been rightly said that Trude's "riches" lay in the small utensils which Hermann had made and in his paintings and sculptures, but she found a particular richness too, in the love that streamed to her so freely from our children. There was a radiant childlike quality to Trude's enthusiasm which seldom failed to draw an eager response from any child, or to raise the spirits of those around her.

In her drama therapy she could elicit very imaginative play and she joined in most activities, running, playing, skipping until well into her later years.

Adjacent to our large, noisy dining room stood Trude's and Hermann's lunch table. It was a special treat for children or adults to receive an invitation to join them for a meal, where, thanks to Trude's care, each one felt himself the most honoured guest.

The journalistic wish to stir up thinking never left Trude: "Let us hear what the young people think," was her frequent request in the Bible Evenings, and woe to those who entered with long faces!

Trude and Hermann made long journeys, usually with their camper van, to the West Coast, to Finland, to France, Spain and even to Egypt! Trude's care made it possible that they travelled and it was Trude's delightful descriptions that meant their enjoyment could be shared afterwards.

Trude has followed Hermann's lead in becoming a member of the Anthroposophical Society and a member of the First Class. Together they joined the Camphill Community in 1980.

After nursing Hermann through his final illness, Trude herself was exhausted and frail. Many will remember her upright courage at the funeral and memorial evening, but soon after the clouds began to build up. It was hard to find the incentive to live on, alone. Doubts, fear of her unworthiness to find Hermann again as well as many anxieties, darkened this time so that sometimes it was hard for us to find her, or for her to find herself. Yet, ever and again, like a lighted candle one was permitted to experience her warm heart.

It was a triumph of this light when she could return from Culter House and some hours later, on June 3, 1991 could peacefully lay down her struggle.

AVRIL BUCHANAN
From Camphill Correspondence, *1992/1.*

Susan Mechie

November 15, 1932 – February 14, 1992

Were we to seek a single word with which to encapsulate the life of Susan Mechie, it would surely be "service," for she gave unstintingly.

Susan was a daughter of the manse, and what is more, of a Scottish manse, so one might glibly assume that all the qualities traditionally associated with such an upbringing must have belonged to Susan, and that we need not search further for the source of her urge to serve others.

To some extent these qualities did belong to her, but that upbringing diverged from the traditional in some important ways. For example, she

went to the newly founded Edinburgh Rudolf Steiner School just as it evacuated to the Scottish Borders owing to the outbreak of war. There, as might be imagined, the children enjoyed a near idyllic existence. Susan was to forge connections then, both human and spiritual which lasted her lifetime, but even this early in her life she felt the tug of duty, and her play-mates often saw her absent herself from the fun, since (as she would tell them), "I am needed at home."

In due course, her father moved to a parish in Glasgow, a city in diffi-culties. It was impoverished and needy. Susan was painfully aware of this; she later told of how she saw deprivation all about her and felt no right to pursue the cultural and social opportunities afforded to one of her gifts and "station" while this situation went uncorrected. I dare say she would have attempted some form of correction, were it not for her much-loved brother's untimely and rapid death from polio. This event established her resolve to take up medicine which she set as her goal in life. She gradu-ated at the beginning of the sixties.

She knew of Rudolf Steiner and anthroposophy through the Steiner School: she had seen and experienced the caring atmosphere and will to do the good, often found among those inspired by anthroposophy. While she had her intellectual reservations, emotionally she was strongly attracted to anthroposophy. As a student she had spent holidays helping out at Camphill in Aberdeen and so met the handicapped, and of course, Dr König. He urged her to join Camphill as a doctor.

She did not immediately do so, partly because of her reservations, partly because of her recognition of needs elsewhere, but chiefly feeling it necessary to properly equip herself for service. She studied homeopathy at the Glasgow Homeopathic Hospital. This was characteristic: Susan always wanted to learn more, in order to serve better. This was so much so that sometimes to general astonishment she was to be found reading medical journals or books, and knitting while listening to a concert she and her friends had come to hear. "We cannot waste time," was her mild rejoinder to their remonstrations. I do not think she ever did waste time, and her own interests were always set aside, perhaps to her ultimate detriment.

At last in 1966 she came to Camphill as Dr König had hoped. She brought to the small group of doctors a spirit of enquiry and research, and made considerable contributions in the fields of child development and therapy, particularly play therapy. At the same time she carried a doctor's commitment to several smaller homes and schools dotted about Scotland, which she regularly toured in her little blue mini. (Her prowess as a driver led to her wry surmise that she must have had not one, but eight, guardian angels). Susan retained several professional connections and was a prime mover in bringing them to Camphill for a series of important, ice-breaking conferences. She taught extensively on the Camphill training course, and regularly gave lectures at Robert Gordon's Institute of Technology in Aberdeen. In terms of professionalism and achievement this period saw Susan blossom. However, the personal impact on Susan herself was to her detriment.

When Dr Peter Engel, who had been Medical Officer to the Camphill Schools, died in 1976, it fell to Susan to take his office. She did so unstintingly as ever, but with a heavy heart as she felt herself unfit for the task. Its responsibilities weighed on her, though she discharged them well. Many recall with appreciation the treatment and counsel she gave them, and the "clinics" she conducted for the children at the Schools.

By 1976, Susan was already weakened by the progressive cancer which was ultimately to lead to her death. There were times in hospital when death seemed near, but she rallied. However, it became clear that she could not continue carrying the task of Medical Officer.

It was painful for those of us who had known Susan at her best, to watch the diminution of her powers by her illness, and to stand helplessly by. It seemed to mask her from us making it hard to meet her, but we may be sure that it was harder and more painful for Susan herself. In the end it seemed as if her wish to serve others had been her greatest sacrifice.

SHIRLEY NAUCKS
From Camphill Correspondence, *1992/3.*

Robin Willes

May 25, 1946 – December 16, 1975

Robin was born in London as a second child. His father's family is of Dutch-English aristocratic origin and Robin was their only son. Already at birth he was very long and soon his parents were warned about the condition he suffered from, which gave him a strange and weak constitution. For the first three years he was looked after by a Nigerian nanny who was very gentle and caring. Later, another nanny cared for him, who being aware that his constitution could ultimately lead to blindness, did a lot to further his education. Robin first attended school in London.

When he recounted his early childhood, the most outstanding memory was his deep love for his mother; he told how he loved both his parents, but truly adored his mother. He was also fond of his sister, and as they both had been brought up in an atmosphere of gentleness, kindness and understanding, these three qualities characterized their relationship. Outstanding also in his memory were their holidays, especially going to the country to the grandparents whom he also loved dearly. There to his great joy, he was for a while able to ride a pony. The death of his grandfather, when he was fourteen years of age, made a great impact on Robin, and through this he found his way to a religious inner life.

He went to Harrow for his further schooling. There he did very well academically and was liked by everyone, including the smaller boys for whom he was partly responsible and who were traditionally meant to be of service to their superiors. For Robin they would gladly do anything. While at Harrow Robin had to go through the painful experience of not being able to partake in the sports and games which played such an important part in the school life.

His greatest interest, next to an intense regard for the social conditions of his school friends, was history and from fifteen to eighteen he studied British and European history very thoroughly; journeys with his family supported his studies. Leaving Harrows at eighteen, he went to Cambridge to study history with a tutor. His eyesight was very poor and he experienced great difficulties. He was also on the search for an inner pathway At that time he also visited a friend at Thornbury and became certain that his way was to find out more about anthroposophy. He came to Glencraig, and my first meeting with him on returning from a holiday was seeing him ill in bed with a stack of bound copies of *The Cresset* by his bed; these he was reading from cover to cover being fired with his characteristic enthusiasm for all that he read.

The way to becoming a curative teacher was a hard and arduous one for

Robin. The demands put on his frail physique by a group of children who needed him from early morning to late at night were sometimes too great but he was determined to become capable in all the practical skills of which he knew so little, and for which his poor eyesight was such a hindrance.

What was taught in Seminar, the Bible Evening and the services meant a lot to Robin, and it was in the realm of our spiritual life that he soon found the well from which he ever and again drew the strength needed to live and work. He formed a deep friendship with Hans-Heinrich Engel, whom he regarded as his teacher in the highest sense of the word. At his death, Robin felt he must return to Glencraig, having been in Germany and Switzerland after completing the Seminar.

In the short time which was left to him he brought to life two impulses which fitted him: the building of Kaspar Hauser Hall, for which he gave his whole personal fortune and which he dedicated to the memory of Hans-Heinrich, and the beginning, in September 1975, of Holywood Rudolf Steiner School.

Robin's family did not see so much of him after he joined Camphill, but in the autumn of 1975 his grandmother celebrated her ninetieth birthday and Robin joined the large gathering of relatives on the occasion. His beloved sister was still in London when he returned there and they still had a week together.

Robin died December 16, 1975. The address given by Baruch Urieli at a memorial service was most beautiful and I would like to pass on an image from it as a conclusion.

It was said of the great sculptor Michelangelo, that with his chisel he freed the figure which he knew was imprisoned within the block of marble. This image of the sculptor freeing the being of man from its imprisonment can be an image for the life of Robin.

Robin was imprisoned in a rock of earthly existence. An unwieldy body, impaired eyes which left him very short-sighted, and a malfunctioning heart, made life for Robin a continuous struggle in order to live up to what was expected of him and what he demanded of himself. Many a burden had to be borne, many a renunciation had to be made, many a sacrifice had to be brought. But with a strong will he took up the chisel and worked on the rock of his existence to liberate the spirit. And from the ungainly body grew strength of will, from the impeded eyesight he gained a Michaelic perception for the aims of the spirit, and from the ailing heart grew a wealth of warm brotherly love.

TURID ENGEL

From Camphill Correspondence, *1976/1.*

Ivan Abner Jacobsen

October 12, 1918 – January 30, 2004

When someone leaves his earthly body, he becomes immensely large. The personality expands, and grows, and it is not so easy to realize what this human being has represented in the life which has just come to an end.

Ivan Jacobsen, who passed over in the early hours of January 30, 2004, had known for some time that the sand was running out of his hour-glass, and he used his last time to the full. His correspondence during the last year bears witness to a lively and expansive network of contacts, and we who stood around him know that he took up contact especially with all those with whom he felt that there was still something unredeemed and did his utmost to make up and come to an understanding.

He spent a lot of his time thinking back on his life, and also taped some ten hours' worth of recollections. A good friend of his, professor Nils Christie, said about him: "He was a man that had lived many lives," and that last year became one of nearness, intimacy, warmth and self-searching. To us surrounding him in this time, he gave freely of the results of this research; something that was very untypical of Ivan, who earlier had been very reserved when it came to revealing anything of himself. He drew us, his nearest family, close to him, wishing for nearness and presence. He called us all, and in the course of the last three days we were all able to take farewell: wife, children, grandchildren and great-grandchildren.

It was as if all things finally came together for Ivan that last year — his bonus-year — as one of his grand children put it. He made contact with many friends, he took part in the Camphill gathering in Pahkla in Estonia and visit the new village in Latvia, where his great interest in the new social ventures in Eastern Europe was affirmed; he even came round full circle, back to Vidaråsen. In a most unusual and generous way the new care-unit, Ita Wegman Hus, opened its doors, and he, together with Phyllis, was able to spend his last months there in an atmosphere of light, warmth and love.

Ivan was born on October 12, 1918 in Tacoma, Washington on the west coast of the United States. Born three months prematurely while his father was lying in the trenches of the Western Front, he was given his name in an emergency baptism, no one believing that he would survive, but Ivan did pull through.

When he was nine, the family had to leave Tacoma and a life in affluence and move out into the sticks, as Ivan used to put it. In the great Wall Street crash in 1929 they lost everything, save for a smallholding in the

logging-town of Morton, Washington, and here the family had to make do, as best they could.

Ivan's father, who had emigrated from a Norwegian fiord when he was fifteen, was used to country-life and started a butchery, but his mother who was a concert-pianist, found it a challenge to leave the nanny and housekeeper behind, and to have the sole and full responsibility for bringing up five children in the backwoods.

Ivan tells of utter poverty and of many hardships, but he never experienced it as a time of need: this was what everyone had to contend with, in this conglomerate of different people. The Norwegians were a heavy influence, but Swedes, Lebanese and of course, the Native Americans, made up for a wide range of cultural influences.

Ivan was a skinny kid, and told how throughout his childhood he tried to become big and strong. He ran and trained but never managed to become "one of the others." but He was good at school, a good musician, and he played for many a dance on his jazz-trombone. He was awarded a scholarship, and was able to go to Seattle University and study political science, a subject that had always interested him: "How are inter-human relationships formed?" Was it right that man's main occupation should be to grab as much as possible for himself, in the most opportune way, and to sell it with the highest possible profit; to climb up in the system at the expense of others?

To manage financially at the university, Ivan had to work for the richer students, washing and ironing their clothes, cleaning their rooms and serving them. His time at university was not an easy one. He told how wounded he felt, when he overheard himself referred to as the butcher from Morton. One day he came back to consciousness, lying on the floor looking up into the shocked faces of his fellow students, and he came to the realization then that he was not like the others. It turned out that he had, at the age of seventeen, developed epilepsy. Not really knowing what it was, he had had no wish to find out what it was, or to contact a doctor, choosing to ignore it. He felt himself so stigmatized and excluded, now that everybody knew about his situation, that he chose to leave university. He managed to get a scholarship to continue his studies at the American University in Beirut, Lebanon. This would also give him something to come home and tell about; something that would maybe impress the others, and give himself some identity. He got work in the galley on a Norwegian freighter. He had some spare time before starting in Beirut, so when he landed in Rotterdam he signed off to visit his relatives in Norway. Five brothers and sisters had emigrated from the small hillside farm in Nordfjordeid and Ivan was the first descendant to make the trip back home.

While he was there, war broke out, and being an American citizen, he was not allowed to travel in the war-zone. The solution was to go to Oslo, and study at the University there. Quickly he became involved in the budding resistance. As a US-citizen he was free to travel to both Sweden and the Soviet Union, and did so several times, bringing secret documents with him. He was offered the job as secretary at the US legation in Moscow, and the evening before leaving he was approached and asked if he would bring some documents to Stockholm. At the border the Gestapo boarded the train, and arrested Ivan. Back in Oslo, he was put into Møllergata 19, the main prison; "I lived for four months in a single-room in Hotel Møllergata," he used to say. Nine months later, just before Pearl Harbour, he was flown to Berlin, and on to Lisbon, in Portugal, to be exchanged for German spies that had been arrested in the US.

Back home, weakened by the time in prison, he was rejected by the army when he wanted to enlist. Instead he was asked by the Norwegian foreign-office to travel around in the US and lecture about the Norwegian resistance in occupied Norway, being the first American to have experienced German imprisonment to return and tell about it. "Look to Norway!" was the slogan coined by Roosevelt.

In Los Angeles, lecturing in the assembly-room of the local branch of the Communist party, Ivan noticed a beautiful girl in the audience who, as well as being pretty, was also able to put intelligent questions, so after the lecture, wishing to "elaborate" on some of the answers, he invited her out for dinner. Phyllis was willing, but wondered if her mother could come along, since she was also there. So Ivan's first evening out with Phyllis was with his prospective mother-in-law in attendance. Later on, dancing together, it was never a question for them *if* they would marry, only *when.* Two days later they were engaged.

The year after they married Ivan took up his studies again. During the day he was in Berkeley at the University, after a quick dinner they both went to Moore's dry-dock to contribute to the war-effort, Ivan doing carpentry-work, Phyllis working in the drawing-department, on the Liberty ships which were being assembled at great speed. Around eleven o'clock they went home, had a snack, a few more hours of study, some sleep, and then back to campus. This went on for several years, until he graduated with honours in 1945. The Phi Beta Kappa key that he wore on his watch-chain signifies his admission to this very prestigious fraternity.

Ivan was offered a job in the Norwegian Foreign Office in New York, and Phyllis became a matron for the Norwegian embassy's guest-house outside Washington DC. In the course of a very short time Ivan acquired a large circle of acquaintances within the Norwegian diplomatic and foreign-office circles.

Nils and Karen were born, and in 1950 Ivan was offered a job for a year in the Norwegian information office in Oslo. The family moved to Norway, and after the year was up they chose to stay on.

Then there followed a string of different jobs. For two years he was employed by Trygve Lie, the first Secretary-General to the UN, to organize and analyse his archives, and help to write his memoirs. Three thick volumes resulted. One can imagine the insights and knowledge that Ivan gleaned from all this. Later, together with a friend from the time in Washington, he formed the first public relations firm in Norway. He was pivotal in the making of the film *Windjammer,* sailing on the square-rigger for eight months, and when the film was shown in Denmark, spent a year there as commentator, while the rest of the family was in California, where Phyllis did the Waldorf-teachers' seminar.

But then, suddenly, enough was enough! Ivan met a wall, and felt that all he had done until now was for nothing. All that he and Phyllis had left behind in the US seemed to have caught up with them. He gave his notice, there and then. He went home and told Phyllis that he was out of work, and that what he really would like to do, a dream he had had all his life, was to become a cabinet-maker. Phyllis supported him: "Do it, Ivan, *do* what you have wanted to do!" And so at the age of 42 Ivan became an apprentice at an apprentice's wage with two teenagers at home.

Phyllis had always had a longing for the spiritual. Her mother was an anthroposophist and she had grown up with questions about the supersensible. She told how, as a child, she used to play with the elves between the bushes and flowers in their garden. They had been her friends, and for her it was a matter-of-course that there was a reality beyond what the eyes can see and ears can hear. Ivan, on the other hand, even though he had had a strong near-death experience connected to his illness, was never able to meet her on this level when she tried to mention such matters. This made for a rough marriage, though we children never had any experience of it.

Ivan's interests had gone outwards, Phyllis' inwards; but now, working as a cabinet-maker his perspectives began to change, as did Phyllis's, who had started as a teacher at the small curative school Hestafivel in Oslo. Ivan let himself be persuaded to take part in an anthroposophical summer conference in Järna in Sweden in the summer of 1964.

The following year, again persuaded, Ivan visited Botton Village and Camphill, and also met and spoke with Dr König. Here it was that after only a few days, he began to sense "that there is something behind all this. What are you not telling me? How is it possible for so many different people, to be able to live and work together in such an extraordinary way and how has this unbelievable place been able to grow?" At last Ivan found an answer to the questions which had led him to study political science. It turned out that Ivan had read quite a lot of anthroposophy; one book after the other, putting each one aside without finding anything that could satisfy him. Now, in Botton Village, when he was given Steiner's books on the threefold social order to read, a new world opened up: "If this guy can say something so sensible and meaningful about something of which I have knowledge, there must be something to the rest of what he says." To cap it all, he experienced and perceived Botton and Camphill as working and functioning manifestations of anthroposophy.

And so it was, that Vidaråsen Village was founded at Whitsun 1966 with Ivan as one of the four founders.

Towards the end of his life, Ivan told us of how he felt that his long, expensive and very specialized education had been for nothing. In Norway it had been of no worth to him, landing him no great jobs. Those of us that have been near to him can, on the other hand, see how the knowledge, experience and network of contacts that he had acquired through all those years constituted just those tools that were needed when he, together with Phyllis, Margit Engel and Trygve Thornæs founded and built up Vidaråsen.

Ivan's meeting with the "person in need of special care" opened up a new area of his soul; an area that for the rest of his life would be his most cherished. He had an immense empathy towards those that we call Villagers, and he was their great friend and champion. Phyllis and Ivan remained in Vidaråsen until 1972, then moved down to Sandefjord to establish Norway's first living-unit for adults with learning disabilities in the wider community. They lived together in a regular house in the suburbs of town, and Ivan got regular jobs (not sheltered ones) for all of the four or five villagers that had moved with them from Vidaråsen.

Some years later they were asked to move to Hogganvik on the west-coast of Norway to help out with the difficult beginning years in a setting of scepticism and mistrust. It was a long and laborious task which called for all his diplomatic talents.

Again they were called, this time to Solborg, north of Oslo, where some older and experienced Camphillers were needed to help carry the cultural life and the services. With every move Ivan brought his tools and wood-working machines along and worked with the villagers. So also in Solborg.

Here Phyllis and Ivan lived for his last 23 years, but their pioneering spirit has had little chance to rest. They were instrumental in bringing a village into life in Iceland, and also lived there for a year. Since the first IVS-camp in Vidaråsen in 1967, where they got to know Mila Moravec from Czechoslovakia, who became a lifelong friend, their interest in Eastern Europe was roused, and when a wish came to start a village in Poland, Wójtówka, they engaged themselves strongly, also living there for a year.

I believe we can say of Ivan, that he was the youngest of us all. Two years ago, when he was in hospital to get "the final verdict," as he put it, he took three days' leave to take part in an international conference on globalization. "This is where we meet the people that want to do some-thing now! This is where the anthroposophists should be! Here are those to whom I feel a soul-connection." It was the same glow that he felt the year before, when he and Phyllis, together with many more from Solborg, marched under the banner "Rudolf Steiner fought for threefoldness" in the large demonstration held against the World Bank and globalization in Oslo. Ivan's view was towards the future, engaged in the development of the future, never stuck in old dogmas and "rusty truths."

Still, at the age of 85, he had the ability to see the potential in each and every one that he met. He managed to make you feel that you were some-one important, no matter what your position was, that you were an impor-tant part of society.

Ivan also had the ability — when the ideas of the threefold social order and what they signified had dawned on him — to hold this spark alive throughout his life. This same faithfulness he also had towards individual human beings. If he had *seen* you, he carried you in his soul and kept con-tact over years and great distances. His will was of the extended type; strength to travel the path to the end, even though it be thorny, dark and full of obstacles. He never lost the belief in the importance of the work that he had taken upon himself. Ivan was one who never let his ideals grow dim.

The extent of his contacts around the world, to so many people, only became apparent during his last year. Going through the papers on his desk we found a thick folder with letters, with "correspondence from my sickbed" written on it. In his calendar he had faithfully written down the names of those with whom he had been in contact that day, be it by letter, a visit or a phone-call. Almost every day there was a list of ten to twelve names.

The intimacy that developed around Ivan during the last year became very real the last few days of his life. He was able to share with us how he experienced himself as being in two worlds at the same time. He described how when we thought he was sleeping, he was on the one hand "somewhere else," but at the same time could hear our voices, and then "come back" and give a relevant comment to something that had been said. The wakefulness, expectation and preparedness that he showed in those last few days, stand as a shining example for us, and we thank him for his strong deeds here on earth and for his continuing care.

KAREN NESHEIM & NILS LANGELAND

Susan Cartwright

February 20, 1914 – November 4, 2001

Born in 1914, the third of four children, Susan's father was managing director of the *Hull Daily Mail.* She grew up in Yorkshire, educated by a governess until the age of fourteen when she went to boarding school. Her talent as an artist led her in the 1930s to study under a well-known portrait painter in London. By 1939 Susan was beginning to make a name for herself as a portrait painter.

When the war came Susan turned her energies to voluntary auxiliary nursing. In 1940 she married Jack Cartwright, a captain in the Royal Navy and the following year their first son was born. Susan moved about quite a lot during this time, setting up house in various port areas so as to be near Jack's ship. As a captain's wife she was involved in the welfare of the families of the crew and I imagine this was the beginning of her life-long task of counselling, advising and comforting. She had a natural gift for this and aided by her ability to listen she could use her warm and genuine interest, her lovely sense of humour and her down to earth attitude to life and its various problems, to help.

In the 1940s it was still a generally held view that Down's syndrome children were ineducable. When her second son Hugh was born in 1946, Susan determined to show that this was not so. She was very active in professional circles where this view was held, and the opinions of these

people carried a lot of weight. She was influential in changing what were then the norms of education in this area.

Hugh was educated and proved to be a vindication of Susan's claims for the right to education for all children. Susan had been called upon by doctors and social workers to speak to mothers who had given birth to Down's syndrome babies. She brought great comfort, hope and acceptance to the parents and helped them to see the positive in the child's future.

Hugh went to St Christopher's School in Bristol, which is where he met Nina Rice. Nina became a very close friend of the Cartwright family.

Her great love for painting was stimulated by her joyful garden work. She continued to paint landscapes and flowers and several examples are in the Grange. Many will be familiar with her floral notelets, designed for Camphill Village Trust fundraising.

Hugh came to Grange Village in 1965 and very soon became a responsible member of the community. Susan lived in Farnham, Surrey, but was often replacing house-mothers, helping with open days, conferences and parents' meetings. She was there wherever she could help and support us. Ursula Gleed called upon her help to establish the Camphill Counselling Service. She became president of the Friends of Camphill Village Trust.

Susan became rather unwell but only took to her bed in the last week of her life. She knew that she was very ill but wanted no treatment or hospitalization. Her wish was to stay in her own home and her own bed. She had a very peaceful end with family and friends around her.

She was a good and faithful friend, with the courage to criticize when necessary. We will miss her.

MARY CANNING
From Camphill Correspondence, *2002/4.*

Irene Durand

September 16, 1944 – March 13, 2005

Some days before she died, Irene said to me, "I was born in 1944, in Switzerland, on September 16." I wondered at the order she chose: first the year, then the country — not the place — of birth, and last of all the exact date. I asked myself whether she had wanted to put forward the fact that she was born during the war, but in a country which had been able to stay at peace, and that she had come to earth under the sign of Virgin, already close to Libra. She bore her name, Irene — peace — consciously, like an aim which she sought to achieve: the city of peace, the new Jerusalem.

She began her path in a happy family. Her father, Jean Robert Junod, philosopher, professor of French, was broad-minded and loved by his pupils. Her mother, Pierette Marguerite Junod, was a dedicated woman who taught rhythmics. And there was Anna, her older sister, and Nicolas, her brother. Born as a third child, Irene couldn't keep herself feeling that she was the fifth wheel on the family wagon.

At two and a half she was sent to hospital with a serious illness, and felt abandoned as her parents only came to visit her once a week. But her first memory was of the happy moments when she saw her parents coming towards her cot. The leitmotifs of her life are in this first memory: reunion, peace, restored balance and communion between human beings.

From the age of three Irene loved dancing and costumes. She took dancing and singing lessons until she was eighteen. She had parents who guided their children towards beauty, goodness and truth. She remembered her father often reading aloud: he was a pacifist who impressed her deeply. His humour comforted her when she was prey to feelings of inferiority, which came, she said, because, "I have always been the daughter of Professor Junod, or the sister of, and never myself." She suffered from severe dyslexia which held her back and did not help these feelings. However, she was quick in finding her husband. Her meeting with Patrick Durand took place when she was thirteen. Both their mothers were *rythmiciennes* at the Jacques Dalcroze Institute. The Durand family came from the Cevennes, where they spent their holidays. Irene spent fabulous times there.

She characterized her youth as calm and carefree. After her baccalaureate in general culture, Irene took up four years of social studies and became a youth leader. Meanwhile Patrick did a practical course in Aigues-Vertes, a village-in-the-becoming, which was to welcome mentally handicapped people.

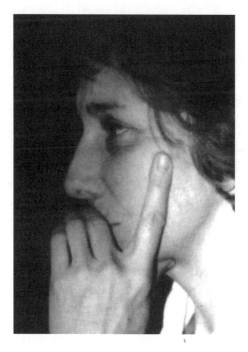

This meeting with anthroposophy and the Camphill movement was decisive for Patrick. He began a course of curative education in England while Irene finished her training in Geneva. He returned after one year to celebrate their wedding and they left together for Scotland, to the source of Camphill where Patrick continued his training and Irene was soon expecting her first child. Corinne was born in Scotland in 1968.

Irene had followed Patrick to a new way of living in community, but at first it was not easy for her. Her family was not accustomed to forms and rituals. Now she had to face a life of rhythm: the festivals, the day, the week and the year.

The artistic life, especially eurythmy which attracted and impressed her, helped Irene to find her place. She soon took great pleasure in the plays celebrating the festivals. She was deeply touched by the children's service, during which each child, even the most deprived, recovers his full human dignity.

All these seeds cultivated during two years in Scotland blossomed in the Village Aigues-Vertes where Patrick and Irene spent twenty years of their lives. Antoine was born there in 1970, followed by Gabrielle and Frederique. Irene looked after her four children while caring for the handicapped members of large house communities.

On several occasions she began a eurythmy training but this dream never came to a conclusion. However, her love of plays, of costumes, her light step and graceful movement had ample opportunity to be called upon in the intense cultural life of the village community.

Her capacity to be attentive to the needs of others was rooted in a deep veneration and gratitude for the social organism, which Camphill and Rudolf Steiner schools attempt to practice.

Irene got to know the Steiner schools more closely after a year in the United States and some time spent with her mother. She was asked by the school in Geneva to take on the kindergarten for very young children. This invitation set an early childhood experience resounding in her. The first time she had been taken to kindergarten at the age of five she had cried all day long and had learned how things should not be done. Out of this experience of pain she said Yes, because she wanted to offer the children a more positive welcome by maintaining sufficient contact with the parents.

After a short time with the little ones she became ill and had to pass on her work to others. Throughout her losing battle with illness she showed her serenity.

Before she died, she said to me, "I never saw the advantage of throwing myself headlong into things, I was looking for balance." These lucid words characterized her well: Virgin, near Libra, the Balance.

WALTER WILD
From Camphill Correspondence, *2005/5.*

Susanna van Eyseren

1905 – December 14, 1976

Susanna van Eyseren rarely talked about herself or her past. Sometimes she would tell of the time she had to spend in a prison camp in Indonesia, and then one caught a glimpse of the tremendous hardships she had gone through as a nurse in this situation. She felt responsible for the health of the many women and children who were interned in this camp. She would fight for food and medicine. Susanna was a true nurse; she lived for others, she wanted to give to others but found it difficult to take for herself.

We lived together in the Sheiling Schools in Ringwood for seven years. I remember how once, when nearly all the houses were infected with scarlet fever, there was Susanna, going from house to house, assisting the house-mothers, giving children a bath, making their bed fresh, taking their temperature, preparing their medicine and having a cheerful word for the children as well as for the house-mother. Nobody would guess that she herself had a very sore throat and was running a temperature. She spoilt her patients. What a wonderful feeling it was when she came into your room! She would quickly clean it, dust everywhere and put a white serviette under your medicines. Then make a really hot water-bottle for you, fresh orange juice, and, if possible, bring some flowers. If one were badly ill, she would not stay too long, but always long enough to make you feel cared for and relaxed.

All who know her, will never forget the sight of Susanna early in the morning or late at night walking through the estate from house to house with her medicine basket, never thinking of her sore feet which she had had for many years.

Out of the impulse to help, she came out to Botswana when our fifth child was born. In so many ways she was a great support for us, and all who know her think of her in gratitude and love.

I was very happy to have been able to see her some months before she died. I will never forget the peace and dignity around her when we spoke together about her approaching death. It was really as if she were sheltered and carried by the light of death. Everybody who met her in that time had this strong experience.

ROSWITHA GROTH
From Camphill Correspondence, *1977/2.*

Lawrence Adler

April 7, 1911 – July 20, 2002

Lawrence Adler was born in Czechoslovakia to German-Jewish parents who had met the work of Rudolf Steiner, in particular the biodynamic method of agriculture. Lawrence's attendance of the local Waldorf School was brought to an end by the move of his parents to South Africa just before the war.

Once Lawrence had finished school he took an apprenticeship in woodwork and set up a small business making picture frames. This was in line with his great interest in art, and before long he opened the first art gallery in Johannesburg. Here he displayed art for exhibition and sale. He became well known for his true artistry, and his gallery needed to expand. He took on a partner, and in time they transferred to new premises.

During this time Lawrence was a conscientious student of anthroposophy and led several study groups. Yet, successful as he was in the realm of art, he nurtured a deep wish to become a Waldorf teacher. In the early

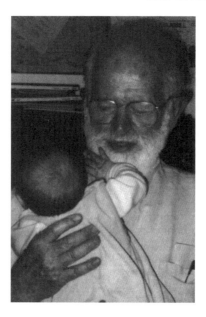

sixties he sold his share of the gallery and went to train as a teacher in Hanover. After three years he joined the Constantia Waldorf School and took on a class. He was very devoted to his pupils and to the school but it gradually became clear that this was not the right profession. His breadth of knowledge and the intensity of his enthusiasm was overwhelming for the primary-school pupils.

He then joined the Camphill School for children with special needs, where he taught adolescents and generally engaged himself in the manifold activities of this residential and therapeutic community. Here he met and married Ingrid Röder, a co-worker from Germany and Camphill, Scotland, who shared his interest in art and music and who was also an earnest student of anthroposophy. This was a very supportive marriage for Lawrence — he had found his soul mate, and together they helped the centre at Hermanus to grow and flourish.

The urgency for more provision for adults with special needs led to Lawrence's main achievement — the founding of the Camphill Farm Community on the farms adjacent to the School. Lawrence virtually moved mountains. First there was the purchasing of the Le Roux farm, which called for a great amount of fund-raising; then the design of the workshop-complex around a majestic oak tree, and finally registering and establishing of the Village Community. There followed the negotiations with the Government for a comprehensive loan to build three large and two smaller houses and the whole complex of farm buildings for milking, dairy, cheese making and storage. Lawrence masterminded the entire development, which involved extensive interviews. Its successful completion put the Farm Community well and truly on the map.

The life of this community thrived under his and Ingrid's guidance and the devoted work of many co-workers and villagers. There was one item missing — a hall for assembly to serve both the Farm and the School Communities. Lawrence poured his interest and his imagination into this project, but unfortunately his suggestions were felt to be unworkable and over-ambitious. He withdrew from the fray; the task and design was given to Wilfried Bohm, and this project was nearing completion when Lawrence died. It was fitting that the building could be used for his funeral service.

JULIAN SLEIGH
From Camphill Correspondence, *2002/6.*

Ingrid Adler

November 22, 1928 – December 5, 1999

Ingrid made everything a work of art. Her whole life was a beautiful translation of spirit into biography. She was born in China as her German father was an academic lecturer. During childhood she lived some years in Turkey before settling back in Germany where she went to school. She trained in fine art, specializing in the making of stained glass windows. This very metier shows how she combined art and craft. She then sought greater depth to her life and found her way both to anthroposophy and Camphill in Aberdeen.

Ingrid joined Camphill in 1954 She worked successfully and cheerfully with severely handicapped children, and later as a teacher of a class. There were many of us who were young friends and colleagues together, including Friedrich Röder, a gardener and philosopher, and a person of great charm. Ingrid and Friedrich married, but this was not to last. Soon Ingrid was one of the younger co-workers who were appointed to replace the older original leaders in the various estates that comprised the Camphill School. Ingrid was made responsible for Murtle House, while Friedrich took on the vegetable garden. Unpredictably this drew them apart. The running of Murtle was an overwhelming task for Ingrid and after some years she found an opportunity to change her work and take on gardening and landscaping at the emerging village of Newton Dee. It was from there that she responded to a call from Michael Lauppe to come and work in South Africa in the Camphill centre near Hermanus. She came and was

one of the stalwart co-workers who saw to it that the work could continue. Times were hard for Camphill in South Africa in 1970, and we almost gave up the Hermanus centre; but Ingrid helped to maintain the determination to continue against all odds, and her cheerful buoyancy won the day.

Early in the seventies Lawrence Adler joined Hermanus. He had run the premier Art Gallery in Johannesburg, had trained and served as a Waldorf teacher, and now entered curative education and social therapy at the Hermanus centre. He played the violin and Ingrid the side flute, and before long their duets turned into nuptials. They married in 1972 and worked closely together to create the Camphill Farm Community, which was soon to become a thriving Village, on the two farms that were adjacent to the Camphill School. All this development was due to Lawrence's enterprise and flair for public relations; and Ingrid contributed her cultural gifts, which permeated that community with a spiritual essence. Over the years since then the Village has become well established.

For many years Ingrid had the responsibility for reading the lessons of the First Class. She rendered this service both at Hermanus and with a Group in Cape Town. Ill health in later years obliged her to give this up, and she and Lawrence retired in a small house. There a magnificent rockery has been constructed, which has been the joy of Lawrence and the workplace of Ingrid.

JULIAN SLEIGH
From Camphill Correspondence, *2000/2.*

Petra Julius

March 12, 1941 – August 12, 1984

Petra was born in Hamburg in the springtime of 1941. The Second World War was raging over Europe. Her father was a soldier in the German army. Petra was an eagerly awaited child, but so frail after birth that she had to remain in hospital for the entire first year of her life. Her mother went to the hospital daily to take her own milk to the baby because breast-feeding was not possible, and after a year Petra was strong enough to be helped by an operation and was then allowed to return home. A year later, her father was captured in North Africa and came, as a prisoner of war, via America and Belgium to Scotland. In a camp near Kintore he heard of Camphill for the first time. He had the option of going to work in Camphill every day, returning to camp in the evening, but he did not take this opportunity.

After his release in 1947 Petra and her father saw each other again, and the little family moved to Schleswig, close to the Danish border. Petra's father took over the family business from his ageing father. In Rendsburg, near Schleswig, a new Waldorf school had begun and he gave support to this new beginning. Petra, on reaching school age, entered this school, greatly enjoying the short train ride every morning. She soon became the leader of the commuting children in all the fun they had. She was a happy, warm-hearted sanguine child, around her everything was movement.

In class she was not a great "learner." Eurythmy lessons became favourite lessons and she adored her teacher. This strong connection remained throughout the school years and so it was fairly clear to her that she would like to take up eurythmy training, which she did in Köngen with Else Klink. Her training completed she decided to follow a small group of eurythmists who had just joined Camphill: Eva Maria Rascher, Angela Haack, and Rosemarie Kampe. About this time Else Klink visited Camphill and mentioned Petra's coming to me, a broad smile on her face: "Oh yes, Petra will also come. Oh yes, Petra is still coming — you wait and see!" Becoming curious, I asked: "What about it, what is so special about her?" But I just received the same refrain in answer.

On the last day of 1966 she came: Tall, with open curious eyes, inquiring into everything, and spreading laughter and gaiety. Wherever Petra appeared there was constant movement, and waves of badly pronounced English mixed with very loud German talk poured over the children and adults. Soon old Camphillers raised their heads: "Who is this new co-worker who wants to join absolutely every activity without waiting for an invitation?"

An eagerness to understand, to be "with it," had got hold of her and it needed very loving understanding to put her at peace and make her see that she would need to learn patience. Teaching our children soon made it clear to her that she would have to add curative eurythmy to her training. It meant leaving Scotland and going to Switzerland. Again she met a personality whose work and school she greatly admired and took as an example: Frau Niederhäuser in Dornach. Having completed her training, she returned to Scotland.

She followed the call to Germany, returned after a time to Scotland, went back again to Föhrenbühl and, after a time of inner struggle decided to remain in Germany.

Petra's sudden death in a rail accident near Heilbronn, Germany, after three weeks of very special holidays in Camphill, Scotland, came as a great shock to her many friends. All who met her in the last three weeks were deeply touched by the light-filled friendship and the warm love she so abundantly offered. Many old friendships were renewed and many young people remarked how reassuring, encouraging and loving she had been when they met her.

TRUDE AMANN
From Camphill Correspondence, *1985/3.*

Paul Marshall Allen

June 26, 1913 – July 8, 1998

Living in Camphill for a time one was bound to hear the name of Paul Allen. We saw the name in articles, book reviews, in many anthroposophical magazines and pamphlets that went through our hands. Later on, we heard that this man had moved to Botton Village, and that he originally came from America. Word went round that he was a very good lecturer; he could lecture on many diverse subjects, and could easily give up to three a day! Then we heard that Paul was a producer of plays, preferred very large casts, always including villagers in his productions; and we heard that Paul was producing Rudolf Steiner's Mystery Dramas in Newton Dee with villagers. What was this man up to? We head all this from a distance: never having met him, I built up a picture of a very wise man who had travelled far and wide, had met many great men, and a man who had read a very great many of the world's books.

The first time I was allowed to really meet this man was when I lived in Mourne Grange, and he had agreed to produce the medieval scenes of

the Mystery Dramas with all of us. When I say "all," I mean it. We were still a small community, and every living soul, man, woman and child was cast into these scenes, whether we liked it or not. It turned out that we all liked it, and it turned out to be a real community experience and a wonderful event.

To help him to cast us for the play he held an audition. He did not look at us and was not interested in what we looked like. He was only interested in listening to our voices as we read the part. His eyes were shut, and in this way he could decide who was to play which part. The voice was all-important. Of course, if there was any evening without rehearsals, Paul gave a lecture. All he needed to give these talks was a small card with a little bit of perfect writing on it, which fitted neatly into his jacket pocket but it usually stayed there, as he hardly ever needed the prompt.

The meeting I remember best was at Halloween. Paul was living in our house and we had asked him to tell us a story for the occasion. We all gathered around the fire leaving a big armchair free next to the fire, eagerly awaiting his arrival. Down he sat, looked earnestly at each one of us in turn. The mood was set, and he pulled out his book and "read" us a most wonderful American story about the devil. I say "read" because he had a book on his lap, but I would wager that he knew the story off by heart. He was a wonderful storyteller: his voice like thunder one moment, and a whisper the next. But look at him, look at Paul next to the fire. A huge head, a noble head, a long beard coming down to his chest, very large hands holding the little book, his brow nearly without a wrinkle. I had often seen Orson Wells in American films, and always thought that this was a real American. Now he was sitting in front of our fire telling a story of the devil bargaining with human souls. It was an experience I will never forget.

Since then I have got to know Paul better. I was amazed to learn of his great love for Russian people and their folk spirit. When speaking about Russia one felt Paul was Russian himself. He also had a deep connection to his home and America, and had far-reaching insights into its people. Then there was a great love and connection to South America which came out when he spoke about the old mysteries of the Incas, for instance, and one felt he was part of that, too.

In his lectures about art, say Italian art, one felt his connection to the whole country and to its people. He often spoke to us about the arts in Scandinavia before he moved to Norway, again giving the impression that he knew more than just the artist and his picture. It was the same when he spoke about his beloved Scotland, when later he lived in Corbenic Community.

When I got to know Paul better after he came to live in Mourne Grange I could experience that this was a universal man. A man whom we could truly call an old soul, in the sense that Rudolf Steiner spoke of souls who knew many parts of the earth and left their mark where they had lived before.

I could not write an appreciation of Paul without mentioning his connection to young people and of their connection to him. They were drawn to him as they soon found that he had their interest at heart. No doubt Paul helped and guided numerous young people who came to him for advice.

I will never forget a moment many years ago when at an Easter conference I sat in the hall at Newton Dee next to Alix Roth, and watched and listened to the scenes from the Mystery Dramas. After the most wonderful and moving performance produced by Paul, she said to me: "I am quite sure that Rudolf Steiner would have wanted his dramas to be performed just like that."

CHRISTOPH KÖNIG
"Happy (eightieth) Birthday, brother Paul," from Camphill Correspondence, *1993/4.*

Strange so it seems, though Paul and I were married for more than forty-five years, I know relatively little concerning the first forty years of his life. However, I shall attempt to set down some salient details which I have gleaned, especially during these last months when his childhood memories arose so much more vividly within him.

Paul was born on June 26, 1913 in a typical white colonial house in the tiny village of Conquest, New York, about 150 miles west of Albany. His mother almost died giving birth, and everyone was so concerned about saving her, that if his grandmother hadn't bundled him down to the kitchen and forced some strong black coffee into him he might not have survived. Because of his mother's ordeal he remained a lonely, single child but had the good fortune to have two sets of close and caring grandparents, who often took him to stay in their homes as he remained the only grandchild.

They were all farming folk, and once, twenty years ago, Paul, Morven, Temora and I visited Conquest and could still see the houses, decaying barns, the neglected land and some of their family tombstones in the village cemetery. At the age of six Paul developed rheumatic fever, which necessitated that he be kept at home for three years. During this time his grandfather Allen (the Quaker side of the family), began to teach him Greek, Latin and most importantly, a great respect and love for literature, history and travel. Grandfather was born in 1838 in Westmorland, England, and had spent three years in Russia as a young man in the late 1850s with a group of Quakers who had gone there to help the Russian serfs to adopt more modern agricultural methods. Later he was to teach Paul Russian when he was twelve, so that he could read the great Russian classics in their original language.

For Morven's twenty-first birthday in 1982, Paul wrote down many of his early childhood memories, especially of his grandfather Allen, and I would like to quote the following from his reminiscences: "One of my precious memories was hearing my grandfather pray aloud, either before meals, in meetings, at home or anywhere. It always seemed so very natural for him to pray. He appeared to be on such friendly terms with God that whenever I heard him pray or say grace at meals, I could be certain that God was actually right there, and my grandfather was talking to him. He really loved God and always prayed out of love, joy and gratitude, never pleading or begging or asking for anything, but simply acknowledging His care and presence."

During these past few years it seemed to me that Paul inwardly turned more than ever to those early childhood years, when the true piety and inner conviction of his Quaker family planted such deep impressions in his soul. Every evening, when we read from the Old and New Testaments and then ended with some of the Psalms, he would often be able to quote long passages from them, remembered from his childhood. Also graces began to emerge from the depth of his memory, which I had never heard before, and often he dreamed vividly of his grandparents in his past years.

When Paul was about thirteen, the little family moved to Auburn so that he could attend secondary school there, and later go on to Syracuse University, where at the age of twenty he graduated with a degree in

Comparative Literature. Paul's grandfather Allen died just after his 21st birthday and he still describes his last meeting with his grandfather when he advised Paul: "There are many things I could say to you, but this includes them all — always remember that you could say *no.*" With great foresight, his grandfather left some money to Paul with the stipulation that he travel abroad and continue his studies there. So in 1935 Paul spent some months in Oxford, but then went on to Florence, Italy, where he immersed himself deeply in the study of Dante's *Divine Comedy* and the Art History of Umbria and Tuscany, including of course many visits to Assisi, Sienna and other towns close by. He often said that if it was not for the impending war necessitating his return to the USA in 1938, he might well have remained in Italy. However, during these three years in Europe he appears to have made a number of interesting journeys, because every so often he would tell of his adventures on a postal boat sailing up to the North Cape, his visit to the Holy Land (Palestine at that time), his journeys up the Nile to see the Coptic churches, and many other fascinating experiences within Europe itself.

Upon taking up residence in New York City, Paul began to offer dramatic readings and lectures on Dickens, Shakespeare and Russian writers — to schools, colleges and various cultural clubs — in a country still attempting to recover from the Great Depression. This soon led to his being recommended to Michael Chekhov (nephew of Anton Chekhov) as a teacher of comparative literature in Chekhov's newly founded studio Theatre. Thus began a whole new chapter and turning point in Paul's life, as Michael Chekhov slowly but thoroughly introduced him to the life and work of Rudolf Steiner, whom he had personally known and recognized as his "teacher and master," and of whom he once told Paul, was that he was "the most human being" he had ever met. This close friendship with Chekhov was to continue until Chekhov's death in 1955 in Los Angeles, where Paul gave the funeral address.

During the war years, Paul became increasingly active as a lecturer and council member of the Anthroposophical Society, including participation in the dramatic work with Hans Pusch, all centred in New York City at that time. This led to his being sent in the late 1940s on three transcontinental lecture tours for the Society, visiting many groups and individual members across the country, holding public and members' lectures and of course having innumerable personal conversations and encounters. At the same time he was teaching in the Scudder Collver School in New York City, a small private "finishing school" for young ladies from well-to-do families, which included summer-school sessions in Guatemala City. This teaching activity also entailed taking groups of students several times on the "grand tour" of Europe, via ocean liners and deluxe rail travel with Paul as the well-qualified art and architecture guide. The prolonged stays in Guatemala gave opportunity for extensive travels to the as yet undeveloped Mayan ruins in Central America, and eventually several journeys to ancient Inca sites in South America. And as with everything that Paul took up in life, he went into it thoroughly and fully, including often learning new languages, at times reading a book a day, and most incredible of all, remembering all that he read and experienced.

Paul had long been a friend of my father, George de Ris, only seven years his senior and one of the early anthroposophists in the USA. However, Paul and I first met in the newly founded Christian Community in New York, when at Advent 1951 he played the role of God Father and I of Eve, in the Paradise play. We married in December 1952 in my family's home in Englewood, New Jersey, which for 35 years was to be a kind of anthroposophical hotel where numerous anthroposophists from Europe and America could always find a home for shorter or longer periods of time. There Paul and I also lived for nine years, during which time he helped and supported me in every possible manner (from typing my papers to making my packed lunches) during my five years' study of architecture at Columbia University, and following that my three years of apprenticeship and final state exams. Meanwhile, he was the official secretary of the Anthroposophical Society at 211 Madison Avenue, besides actively lecturing, translating and writing, all in connection with Rudolf Steiner's work. Looking through his small pocket diaries, which he kept throughout his adult life, I estimated that Paul must have given at least eight thousand lectures and seminar sessions during the past sixty years.

In the summer of 1960 we heard Karl König giving a talk at the Christian Community in New York, describing the early beginnings of Botton Village — hardly dreaming that eight years later we would move there. Summer 1961 saw us settling in the little summerhouse we had built in South Egremont, Massachusetts. In early October, two weeks after Morven was born, we visited the first group of "pioneers" who had just moved to Sunny Valley Farm in Copake: Carlo Pietzner, Renate Sachs, Mary Collins and Karin Waldstein. Slowly our future with Camphill began to unfold: meetings and talks with Dr König in summer 1962, increasing involvement with Camphill Village Copake and Beaver Run in Pennsylvania, and many friendships formed, especially with the numerous Camphillians who visited from abroad. Peter and Kate Roth came to the USA in 1964, a few months before Temora was born, and sitting on our terrace in South Egremont, Peter suddenly turned to me and said: "Someday you will move to Botton and design our new church." And thus from 1968 onwards, the lives of our family became entwined with Camphill's unfolding history, first in Botton, then in Newton Dee, Mourne Grange, Vidaråsen and Corbenic.

Knowing Paul's sense of timing was always superb, none the less it was overwhelming for me to realize how incredibly beautifully he drew all the threads together for this final act of his earthly life's drama.

In the last year many friends came and we made a number of journeys. In late February we spent two weeks with our many friends in Mourne Grange and Clanabogan. And then came our journey to the States for a month, where we had the great joy of welcoming our first grandchild, Ian Paul Allen, and being there for his christening on Easter Sunday, an event which became an occasion for a large gathering of family and friends. At the end of May, together with Gene Gollogly from New York City and Norman and Jessie Young, we made a weekend visit to Fingal's Cave on Staffa, Mull and Iona.

All this happened while Paul was feeling increasingly frail and at times quite unwell, with the added sadness that his eyesight was steadily failing. Between it all we completed our third book, *Fingal's Cave, Celtic Christianity and the Poems of Ossian*. Then on the morning of July 8 all our earthly belongings were packed into a container for shipment to Norway and we travelled up to St Devenicks. There he told Gisela Schlegel that here he felt "at home," and that evening, in full consciousness he closed his eyes and breathed out his spirit in his beloved Scotland. Timed to perfection, the curtain descended on his earthly life.

JOAN DE RIS ALLEN
From Camphill Correspondence, *1993/4.*

Joanna van Vliet

September 30, 1939 – March 29, 1993

So many images flood my inner eye when I think of Joanna: a questioning look, sparkling laughter, beautiful and often almost holy eurythmy, indomitable inquiry, childlike joy over something beautiful, devotion to the perfect completion of a task, migraines, playing the violin, the little blue motorbike and her busy guardian angel, a humorous twinkle in her eyes, research into anthroposophical topics, the clown at Carnival that makes little children feel safe and happy, a shared discovery — and much more.

Joanna was deeply connected with the Middle European impulse; she also spoke German fluently. I met Joanna when we were both asked to be part of Carlo Pietzner's Art Retreats between autumn 1972 and Easter 1973. At that time she lived in Beaver Run. Joanna brought to these

retreats her manifold and outstanding gifts, in particular the specific kind of eurythmy she developed, which almost became a meditative experiences. Yet, at mealtimes her humour and bright laughter lit up everyone! In 1987, Joanna decided — largely for the sake of her mother Eleanor — to become part of village life in Copake. She had spent approximately seventeen years in Beaver Run as a teacher and artist. It was a very big step she took, which brought her many a struggle.

We will always remember her when recalling several New Year's Eve celebrations showing the stars of the old and the coming year, with a large group of farmers clad in the colours of the zodiac and the planets. Joanna was ingenious with such creations.

Another important memory was when she performed a section from St Paul's Letters to the Corinthians as well as Ephesians.

RENATE SACHS
From Camphill Correspondence, *1993/4.*

Rudolf Ernst Bartsch

May 17, 1927 – December 12, 2000

Rudolf Bartsch moved to Föhrenbühl in 1968 to work with Georg von Arnim. He was one of the many friends who accompanied Georg during the autumn weeks of the year 2000, from the celebration of his eightieth birthday to his death. Rudolf was present at all times with his usual deep sincerity and faithfulness: a brother. Little more than a month later he followed Georg into the spiritual world.

Rudolf Ernst Bartsch was the youngest of three brothers who grew up in East Prussia, in Elbing near Danzig. The father was president of Elbing Sailing Club and of the Chamber of Commerce. Many diverse cultures of the Baltic countries, met at both these institutions. His father's standing and the large family business, gave ample opportunity for Rudolf to experience inter-cultural activities from an early age. He could have followed in his father's footsteps but just after his apprenticeship as a tradesman he was called up for war service. On January 22, 1945 Russian troops entered Elbing, and the next day Rudolf managed to escape across the Baltic with his mother. The ship in front of them, filled with refugees, sunk. His father had moved south earlier for health reasons, and both brothers had fallen at the front.

After a few months in an English prisoner of war camp in Denmark he worked on a farm in northern Germany. He was enthusiastic about farming and kept contact with this profession all his life, although it soon became clear that it was not his task in life.

From 1947 he trained as ship's carpenter in a large dockyard in Hamburg for three years before following his parents to southern Germany where he worked as a carpenter for various companies in Allgäu and at Lake Constance. On the way south, however, he met Herbert Hahn in Stuttgart. This gave his life a new direction and new meaning.

After a time at the seminary of the Christian Community, he studied education and became a class teacher, at the original Waldorf School in Stuttgart from 1964 to 1968. Following this he went again to Lake Constance, to Föhrenbühl where he arrived at a pioneering time and could set hand to many developments, including the building of the House of Childhood, the new schoolhouse with Kaspar Hauser Hall. With his building experience he took on the task of modelling the beautiful stage, following the ideas of Georg von Arnim and Else Klink, the eurythmist, with whom he kept in close contact.

Three new impulses arising out of anthroposophy kindled a fire of enthusiasm in Rudolf and he carried them untiringly through the rest of his

life. First he made religious life his responsibility and cared for it on every
level with incredible faithfulness. Even a week before his last visit to hospital, without help he still took a religion lesson with 28 severely handicapped youngsters. Secondly, he devoted all his strength to education and
healing, in which he always included the necessity of healing the earth. He
took two classes through nine years of schooling and taught in the upper
school. He was always able to find a deep relationship with the children.
As a teacher he was anything but conventional — some said chaotic —
but nevertheless all pupils loved him dearly. They learned much from him
and were nourished by his enthusiasm. He experienced their humanity,
and they experienced a brother. Again and again he would forgive his colleagues for their doubts, criticism and impatience. He opened his classroom to take in anyone who sought his guidance, and many took up this
opportunity. This points to the third impulse which was his love for
Eastern Europe.

Long before the Iron Curtain disappeared Rudolf helped with many
anthroposophical initiatives, first of all in Poland and East Germany. He
made contacts in many countries, visited homes, hospitals, state schools,
found partners for assistance and opened ears and hearts for new ways in
care work and education. He went to Czechoslovakia, Hungary and
Russia, spoke to professors, government officials and farmers, showed
slides of Föhrenbühl, the Goetheanum and Botton Village, gave away

books and anything he could carry. I remember visits to Olga Havel and to world-famous musicians. And after "retiring" he spent most of his time in the Baltic region, including Svetlana east of St Petersburg, as well as Siberia. Rudolf was one of the driving forces of the East European Conferences for educational and healing professions which of course included farmers. These conferences have taken place in a different Baltic country each year since 1992. In a letter of preparation he wrote: "My encounters in 1950 with Herbert Hahn, who was a colleague in Stuttgart, and our conversations after the Sunday services became my guideline to the East."

He made many a sacrifice on his way, taking little heed of his own diminishing health. After months of preparation work, sleeping in cold offices, he signed a letter to Dr Ossopofsky, "your camp-bed companion that time in Gdynia."

During his last two years, Rudolf never recovered completely from a number of operations. He did not make too much fuss about it and continued his journeys, ever further afield, to Kyrgystan and Kazakstan which did, however, cost him too much strength. He had two short weeks during his last hospital visits to prepare for the greater journey and to take leave of friends. Although in pain, he had an inner calmness and certainty.

RICHARD STEEL
From Camphill Correspondence, *2001/2.*

Some who Came Later

Faith Brosse

February 12, 1933 – March 28, 2006

Faith joined Camphill in her late thirties and for the next 35 years she lived the Camphill way of life fully, imbued with its aims and values and taking up the opportunities it offers. Faith was instrumental in bringing about Clanabogan Community in Omagh, Northern Ireland and, having become ill at Christmas time, on March 28 she died peacefully there, surrounded by friends.

Faith spent her years in Camphill caring for and about people, befriending them in a special way. She made all sorts of friends and many a person needing special care and attention was taken under Faith's wing. She shared trips and holidays, gave cards and gifts, offered hospitality and thoughtful kindnesses. Faith really enjoyed her friends and at the end, the love she had given them flowed back to her.

Faith was born in London in 1933 and with her younger brother had a happy childhood despite the outbreak of the Second World War. She enjoyed a successful career as a teacher of dance — ballet, ballroom, Scottish and modern — until her mid-thirties when she went to teach at Delrow College near Watford. Through reading philosophy and psychology, Faith had been searching for something more meaningful and she was attracted to life in Camphill.

In 1970 she joined Newton Dee Village in Scotland as a house-mother and that was henceforth her primary role, supplemented over the years by running workshops and teaching dance to adults and later children.

A couple of years later she moved to Glencraig in Northern Ireland which was initiating the pioneering vision of a community in which disabled children and adults were part of the same house community. She was busy there for nearly a decade. As Mourne Grange developed it needed more help and, seeking a less demanding lifestyle, Faith moved there at the end of the 1980s until her mother's increasing age and illness necessitated a move back to England.

After a while Faith was able to live with her mother in Delrow which Mrs Brosse enjoyed until her death aged 92.

All this time the seeds of further destiny were germinating. While in Glencraig Faith had received into her house a young man who had suffered a serious head injury. Donald Stewart was a brilliant mathematician who became disabled through a fall, and it was Faith who was determined that he could find a place in Camphill. Her friendship with Donald's mother and aunts grew over the years and she spent holidays with them in their family home at Clanabogan outside Omagh.

By the early 1980s Camphill in Northern Ireland was considering starting another village community for pupils leaving Glencraig and the idea
grew among Faith and Donald's family that their property might be suitable as it comprised a rundown farm and a fairly large house with out-
buildings. Eventually this property was bought for the work of Camphill
and in 1989 Faith left Delrow to join the new village as the community
expanded.

There followed another rich and happy time for Faith. She knew many
of the co-workers and villagers from former times and she also established
friendships with the local people who supported the community at
Clanabogan.

So we can say that Faith accompanied Clanabogan from its conception
and birth as a Camphill community until it came of age in 2005 with its
twenty-first birthday. All Faith's abilities blossomed during her life in
Camphill. She was able to use her gifts for the enrichment of others: bak-
ing, jam and juice-making, sewing, embroidery, flower arranging, home-
making, writing and telling stories, giving talks and lessons.

Faith was especially connected to all the Christian and seasonal festivals and decorated her house and the Hall most beautifully. The Christian
Community, the Offering service and Bible Evenings were very dear to
her.

In particular Faith's dramatic gifts flourished. As well as producing
Karl König's festival plays she used her abilities in dance, mime and recit-
ing poetry to bring about magnificent plays, tableaux vivants and
masques, as she called them, of her own. These were enactments of Bible
texts or Camphill themes written and produced by Faith herself, involving
large numbers of co-workers and villagers. They were usually presented

at festivals for the enjoyment and admiration of neighbours and families. Her final achievement in this area was a modern Nativity play in which Mary, dressed in jeans, gave birth among homeless people against the threats from entertainment culture, one-sided science and materialistic commerce.

Blessed with a bright, sunny disposition Faith had a positive outlook on life and her radiant smile brought light into many situations. She met life with interest, energy and enjoyment, and her sense of fun made her shine at parties and skits. In her last years after she retired from running a house, Faith enjoyed herself immensely: holidays at the Mediterranean, walking in Switzerland, outings on local buses, gardening, while faithfully carrying out her remaining tasks in the community.

For, as Ben van Lieshout said, Faith lived up to her name. Everything she did was gracefully and properly done, an expression of her commitment and love for Camphill and her belief that ordinary life can be Christianized by hard work and dedication.

CHERRY HOWE
From Camphill Correspondence, *2006/4.*

Lenie and I are very thankful to Faith for the special part she played in our lives during the last 33 years. In the course of time it became ever clearer that it was no mere coincidence that I was invited in March 1973 to come for three months to Glencraig and to help Faith as house-father in her house community. Neither was it accidental that this invitation reached me in Botton Village on the first anniversary of the day on which we had buried my mother's ashes in Germany. My mother must have had a subconscious presentiment that the last part of my life would be connected with Ireland, because in September 1971, during what became unexpectedly my last holiday with her, my mother spoke with me several times about Ireland. Yet, I can never imagine my connection to Ireland without our close connection to Faith Brosse.

I have to thank Faith also, for inviting me again to help her as housefather in 1974 and 1975, when she became house-mother in Dell O'Grace. At that time Donald Stewart joined Glencraig and lived with us in Dell O'Grace. I will never forget our very first excursion to Clanabogan, with the whole house community, when we walked over to the local church and were shown the beautiful and ancient baptismal font. In retrospect this seems to me like a land of baptism for us and for Camphill.

In recent years Faith mentioned to Lenie and me a few times that, already at that time when I lived with her in Dell O'Grace and Lenie would occasionally come to have a meal with us, she had a strong feeling that Lenie and I belonged together. This was a few years before even we ourselves realized it. We were deeply moved when she told us this, and invited Faith to be the witness at our silver wedding. Yet we could never have imagined that she would be called back to the spirit land before us.

Finally, we must thank Faith for all the beauty she created around her, both outside and inside.

MANFRED SEYFERT-LANDGRAF
From Camphill Correspondence, *2006/4.*

Max Abraham

October 27, 1917 – July 27, 1997

Max Abraham was born in Port Elizabeth, South Africa; the youngest of five children in a prosperous orthodox Jewish family, and grew up in the comfort that a loving and wealthy family could provide.

Max was a very sensitive child. When he was a young boy he was made to dress inappropriately for a rugby match at school. This was such a traumatic experience for him that from then on he developed a very serious stammer, a burden that he had to carry for the rest of his life. Max twice failed classes in the lower school, but in the secondary school, under the guidance of understanding teachers, he began to shine, became prefect and did a first class matric.

As a young man he enjoyed driving fast cars and spending money, but also realized that there was more to life than the wealth and status most other members of his family were pursuing.

In his early twenties, Max met Lorna. She had lived for the first nine years of her life in Lithuania in a highly respected, cultured Jewish family. Many of her relatives lost their lives in the Holocaust and those who could flee to South Africa found themselves impoverished and suffering complete loss of status. After her education at a convent school Lorna had to work in order to support the family. Hence Max's family definitely disapproved of a marriage to her, but he was not to be deterred.

The wedding was celebrated in 1941 — the beginning of a new phase in Max's life. In the following twelve years their three children were born and Max was always a loving father to them. He was in business, always concerned that the family was provided for. His extended family continued to expect assistance and thus finances had to play an important part in his life.

In the 1950s and 60s Max and Lorna were running the Royal Hotel in Hermanus, a small coastal town 80 miles east of Cape Town. They loathed everything that the apartheid regime stood for, and every day they were distressed by having to apply the inhuman laws. Wherever possible they tried to improve conditions for their staff as well as for the so-called Coloured population in the area. The business was successful, but these were very stressful years for them.

In the middle of the 1950s, a few miles further inland from Hermanus, a Camphill school for children in need of special care had been established. Lorna took up contact with the school, offering help. As a result, a deep friendship developed between those living at the school and Max and Lorna. She was invited to join the Third Year Seminar there and Desiree, one of her daughters, became involved in weekend work. Max had initial difficulties meeting handicapped children but later, when Desiree fully joined the work there by marrying Melville Segal all that changed. He became a member of the School's Council.

During those years Max and Lorna were something of a living legend in the South African Camphill centres. Co-workers would come for meals to the hotel, birthday parties for the children and weekends away for the co-workers in their house were arranged — in short it was wonderful for those living at the school to know that at all times Max and Lorna's friendship and hospitality could be counted upon.

In about 1969 the family Abraham could no longer remain safely in South Africa because of their continued disregard of apartheid laws. They sold the hotel and a tremendous burden appeared to fall from Max's shoulders. He was radiant, as if newly born. This was also the time that he succeeded — with Dr Lotte Sahlmann's help and tremendous will power — in putting an end to heavy drinking and smoking. He was ready to start a new phase in his life.

Max and Lorna sailed to Britain in March 1970. To their surprise, they met their old friend from the Hermanus Camphill School, Irmgard Lazarus, on board ship, on her way to Norway.

The move into such a setting as Camphill was naturally an unsettling, even painful experience, but before the end of 1970 Max and Lorna were settling down at the Sheiling School in Thornbury. After having spent about half of their married life in South Africa, Max and Lorna were to live the other half in Thornbury.

Max fully joined the work at the school and became a member of the Camphill Community. It was not in an intellectual way, but deep in his heart that he could unite with the new way of life and the striving he met at the school. To the end of his life he followed with the keenest interest everything to do with pupils and co-workers. He loyally attended the Sunday Offering service for as long as he was able to do so. With his expertise and dedication to all things financial, he made an invaluable contribution to the financial side of the small community's life.

For years he chaired the Finance Group and until his last weeks he felt that, in the mornings, his place was in the office. He was also a Council Member of the School. Often his deeply ingrained past as a South African "boss" could make life difficult for others, but one always knew that behind all this beat a heart of great generosity and loyalty.

After having fought his final illness for four years, Max passed away peacefully on July 27, 1997, surrounded by his beloved family.

ELLA VAN DER STOK
From Camphill Correspondence, *1998/4.*

Margarete MacDonald Bain

February 8, 1919 – October 12, 2004

Margarete was born near Newcastle into a well-to-do family, the third child of four. She had two brothers and a sister. She enjoyed a happy childhood, always with lots of children around. She went to a private girls' school, and every week the family went to church. All four children learned to play the piano and sometimes concerts were held with duets on two pianos. When she was six years old her father died. She joined first the Brownies, then the Girl Guides, and at nineteen, the Sea Rangers. It

was one of Margarete's characteristics throughout her life that she was always well prepared for any eventuality!

At the age of thirteen she became very ill with pneumonia and pleurisy. An operation was performed and she was in hospital for a long time. In later life, and probably as a consequence of this illness, Margarete was prone to chest infections.

Margarete was twenty when the Second World War started and she was soon involved in ambulance driving. Around 1940 she was set to sail on a ship as an escort for children. For some unknown reason she did not embark, which was fortunate, for the ship sank.

In her twenties Margarete trained as a teacher of the deaf, and afterwards had a year at Durham University where she gained a Diploma in Service of Youth. While in Durham she must have first visited Camphill in Scotland. For three years Margarete was involved in an orthopaedic hospital school and for two years she was the Education Secretary for the YMCA in the South West.

In 1947 when she was 28, Margarete was involved in relief and post-war reconstruction work BAOR (British Army of the Rhine), and met her husband to-be, Hector Duncan MacDonald Bain, known simply as Mac, who was working in Germany as a supervisor for the YMCA. Mary was born there and Hamish later in England.

It was when living near London that Margarete went to hear a talk at the local Women's Institute about Camphill given by Morwenna Bucknall. This it seems must have been the trigger which brought the Bain family to the Sheiling School at Ringwood in 1961. Margarete was then 42 years old. They lived in Ringwood for some eight years. Mac died in 1968 and after this loss she and the children moved to the Grange Village and then to Delrow, within the space of a year, and in 1970 to the Sheiling School in Thornbury.

In Tyndale House, Margarete as house-mother and also as a teacher had very lively children which included some deaf pupils. Margarete's previous training now stood her to good stead.

When eventually she handed her class over, she very actively engaged herself in the organization and running of the Camphill Training Course as well as attending meetings internationally. She made a special and very important contribution in teaching of lyre-playing. Margarete also procured a set of hand-bells and directed their use.

For some time she was responsible for all new co-worker applications; she was a service holder; an active member of the Camphill Community; a Council member; and also for some twenty years was the librarian for the extensive library in Thornbury Park. Her disciplined, conscientious, and ordered approach, as well as her genuine warm interest and thoughtfulness in the welfare and care of others equipped her well for these different tasks. She was always interested in leading young people into roles of greater responsibility and could see something of their future potentials, even if these were rather hidden to themselves!

Margarete was, typically, not short of new ideas, enthusiasm, willingness to help, and optimism. There was something very light, joyful, conscious and aware about her being, and she had a good sense of humour. On the other hand Margarete was also a private person who kept any more personal concerns or worries very much to herself. As in her nature she was tactful and sensitive, so those who came into close contact with her also needed to learn to exercise a certain tact and sensitivity in their relationships with her.

Particularly in the last year of her long life Margarete became increasingly frail and required the help of others, both from within the community and from outside. She often experienced difficulty to find the words needed to express clearly her thoughts, and she then relied on others to supply the words which eluded her memory. Even with these difficulties, she still retained her dignity.

Around Michaelmas Margarete contracted a cold which went to her chest, and she became quite unwell. She passed across the threshold peacefully in her sleep, at the age of 85, on October 12, 2004.

BOB WOODWARD
From Camphill Correspondence, *2005/1.*

Marjorie Rosenthal

December 6, 1907 – April 15, 2002

Marjorie's keen interest and outstanding ability to reach out to anyone and everyone made her the focus of attention whenever she came for a visit. She gave advice willingly and sensitively, a listening ear to other parents, sharing freely the experiences of joy and despair she had with her own daughter. During parents' interviews at her home in London, she looked after the children — a testing task which she took in her stride.

The parents of other pupils remained the focal point of her life. In her early eighties she participated in the first seminar for parents and contributed throughout the course of eight long weekends over two years. Marjorie's interest was equally directed to the Camphill philosophy and ethos and she tried to learn as much as possible about this. Participation in the yearly festivals gave a starting point for deepening her understanding of what stands behind Camphill ideals. Later on, when she had made St Devenicks in Murtle Estate her permanent home, she did not miss any lectures, talks, concerts or plays. Her outlook remained positive, as she seldom voiced disapproving questions or criticism.

Seeing Camphill throughout her life in a positive light gave her the conviction to speak openly to reluctant parents, social workers or other officials. Often this brought about a change in their attitude.

MARGA SCHNELL
From Camphill Correspondence, *2002/6*

Marjorie was a social worker and mother of a severely spastic girl through whom she made her connection to Camphill.

Kari Krohn

June 5, 1926 – August 10, 1984

Kari Krohn was born in Finland to a famous and cultured family which was known for many poets, authors and philosophers. He was also very gifted. He graduated as a very young man and was a judge already at the age of twenty-one. But then the will that lived in his deep unconscious awoke and he decided to study medicine.

Only then did he feel in harmony with himself and so he could start to acquire knowledge of healing. His wish to heal led him honestly and without prejudice to look for old and new methods of treatment. His serious aim was to work together with man's hidden natural regenerative powers. Homeopathy, acupuncture and anthroposophical medicine helped him to widen the boundaries of usual, conventional medicine.

But he was alone in Finland on his path, though he often travelled abroad to make contact and acquire friends. In the beginning he met resistance from his Finnish colleagues: He was a lonely knight, a real Michaelic knight. When his colleagues did not want to share his experiences of new types of medical therapy, he wrote a book, *Doctor on the New Ways of Healing*. This was a bestseller in Finland a few years ago. After this he made new friends, and gained acceptance and appreciation. Through Kari, many younger doctors found a new possibility to deepen and widen their knowledge of medicine.

Kari was the person who led Freddy and Kaarina Heimsch to the first Sylvia-koti. When Sylvia-koti was started in Lahti in 1970 as a Camphill home, he became its doctor. He worked there one day a week and knew all the children well. He had a very special relationship to the handi-

capped, for one of his own children was handicapped and now lives in Tapola, the Camphill Village near Sylvia-koti.

Kari also taught in our Seminar. His advice was always simple and natural. He always celebrated the festivals with us and took part in our Bible Evenings.

Kari loved music and was very gifted in languages. He could speak all the main languages of Europe, as well as Chinese. He went in for sailing and sailed as much as possible. A couple of times he sailed over the Baltic Sea to Sweden and through its canals to Norway.

For seven years he helped with enthusiasm and diligence in our curative educational work and then he had to withdraw because of serious illness. Again for seven years Kari fought with cancer and prepared himself to step into the spiritual world in full consciousness and with joy. Kari Krohn left his earthly dwelling on August 10, 1984.

FREDDY & KAARINA HEIMSCH
From Camphill Correspondence, *1985/3.*

Edelina LeFevre

August 6, 1948

It was a beautiful sunny morning in June 1971. In a large flower-filled garden in a wooded area outside a small town in the north west of Holland I was having coffee, strawberries and cream with a dear friend, the owner of the house, and a neighbouring couple. It was a defining moment in my life, which up to then had been quite stormy and not altogether easy. How I had come to be there in that garden I still consider to have been something close to a miracle. My childhood and youth had been rather uneventful, often even boring. At the age of sixteen I met a young man who would weave in and out of my life, at ever-increasing frequency and intensity, shaking it up and making me think about things like life and death, art, music, and myself.

He reappeared suddenly when I was well settled at university, disturbing my nice student life by bringing along his personal problems, doubts and failures. I began to smoke and drink and miss lectures and try to help him by listening to his endless conversations, which often became quite hopeless and negative. I was pulled into this world of negativity and hopelessness, and realized that my ambition to help him and change him was not coming to anything at all. After I had managed to scrape through my BA English exam, my father, who had become quite concerned about the relationship I had got myself into, decided to withdraw his financial support. I had to find myself a job as a teacher and a place to live. My boyfriend continued to visit frequently and my work was severely affected by my personal situation. I was not a great success as a teacher.

One day a colleague took me to an open day at the local Waldorf School, and this is where the miracle happened. She introduced me to a lady in her fifties, who was trying to teach English in the school but was not very good at it and asked me a few questions about English words. This was the extent of our conversation and I went home, not thinking about it any more. The next day my colleague said that this lady wanted to meet me and that I was invited for dinner in her house. I went, not quite knowing what to expect, and when I had found the house, a dream house in the middle of the forest, she answered the door, looking very busy and inviting me into her kitchen where she was cooking the meal. She explained that she was not very good at cooking and always needed to smoke a cigarette to make it more bearable! Very soon the conversation intensified and we were discussing life and death and our relationships and problems. It was the first time I had been able to speak about these

things with someone who really understood me, in fact it was the first time that I admitted that I was having problems!

After a few visits to my new friend she asked me to bring my boyfriend, whom she received very warmly so he also felt quite at home there! When my landlady threw me out of my room because she could not tolerate my boyfriend being there, my new friend let me stay in her house while I tried to find a new place to live. We had many deep conversations in which she pointed out to me that I lacked will power and that I should not let myself be used by my boyfriend. She also explained to me that, when we met for the first time, she had a very strong premonition that she was meant to help me with something, and that this is why she invited me for dinner.

Only much later I discovered that she was a student of anthroposophy and one morning at breakfast the conversation turned to reincarnation. I will never forget the flash of light, which went through me when hearing this word, a light of recognition. Everything suddenly seemed to fall into place, began to make sense and become positive. I asked her for books to

read and she gave me *The Education of the Child,* which I read while listening to the boring English tapes which I had to play to the poor children
in my (probably very boring) lessons. One of the other books I was very
much taken by was by Zeylmans van Emmichoven, in which he related
Christianity to the other world religions in a very clear way, which made
a lot of sense to me and answered many of the questions which had made
me step out of the Protestant church a few years previously.

Soon afterwards I found the courage to end my relationship. When the
end of the school year approached I was told that my performance as a
teacher had not been good enough and I was politely asked to leave the
school. When I discussed this with my friend on one of my frequent visits, she invited the neighbouring couple for strawberries in the garden. She
explained that these people had just returned from Scotland where they
had done a training in a place for "mentally handicapped" children called
"Camphill." She thought I might like to meet them. So there I was on this
hot summer's day in June in her garden, listening to a very enthusiastic
description by these two people. They were now back in Holland, trying
to find a suitable site to start a new home like the one in Scotland. I listened to their story and for some reason did at first not connect it to myself
but to my sister, who at that time had just gone through a crisis. I felt this
would be just the thing for her, to get away from it all! Only the next day
it began to dawn on me that maybe I myself was the one who needed to
get away! As I had failed as a teacher, mainly because I had never learned
anything about children or teaching, but had only studied English, I realized that this might well be an opportunity to learn about all aspects of
childhood. I decided to write to Aberdeen. Very soon I received a reply
saying that they were full, but that Glencraig in Northern Ireland needed
people. I applied to go to Glencraig for half a year and arrived the day
before my 23rd birthday. It was the birthday of a new stage in my life.

When I sat in the bus with the one suitcase of belongings, which I had
brought along from my old life, I saw a young man holding a plastic bag
with some fish in water. After looking at me a few times he asked if I was
going to Glencraig, and then offered to carry my suitcase if I would carry
the fishes, and so we walked down the long, beautiful drive of Glencraig
and I felt like coming home. I just loved it there — I loved the children,
the atmosphere, my "birthday table" the day after my arrival, the peace
and the simplicity of the life. For the first few months I felt as if I had
entered a monastery where I was able to purify myself of all the nonsense
and negativity of my past, and regain my sanity in a very new and meaningful way.

The "half a year" turned into the full three years of the Training Course.
I found myself a husband in Glencraig, and after having spent six years
away, in England and Australia, we returned in 1980, now with two

children, and we are still here 25 years later (with four grown up children)! The monastery experience has long since faded and life has become complicated enough, but with the help of my brothers and sisters in the Camphill Community and through anthroposophy, it has become possible to face any problems in a positive way. I feel that I am on a path of life-long learning and have never been bored since I put foot here! Life has become worthwhile and I hope that I may have been allowed to give a tiny contribution to the good of mankind through meeting anthroposophy and becoming part of the striving of the Camphill Community.

AUTOBIOGRAPHICAL

Steve Lyons

August 22, 1946

I arrived in the Camphill Rudolf Steiner Schools at the beginning of my 28th year. Learning only later of the significance of biographical rhythms I was at that time only pleased to be learning about curative education and that impulse still dearer to me: community.

During the three years of the training in curative education I simultaneously undertook the new training course in Camphill Nursing. These two together introduced me to practical caring skills and to two approaches to inner training. Reading for these courses included quite a bit of Rudolf Steiner's books, essays and lectures. Thus my introduction to anthroposophy was through practical work combined with classroom instruction, in two distinct professions.

The nursing work and study led eventually to my helping to found Simeon Care for the Elderly, a Camphill community in Aberdeen. My curious path to Simeon and beyond is partly traceable through my interest in Steiner's lectures on the human life between death and rebirth. This interest was fired first in the course in nursing and strengthened via the Camphill Community. A very agreeable relationship began to appear to me between activity beyond the threshold and the creating of social organisms on earth. This recognition had a direct bearing on our caring for and living with older people. The study of the later stages of biography had been illuminated by very few up to this time. I wanted to do more studying in this direction but time and energy were wanting.

Instead of working more with the building of community for the fostering of an appreciation of human ageing, I have been asked to turn my attention to community building generally. I now work with others in

Camphill Scotland to build on the earlier Camphill success of associating (another of Steiner's little-understood social ideas). Here I am increasingly engaged in the study of those forces through which social organisms thrive. I do this via *Ways to Quality*, one of anthroposophy's recent initiatives. Camphill Scotland is encouraging our communities to take up *Ways to Quality* as a study of the forces mentioned, to be able to use such study as a diagnostic tool for self-determination.

    Autobiographical

Peter Bateson

June 27, 1953

In the early seventies I was living in London after finishing university, following a series of different jobs and with absolutely no sense of direction. I found life in the capital exciting and was free to enjoy its many and varied pleasures to the full, but my existence was strongly coloured by a feeling of transience and uncertainty. At university I had become a wholehearted member of the "hippy" generation with its joyful idealism and transcendent vision, underscored at the same time by a dark streak of pessimism about human nature and the state of the world.

In London I formed various circles of friends and acquaintances, usually related to my current place of work, in offices of an oil company, an advertising agency, a recruitment agency, a publishers, and even for a spell at the Old Bailey. However, after a time I would always come to a point when I felt I was at a dead end and had to free myself again, and then I would simply move on, dropping everything and everyone in my wake. It was a very self-centred attitude, but born partly out of youth and inexperience and partly out of the longing to find something worthwhile and valuable. I could have recited countless examples of what I did *not* want to do with my life, but was utterly at a loss to know how I might put myself into something really positive and constructive.

During my first fourteen years I had grown up in a very harmonious and settled family background steeped in the traditions of the Church of England, the celebration of the Christian year, a thorough knowledge of both the Old and New Testaments and surrounded by people living out of a quiet and self-effacing attitude of service to humanity, not least my own parents. My mother had for many years worked in the Cub Scout movement and with physically disabled children, including at one time a combination of the two, and my father worked for many years in a promising career as a highly qualified engineer before giving up to start work on the bottom rung of the social work ladder. My father was also a gifted church organist and choirmaster, and my younger years were illuminated by the sublime tradition of English church music. At the age of fourteen, on the actual day of my Confirmation, I rejected all this entirely.

Just over seven years later, drifting in the maelstrom of London life, I went in my lunch hour from the Old Bailey to a dusty little bookshop in the shadow of St Paul's Cathedral and bought a slim volume of the New Testament for 50p. I had been reading about a man in prison who had found his only light and hope through the Gospels which were the only thing allowed to him in his cell. Like him, I began to read a little each day. Like him, what had for me in the past been external religious culture and tradition became an urgent inner and personal necessity. A wellspring opened up in me again which has continued ever since to grow stronger and stronger, and has been at the heart of many years of religion teaching and the holding of lay services.

I soon realized that in order to find my way I would have to turn away from myself and look outwards to the needs of other people. It seems so obvious but to me it was a revelation. At first I had grandiose ideas and an almost missionary zeal to go far away to an exotic location where I could help to make a real difference to the lives of people in need. Of course, I was deluding myself, a fact which came to light as soon as I tried to contact Voluntary Service Overseas (VSO). By some sequence of events which I can no longer remember or explain but which seems to have been

brought about by a power above and beyond my knowledge, I got in touch
not with VSO but with Community Service Volunteers, an organization
which I did not even know existed. They told me straight away that I had
nothing to offer VSO but encouraged me to think of doing voluntary work
in Britain. They happened to have a central office just a short walk away
from my current home near the Angel, Islington. I went for an interview,
and a few weeks later arrived in Camphill, at the Sheiling School
Thornbury, knowing nothing of Rudolf Steiner or the Camphill movement.

I found something totally new and unexpected in Camphill and realized
almost immediately that it was what I had been looking for. It was a real
synthesis of all the richness I had experienced in my upbringing with a
modern and forward-looking respect for the freedom of the individual
spirit. Even so, during my first eighteen months there were many times
when I felt as if I might repeat my previous pattern of behaviour, to simply give up and move on from a situation which I found too demanding or
restricting.

At a surprisingly early stage I, and some others of my generation, were
admitted to the large central decision-making group and were able at first
hand to witness the struggles and human difficulties of life in community.
One night, after a particularly difficult and controversial meeting, a group

of us younger people, including my future wife, sat together to dissect what had been going on. It was disheartening and there was again the feeling of wanting to escape. Then at one point there came a sudden revelation — we should not run away but decide to stay and commit ourselves to being part of the community, to help to bring about change and to build the future together with others. It felt true and right. At last I had found the commitment for which I had been searching.

AUTOBIOGRAPHICAL

Bob Clay

April 12, 1949

I can identify three stages in the deepening influence of anthroposophy in my life. As they are spread over twenty-five years of my life perhaps I had better speak about turning points rather than a single turning point, though in my biography they are clearly experienced as stages in a single process.

My first contact with Rudolf Steiner's work came some thirty years ago in 1976 when my wife, Fran, went for a ten-week placement to the Camphill community at Newton Dee, near Aberdeen, as part of her Social Work training. We were living in Edinburgh and out of curiosity I wandered into the small anthroposophically inspired craft and bookshop in Morningside, close to the children's home in which I worked. I came out having purchased a beautiful hardback copy of *The Four Seasons and the Archangels* by Rudolf Steiner, and a simply bound typescript of biodynamic preparations by Lievegoed. I was a keen organic allotment gardener, which accounts for the second choice, and to the first I was drawn by its beauty; it seemed worthy of reverence as I held it in my hands. I still have both books today: the slim volume of Steiner's lectures cost £1.95, which was at least ten per cent of my weekly wages!

The experience of being drawn to something which was beyond my understanding continued and became more tangible when I visited Fran at Newton Dee a few weeks later. I will simply recall the experience of arriving, of walking into the community, of meeting people: an indivisible mixture of strangeness and complete familiarity.

Some five years later, by now living in Newton Dee, with two young children and a host of responsibilities, I became quite seriously ill. During my slow recovery I became a regular server for the Act of Consecration of Man. I would liken this time to a child gaining speech — welcoming language yet not truly living in the realm of thinking. The words and actions

of the service lived in me and gave me a foundation I had lacked.

Twenty years later, I again became significantly unwell and it was this crisis, which allowed me to take a step into a more mature experience of my human nature and my personal destiny. My inner life opened up, as the loving power of thinking quietly entered my being. I think particularly of the meditative verse given by Rudolf Steiner, which is often called "The Holiness of Sleep" and which begins:

> *I go to sleep till I awaken;*
> *My soul will be in the spiritual world*
> *And there will meet the higher being*
> *Who guards me through my earthly life.*

I was allowed to feel the reality of such mighty but simple truths.

So, this latest stage in my turning point was connected with the world of sleep which informs and inspires our waking experience. Seen in this light it is then not surprising that a turning-point, which we would associate with waking-up, expresses the deeper currents of the world of the spirit. Anthroposophy has opened for me an awareness of the width and depth of the environment in which our lives unfold and in such a context twenty-five years is but a moment.

AUTOBIOGRAPHICAL

John O'Connor

October 2, 1961

Michelangelo painted a wonderful image of creation in the Sistine Chapel. The dynamic of this painting portrays enormous power. An outstretched hand reaching towards Adam, two hands which do not quite meet. The small gap could be the world, the universe or merely the effort needed to reach beyond our physical and earthly limitations. This painting challenges us to do just that.

Frequently in community life I have met this little gap between inner and outer life, ideal and reality, processes and forms. Brother and stranger, realizing hopes or half-hearted aspirations in pursuit of them.

This idea of community has been close to people's hearts in Ireland for thousands of years. To the present day the "community spirit" still lives strongly in areas of Irish life but the contentious question of the individual and the community does not sit harmoniously together. The old form of community which had the individual subservient to the greater goal does not fit any longer, and the search for a new form of community where the growth of individuality and the common purpose go forward in tandem is called for and is emerging slowly.

My own experience of the search for community leads me directly to this realization. On reflection I have seen the emergence in the last forty years of a new type of community where the dynamic between the individual and the community find some way to converse and grow together. In the move from my parents' generation to my own huge strides have been taken.

My own biography has had the motif of bridging the gap throughout various stages of childhood, young adulthood and now middle age. My path of community life started in Dublin in the sixties and seventies. Growing up in Dublin at this time was a wonderfully ordinary affair. Suburban Dublin was a changing place, but neighbours were real neighbours, and the children — huge numbers of us — played out our childhood with great gusto.

Many, if not all of the adults around us had strong virtues, the ability to sacrifice personal wishes for the sake of the family was evident. Affluence had not yet arrived and a tinge of poverty kept life in perspective and maintained social bonds. My family had strong roots in the rural parts of Ireland — so trips to the countryside and the rural communities were an ever-deeper experience for me of community life that was slowly being lost in suburban Dublin.

We had special traditions at different times of the year and when we met with the extended family we informally went over our common history, stories about relations from the past became family myths and strengthened the bond.

It was common for the members of many families to fall out with each other. Disputes over the wills left by deceased relatives were often the focal point. The perceived loss of integrity by a relative who became greedy around land, houses or contents would often lead to long feuds often carried to the grave.

Another form of extended family and local community was the Gaelic Athletic Association, G.A.A. or "Gah." The organization promoted Gaelic sports and related culture. My favourite aspect of this was the Gaelic football where, unlike soccer you could catch the ball, shoulder an opponent and run with the ball touching it from toe to hand every three steps. Being part of the G.A.A. community fulfilled some aspects of the search for identity during the teenage years; stories told in the local pubs after a match by older club members about the great feats achieved by great players provided iconic heroes to mould our sporting lives on.

In later years when I left school and had taken up vegetarianism and yoga I was unable to compete with enough aggression and I lost my appetite and motivation for chasing the ball around the park. It was around this time I read a story about two frogs sitting by a well discussing the Atlantic Ocean. The younger frog asked the elder how big is that ocean — four of five times the size of the well? No, replied the elder, much bigger, ten or fifteen times the size — and so they continued to compare the vastness of an ocean and their own well. Life in my blood-related community had grown too small for me. The community of work and young adulthood beckoned.

In Dublin's inner city there is an area of cobbled stone where the smell of the famous Guinness brewery fills the air. For me as a child this was the heart of Dublin. Not too far away from the brewery on the other bank of the River Liffey, every evening at around 5 o'clock a group of bedraggled individuals would meet outside a steel door which led into a three-storied hostel, home of the Simon Community. These forty or fifty individuals were some of Dublin's most forgotten people.

The fact that these individuals had a door to open to them, a good meal, a bed and most importantly a listening ear was due to Anton Wallich Clifford, a founding member of the Simon Community. This type of social activism as personified by him and others who followed on was very impressive to a nineteen-year-old like me. To experience life at the fringes of society seemed more appealing than the stability of a job in a good company.

One of the first people I met after I decided to join the work of the Simon Community was an ex-monk who had stepped out of his monastery

to work for the organization. As director he received £10,000, half of this he put back each year into the community and lived a very frugal life. This type of conscience and free action out of ideals greatly inspired me.

Long conversations with residents in the back alleyways and the hostel at night led me to see beyond the bedraggled appearances. Incredible stories lay at the heart of these people. Many had been successful at one point of their lives: the boxer who represented Ireland, the teacher who had had a breakdown, the daughter of aristocracy who had lived on an estate in India and later was travelling up and down the country with the travelling community. This was a disenfranchised group of people in Ireland many of whom experienced poverty and discrimination as they lived on the fringes of society.

Another big part of the heritage of Dublin at that time was Bewley's Oriental Cafes which had been set up by the Quaker Bewley family in the 1840s. If the area around the Guinness Brewery was the heart of Dublin, Bewleys was the lungs where you could breathe in the good conversation of the many diverse characters and the rich aroma of oriental teas and coffees. For anyone who lived in Dublin around this time Bewley's held a special place in their hearts. These coffee houses were like cultural community centres and James Joyce, Brendan Behar and Patrick Kavanagh were frequent visitors. On any given morning you could find the banker, the baker, the candlestick maker, the poet or the lonely individual sitting for hours over their coffees — at home in the plush red velvet and dark wooden interiors. I met Victor Bewley in the 1980s and heard about the work he was carrying out. He used some of the profits to help finance the early stages of his social work. Meeting this Christianity and its application to the commercial and social world and the quiet humility of the Quaker religion as personified by Victor Bewley was an experience of another bridge builder whose quiet activity inspired faith in humanity.

I worked with the Dublin group which Victor Bewley had set up and experienced the necessity of this work. He was trying to break the vicious circle of children of problem families caught up in glue sniffing, drug abuse and the illegal activities to support an alcohol or drug-dependent life. His inspired interventions seemed to have some success by offering an alternative to the ghetto where many of their families and older siblings were stuck.

Meeting socially active organizations and the ideals behind them was showing me my outer task, but inwardly, as I reached 21, the search for my spiritual home led me to my next step.

In October 1983 I travelled to India and the surrounding countries of the Himalayas. I travelled there to meet the cultures and work on some projects supporting the change of attitudes and conditions experienced by the huge underclass in India and Bangladesh. One of the highlights of this trip was a three week stay at a community called Anand Nagar in Madhya Pradesh. The community was enabling people who had leprosy to rebuild their lives. The project had started with four families on a remote ten-hectare belt of fallow land in the province. Wells had to be dug, simple houses were built and gardens established. The residents, most of them leprosy patients, formed new families and developed some degree of ownership for the project.

Although on a physical level a lot of success was apparent, equality in relationships was difficult to establish. The invisible caste system, which still lives on in the habits of the Indian culture, created a huge division between the participants. Giving charity or receiving it, these polarities could not easily be bridged.

In a number of projects, communities and monasteries I visited and stayed while travelling the country I began to discover the gulf between aspirations and deeds; so many noble causes appeared to be crippled by corruption or weak resolve.

The aura of grandeur in which I had placed eastern religions and philosophies began to take on a more real perspective. Human grappling with ideals and reality began to emerge as a path. At the age of 22 I had discovered that Utopia or Nirvana — that perfect place in our imagination — is no easy place to find or build. This was no easy truth to swallow.

On my travels the experience of poverty was beyond anything I could have imagined — this was difficult enough — but more frightening was the social and spiritual poverty which hit even harder at my heart.

On return to Dublin I sat in a small gallery in the newest exclusive shopping mall. A lady came out of a beauty parlour with her nails painted; and having only two days before walked in the shanty towns of the suburbs of Bombay I felt that huge gulf again. An experience of homelessness descended on my soul, a deep disappointment with the world with that great gap between cultures and classes and the difficulty in realising ideals.

This moment of low tide in my life was a turning point: two days later I sat with a friend in a sunny suburban garden and we shared our experiences of the previous months. He described a visit and a short stay in an unusual community with disabled people in County Kilkenny. What he said was both good and bad but one description sounded above the rest. He described how, while sharing the meal with the house-community he could not differentiate between the disabled friends and the co-workers. His lucid description called up an image in me of a large wooden table and I pictured these people sitting there in a united and harmonious mood, a quality that reminded me of Leonardo Da Vinci's painting of the Last Supper. Coloured by my imagination of what my friend had described I visited the place later and was affirmed by what I met in the people.

Arriving in a small rural community, which was at a pioneering stage, was a good first meeting with Camphill. I loved the country setting with animals, plants, trailers and tractors, with hay and straw, and all the farm labour. It seemed like the therapy I needed after all the travels in India.

This community was building from within and had laid firm foundations. I joined in the preparations for celebrating Michaelmas — we dramatized the parable of the kingly wedding.

With this I had my first taste of Camphill and was interested in finding out more in a larger community north of the border. What I found was, what can be called, "a culture of consciousness building." They practised "devotion to the detail." This was not a strong point in Ireland where there was much more sensitivity of listening to the words of others, to music, and to the voices of older relatives and friends, their wishes and traditions. What I found here was this devotion to the detail as perceived by the eye. Things had to look beautiful; the culture of beauty was applied to all the places you lived in, both inside and around the house.

The rhythm of life was almost monastic and disciplined: to be "on time" was of utmost importance. In the busy life, however, moments of peace were carefully etched out to enable the individual to find himself again.

Spontaneity and fun were at times held in check by this consciousness and custom. A culture of letting go was not encouraged or was diverted to aesthetic endeavours in nature and constructive social forms. In attempting to guide the exuberance of some of the young and energetic children I firstly had to take hold of myself. The path of self-education was central to life in Camphill.

The vision-building process in the community was deep going and thorough; decisions were mulled over in plenum meetings: the spiritual and practical perspectives were given a good airing. The attempt to bridge ideal and reality was an active and earnest one.

Within this new culture I wondered about my own place; to live with people with whom I did not especially choose to live was an interesting challenge. For me, the centre point that helped to root myself in the life and work was that I felt recognized, my virtues and gifts were openly appreciated, and warmth was offered in the process of schooling those sides of my character that needed to change.

In these processes of change on all levels of my life I became very ill, as I had never been before. It happened around midsummer, and as I lay in my bed for a week I listened to the sounds of the St John's Play rehearsed nearby. The theme of *Change your ways* rang out and poured into my fevered and exhausted shell.

A little nine-year old boy who was part of my responsibility in the house became my main visitor. He could not talk or stay still for long but would rush into my room at every chance and look anxiously at me in bed. I could feel the influence I had on his life, his security and well-being. What he needed I was not able to fully give: he was the reason why I had to "change my ways," discard the old and become something new. I began to see the path that lay before me. Thoughts and plans I once had of joining a religious order had faded away; what I had found was closer to reality and closer to the ideals I held.

That first year is still very clear for me: so much had happened. I have since spent over twenty years experiencing community living and the challenging reality of self-education and transformation as a cornerstone of community life.

My search for community has led me to this truth again and again. The little gap in Michelangelo's painting can be a space for this imagination.

AUTOBIOGRAPHICAL

Bibliography

Allen, Joan de Ris, *Living Buildings,* Camphill Architects 1990.

Arnim, Georg von, *Bewegung, Sprache, Denkkraft,* Goetheanum, Dornach 2000.

Bock Friedwart (Ed), *The Builders of Camphill,* Floris Books, Edinburgh 2004.

Camphill Correspondence, Journal of the Camphill movement from 1975.

Cresset, The, Quarterly journal of the Camphill movement from 1954 to 1972.

Nauck, Erika, *Biographic Sketches of the Twenty-Five Participants of the First Camphill Seminar 1949–1951,* privately published 2007.

Pietzner Cornelius (Ed), *A Candle on the Hill,* Floris Books, Edinburgh & Anthroposophic Press, New York 1990.

Schilling, Karin von, *Where Are You Now?* Anthroposophic Press, New York 1988.

Segal, Melville, *Turn Right at Magnolia Street,* Tiferet Publishing, South Africa 2006.

Sleigh Julian, A Walk Through my Life, Visual Junction, Cape Town 2006.

Steiner Rudolf, *An Autobiography,* Rudolf Steiner Publications, New York 1977.

Glossary

Anthroposophical Society promotes anthroposophy and the work of Rudolf Steiner. International centre at the Goetheanum, Switzerland.

Bible Evening, Saturday evening festive meal followed by study of a Bible passage. A Camphill tradition kept in most of its institutions during the first decades.

Camphill Community, the spiritual carrying group of those committed to the ideals and aims of Camphill.

Christian Community, the, a movement for religious renewal founded in 1922 with the help of Rudolf Steiner.

Class, First Class (of the School of Spiritual Science) a course of lessons on spiritual development including a sequence of meditative verses, open to members of the Anthroposophical Society on application.

Class reader, person holding Class lessons

Children's service, service, a short non-denominational Christian Sunday service for children, originally given by Rudolf Steiner for the first Waldorf School in 1919.

Goetheanum, the international centre of the Anthroposophical Society in Dornach, Switzerland.

Offering service, a short non-denominational Christian Sunday service for people over sixteen, originally given by Rudolf Steiner for the first Waldorf School in 1919.

Section, division of anthroposophical work of the Goetheanum. Curative education is part of the Medical Section.

Seminar, the Camphill training course in curative education.

Service holder, lay person holding children's, youth or offering service.

Youth service, a short non-denominational Christian Sunday service for young people between fourteen and sixteen, originally given by Rudolf Steiner for the first Waldorf School in 1919.

Main Centres of Camphill

Following is a list of the main Camphill centres mentioned in this book. It is not a complete list. A current directory can be found at www.camphill.org.uk/directry/directory.pdf

Alpha former name of *Camphill Village West Coast*

Beaver Run, Pennsylvania, USA.

Botton Village, near Castleton, North Yorkshire. The first Camphill Village began in 1955.

Brachenreuthe, school and farm community, near Überlingen, Germany.

Cairnlee House, just north of Newton Dee in Bieldside, Aberdeenshire was initially used for severely disturbed adolescent girls.

Camphill House and estate, Peterculter, Aberdeenshire was purchased by Mr Macmillan and the move from Kirkton House was completed on June 1, 1940. Close by are Murtle, Newton Dee and Cairnlee.

Camphill Village West Coast (formerly called Alpha), Dassenburg, Western Cape, South Africa, see *Julian Sleigh*

Christophorus, in Holland, see *Leonie van der Stok*

Clanabogan, Co Tyrone, Northern Ireland, see *Faith Brosse.*

Coleg Elidyr, Llandovery, Carmarthenshire is a place for further education for sixteen to nineteen-year-olds. See *Birthe Hougaard.*

Copake, Camphill Village in New York State, USA.

Corbenic near Dunkeld in Perthshire.

Cresset House, between Pretoria and Johannesburg, South Africa.

Delrow House, Watford was started by Ann Harris. It is the Camphill Village Trust offices and is also used for clinics for applicants for CVT places.

Föhrenbühl, school, near Überlingen, Germany.

Glencraig, school, Co Down, Northern Ireland.

Grange, village at Newnham-on-Severn, Gloucestershire.

Hapstead, a village in Devon, England, see *Leonie van der Stok.*

122 **Harley Street,** London. The consulting rooms used by Dr König in London until the early 1960s. See *Ursula Gleed.*

Heathcot House on the south side of the Dee in Aberdeenshire, Scotland was rented from 1942 to 1957.

Hermanus, Farm and School Community in Western Cape, South Africa.

Hogganvik, Vikedal near Bergen, Norway, see *Margit Engel* and *Ivan Jacobsen*

Humanus-Haus, Beitenwil near Bern, Switzerland

Kimberton Hills, village, Pennsylvania, USA.

Kirkton House, Aberdeenshire, Scotland, was where Karl König's work in Scotland began in 1939 until Camphill House was purchased soon afterwards.

Kyle/Callan, Co Kilkenny, Ireland, see *John O'Connor.*

Lehenhof, village, near Überlingen, Germany.

Mourne Grange, village, Co Down, Northern Ireland.

Murtle House and estate, close to Camphill, in Bieldside, Aberdeenshire, was acquired in April 1944.

Newton Dee estate, adjoining Murtle in Bieldside, Aberdeenshire, Scotland, was acquired in 1945. Initially used for delinquent boys, it is now a Village.

Ochil Tower School, Auchterarder, Perthshire was acquired in 1972. See *Johannes* and *Jean Surkamp.*

Pahkla, Estonia, see *Margit Engel* and *Ivan Jacobsen.*

Rankoromane, Botswana, see *Werner Groth.*

Ringwood, Hampshire, one of the two sites of the Sheiling Schools.

St Christopher's School, Bristol. Though not a Camphill school, this anthroposophical school for children with special needs features in some of the earlier stories.

St John's School, the Waldorf school for co-workers' children at Murtle, later it was open for all Camphill children.

St Prex, near Geneva, Switzerland, see *Hans and Johanna Spalinger*

Sheiling Schools comprise two separate schools, Thornbury, north of Bristol, and the Sheiling near Ringwood in Hampshire.

Simeon Care for the elderly is at Cairnlee Estate, Bieldside, Scotland.

Solborg, north of Oslo, Norway, see *Nina Oyens* and *Ivan Jacobsen*

Svetlana, near St Petersburg, Russia, see *Margit Engel.*

Sylvia-koti, Lahti, Finland, see *Kaarina* and *Freddy Heimsch*

Thornbury House, north of Bristol, acquired in 1948. Part of the Sheiling Schools

Thornbury Park, adjoining Thornbury House, acquired in 1952.

Vidaråsen, south of Oslo, Norway, see *Margit Engel, Ivan Jacobsen* and *Martha Hönig.*

William Morris House, near Stroud, Gloucestershire, a community for trainees and students. See *Michael Lauppe.*

Wraxall House, near Bristol, first Camphill offshoot serving as a boarding house for St Christopher's School, Bristol.

Index